GENDER AND PO

By the same author

Staking a Claim:)Feminism, bureaucracy and the state (1989), with S. Franzway and D. Court

Teachers' Work (1985)

Which Way Is Up? Essays on sex, class and culture (1983)

Making the Difference: Schools, families and social division (1982), with D. J. Ashenden, S. Kessler and G. W. Dowsett

Ockers and Disco-Maniacs: Sex, gender and secondary schooling (1982), with S. Kessler, D. J. Ashenden and G. W. Dowsett

Class Structure in Australian History (1980), with T. H. Irving

Socialism and Labor (1978)

Ruling Class, Ruling Culture: Studies of conflict, power and hegemony in Australian life (1977)

Twelve to Twenty: A study of teenagers in Sydney (1975), with W. F. Connell, R. E. Stroobant, K. E. Sinclair and K. W. Rogers

The Child's Construction of Politics (1971)

Politics of the Extreme Right: Warringah 1966 (1967), with F. Gould

GENDER AND POWER
Society, the Person and Sexual Politics

R. W. Connell

Polity Press

First published in 1987 by Polity Press in association with Blackwell
Publishers Ltd.
Reprinted in 1991, 1993, 1995, 1996, 1998

Editorial office:
Polity Press
65 Bridge Street
Cambridge CB2 1UR, UK

Marketing and production:
Blackwell Publishers Ltd
108 Cowley Road
Oxford OX4 1JF, UK

ISBN 0–7456–0467–6
ISBN 0–7456–0468–4   (pbk)

A CIP catalogue record for this book is available from the British Library.

Typeset in 11 on 12 pt Baskerville by Photo·graphics, Honiton, Devon
Printed in Great Britain by TJ International, Padstow, Cornwall

Contents

Preface   ix
1 *Introduction: Some Facts in the Case*   1
   A teenager and her family   1
   The public world: wages, education, jobs   6
   Violence, prejudice, the state   11

Part I: Theorizing Gender

2 *Historical Roots of Contemporary Theory*   23
   Secular morality   23
   Science and radicalism   26
   Sex roles and syntheses   29
   Feminism and gay liberation   32
   Reaction and paradox   37
3 *Current Frameworks*   41
   Extrinsic theories: from 'class first' through 'social
     reproduction' to 'dual systems'   41
   Sex role theory   47
   Categorical theory   54
   Towards a practice-based theory   61
4 *The Body and Social Practice*   66
   The knot of natural difference   66
   Transcendence and negation   78
   Practical transformations of the body   83

Part II: The Structure of Gender Relations

5 *Main Structures: Labour, Power, Cathexis* 91
    Structure and structural analysis 92
    Labour 99
    Power 107
    Cathexis 111
    A note on 'system' and composition 116
6 *Gender Regimes and the Gender Order* 119
    Institutions 119
    The family 121
    The state 125
    The street 132
    The gender order 134
    A note on the definition and institutionalization of
      gender 139
7 *Historical Dynamic* 143
    Historicity and 'origins' 143
    The course of history 150
    Crisis tendencies 158

Part III: Femininity and Masculinity

8 *Sexual Character* 167
    Unitary models and sex difference research 167
    Masculinity/femininity scales 171
    Multiple models: from typology to relationship 175
    The effect of structures 180
    Hegemonic masculinity and emphasized femininity 183
9 *The Mystery in Broad Daylight: Gender Formation and
   Psychoanalysis* 191
    Socialization 191
    Classical psychoanalysis: the dynamic unconscious 196
    Existential psychoanalysis: the project 211
10 *Personality as Practice* 219
    Personality, society and life history 219
    The historical dynamic in personality 224
    Politics of personality 228

Part IV: Sexual Politics

11 *Sexual Ideology*   241
    Discourse and practice   241
    Ideological processes   245
    Cultural dynamics   250
    Ideologists and interests   253
12 *Political Practice*   259
    The scope of sexual politics   259
    The articulation of interests   262
    Working-class feminism   265
    Liberation movements: birth and transformation   270
13 *Present and Future*   278
    The present moment   278
    Strategies   280
    Concluding notes on the world to which a social
      theory of gender might lead   286
Bibliography   294
Index   317

Preface

The radical movements of the 1960s and 1970s opened debates about a range of practical issues to do with sex and gender, ranging from sexual expression to economic inequality, police violence against gays, and rape. Naming these issues, the new feminist and gay politics also posed theoretical questions and began to grow a theoretical language: 'sexual politics', 'oppression', 'patriarchy'.

By the mid 1970s when these terms were common currency, it was clear to anyone willing to listen that women's liberation and gay liberation required a profound change in our ways of understanding society. Sexual politics brought to light patterns of power, interest and conflict which made little sense in terms of socialist class analysis, conventional economics, political science pluralism or sociological functionalism. A theoretical revolution in the social sciences was called for.

This has been slow in coming. It was not clear what kind of theory would be adequate to understand the world of sexual politics. Attempts were made to adapt existing ideas. A quiet academic backwater, 'sex role' research, suddenly found itself enormously popular and influential. Biology was roped in to explain matters the biologists themselves hardly dreamed of. Rival schools of thought emerged within feminism, debating the universality of patriarchy, the usefulness of psychoanalysis, the impact of capitalism, the significance of men's sexual violence. Theorists of gay liberation searched for inspiration through psychoanalysis, Marxism, anticolonialism and the emerging theories of discourse. By the early 1980s one influential school of feminism was abandoning the basic theoretical assumption of ten years before, the fundamentally social character of gender.

This book is an attempt to resolve some of the difficulties raised by these controversies and to propose the outline of a systematic social theory of gender. That is a generous ambition and one person's work can only be a fragment of the enterprise. But given the state of the problem it seemed timely to try out a large synthesis, to suggest how the different issues about gender might fit together. The argument, accordingly, ranges over a very wide field and the research has led me into some unexpected corners – from the archaeology of ancient south-west Asia (trying to get some grip on the evidence for feminist 'origins' arguments) to the lesser-known followers of Freud. It is inevitable that some parts of the analysis are thin, and some are relatively abstract or speculative. When there was a choice I put more time into problems that seemed relatively neglected, such as the institutionalization of gender, than into issues now widely studied, such as sexual ideology.

The basis of the synthesis, the logical starting-point, is the nature of social reality itself. Arguments about gender are plagued by an assumption that what is biological or 'natural' is somehow more real than what is social. For instance it was often suggested in the early 1970s that sex roles were 'artificial' because they were socially created (by media, schools or whatever). There was a sense that if you poked a finger at them it would go right through. Since then a good many fingers have been poked and they did not go through. Sexist stereotypes are still with us, showing impressive toughness and resilience. Social process has its own power to constrain, its own resistance to dissolution. And yet it is entirely human. The oppression of women and gays is a matter of human agency, not of nature.

How to get a good understanding of these qualities has been a central issue in social theory over the last thirty years, and an uncommonly difficult one. The debates around structuralism in the 1970s got badly hung up on a contradiction between the impersonality and the humanness of social process. There is, however, an approach emerging in social theory that has a more convincing answer, though it is still not widely known outside a technical readership. One of its sources is the theory of practice derived by philosophical critiques of mainstream Marxism; another is the dualist or recursive models of the relation between structure and practice developed in theoretical sociology; and a third is the contextual analysis of the self, personal action and intersubjectivity developing in social psychology.

There is no commonly accepted term for this approach; I will call it the 'theory of practice' for short. It seems to me consistent with the best current research on gender and sexual politics, and to offer resolutions of some of the dilemmas the theory of gender has run into. Accordingly the general approach of the book is to bring together the theory of practice with the problems of sexual politics. This is far from being a one-way trade, an 'application'; it has involved reformulations of both. One of the unexpected outcomes was a demand for a practice-based approach to personality, which grew equally from a general principle of historicity, the findings of psychoanalysis and the experience of sexual liberation movements.

The reasons for undertaking the enterprise were partly that I wanted to understand the problems myself and partly that theory is important, at least in the long run, for practical politics. Bad theories will do harm. There are enough dilemmas and strategic conflicts in sexual politics to make a decent theory of gender a tangible asset for progressive politics of many kinds.

But theories don't grow on trees; theorizing is itself a social practice with a politics. Most of the radical theorizing of gender has been done by women or by gay men. I am a heterosexual man, married, middle-aged, with a tenured academic job in an affluent country – in world terms one of the very rich and secure. I owe an account of what I am doing here.

There is a view put by the 1970s 'men's movement' in the United States that 'men are equally oppressed'. This claim is demonstrably false. Some of the relevant evidence is set out below in chapter 1, which is intended as an introduction to the facts of gender inequality for those not already familiar with the issue.

Men in general are advantaged by current social structure, heterosexual men more so than others. What the debate about 'men's liberation' nevertheless showed is that there are costs for men in their social advantages, sometimes serious ones. It also showed that there are some groups of men who can recognize injustice when they see it and are far from comfortable with the position they have inherited.

For me, this discontent had several sources. I have been uneasy with conventional masculinity almost as long as I can remember, certainly since I was a teenager. I am not sure why; there may be an answer in what Dorothy Dinnerstein says in *The Mermaid and the Minotaur* about the men who became student activists in the 1960s. At all events my attachment to masculinity was sufficiently fractured to make me sit up and take notice when the women of that generation mobilized in their own liberation movement. I read books like Shulamith Firestone's *Dialectic of Sex* as well as those of the 'Freudian Left' and listened to a great deal of discussion about feminist principles and programs. A commitment to a socialism that stressed the theme of equality rather than textbook Marxism was probably important. Certainly important was the fact of living with a woman who was working on projects like setting up a women's health centre, and the fact of working in university departments alongside people engaged in feminist research.

I became convinced fairly early that the main feminist arguments about inequality and oppression were right. Somewhat later, I became convinced that they required a thoroughgoing reconstruction of socialist politics and the social sciences. Later again, that gay liberation raised crucial theoretical questions that were part of the same set of issues. Finally, that this was also the business of heterosexual men, who have some specific jobs to do (e.g. in the politics of masculinity) but also ought to be involved in the general analysis of sexual politics.

That is not necessarily easy to do. On the one hand men's settled ways of thinking have to be disrupted. The slow progress in getting issues of gender recognized in the mainstream of academic disciplines like history, economics or psychology, long dominated by men, illustrates the resistance. On the other hand there are currents in feminist thought which do not welcome men's involvement, and there is a fine line to tread between intruding on women's business and sharing the work on common problems. Even sympathetic men writing about feminism have attracted some pretty fierce responses. I do things in this book that a purist might not do, such as discussing the strategies of feminist movements. The reason is that no one of either sex can make an extended analysis of sexual politics without touching on these issues.

The number of heterosexual men working on these issues is still small. I don't think there is anything in itself admirable about being a dissident. I look forward to the day when a majority of men, as well as a majority of women, accept the absolute equality of the sexes, accept sharing of childcare and all other forms of work, accept freedom of sexual behaviour, and accept multiplicity of gender forms, as being plain common sense and the ordinary basis of civilized life.

If the number of people working to turn these principles into practice is to grow into settled majorities, there have to be good reasons why people will accept them as principles. These reasons need not all be the same. Sexual politics, like politics in other fields, is a matter of constructing coalitions. For some groups the reasons flow straightforwardly from a collective interest in change. The catch is always with heterosexual men, whose collective interest – as the evidence through the book confirms – is broadly to maintain the existing system. What reasons for change have enough weight, against this entrenched interest, to detach heterosexual men from the defence of patriarchy? There are, in my experience, five.

(1) Even the beneficiaries of an oppressive system can come to see its oppressiveness, especially the way it poisons areas of life they share.

(2) Heterosexual men are often committed in important ways to women – their wives and lovers, mothers and sisters, daughters and nieces, co-workers – and may desire better lives for them. Especially they may see the point of creating more civilized and peaceable sexual arrangements for their children, even at the cost of their own privileges.

(3) Heterosexual men are not all the same or all united, and many do suffer some injury from the present system. The oppression of gays, for instance, has a back-wash damaging to effeminate or unassertive heterosexuals.

(4) Change in gender relations is happening anyway, and on a large scale. A good many heterosexual men recognize that they cannot cling to the past and want some new directions.

(5) Heterosexual men are not excluded from the basic human capacity to share experiences, feelings and hopes. This ability is often blunted, but the capacity for caring and identification is not necessarily killed. The question is what circumstances might call it out. Being a father often does; some political movements, notably the environmental and peace movements, seem to; sexual politics may do so too.

These are, at least, among the reasons for this book. It is also motivated by personal experience. Over the last fifteen years I have tried to work through issues of sexual politics with other people in my household, my workplaces and the labour movement. Some of this has been very difficult indeed and has convinced me, as no theoretical writing could, of the sheer intractability of gender relations. It has also convinced me that relationships and customary practices do change, that collective projects of reconstruction are possible, and that oppositions of interest can be worked on and sometimes worked through, within such projects.

If social research is to have major value for that enterprise, it must do something more than show where we have come from or describe where we are now – useful as those jobs are. It must also concern itself with strategic issues: with where it is possible to go and how it is possible to get there. It is easy to speculate on these matters, difficult to produce well-founded arguments. Much of the literature on gender cannot do this job because of the way its theory is constructed. It has been one of my main aims to develop forms of analysis that are credible as social theory and which also key in to strategic argument. This is behind the following analyses of interest articulation in sexual politics, crisis tendencies at the level of the whole society, and the means of reconstructing personality 'from below'. A social theory should also help to formulate the general goals of politics. I think the kind of theory developed here can do this, and the book ends with a discussion of what the ultimate outcomes of progressive sexual politics might be.

This book is the product of ten years' work, not all of which has proceeded smoothly in one direction. My first attempt to get the issues together was an unpublished essay of 1976 called 'Another Coup d'Etat Among Men' (Robin Morgan's joke about socialist revolutions), which sketched a theory of 'hegemonic sexuality' as a meeting-ground for socialism and feminism. About that time I began work with Dean Ashenden, Sandra Kessler and Gary Dowsett on a study of social inequality in secondary schooling, eventually published as *Making the Difference* and *Ockers and Disco-Maniacs*. We started with class inequality but developed an interest in gender and sexuality among teenagers. The interviews and case studies from this project have been important in my thinking ever since and are discussed at several points in this book. How femininity and masculinity are realized among adults, especially in the workplace, became a major theme in the study of teachers that grew out of the same project, *Teachers' Work*. In 1979 I began very hesitantly to work on issues of masculinity, attempting a self-analysis *à la* Karen Horney and writing about the politics of my own relationships and experience of the body. Less hesitantly I began a series of essays on the theory of patriarchy and how to connect it with socialist theory. The few publishable products of these two enterprises were collected in *Which Way is Up?* from which the idea of this book developed. The detailed studies in that book on the concept of social reproduction, Sartre's theory of practice, the connection of patriarchy and capitalism and the nature of role theory, underlie parts of the argument here, as indicated in the notes. In the 1980s the work on masculinity turned into two new projects. One was a theoretical study, done with Tim Carrigan and John Lee and published as 'Toward a New Sociology of Masculinity', which reworked social-scientific studies of masculinity in the light of gay liberation, psychoanalysis and feminism. The other is an empirical study of changes in contemporary masculinity, done jointly with Pip Martin and Norm Radican, which is still in the field. These two projects underlie a good deal of the discussion of personality in Part III.

My work on these issues has been strongly influenced by the work of other people at Macquarie University. Rosemary Pringle's work on sexuality, on gender and capitalism, and the industry studies that became Ann Game and Rosemary Pringle's *Gender at Work*, have been a constant point of reference. Sue Kippax introduced me to the new social psychology; Sheila Shaver to the intersections of gender with welfare policy. I have learnt a great deal from several doctoral students with whom I have worked as supervisor: Teresa Brennan, who introduced me to feminist psychoanalysis; Clare Burton, whose book *Subordination* develops a detailed critique of socialist-feminist thought; Tim Carrigan's work on gay liberation theory; Carol O'Donnell's work on labour markets in *The Basis of the Bargain*; and the late Di Court, whose work on feminism and the state highlighted the problem of the central structures of power. The continued interest of several generations of undergraduate students has been both a stimulus to do the work and a test of what was produced.

The final stages were made possible by research assistance from Thea Welsh, who is responsible for much of the detail in chapter 1, and Pip Martin, on questions ranging from the membership of the Soviet Communist Party to the recent history of Sydney theatre.

Many people have given feedback to working papers and drafts. I have been helped particularly by comments from Glynn Huilgol, Elizabeth Reid and Hester Eisenstein. Gary Dowsett, Lynne Segal, Rosemary Pringle, John Iremonger and Venetia Nelson read and criticized the whole manuscript. The bulk of the typing in the last few years has been done by Helen Easson, as it was in earlier stages by Heather Williams; the project would not have moved without their skill and critical interest. And I am deeply grateful for the tolerance and friendship of Robyn Dasey, in whose house the whole first draft was written.

Part of the work for this book was funded by the Australian Research Grants Committee with a grant for a study called 'Theory of Class and Patriarchy'. Grants for purely theoretical work are sufficiently rare that this should perhaps be celebrated. Part has been funded by Macquarie University Research Grants and by two periods of study leave from Macquarie University.

My greatest debt by far is to Pam Benton, who has been involved with the project through its whole development and at all its levels – intellectual, practical and emotional. I would like to dedicate the product to our daughter Kylie, in the hope that we can get enough right in this generation to make the world she grows up in a more equal, safe and rational place: less patriarchal and more human.

The plan of the book is straightforward: an introductory sketch of the facts of gender inequalities; three chapters on theories of gender; three chapters on gender as social structure; three chapters on gender as personality; and three chapters on politics and ideology. This plan, however, risks exaggerating the separateness of the parts. A central theoretical idea is that the social and the personal depend on each other and in an earlier draft of the book the chapters on personality came before the chapters on social structure. I would emphasize that Parts II and III should each be read in the light of the other.

Referencing is a problem with a complex and wide-ranging text, so I have invented my own (condensed) version of the Harvard system. The names of authors are mentioned in the text without dates and the details can be found in the alphabetical bibliography at the back. Any ambiguity about which work of a particular author is cited is explained in the bibliographical notes at the end of each chapter, which are compiled section by section. Here also are references which would have been awkward to include in the main text and discussions of some technicalities which would have interrupted the flow of argument. These notes refer, as in the conventional Harvard system, to the bibliography; with the exception of the notes to chapter 1, which give directly the sources of statistical data used in that chapter alone.

NOTES

For an example of the trouble a man can get into when writing about feminism, see the criticisms of David Bouchier's *The Feminist Challenge* by Janet Bujra and others (1984). For the gender dimension of our educational research see Kessler, Ashenden, Connell and Dowsett (1982, 1985).

1
Introduction: Some Facts in the Case

This chapter attempts to show why a social analysis of gender is needed for a comprehension of personal life, politics and society as a whole. It makes out a prima-facie case for the enterprise. Accordingly the facts are set out here with little commentary. Their interpretation is provided by the rest of the book.

The first part of the chapter takes one person – an Australian teenager called Delia Prince – as a point of departure and explores how her circumstances and choices are shaped in terms of sex and gender. Delia has not been chosen to represent a particular 'type'; the point is, rather, that the same kind of analysis would be needed to understand any individual life. The second part of the chapter looks at the collectivities Delia lives in: city, state, country, world. Here I discuss some of the statistical and institutional evidence about sex inequality and sexual politics. This too is illustrative. The topic is vast and only a fragment of the evidence can be recited in a single chapter. But it is perhaps enough to demonstrate the scale and importance of the issues.

A Teenager and her Family

Delia Prince (the name is a pseudonym) is one of the teenagers my colleagues and I interviewed in 1978, along with their parents and teachers, in the research project later published as *Making the Difference*. The research was an attempt to understand the circumstances, in school, family and workplace, that lay behind the massively greater drop-out rate from working-class high schools compared with ruling-class secondary colleges.

Delia was one of a sample of students from a working-class outer suburb, where she lives with her two parents, older sister and older brother. Like a large proportion of the Australian working class the family owns its own house, a comfortable brick-veneer one, set back behind a high fence. The house was built mainly by Delia's father and a great deal of her mother's energy over the years has gone into keeping its interior gleaming and its garden attractive.

Delia, fifteen at the time we interviewed her, is a cheerful if rather quiet person, past puberty, and already equipped with a steady boyfriend. From her parents' point of view she is doing well, especially as she has come through some serious medical problems and periods in hospital. She 'chatters' with her mother in the kitchen about what goes on at school, does her share of housework without much grumbling and, unlike many of her peers who sneak out at night, observes the family rules about when she can go out. 'Basically just a normal kid' is her mother's summary. Certainly Delia seems everyone's picture of a nice girl.

She loves animals and so would like to become a vet. That is, if she gets good enough marks at school; otherwise she will try for a clerical job in a bank. Her school test results at present are no better than moderate; she is having trouble with maths. She gets along easily with most of her teachers, though there are a couple she has disliked. From their point of view she is not very visible – not a problem, not a star. Apart from her parents' wishes and her own vague ambition to be a veterinarian, there is nothing much to attach her to the school. She confesses that she would prefer to leave this year, though she expects to go on to the School Certificate assessment and leave at sixteen.

'Just a normal kid', yes; but where does that 'normality' come from? How is it produced? And isn't there a little too much of it? If we push back behind the somewhat bland appearance of Delia's adolescence, some more complex and tension-laden processes might come into view.

To start with the economic circumstances of Delia's life, Fred Prince, her father, is a tradesman with a certified skill. He does not use this trade in his current job working for a public authority as leading hand in maintenance, in charge of a gang of five men. He left his trade a good many years ago to cash in on the television boom, setting up a small business installing aerials. Working very long hours he made enough money to buy a block of land and starting building a house. He eventually gave that job up because it kept him away from the family too much, and went back to work for wages. Rae, Delia's mother, also has a paid job. She is clerk, typist and office dogsbody for a small business selling motor parts. As a young woman in the late 1950s she started clerical work in a bank but was dismissed, as a matter of bank routine, when she married. She took other jobs and kept up paid work even when the children came along, in order to finance the house. Her current job is (theoretically) part time. She does the family's cooking and cleaning, washing, ironing and most of the childcare.

While there is a strong element of 'tradition' in this arrangement, it is also economically rational for the Princes to organize their employment this way. The base rate of pay in Fred's occupation is $10 a week more than in Rae's, and actual earnings differ much more than that because of overtime and various penalty rates. Equally important in a recession, Fred's job is much more secure. He is a member of a strong, though not exceptionally militant, trade union, run by men with experience much like his own, which has established virtually lifetime tenure for jobs at his level. Rae is covered by a union also run by men (though about two-thirds of its members are women). As it happens, this is a union dominated by conservative Catholic men who are not very keen about women being permanent members of the work-force at all. It has not established any rights of tenure or redundancy entitlements in jobs like hers.

When I first arrived at their house to arrange the interviews, Fred came to meet me with his hands covered with oil. He had been stripping down his lawnmower which had broken down because he was trying to mow wet grass in time for a christening party. Rae was inside the house cooking for the party. As this illustrates, Delia is growing up among clear-cut definitions of what is men's work and what is women's, at home as in the workplace. The sense of what work is appropriate for a woman feeds into Delia's ideas of possible futures. This is evident in her sex-typed interest in animals, and her idea of an alternative as a bank clerk, which is modelled directly on her mother's work history.

Despite a formal commitment to 'equal opportunity', her schooling does little in practice to change these ideas about work and the assumptions about marriage to which they are closely tied. Most of Delia's female friends and peers expect to get married fairly young and have children quite soon. So does she; she can even name the age – twenty – at which she expects to get married. There are some feminist teachers at her school who have different notions of what women might aim for. But as their ideas centre on 'careers' for women and advancement through higher education, they only make much sense to the girls in the 'A' stream – who are the only ones, in a working-class school, likely to have any chance of going to college or university. Delia is not one of them.

Yet Delia's future is not being constructed in a closed system. There are changes going on, even in small details. Her mother Rae, for instance, has taught Delia's brother, as well as the two girls, to cook. On larger issues there is significant tension, even contradiction. Rae herself had done well at school and was obliged to leave before she wanted to, to help her widowed mother. She had wanted to become a nurse but her boyfriend (Fred) did not like the idea, so she gave it up. Her mild comment, 'it's my only regret now', is the nearest she gets in the interview to expressing anger against Fred.

Even more striking is the fact that Rae kept a job when the children were young. This was for a 'good' reason, to pay for the house, but still violated an almost universal Australian doctrine that mothers should stay home with their pre-school children – a doctrine duly recited and endorsed by Delia. Rae was defensive and 'guilty' (her word) about this and has probably come in for a lot of criticism from relatives. She seems to have tried to compensate by being the perfect wife-and-mother ever since. One result is overload, doing a full-time job at home and a nearly full-time job at work. At thirty-eight she already looks worn and her manner is a little stressed and abrupt. Even Delia, with perception unusual in a fifteen year old, thinks that the job is good for Rae but that she is working too hard.

Both Rae and Fred have a clear idea of what a good family is. Both have sacrificed something in their own lives to make it possible and both have invested a lot of emotion and energy in trying to produce it. Delia, the youngest child, is now the focus of that process. Where Rae's mother had never spoken of sex, Rae and Fred have organized 'round-table sex talks' with their children. They have tried to be more humane than their own parents without losing control of the kids. They closely monitor what is going on in the teenage peer groups. Fred heard rumours of 'sex, drugs, playing up in toilets' at the school, so he went and challenged the teachers about it, to be reassured that Delia and her sister were not involved. Earlier this year Rae leant that Delia was in a group that smoked and got drunk at weekends; she exerted herself, successfully, to separate Delia from them. Yet Fred and Rae are not opposed to Delia having an active social life. The boyfriend is not only approved of, but, astonishingly, he seems to have been chosen by the parents. At least they introduced him to Delia.

Behind this constant management of the children is a structure of authority that makes Fred, very definitely, the 'head of the household' and Rae the second-in-command. He is self-confident in public, she is not. He contrasts his own behaviour with that of his father, 'a hard man' (read: violent) who would belt even an eighteen year old for bad manners at table. Fred reports with some complacency that he has thrashed each of his children once, hard, and never needed to again. Now he is able to control them by 'applied psychology'. We did not ask if Rae was included in the thrashings. (Statistics on domestic violence suggest that at least a quarter of all wives have been assaulted by their husbands at some time.) Fred puts a lot of energy into coaching local junior football teams and is president of their club; Rae is the treasurer. He takes, as a right, a couple of nights out for beers with the boys each week. Rae, even if she felt it the thing to do, does not have the time.

Clearly this is only the beginning of an analysis of Delia's circumstances. It is perhaps enough to show that what lies behind her relationship with school and intentions about leaving, the original question in our research, is a very complex interplay of personal and social forces. Much of this has to do with her family's class situation, as educational sociology has long insisted. But as much has to do with the fact that she is a young woman, growing up in a setting where relations between women and men work in a particular way.

We cannot understand Delia's life without having a way of understanding the division of labour between women and men in her household, in other families she encounters, in Rae's and Fred's workplaces and in the school. We need to understand the power relations between husbands and wives, between men and women in trade unions and companies and in voluntary organizations like the football club. We need to understand how Rae's femininity and Fred's masculinity are constructed, how Delia's sexual awakening is being managed, how images of

femininity are conveyed to her. We cannot understand Delia
without having some grasp of the tensions and contradictions in
these processes and the ways they change between generations.

These are not independent issues. They interact; indeed they
define a sphere of social life that is strongly patterned. As soon as
this is recognized, it is obvious that the pattern is not peculiar to
Delia, Rae and Fred. What happens in their milieu is part of a
much wider set of social processes, which must be analyzed to
understand what is happening in Delia's life. Let us turn, therefore,
to evidence about these patterns on the larger scale.

The Public World: Wages, Education, Jobs

The division of labour in Delia's household and the kinds of jobs
her mother and father hold outside, have roots in the conventional
images of man-as-breadwinner and woman-as-home-maker. They
also have a hard material base. We do not have Fred and Rae
Prince's tax returns but the general position is known. In 1978,
the year of these interviews, the average wages for adult full-time
employees in Australia were $239 a week if they were men, $183
if they were women. That is to say, a decade after the Equal Pay
Case that established a notional policy of sex equality in pay rates,
women got 77 per cent of what men got. By 1985 this had moved
up to 82 per cent.

These figures greatly overstate the general level of equality. In
the mid-1980s more women than men earn less than a full wage
because they are less than full-time workers. About 36 per cent
of employed women in Australia are part-timers (Rae Prince being
one), compared with 6 per cent of employed men. Taking all
employed people, women's average earnings are 66 per cent of
men's (1985 figures). Further, a higher proportion of women
workers earn no wage because they are are unemployed, and many
more women than men have very low incomes because they are
dependent on a pension or welfare benef.t. Figures for 1981/2
show that 1.97 million women have social security as their main
source of income compared with 0.78 million men. The result is
that the average income of women who have any income at all is
48 per cent of the men's average (1981/2). And even that overstates
the degree of equality, since a higher proportion of women have
no income at all. Adjusting for that, the average income of all

women is 45 per cent of the average income of all men.

Statistics on wealth are harder to come by, as wealth is better concealed. But there is no doubt at all that men control the major concentrations of wealth in the Australian economy. The magazine *Business Review Weekly* compiles, from a miscellany of sources, an annual list of the 200 richest people in the country. In the 1985 list just four of the listed names were women.

Australia has a reputation for putting women down; are these figures exceptional? There are no systematic statistics on men's and women's incomes on a world scale. But there are many pointers to the state of affairs in individual countries. A recent International Labor Office study of manufacturing industries in twenty countries, for instance, shows that women's wages are less than men's wages in every country studied. As examples:

	Women's wages as % of men's
West Germany	73
Japan	43
Egypt	63
El Salvador	81

Figures for Eastern European economies show much the same pattern as in Western Europe:

	Women's median full-time earnings as % of men's
Czechoslovakia	67
Poland	67
Hungary	73

A comparison of Latin American countries uses a different measure, setting cut-off points and showing what percentages of women and men fall above and below them. These figures show the percentages falling in the *lowest* income category in each country:

	Women	*Men*
Colombia (all employees)	47%	38%
Chile (non-agricultural)	27%	7%
Panama (non-agricultural)	34%	6%

Clearly the pattern of unequal income is international, though the level of inequality varies from place to place.

One of the reasons for these differentials (though certainly not the only one) is unequal access to education and training. There are relatively systematic international statistics on literacy and participation in schooling. Though the overall levels of literacy claimed have to be taken with a certain scepticism, there is no reason to doubt the overall pattern of sex differences that emerge within each country.

To get a global picture in these and following comparisons, I have taken countries from six broad groupings: (1) United States (a group in itself); (2) EEC + Japan; (3) Soviet Union and Eastern Europe; (4) China + India; (5) second-tier capitalist; (6) poorest.

Access to jobs outside subsistence agriculture – as well as other sources of social power – is very much affected by whether you have been taught to read and write. Almost everywhere in the world, more men than women have been. Table 1 shows a selection of illiteracy rates, the percentage of the population reported illiterate.

Access to higher-level jobs is very much affected by advanced education. Men generally get more of this than women. The figures in table 2 are percentages of the adult population who have post-secondary education.

The differences in earnings shown on page 7 are compounded by massive differences in the numbers of women and men able to earn any income at all. There are systematic figures on this, because of the close interest taken in the size and composition of the 'labour force' by official agencies concerned with economic development. The World Bank, for instance, has statistics on what percentage women make of the (paid) labour force in every country,

Table 1 Percentage of population reported illiterate

Country	Women (%)	Men (%)
(1) United States	Not given	
(2) Italy	7	5
(3) Poland	2	1
(4) India	81	52
(5) Brazil	26	22
(6) Indonesia	42	23

Table 2 Percentage of adult population with post-secondary education

Country	Women (%)	Men (%)
(1) United States	28	37
(2) Japan	10	19
(3) Poland	4	7
(4) India	0.3	2
(5) Brazil	3	5
(6) Egypt	1	5

Table 3 Women's share of the total paid labour force

Country	Percentage share
(1) United States	38
(2) West Germany	36
(3) Soviet Union	50
(4) China	38
(5) South Korea	33
(6) Colombia	25

and has even totalled them across four groups of countries (the categories neatly reflecting the Bank's own preoccupations). The figures are: for 'developing countries', 25 per cent; for 'capital-surplus oil-exporting countries', 5 per cent; for 'industrialized countries', 35 per cent; for 'centrally planned economies', 45 per cent. Examples of women's share of the total labour force in countries selected from the six groupings defined earlier, are shown in table 3.

Only in the Soviet Union and Eastern Europe, and some parts of Black Africa, is women's participation in the paid labour force close to that of men. In the rest of the world, men's participation rates run at roughly twice those of women. The differences are startling in Arab countries, where it is exceptional for more than 15 per cent of the paid labour force to be women; here men's participation rates are from five to twenty times as high as women's.

A low labour-force participation rate certainly does not mean that large numbers of women do no work. What it means is that their work is not paid. They work mainly outside the cash economy, in housework, childrearing, subsistence agriculture, or labour for a husband or father who markets the product.

This is one aspect of an economic segregation between women and men that also runs through the money economy. In Australia, for instance, men hold 86 per cent of the jobs as administrators, executives and managers, but only 28 per cent of clerical jobs; 88 per cent of jobs in trades, process work, labouring and mining and 47 per cent of jobs in sales (1983 figures). A study by the Organization for Economic Co-operation and Development (OECD), covering the richer capitalist countries, shows that this pattern is international: 'The coefficient of female representation shows that women are most under-represented in administrative and managerial occupations in all countries ... Women are over-represented in clerical occupations in all countries ... They are also over-represented in service occupations in all countries.' When the broad groupings are broken down, as the OECD study also notes, the degree of concentration can be even more striking: 'For example, in the United States in 1978, 97 per cent of registered nurses and 94 per cent of elementary teachers within this group were women, while 91 per cent of industrial engineers and 99 per cent of airplane pilots were men.'

One reason why women rarely appear near the top of the economic tree is that in a capitalist economy the ability to accumulate wealth is very much dependent on one's ability to command credit. There is reason to think that lenders – banks and other financial institutions – do not extend the credit to women that they do to men. The New South Wales (NSW) Anti-Discrimination Board, currently studying this issue, cites cases such as this in the early 1980s: 'A married couple ... had a joint cheque account with the same suburban bank. They separated and then took out individual accounts with the same bank. They both overdrew. The man's cheques were honoured though he overdrew by $1500. The woman's cheques were bounced although she overdrew by only $300.'

Direct discrimination in terms of sex, marital status and the assumption that a husband is necessarily 'head of the household' and therefore a wife is not an independent agent, is compounded by the fact that several categories of people who are usually not given credit at all consist mainly of women. This includes people dependent on welfare payments and those with no current cash income. The difficulties this situation creates for women in getting finance to buy a house are familiar in the experience of women's refuges.

Violence, Prejudice, the State

The lack of alternative housing is one of the reasons women may stay in, or return to, a violent marriage. Domestic violence is a very large part of all violence. It is difficult to get reliable statistics, but a good many pointers exist. A study of four police stations in different suburbs of Sydney in 1977–8 showed that calls to domestic assaults exceeded calls to other assaults – in some areas by a factor of three. (The notorious reluctance of police to intervene in domestic violence has some basis in the risk to the police themselves: in the United States about 20 per cent of police deaths in the course of duty occur in such cases.) A widely quoted study in Scotland found that 25 per cent of violent crimes reported to the police were assaults against wives and girlfriends. A national sample survey in the United States in the mid-1970s reported that 28 per cent of couples acknowledged at least one violent incident and estimated that the true figure was closer to 50 or 60 per cent. In a recent phone-in in Victoria 22 per cent of women had experienced domestic violence but did not report it. While violence by women against men is far from negligible, the majority of serious domestic assaults are by men against women.

This is part of a larger pattern of violence against women. Rapes reported to the police in Australia rose from around 600 a year in 1972–3 to over 1,200 in 1981–2. In the United States the figure rose from 47,000 in 1972 to 79,000 in 1983. There is reason to think that these figures are still very much understated and that most rapes are not reported to the police. An alternative approach is to conduct a survey of the general population asking people if they have been victims of various crimes. One such survey, done on a very large scale by the Australian Bureau of Statistics in 1983, estimated 26,700 sexual assaults on adult women during a year, including 8,600 rapes or attempted rapes. (Attacks on teenagers would have to be added to this figure.) This gives a rate of five sexual assaults for every 1,000 adult women, which may not seem very many until it is seen in its context of very widespread intimidation at a lower level, from wolf-whistles and shouted jokes to sexual harassment in workplaces. A number of the mothers we interviewed in Delia Prince's suburb will not let their daughters go out on the neighbourhood streets at night because of the fear these assaults generate.

Homosexual men also have reason to fear assault in public places – and one of the main groups they have to fear are the police. There are no official statistics on these matters, but police violence on a considerable scale has been carefully documented for New York from 1960 through a twenty-year period in which the growing political strength of gays led to a decline in the attacks. The murder of Dr George Duncan in Adelaide in 1972 was almost certainly the result of an entertainment for off-duty police which consisted of bashing homosexual men and throwing them in the River Torrens; Dr Duncan could not swim.

Other groups also are involved in attacks on homosexuals. A 1985 phone-in conducted by Gay Hotline in Sydney (sponsored jointly by the police) over two days received calls describing fifty-three episodes of assault on homosexual men. In almost all these cases the attackers were groups of teenage boys or very young men, a fact that raises disturbing questions about the role of violence and homophobia in the construction of masculinity.

These attacks occur in a context of general hostility towards homosexuals that ranges from discrimination in housing to legal danger. Antagonism to lesbians is less explicit than to gay men – there is a tendency to make lesbians socially invisible. Nevertheless it becomes very clear in such cases as a lesbian mother fighting a custody battle in the courts. Lesbianism itself is liable to be offered as evidence that a woman is unfit to have custody of a child. Gay men face the criminal law because of their sexuality. In most of Australia it is still illegal for adult men to commit 'the abominable crime of buggery' or 'indecent assault upon a male person'. In 1985 the state of Queensland even legislated to prevent hotels from serving beer to 'sexual deviants or perverts', meaning gays, along with 'drug dealers' and 'child molesters'. This degree of legislative stigmatization is exceptional; the attitudes underlying it are not.

Statistics on the operation of these laws are patchy but an indication is given by a study of Sydney court cases by the NSW Bureau of Crime Statistics and Research. This showed 100 to 200 prosecutions a year in the 1940s, rising to 400 to 500 prosecutions a year from the mid-1950s to the late 1960s. Great peaks and troughs (117 cases in 1966, 1,204 in 1968, a lull in the early 1970s) reflect changes in the intensity of policing. In the mid-1970s, when Sydney was well on the way to recognition as one of the 'gay capitals' of the world, the rate was rising again. In 1975 NSW courts processed 300 homosexual prosecutions under the Crimes Act and Summary Offences Act (plus others, their number uncertain, under the Child Welfare Act).

Police surveillance in pursuit of these laws merges into police harassment. 'Decoy' squads on homosexual beats produce a stream of individual prosecutions; there were said to be two such squads operating in Sydney in the mid-1980s, one in Adelaide. Much more publicity is gained by large-scale police raids on homosexual bars and baths, such as the 1977 raid on the Truxx bar in Montreal (146 arrested), the 1981 raid on bath houses in Toronto (304 arrested), or the 1983 raids on Club 80 in Sydney (over 100 arrested, though few charged). These patterns of intervention in turn merge into the violence already discussed.

While there are clear patterns of domestic assault and sexual assault against women and of violence against gays, there are other patterns of violence which affect men more drastically than women and heterosexual men as well as gays. The 1983 Australian national survey already mentioned estimated 113,000 assaults in a year against women and 278,000 assaults against men. In the same year there were 294 reported homicides in Australia: 41 per cent of the victims were women and 59 per cent were men. In the United States the 1978 rate of assaults per 1,000 people was 12 for women and 22 for men. In 1981 the United States had 23,600 homicides: 21 per cent were of women and 79 per cent were of men. In that year the rate of death by homicide per 100,000 people was 3 for white women, 13 for black women, 10 for white men and 65 for black men.

Those charged with or convicted of violent crime are overwhelmingly men. For instance, in NSW in 1983 some 519 people were convicted in the higher criminal courts of homicides, assaults and like crimes; 93 per cent of them were men. A study of homicide in NSW over a 50-year period found that between 80 per cent and 85 per cent of those charged were men. In the United States in 1983, 87 per cent of the people arrested for murder were men. In the same year men were 87 per cent of those arrested for aggravated assault, 88 per cent of those arrested for arson, and so on through other crimes of violence. Figures for other recent years are very similar.

So far as the official and semi-official figures go, then, it appears that men are more commonly than women the victims of serious interpersonal violence, and even more commonly the perpetrators.

The same is true of the institutional violence represented by the police, the prison system and the military. At the census of 1981 Australia had 30,200 police officers; 94 per cent of them were men. In June 1983, the most recent figures, there was a national prison population of 10,200; 96 per cent were men. The United States in 1983 had a prison population of 224,000; 93 per cent were men. This pattern too is international. The following figures are the percentage of prisoners in 1974 who were men:

Canada	97%
West Germany	97%
Japan	98%
Italy	95%

The situation in the military is similar. In June 1984 the Australian army, navy and air force between them had a total strength of 71,600, of whom 93 per cent were men. A comparison of the major NATO forces in 1979–80 shows the same pattern:

United States	92%
France	95%
West Germany	99.9%
Britain	95%

The dominance of the military by men was even more complete in the past. The United States armed forces, for instance, were 99 per cent men in 1960, 1965 and 1970. The percentage of women began to creep up in the early 1970s, with a formal policy of expanding women's role in the military starting in 1973. In most armies, nevertheless, women are forbidden to have a combat role. In anti-aircraft units in Britain during World War II women were allowed to do every job, including aiming the guns at the German planes – but not to pull the trigger.

What of those who control the machinery of state, who direct

Table 4 Women at upper levels of the state

Country	Date	Body	Percentage
Parliaments			
(1) United States	1984	Congress	4
(2) Japan	1985		4
(3) Soviet Union	1985	Supreme Soviet	33
(4) India	1985	(federal)	9
(5) Australia	1985	(federal and state)	9
(6) Colombia	1975		3
Judges			
(1) United States	1985	state and federal courts	7
(2) Britain	1984	high, circuit and county courts	3
(3) Soviet Union	1984	People's courts	36
(4) India	1986		2
(5) Australia	1985	all federal courts	5
Generals			
(1) United States	early 1980s		0.6
(2) Japan	1986		nil
(3) Italy	1986		nil
(4) Australia	1986		nil

the police, the bureaucracies, the soldiers? It is notoriously difficult to locate actual power-holders with any precision, but a reasonable first approximation is possible, by looking at three groups from whom some key power-holders are certainly drawn: judges, generals and members of national parliaments (see table 4). The statistics on parliaments are relatively easy to get, and are shown for countries chosen from the six groups defined earlier. Figures for judges and generals are scrappy but illuminating. As a change, the figures given in this table are the percentages of *women* in the groups named.

The Soviet Union looks rather good on these figures. But in the communist systems power resides more in the Party than the parliament – and in the Central Committee of the Communist Party of the Soviet Union, the participation of women in 1981 was 4 per cent.

At the end of an excellent review of the world-wide evidence on women in politics ten years ago, Kathleen Newland argued that a global change in the political position of women was under way. Legal equality (for example the right to vote) was now established and there was extensive participation in grass-roots politics. 'Yet women have only rarely surfaced among the leaders in politics. They are nearly absent from the positions where policy is hammered out, where decisions are made, where real power resides.' Ten years later it seems that not a great deal has changed. The levers of state power are still in men's hands.

The facts just recited are a very small fragment of the evidence now available on the social positions of women and men and on relationships surrounding different forms of sexuality. Though some of the details will be relevant to later steps of the argument, just one conclusion needs to be drawn here. The patterns of gender and sex that appear through this evidence are not just an important feature of human life; they are specifically *social*. They involve inequalities of income, the working of institutions, the distribution of power, the division of labour and other distinctively social facts. Whether these social facts have non-social causes will be considered in chapter 4.

Two assumptions or working hypotheses underpin the argument that follows. First, that the facts set out in this chapter are connected with each other; that is, we are dealing not with a shapeless heap of data but with a social *structure*, an organized field of human practice and social relations. This hypothesis is needed to get the analysis under way, though the evidence cited already suggests that it is sound, given the way similar patterns reappear across different fields of social life. A general concern of the book, and the specific topic of Part II, is how this structure can be understood.

There is no convenient name for this subject. Terms like 'sexual politics' and 'patriarchy' are useful in pointing to parts of it but not to the whole. An American conference in the mid-1970s managed to invent a whole new science of gender and call it 'dimorphics'; luckily no more was heard of that. Gayle Rubin wrote of 'the sex/gender system', which is better but begs questions about what exactly a 'system' is. Kate Young and her co-authors speak of 'the social relations of gender', the most precise term but an awkward phrase. 'Gender relations' is a reasonable abbreviation and I will use it as a name for the whole domain.

The second assumption is that the two 'levels' of fact discussed in this chapter – personal life and collective social arrangements – are linked in a fundamental and constitutive way. It makes no sense to theorize one without also theorizing the other. I introduced this chapter with a case study, not to humanize the statistics, but because of this basic point about method. The large-scale structures of gender relations are constituted by practices such as those Delia Prince and her family are engaged in. At the same time their practice cannot float free; it must respond to, and is constrained by, the circumstances which those structures constitute.

This is an abstract point in theory, but it is also a tangible reality. A final point about Delia will illustrate this. Delia told us she wanted to be a veterinarian. Her parents knew of this and were willing to bear the cost of her training, not a small matter for them. When we returned to that school several years later to report back and follow up, we learnt how things had turned out. Delia had left school at sixteen, as she had predicted; and she had found a job. It was a notable one both in terms of the general sexual division of labour and the specific history of her parents' marriage. She was not a veterinarian but a veterinary nurse.

There would be value in thinking through a life history in greater depth, as will be argued in Part III; but it is also important to know that conclusions go beyond the one case. Accordingly I will leave the Princes at this point and move on to other sources in later chapters. The approach to personal life that their interviews helped to develop nevertheless remains basic to the treatment of historical, psychoanalytic and other evidence.

It has been difficult, and remains difficult, to get the field of gender relations into focus. Strong emotions are involved. For many people it is threatening even to see these patterns as social. It is comforting to think the patterns are 'natural' and that one's own femininity or masculinity is therefore proof against challenge. Western intellectuals, by and large, have helped this evasion. The grand systems of philosophy and social analysis, from Thomism through Marxism to functionalism and systems theory, have taken the gender arrangements of the day pretty much for granted. Conventional politics marginalizes 'women's issues' equally firmly.

Nevertheless feminism, gay liberation and the research they have stimulated, have now made a case that cannot be ignored. A vast field has been opened up and existing theory and practice must be reconstructed in the light of it. The habit of mind that treats class, or race, or North–South global relationships as if gender did not matter, is obsolete – and dangerous. For the facts of gender do not go away. Aid programs to Third World countries, by ignoring gender in principle, in fact give resources to men rather than to women. Industrial and nationalist militancy that ignores questions of gender reinforces men's violence and the patterns of masculinity that lie behind it. The question of human survival, in the face of a global arms race and widespread environmental destruction, requires us to understand a play of social forces in which gender has a major part.

NOTES

Introductory

(p. 1). On how easy it is to fall into stereotypes about 'typical girls', see Griffin's book of that name (1985).

A Teenager and her Family

(pp. 1–6). This study is based on interviews from the research described in Connell, Ashenden, Kessler and Dowsett (1982). See two papers with a focus on gender and education: Connell et al. (1981) and Kessler et al. (1985).

The Public World: Incomes and Wealth

(pp. 6–7). Statistics on Australian earnings and work-force from the Australian Bureau of Statistics (hereafter ABS) Catalogue 6101.0, *Labour Statistics*, (1978), p. 71; and from ABS Cat. 4101.0, *Social Indicators*, 4 (1984), pp. 171, 192, 213, 214. The adjustment for people with no income is based on 1981 census figures for women and men aged fifteen and over, in ABS Cat. 2443.0, *Census – Summary Characteristics of Persons and Dwellings*, (1983). The ILO study is summarized in *Women at Work*, 1 (1983), pp. 4–5. Eastern European figures quoted by Molyneux (1981). The Latin American study, with figures dating from 1968–72, is summarized in Latin American and Caribbean Women's Collective (1980), p. 182.

Education, Labour Market and Finance

(pp. 8–11). Figures on illiteracy and post-secondary education (recalculated) from UNESCO *Statistical Yearbook*, (1984), tables 1.3 and 1.4: various years for different countries. Labour-force participation statistics from the World Bank's *World Tables*, (1980), pp. 460–5. Australian occupational segregation figures from *Social Indicators*, (1984), p. 178; for a review of segregation in the Australian labour market see the Women's Bureau report on *The Role of Women in the Economy*, (1981), pp. 22–33. International data and quotations from OECD document *Women and Employment*, (1980), p. 42. Newland (1980) is an excellent short introduction to the sexual division of labour on a world scale. Material on financial discrimination from Niland (1983) and report in the *Australian*, (4 February 1983).

Crimes of Violence

(pp. 11–14). Domestic violence statistics: United States, Straus (1978), p. 446. Scotland, Dobash and Dobash (1979). Police station figures from *Report* of the NSW Task Force on Domestic Violence (1981). This report, and Scutt (1983), compile the scattered Australian evidence. Rape statistics: Australia, *Year Book Australia*, (1985), p. 221. United States, *Statistical Abstract of the United States* (1985). National sexual assault estimate from ABS Cat. 4505.0, *Crime Victims Survey, Australia, 1983, Preliminary*, (1984). Homicides and assaults: ABS Cat. 4505.0; ABS Cat. 3303.0, *Causes of Death*, (1983); ABS Cat. 4502.1, *Higher Criminal Courts, NSW, 1983*; NSW Bureau of Crime Statistics and Research longitudinal study on homicide by Wallace (1986); *Statistical Abstract of the US*, (1980, 1985).

Homophobia

(pp. 12–13). Sydney and NSW statistics on court cases in Bureau of Crime Statistics and Research (1978/9), pp. 10, 33–7. Patterns of oppression of homosexual people are documented in the remarkable report of the NSW Anti-Discrimination Board (1982). Canadian raids documented in *Body Politic*, 94 (1983); 105 (1984); 117 (1985). New York beatings and other harassment are documented by Rosen (1980–81). Gay Hotline phone-in 19 to 21 July 1985 report by Police Gay Liaison Unit (NSW Police Community Relations Bureau press release).

Police, Prisons, Military

(p. 14). Australian figures from *Social Indicators*, (1984), pp. 263, 273. United States figures from *Statistical Abstract*, (1980, 1985). International comparisons on prisons from Heron House *Book of Numbers* (London: Pelham Books, 1979), p. 323. Military figures: Australia, *Year Book Australia*, (1984), p. 45; NATO, Chapkis (1981), p. 88; United States *Statistical Abstract*, (1980), p. 375.

State Office-holders

(pp. 14–16). Newland (1975) is an excellent general source on women's participation in the political system, though narrowly defined; the quotation is from p. 33. Other sources of figures quoted: Australia, Federal Court Library; Sawer (1985). United States, Stille (1986); Hacker (1983) and *Congressional Quarterly Weekly Report*, (10 November 1984). India, Japan and Italy, letters from respective embassies. Soviet Union, Perchenok (1985). Britain, Central Office of Information, *Women in Britain*, (1984).

Part I
Theorizing Gender

2

Historical Roots of Contemporary Theory

There is no widely accepted framework for understanding the facts set out in chapter 1. There are several conflicting ways of looking at them. The aim of the next three chapters is to come to grips with these approaches and derive from them a systematic basis for understanding gender.

The first step is to ask where they came from and how they gained their present shape. The outline in this chapter is far from being a complete history of ideas. That would be a massive undertaking in its own right. Yet we need some kind of historical framework, on the principle that social theory never occurs in a vacuum. It must always be understood, and evaluated, as itself a practice with a context.

Secular Morality

Social-scientific theories of gender are a Western invention, as far as I know, and definitely a modern one. Other civilizations have had their own ways of dealing with human sexuality and the relations between the sexes. As Indian eroticism and Chinese family codes illustrate, these can be as sophisticated and elaborate as anything the West has created. But they are different kinds of cultural formation.

Nor was this perspective part of European culture from the start. Sex and gender in the writings of medieval and Reformation intellectuals were, by and large, items in a debate about the *moral* relationships among men, women and God. Such a framework was not necessarily a constricting one. It could recognize the complexities of passion and treat them with great subtlety. Witness the theme of frustrated love from the romance of Tristan and Isolde, through Dante's story of Paolo and Francesca, to Shakespeare's *Romeo and Juliet*. Yet the well-spring of these stories was much more often a dilemma of conflicting obligations than a curiosity about motive. Similarly the discussion of sex by theologians and philosophers was intended to lay down what people ought to do, rather than consider why they did something else.

The first major change in this framework followed the corrosion of the belief that God laid down a path for women and men to follow. Among intellectuals of the Enlightenment we find the same topics as before, but now secularized. There is a debate about the moral justification of prevailing gender arrangements and – especially in the newly invented literary form of the novel – drama about the lives of people who bent the rules. The framework of a secular moralism, with Society in the place formerly occupied by God, could admit a fair range of positions, among them early feminism and libertarianism. The shock of the French Revolution pushed this debate suddenly in a radical direction. In both France and England clear statements of the 'rights of women' were published in 1791–2, hard on the heels of the 'rights of man'. The text best known to English-speaking readers, Mary Wollstonecraft's *Vindication of the Rights of Women*, laid heavy stress on the distortion of women's moral character by the oppressive conditions under which women lived. The same historical moment saw the bitter satire of conventional sexual morality by the Marquis de Sade in *Justine*, who went on in the monumental *Juliette* to explore the libertine sexuality that became possible when divine law was wholly replaced by human will.

For a good while these remained the high-water marks of sexual radicalism. The reaction against the French Revolution was legitimist in sexual as well as class terms. Most nineteenth-century intellectuals were hostile to Wollstonecraft and Sade if they knew of them at all. But the secularization of the moral argument about gender did stick. In the high tide of liberalism it took the form of a doctrine of equal rights, a claim for citizenship. When the first political mobilization of women on a significant scale began, at the Seneca Falls convention in the United States in 1848, it was centred on this doctrine. Within the liberal and utilitarian framework it became increasingly difficult to see any objection to women's citizenship. When John Stuart Mill wrote in *The Subjection of Women*, 'Under whatever conditions, and within whatever limits, men are admitted to the suffrage, there is not a shadow of justification for not admitting women under the same', the phrasing marked a decisive shift in the terms of argument. The logical presumption was now *for* equality. By the turn of the century in some colonies of settlement on the fringes of the capitalist world (Wyoming, Utah, New Zealand, Colorado, South Australia, Idaho), white women did have equal voting rights, and the struggle for the suffrage in countries of the industrial centre was well under way.

To speak of a 'secular moralism' is not to deny that religious moralism continued. It is a striking fact that nineteenth-century North American feminism only became a mass movement when tied in with religion, especially in the form of the Women's Christian Temperance Union. It is equally striking how the reaction against feminism and gay liberation in the United States in the late 1970s was closely tied to fundamentalist Protestantism. The history of ideas about gender is far from being a succession of neatly defined stages. However radical a new development, earlier frameworks are carried forward with it.

Yet the Enlightenment did see a basic restructuring of the field of argument and by the end of the nineteenth century a second restructuring was under way. The doctrine of equal rights fuelled a feminist mobilization in Europe and in North America and other colonies of settlement. By the 1920s women in these countries had searched out, attacked and often broken the worst of their formal or legal disabilities, most notably in suffrage, property ownership and access to education. At the same time the concept of equal rights led to a different kind of question. If the subordination of women was not natural or just, how had it come about? How was it sustained? These are no longer questions of ethics but empirical questions – and in the framework of secular moralism, empirical questions about 'society'. The logical consequence of the doctrine of rights, then, was a social science of gender.

In one sense this had been evident from the start. Wollstonecraft spent much of her time discussing how women's moral character was formed. She attributed women's character to their education, in the broad sense, and argued for reforming both. In the same vein early socialists like Robert Owen noted how women's and men's characters were distorted by oppressive conditions and deduced a need for educational as well as economic reform. A thread of sex egalitarianism ran through the Utopian socialist movement of the early nineteenth century. It became part of the mainstream socialist tradition through the writings of August Bebel and Friedrich Engels. In Engels this current met the speculative history of kinship being constructed by theorists like Morgan (*Ancient Society*) and Bachofen (*Mother Right*). Engels's famous *Origin of the Family, Private Property and the State* rested on ethnography that was soon superseded and as historiography was obsolete when it was written (see chapter 7 below). But it remained important because it crystallized once and for all the idea of relationships between men and women as a social system with a definite historical trajectory. The argument dramatized the differences between gender relations in the remote past, in known history and in the hoped-for future. Engels tied the trajectory of gender to the dynamics of class, but the basic idea did not depend on this link.

What Engels still took for granted, as did all the reformers of that generation, was the naturalness of the *categories* of 'women' and 'men', and indeed the conventional attributes of women and men. Radical doctrines of equal rights could easily coexist with highly conventional views about 'true womanhood', about the proper work of women and men and about their heterosexual destiny. Women's suffrage campaigners at the turn of the century routinely argued that the public realm needed the moral uplift, domestic virtues and nurturance that were the natural attributes of women. Along this track it was easy for upper-class feminism to merge into charity or moral surveillance of the poor, in the kindergarten movement and campaigns for infant health and mothercraft centres, eugenics, domestic science teaching and the like.

Science and Radicalism

These assumptions of naturalness were nevertheless challenged from several directions. One was evolutionary biology. Charles Darwin's *Descent of Man* in 1874 offered a detailed account of 'sexual selection' as a mechanism of evolution alongside the 'natural selection' emphasized in the *Origin of Species*. In his unemphatic style Darwin took the issue of sex out of the hands of theologians and moralists and made it a question of observation and comparison of the behaviour of different species. More, biologists became interested in why sex existed at all, and gradually developed an account of the evolutionary advantages given by sexual reproduction. Though one spin-off from Darwinism has been the 'naked ape' claim that men's supremacy over women is an evolutionary law, in the long term the effect has been unsettling for patriarchy. Merely by offering explanations of sexual behaviour, evolutionary biology entrenched the idea that these patterns were *in need of* explanation, that they were somehow problematic.

The scientific impact on the field of argument deepened with the advent of doctors interested in sexuality and gender and the creation of a semi-medical speciality which later came to be called 'sexology'. Medical and medico-legal case histories provided the first base for an exploration of the forms of human sexuality as a natural phenomenon. The first monument of this work was Krafft-Ebing's *Psychopathia Sexualis* (first edition 1886, numerous expanded editions later), which catalogued with horrified fascination the many forms of 'degeneracy' from transvestism and homoeroticism to eating shit and liking to be whipped. The anthropology of sexual variation was developed much more lovingly by Havelock Ellis, whose *Sexual Inversion*, the first volume of *Studies in the Psychology of Sex* to be published, appeared in 1897. But the central figure in this movement of thought was undoubtedly Sigmund Freud.

Particularly in 'Three Essays on the Theory of Sexuality', Freud's arguments wrecked the notion of natural fixed characters for the two sexes. His emphasis on 'bisexuality' in human emotions, and his insistence on the importance of conflict within emotional life, made it difficult to see any pattern of sexual character as completely settled. More, in his analyses of the 'Oedipus complex' he showed how patterns of emotion in adulthood could be grasped as resolutions of the conflicts of development, and how different childhood situations could twist and reconfigure every aspect of emotional life.

Freud's importance in the history of ideas was not so much in popularizing the theme of sex, which a good many others were also doing. It was in providing a method of research – 'psychoanalysis' itself – which generated masses of new information about emotional life and human development, and led to a focus on the *life history* as the unit of analysis rather than the species,

the body or the syndrome. The psychoanalytic life history forced
attention to the details of relationships, the configurations of
families, in short to the social contexts of emotional growth.
Psychoanalysis thus produced detailed and sophisticated accounts
of femininity and masculinity as psychological forms constructed
by social processes. Ironically this was not Freud's intention – he
clung to the hope of biological explanations of psychology – but
the logic of his methods led inevitably towards the social.

The concept of bisexuality was one of Freud's devices for
understanding homosexual attraction. This was a standing problem
for accounts of gender which based everything on biology or on
the attraction of opposites. And it was a 'problem' whose salience
was increasing, as the late nineteenth century sharpened the social
definition of 'homosexuals' as a group apart. This was partly by
new forms of criminalization (one of whose first victims was Oscar
Wilde), partly by medical definitions of homosexual behaviour as
pathology and partly by the political and cultural response of
homosexual people themselves. Authors such as Karl Ulrichs in
the 1860s and 1870s, and more famously Magnus Hirschfeld from
the 1890s on, had one foot in scientific sexology and the other in
the movement to liberalize social attitudes and laws. Hirschfeld's
Scientific Humanitarian Committee expressed the blend nicely.
The immediate outcome was a naturalistic theory of homosexuality,
the idea of a 'third sex'. This ran counter to the direction Freud
was taking, and so far as it supposed a physiological basis for
homosexual preference, can now be regarded as falsified. It was
a politically defensive idea, a reply to denunciations of homosexuals
as moral degenerates. Yet in the context of the early twentieth
century it had force as the only explanation of the stability of
homosexual desire over a lifespan. In this sense it added to the
voices questioning the taken-for-grantedness of the dichotomous
sex categories.

Freud lacked, notoriously, a theory of social structure. If the
conventional family were taken as a given, both his analysis of
psychosexual development and his medical treatments could
become a defence of the patriarchal status quo. They certainly did
among his followers, especially after the emigration of psychoanalysis to North America in the 1930s. Freud himself was a kind of
libertarian but not a political radical – and it was mostly among
radicals that the conventional family, and especially its division of
labour, came into question.

The issues raised by the Utopian colonies in the early part of the century, and by socialist theorists of the mid-century, gained extra force in the context of the 'new unionism' of the 1880s and 1890s, the unionization of unskilled workers. Attempts to form unions of working women ran into obstacles that were not met when unionizing men. Partly this had to do with direct resistance from men: unions controlled by men often would not accept women members. It also had to do with the specific kinds of paid work that women were usually employed to do, in domestic service and food and clothing industries, and with the demands placed on them for work in their own homes by husbands and other relatives.

Women in the socialist movement, for example Clara Zetkin, argued that socialist ideas and practices must be rethought to deal with the oppression of working-class women. They assumed that the sexual division of labour could be changed and began organizing to do it. In the first decade of the twentieth century strong women's movements developed in the socialist parties in Germany, the United States and elsewhere. Under their pressure, working-class organizations cautiously began exploring co-operative childcare, public laundries, communal living arrangements and community-controlled education as practical forms of the socialization of childcare and housework. For a short while this became the policy of the revolutionary government in the Soviet Union, urged on by Alexandra Kollontai.

It did not last. With Stalinism in the Soviet Union and the freezing of Western socialism after the 1920s, these policies were completely marginalized. (By 1937 George Orwell could include 'feminists' with sandal-wearers, nudists and vegetarians in a list of unwanted cranks haunting socialist conferences.) Socialist feminism had, nevertheless, made a theoretical breakthrough. It had placed what we now call the 'sexual division of labour' on the agenda for analysis and explanation, as firmly as the question of sexuality had been placed there by Darwin and the sexologists.

Sex Roles and Syntheses

The ebbing of the radical tide in the 1920s drained practical urgency from these debates about gender. In the next generation the main developments were academic. The 'woman question' in politics had already produced a response from the new sciences of psychology and sociology. One line of research asked what were the psychological differences between women and men and how they were caused. Starting in the United States about the turn of the century, 'sex difference' research gradually accumulated in huge quantity, though highly variable quality. In the 1930s this tradition intersected with the new technology of standardized attitude and personality tests, in attempts to measure 'masculinity/ femininity' directly as a psychological trait. Paper-and-pencil scales of masculinity and femininity (M/F) were devised and soon put to work diagnosing gender deviance.

Gender-scaling was on the face of it neutral as to the sources of the characteristics being 'scaled'. Academic social science was addressing that question on other terms. Jessie Taft developed the idea of women's *cultural* marginalization, an approach notable because it placed power and exclusion at the centre of a social analysis of gender. The main line of academic thought, however, followed another path with the propagation in the 1930s of the concept of 'social role'. The notion of a socially provided script for individual behaviour, first learned and then enacted, was easily applied to gender.

By the 1940s the terms 'sex role', 'male role' and 'female role' were in use. By the end of that decade American sociologists such as Mirra Komarovsky and Talcott Parsons had spelt out a functional theory of sex roles and the cultural contradictions surrounding them. These ideas converged with the growing industries of counselling, marriage guidance, psychotherapy and welfare case work. The concept of a normative 'sex role' and various patterns of 'deviance' from it became enormously influential, providing a practical warrant for intervention to straighten out deviants, and theoretical justification for the 'helping professions' as a whole. 'Sex role' has remained the central category of academic thought about gender ever since, with the sex-difference literature gradually slipping under the 'role' rubric as well.

In the meantime psychoanalysis had stirred anthropology in new directions. Freud and his follower Geza Roheim argued that the Oedipus complex was universal, some form of it appearing in every culture. In the 1920s and 1930s writers like Bronislaw Malinowski in *Sex and Repression in Savage Society* and Margaret Mead in *Sex and Temperament in Three Primitive Societies* drew on their own fieldwork to argue a general case for a connection between social structure and the emotional dynamic of sexuality. Malinowski, truer to Freud, centred his argument on the functional necessity of repression and the elaboration of kinship customs as a means to that end. Mead was more interested in the emotional colouring of a whole culture, and her approach was formative in the 'culture-and-personality' school of American anthropology. Perhaps the most important effect of their work was simply to document the range of ways in which different cultures dealt with sex and gender. The exotica of life in the Trobriand Islands, Samoa and New Guinea dramatized for Westerners the idea of social scripting; it was difficult in the face of this to take any aspect of gender relations for granted.

By the mid-century a number of intellectual currents were converging and the stage was set for reflective synthesis. Three theorists published major works, covering remarkably similar issues, within five years of each other; one starting from field anthropology, one from theoretical sociology and one from existential phenomenology. With them the social analysis of gender took its contemporary form.

Mead's *Male and Female*, Talcott Parsons's essays in *Family Socialization and Interaction Process* and Simone de Beauvoir's *The Second Sex* had very different intellectual programs and politics. That perhaps makes what they had in common more notable. All took a psychoanalytic view of the making of personality. All tried to integrate this (though on different terms) with analysis of the division of labour conceived mainly in terms of sex roles or gender roles. Parsons was most systematic about this, as 'role' had become a fundamental term in his general sociology. In all three authors the sense of the social contingency of sexual character and gender relations had gone very deep. Mead's deliberate cross-cultural contrasts dramatized the point most. But it was also assumed by Parsons, who in earlier essays had laid emphasis on the modernization of the female role in American society, and by de Beauvoir, who attempted a phenomenology of different kinds of femininity. Yet all three theorists tried to limit the free play that a complete sociologizing of gender would imply. Parsons did this by appeal to functional imperatives of society, Mead (the most conservative on this issue) by appeal to some rather ill-defined biological regularities in human development and de Beauvoir by the self/other structure of relations between men and women. All three defined gender patterns mainly in terms of relationships within the nuclear family, which all took to be, effectively, universal.

What de Beauvoir saw, and the others did not, was the dimension of power running through these relationships. Mead and Parsons, to put it in a phrase, synthesized the field of gender around the idea of custom and social stability. De Beauvoir synthesized it around the subordination of women.

In the short term the former was the more influential approach. Parsons's analysis of the family, particularly his distinction between 'expressive' and 'instrumental' roles, laid the basis for a conservative sociology of gender which took its place in the great expansion of American social science in the 1950s and 1960s. Its themes were the necessity of the nuclear family, the problems of personal adjustment to sex roles and techniques of intervention to keep the family in good repair. With 'family' and 'sex role' conflated, the actual focus of most of the resulting research was women as wives-and-mothers (the 'female role'). Sex-difference and gender-scaling studies continued and were generally taken to confirm the role paradigm. Despite Parsons's prestige, the area remained rather an academic backwater during these decades. It produced some notable pieces of field research, such as Komarovsky's *Blue-Collar Marriage* and Young and Willmott's *Family and Kinship in East London*. While these studies had considerable influence in social work and sometimes on social policy, they had little impact on social theory or the intellectual world of social science in general. It was not until the arrival of the new feminism at the end of the 1960s that a wider interest in gender was kindled, and then it was Simone de Beauvoir's perspective that became central.

Feminism and Gay Liberation

In the context of this history, the research and the theoretical work inspired by feminism and gay liberation in the 1970s was not as novel as many activists believed. A number of its concerns were already widely debated: the nature of femininity, the power relations between women and men, the socialization of children, the dynamics of desire. The domain of the argument, we may say, had been mapped out. Yet it would be equally wrong to see the new wave of theorists as simply replaying old themes, or as rediscovering an eternal feminism. The history sketched above has seen several transformations *within* a field of debate, and this is basically what happened around 1970. There was a reconfiguration of a wide intellectual field around the themes of power and inequality. Its impulse was a reconnection between theory, which had become largely academic, and radical politics. The existence and strategic problems of sexual liberation movements defined the central issues for a new generation of theorists. The theory of gender thus became, to a degree it rarely had before, a *strategic* theory, centering on how, and how far, the social relations of gender could be transformed. Even if most of the issues were long-established, they were now being questioned with an intensity and depth that made the analysis of gender the most disturbing force on the whole cultural scene.

One of the first effects of feminism on academia was simply to increase the volume of sex-role and sex-difference research. In 1969 sex-role studies accounted for 0.5 per cent of articles published in sociology journals; by 1978 they accounted for 10 per cent, around 500 titles a year. Eleanor Maccoby and Carol Jacklin's massive compilation *The Psychology of Sex Differences*, which cautiously advanced social-moulding ideas, shows the volume of research being done in the United States in the early 1970s. In 1975 a specialized journal appeared, called *Sex Roles*. The field subdivided into specialities: socialization (Maccoby's interest); men's roles as distinct from women's (Joseph Pleck's in *The Myth of Masculinity*); androgyny (popularized by Sandra Bem); and therapies concerned with gender adjustment ('assertiveness training' for women, and for men a kind of masculinity therapy promoted by growth-movement psychologists such as Herb Goldberg in *The Hazards of Being Male*).

With the exception perhaps of the androgyny literature, there was not much intellectual novelty in this literature (for reasons to be explored in chapter 3). There was however a highly significant politics. The sex role approach provided the theoretical ideas that underpinned liberal feminism, the most influential form of feminism in the United States at least. Betty Friedan in *The Feminine Mystique* (1963) criticized Parsons and Méad, but her call for women's emancipation was made from within the same framework. What is needed for reform, in Friedan's argument, is a change of women's identity and expectations.

In liberal feminism generally, women's disadvantages are attributed to stereotyped customary expectations, both held by men and internalized by women. These stereotypes are promoted through families, schools, mass media and other 'agencies of socialization'. In principle the inequalities can be eliminated by breaking down the stereotypes: for instance by giving girls better training and more varied role models, by introducing equal-opportunity programs and anti-discrimination legislation, or by freeing labour markets.

A large volume of literature appeared in this vein, much of it academic but a good deal of it focusing on policy. Sex role theory rapidly became the theoretical language of feminist reform within the state, such as the influential 1975 Australian Schools Commission report *Girls, School and Society* and the 1980 OECD report *Women and Employment*. It was even discovered that freeing sex-role conventions might be good for men. Such was the claim of the 'men's liberation' movement in the United States in the mid 1970s, through publicists like Jack Nichols, the author of *Men's Liberation*.

The more radical wing of the feminist movement soon moved beyond the concept of 'sex roles' and the strategy of changing expectations. These ideas were seen to be inadequate because they missed the significance of power in gender relations. Women's Liberation groups argued that women are oppressed because men have power over them; and that changing the situation of women means contesting, and eventually breaking, this power. Analyses that started from these assumptions initially found much less acceptance in academia and very little in the bureaucracy. They became common in the social movement and drew from movement experiences of political campaigning and consciousness-raising groups.

In its simplest form the power analysis of gender pictured women and men as social blocs linked by a direct power relation. This implies as a strategy for change a direct mobilization of women emphasizing their common interest against that of men. There have been varying accounts of the relation between the two blocs. Christine Delphy's *The Main Enemy*, with French farming households in mind, stressed the economic exploitation of wives by husbands. American theorists tended to bypass economics for politics. Shulamith Firestone in *The Dialectic of Sex* saw a collective power-play by men with the childraising family as its central institution; sexual reproduction rather than housework was the key. Mary Daly in *Gyn/Ecology* pictured a global patriarchy sustained by force, fear and collaboration. Radical-feminist analyses of rape, such as Susan Brownmiller's *Against Our Will*, and of pornography, such as Andrea Dworkin's *Pornography: Men Possessing Women*, have generally followed this model.

A rather more complex line of argument treated the power of men and the subordination of women as effects of imperatives outside the direct relationship between the two. The more general form of this argument started from the need for 'social reproduction', that is, the reproduction from generation to generation of social structures as well as bodies. This was the perspective of Juliet Mitchell's *Psychoanalysis and Feminism*, strongly influenced by Marxist and anthropological structuralism. It was also the perspective of a more humanist psychoanalysis in Dorothy Dinnerstein's *The Mermaid and the Minotaur*. Dinnerstein's argument deduced both the power of men and the acquiescence of women from women's monopoly of early childrearing – itself seen as a technical imperative through most of human history. The theory of social reproduction has recently been given its most sophisticated statement by Clare Burton in *Subordination*. Her argument connects the cross-cultural analysis of women's subordination to the critique of education and the theory of the state – the latter theme treated surprisingly little in radical feminism generally.

To most socialist feminists the question was not the reproduction of society in general but of capitalism in particular. The exploitation of women was connected with capitalism's drive for profit and its general need to reproduce itself: pressures that led to a sex-divided work-force and the oppression of the housewife. These arguments too were linked with ideas about movement strategy. While sectarian Marxists argued against a separate women's movement of any kind, the majority of socialist feminists worked for an autonomous women's movement which would connect with other movements of resistance to capitalism, especially the labour movement.

Socialist feminists directed attention particularly to the situation of working-class women. A long argument arose in the 1970s about the economic significance of their unwaged work at home as a hidden subsidy to capital. The 'domestic labour debate' eventually petered out in a morass of Marxist exegetics, though not before a 'Wages for Housework' campaign had given an industrial dimension to feminist critiques of the family. Another, and eventually more fruitful, line of attack was on the politics and economics of women's waged work. At first sight this appeared as an issue of simple discrimination, or an aspect of the economists' 'dual labour market'. But studies like Louise Kapp Howe's *Pink Collar Workers* gradually revealed the gendered economy as a system of segregation, control, exploitation and social struggle of awe-inspiring scope and complexity. In recent research like Ann Game and Rosemary Pringle's *Gender at Work*, Cynthia Cockburn's *Brothers* and *Machinery of Dominance*, and Carol O'Donnell's *The Basis of the Bargain*, the workplace is treated as a major site of sexual politics in its own right. It can be analysed as an institution, as the point of junction between labour markets and the distribution of income, or as the object of ideology and education.

The problem of the general conditions for the reproduction of capitalism led back to sexuality and the family. Here arguments converged from feminism, from the 'Freudian Left', from the 'New Left' and counter-culture of the 1960s and from gay liberation. Texts like David Cooper's *The Death of the Family* inverted the conventional sociology of the nuclear family, presenting it as an authoritarian institution and the main tool by which a repressive society could control sexuality and create conformist populations. Feminists in the early 1970s widely considered the family to be the main site of women's oppression. Lee Comer's *Wedlocked Women* was perhaps the sharpest statement of the analysis of marriage, housework, motherhood and family ideology that sprang from this.

The most radical departure in the critique of the family was made by theorists of gay liberation. Sex-role theory and socialist theory alike presumed that the vast majority of people were naturally heterosexual; even the early homosexual rights movements had accepted that. The new movement did not. An early slogan declared 'Every straight man is a target for gay liberation'. The changed assumption, and the energy of gay politics in the early 1970s, led to a remarkable surge of theoretical work in several countries. The Australian Dennis Altman in *Homosexual: Oppression and Liberation*, the Italian Mario Mieli in *Homosexuality and Liberation*, and the 'gay Left' in England and the United States all developed variants of a critical theory of sexuality. They generally saw the family as the factory of heterosexuality, meeting capital's need for a labour supply and the state's need for subordination. The repression of homosexual desire, while certainly part of a general authoritarianism, thus had quite specific reasons. Yet it was necessarily imperfect; and imperfectly repressed desire was a prime source of the hatred directed against homosexual people. The liberation of homosexuality was therefore not the traditional campaign for equal rights for a persecuted minority. It was the cutting edge of a more general liberation of human potential.

Whether this blend of Marx, Freud and gay activism could be linked to the feminist critique of patriarchy, and if so on what terms, was a major concern of gay theorists through the 1970s. One of the difficulties was the analysis of masculinity. Early gay liberation theorists treated gayness in men as a kind of dissent from masculinity. This became less and less credible with the spread of 'gay machismo' and the 'clone' style in the homosexual subcultures of the late 1970s and early 1980s. A strong current in radical feminism emphasized the differences between lesbianism and men's homosexuality and wanted no truck with gay men. By the early 1980s gay theory, like feminist theory, was internally divided. David Fernbach's *The Spiral Path* emphasizes the theory of patriarchy, the importance of violence and the patriarchal state, treating homosexual men as necessarily effeminate. Dennis Altman's *The Homosexualization of America* focuses on the new sexual communities and the terms on which they can create solidarity and defend themselves. A third tendency, strongly influenced by Michel Foucault, questions the very notion of 'homosexual identity' as a form of social regulation, and sees progress in the deconstruction of homosexuality itself.

Reaction and Paradox

As radical theories of gender multiplied and divided, and strategies for change became more sophisticated and controversial, a counter-current of reaction also gained strength. Its highlights included the rise of the anti-abortion movement in the 1970s, the narrow defeat of the Equal Rights Amendment in the United States, the squeeze on the welfare state (and therefore services to women) in most capitalist countries, and the international moral panic created around AIDS in the 1980s.

The theoretical expression of this movement has been patchy. Its doctrine is most often religious dogma, or a decayed Darwinism asserting that men's and women's conventional roles reflect biological necessity and that social variation from this must be pathological. The more sophisticated forms of biological reductionism, like Steven Goldberg's *The Inevitability of Patriarchy*, appeal to genetic or hormonal differences between women and men – in Goldberg's case to explain an 'aggression advantage' men have over women, which in turn explains their social positions.

Biological reductionism has been a popular genre in the age of the territorial imperative, the naked ape and the rise of 'sociobiology'; but it was not an adequate response to radical arguments pitched at the level of the social. Conservatism too was obliged to develop a social theory. In texts like the American historian Peter Stearns's *Be a Man!* the emphasis is on social tradition and civility: the nuclear family, somewhat idealized, becomes the basis of a civilized and equable way of life. Compared with this urbane conservatism a more urgent note is struck by the New Right theorist George Gilder. In *Sexual Suicide* Gilder develops an analysis of the mother–child bond as the basic social linkage, which leaves men (as fathers) floating loose. The family as an institution is essential to prevent the destruction of social order by unbound men; and society must provide the economic and managerial roles for men. Anti-feminist conclusions are thus deduced from a strictly social analysis. There is an echo of Parsons's functionalism in this argument; as in the neo-conservative economists who explain the conventional family as the outcome of choices by two rational individuals each bent on maximizing their own welfare.

The state of the field in the mid-1980s is a paradox. The impulse of the last two decades has produced a mass of factual research and a lively theoretical debate, including some theorizing of very high quality indeed. It is difficult to think of any other field of the social sciences where work as penetrating and original has been going on. Yet as the social theory of gender has blossomed, the differences between lines of thought have become more distinct, the conceptual and political distances greater. Current theories of gender are not converging. Rather they present incompatible accounts of the issues, sometimes by marking off separate parts of the field. To move on, it would seem, it is necessary to move back, to reconsider the foundations of the theories now on offer. This is the business of the next chapter.

NOTES

The account in this chapter has been put together from a great many sources; even so I am conscious of its tentative and preliminary character. The main primary sources are the books and papers mentioned in the text. For discussion and interpretation see the following:

Early Feminism and Sexual Radicalism

(pp. 24–6). On the origins of liberal feminism see Martin (1972) and Rosenberg (1982). The view of Sade as a sexual radical is debatable; justification can be found in Carter (1979) and Thomas (1976). On early socialist feminism see Taylor (1983).

Sexology and Psychoanalysis

(pp. 27–8). Weeks (1985) gives an excellent summary of the history of sexology. His *Coming Out* (1977) is fundamental to the history of homosexual movements. For the bases of my interpretation of psychoanalysis see 'Dr Freud and the course of history' in Connell (1983). For the encounter with the Left and with anthropology see Robinson (1972).

Socialist Feminism

(pp. 28–9). For the general story see Rowbotham (1974). Conditions of women's unionization are explored in exceptional detail for the city of Hamburg by Dacey (1985). On the strength of the women's movement in turn-of-the-century socialism see Dancis (1976) on the United States. Its impact in the Russian Revolution can be traced in the writings of Kollontai (1977). Orwell's famous sneer is in *The Road to Wigan Pier*, (1962), p. 152.

Academic Theorizing

(pp. 29–32). Klein (1946) is a pioneering and still useful account of the development of academic thinking about gender; Rosenberg (1982) gives more detail on early sex difference studies. The emergence of sex-role theory is sketched in Carrigan, Connell and Lee (1985). For its classic statement – apart from Parsons – see Komarovsky (1946, 1950).

'Second-Wave' Feminism and Gay Liberation

(pp. 32–7). The recent development of radical theory is itself hotly disputed. Notable beginnings in charting this history have been made by Hartmann (1979) and Burton (1985) on Marxist feminism; Molyneux (1979) on the domestic labour debate; Eisenstein (1984) and Willis (1984) on American radical feminism; Walter (1980) and Carrigan (1981) on gay liberation theory.

3

Current Frameworks

This chapter tests the major frameworks for the social analysis of gender that have emerged from the history just discussed. The focus is on the general logic of different kinds of theories rather than on particular applications or particular concepts.

I take this rather formal approach as it seems the best way to get a grip on the possibilities for theoretical growth, to define both the potentials and the inherent limits of existing frameworks. This leads to a rather unusual classification of theories. Commonly recognized 'schools' of thought turn out to contain logically disparate theories. Socialist feminism for instance contains several of the types of theories discussed below. The concept of 'patriarchy', approached in this way, does not stand for a particular school at all. It appears in several logically different forms of theory and takes on different meanings according to its context.

Three distinctions are basic to what follows: (a) between extrinsic and intrinsic accounts of the determinants of sex inequality; (b) within intrinsic theories, between those that focus on custom and those that focus on power; (c) within power theories, between those that see categories as prior to practice and those that see categories as emerging from practice. I start with extrinsic theories, not because they are less sophisticated but because they do seem the least promising for the general project of a theory of gender.

Extrinsic Theories: From 'Class First' through 'Social Reproduction' to 'Dual Systems'

Chapter 2 noted the divergence between feminist theories that saw direct power relations between men and women as the main determinant of women's oppression, and those that looked elsewhere. The most influential extrinsic theories (apart from biological determinism, which will be discussed in chapter 4 and is not a form of social theory) have been Marxist analyses that locate the fundamental determinants of women's oppression in class relations, the capitalist system, or the 'relations of production' understood in class terms.

The simplest version of this idea is the view that 'women's liberation depends on the class struggle' because capitalism is the root cause of all social inequalities and class struggle against capitalists is therefore primary. In *Women's Liberation, Class Struggle*, an American booklet circulated in the early 1970s, Karen Miles summarized a widespread view of how women's oppression serves the ruling class. Capitalists get higher profits because women workers get lower wages; sexism divides the working class; women's oppression maintains the family, which in turn maintains capitalism. This simple synthesis of socialist and feminist ideas proved too much for more orthodox Marxists to digest. Recent evidence is the rousing restatement of the class-first view by the British Trotskyite Tony Cliff, *Class Struggle and Women's Liberation*. At remarkable length (the book is one of the longest analyses of modern feminism yet published by a man) Cliff argues that there can be 'no compromise' between Marxism and feminism: the latter is a bourgeois deception of honest working women. Essentially similar views are official doctrine in the Soviet Union and China, one of the few points on which these regimes still agree. In China the regime has tried to break women free from the extended patriarchal family by substituting the ideal of a harmonious nuclear family, with the sexual division of labour remaining unchallenged. The Soviet regime is equally complacent about women shouldering the social burden of childcare and other work in the home. Policy on sexual politics has been consistently subordinated to the twists and turns of the class line.

As theory, these views give little to bite on. The priority of class struggle is, as Christine Delphy comments on similar arguments in France, 'a postulate, a dogma'. There is an obvious objection: the subordination of women started long before capitalism, occurs in all classes under capitalism, and has continued in countries that have ceased to be capitalist. The fact that women of different classes have different interests is of great importance. But it does not need a dogma of the theoretical priority of class to recognize this.

Nevertheless, the seeds of a much more powerful analysis were present in Miles's remarks about the family. In the middle and later 1970s this was developed by a number of theorists, particularly in Britain, under the influence of structuralist Marxism.

The central idea was that the family, sexuality or gender relations at large were the site of the *reproduction* of 'relations of production'. A particular pattern of relations of production (which mainly means class relations in industry) is taken in Marxist theory to define a 'mode of production' (capitalist, feudal, etc.). A mode of production provides, so to speak, the backbone of a whole historical epoch. These relations of production could not exist without being reproduced, from day to day, year to year, generation to generation. This need calls into existence social processes centering on the family, domestic life and the raising of children. Different theorists gave somewhat different accounts of these processes. Juliet Mitchell saw patriarchy as the sphere of ideology, inserting people into their slots in the world of production. Other English theorists traced a whole new set of social relations here, the 'relations of reproduction'. There was agreement, nevertheless, that these processes or this sphere was the main determinant of the subordination of women.

Social reproduction theory in this form represented a major advance over simple class-interest theories of patriarchy and offered a synthesis of several important lines of thought. 'Reproduction' could be understood as bearing children to fill places in production and servicing the tired worker at the day's end. Here theory could connect with the basic facts of life documented by working-class women themselves, in autobiographical writings from Margaret Llewelyn Davies's *Life As We Have Known It* to Gwen Wesson's *Brian's Wife, Jenny's Mum*. Alternatively 'reproduction' could be seen as a matter of culture and psychology, of 'socialization', making square people to fit square holes in capitalist industry. This picked up themes that were familiar in socialist critiques of the ways education and culture were distorted to fit the needs of capitalism. When Andrew Tolson argued a connection between competitive masculinity and the functional requirements of capitalism, the material was new but the form of argument was very familiar to socialists.

Above all, reproduction theory argued a *systemic* connection between the subordination of women and economic exploitation in capitalism. The link was seen as embedded in a whole integrated structure of social organization, not in particular interests or groups. The bourgeoisie-as-devil faded from the picture. This allowed the tremendous complexity of the issues to be recognized; some subtle and important researches resulted. But it also made the target of reform seem much more formidable and less vulnerable than the politics of the early 1970s had assumed. There was more than a flavour of pessimism about social reproduction theory.

As this is true of reproduction approaches in other fields of social analysis, such as Bourdieu's work on education and Althusserian class theory, it is likely that it flows from some general feature of the approach. It is, I think, inherent in the concept of 'social reproduction' itself, which makes sense only if an invariant structure is postulated at the start. History enters the theory as something *added on* to the basic cycle of structural reproduction. For history to become organic to theory, social structure must be seen as constantly *constituted* rather than constantly reproduced. And that makes sense only if theory acknowledges the constant possibility that structure will be constituted in a different way. Groups that hold power do try to reproduce the structure that gives them their privilege. But it is always an open question whether, and how, they will succeed.

'Social reproduction,' therefore, is an *object of strategy*. When it occurs, as it often does, it is an achievement by a particular alliance of social forces over others. It cannot be made a postulate or presupposition of theory. And the concept cannot take the explanatory weight that reproduction theories of gender place on it.

The second major difficulty in these approaches is making a convincing connection between the needs of capitalism and what is specific about gender. It is clear enough that if capitalism is to continue, its dominant groups must succeed with some kind of reproduction strategy. But it is not at all obvious that doing this must produce *sexual* hierarchy and oppression. Much the same might be argued (and sometimes is) about racial and ethnic hierarchies or about hierarchies of age. There is historical evidence, known to early socialists like Engels and Bebel, that in some respects capitalism has broken down existing patriarchal customs and given women greater personal freedoms and more chances for equality. Recent experience in countries like the United States and Australia shows that the feminist attack on the restrictions on women's lives and careers may unlock their talents for capitalist purposes. Witness the co-optations not only documented but celebrated in magazines like *Ms* and *Portfolio*. Clearly the relationship between capitalism and patriarchy is not simply functional. The fit is looser, the relationship more contradictory, than reproduction theory has supposed.

In trying to bridge this gap, Marxist-feminist reproduction theory sought explanatory principles mainly in cultural theory: Lacan's reworking of psychoanalysis, Lévi-Strauss's structural anthropology and various developments of semiotics. A consequence of this was a strong tendency to treat gender relations as a *truncated* structure by comparison with class relations. In some versions, social reproduction and patriarchy were regarded as occurring entirely in the realm of ideology, and not part of the sphere of production at all. In other versions 'reproduction' was connected with a social division of labour, but only one kind of labour, housework. This sense of gender relations as being less comprehensive than class relations underpinned a view of the history of gender which saw its major turning-points in terms of a class periodization of history. For in Marxist theory it is the history of class relations in production that defines the 'modes of production' and the transitions between them.

In this tendency to truncate the concept of patriarchy the logic of reproduction theory led steadily away from the developing *practical* concerns of socialist feminists. In Australia and Britain at least there was increasing involvement in the late 1970s and early 1980s with issues that were very much about the material world and the sphere of production: women's employment, wage rates, unionism, health care, state regulation and like matters. At the same time there was an increasing flow of research studies, inspired by socialist-feminist concerns but not by reproduction theory, into women's experience in factories and labour markets. Studies like Claire Williams's work on open-cut mining towns in Australia and Ruth Cavendish's work on a motor vehicle components factory in Britain, rapidly demonstrated that gender relations and sexual divisions were deeply embedded in the production system of advanced capitalism – the traditional heartland of class theory. The clear implication is that gender relations are not a truncated structure. Gender is *part of* the 'relations of production', and has been from the start; it is not just mixed up in their reproduction.

Along this track lay a different answer to the question of how capitalism and patriarchy were connected. Socialist feminists in

several countries in the 1970s pointed in this direction. Mariarosa
Dalla Costa and Selma James wrote that 'class exploitation has
been built upon the specific mediation of women's exploitation'.
Barbara Ehrenreich argued that socialists must see women at the
heart of the working class. Anja Meulenbelt contested the idea
that the class struggle was the 'general' struggle and feminist
organizing was a diversion. Nancy Hartsock argued for a fundamental rethinking of the category of class in the light of gender issues.

To start with, these arguments were unrelated; but they had in
common the implication that gender relations are parallel to,
interacting with, and in some sense constitutive of, class relations.
Heidi Hartmann's paper 'The Unhappy Marriage of Marxism and
Feminism' and Zillah Eisenstein's collection *Capitalist Patriarchy and
the Case for Socialist Feminism*, both published in 1979, crystallized an
approach that came to be called 'dual systems theory'. The basic
idea is that capitalism and patriarchy are distinct and equally
comprehensive systems of social relations which meet and interact.
The present form of their interaction is the social order which
Eisenstein calls 'capitalist patriarchy'. Understanding the contemporary world requires the simultaneous analysis of its class and
gender structures. The analysis of gender requires in principle an
intrinsic theory logically independent of the theory of class.

In terms of our present knowledge of gender, this is better
founded than social reproduction theories. It is consistent with the
fact that gender relations appear in all domains of social practice
and pre-date capitalism and possibly class societies of all kinds.
The approach meets Meulenbelt's practical criterion of giving
full weight to women's experience of sexual politics, without
abandoning the politics of class. Yet it has two considerable
difficulties. One is the idea of a 'system'. It is not immediately
clear what makes the patriarchal 'system' systematic, and in what
sense capitalism and patriarchy are the same kind of thing. The
other difficulty is how to understand the 'interaction' between
capitalism and patriarchy. The link may be seen as a boundary
exchange (in the sense of Parsons' systems theory), or as a more-
or-less chance intersection of structures. Neither idea gives much
grip on the task that socialist-feminist theory is presumably *for*,
that is, explaining oppression and developing a strategy of
liberation.

These difficulties are substantial. It is unlikely that formulations
of the class and gender problem like Hartmann's and Eisenstein's

can stand in their present terms. Yet the overall direction they are taking does seem right. If we regard them as first approximations within a general type of theory their potential can be developed in new ways. The first thing required is an adequate *intrinsic* theory of gender. Accordingly the rest of the chapter considers the main versions of intrinsic theory.

Sex Role Theory

The literature on 'sex roles' is very large. It is also more than a little confused, especially over the differences between 'sex roles', 'sex differences' and 'sexual character'. An example is the well-known research on androgyny by Sandra Bem, which attempts to measure psychological traits of masculinity and femininity. Her questionnaire is entitled the 'Bem Sex Role Inventory' though it does not include questions about *roles* in any strict sense of the term. In literally hundreds of other studies, information on sex differences is presented with a loose assumption that role phenomena explain the differences observed. So it is often quite difficult to specify exactly what theory is contained in 'sex role' literature.

There is, nevertheless, a definite body of social theory organized around the concept of 'role'. While formulations of the concept (which go back to the 1930s) differ in detail, most have five points in common which form the logical core of role theory. The first two state the essential metaphor, an actor and a script:

1   an analytic distinction between the *person* and the social *position* she occupies;
2   a set of *actions* or role behaviours which are assigned to the position.

The other three state the means by which the social drama is set in motion and held to its script:

3   Role *expectations* or norms define which actions are appropriate to a given position;
4   they are held by people occupying *counter-positions* (role senders, reference groups),
5   who enforce them by means of *sanctions* – rewards, punishments, positive and negative reinforcements.

These concepts are the tools by which role theory attempts a general analysis of social interaction. Broadly, role theory is the approach to social structure which locates its basic constraints in stereotyped interpersonal expectations.

This paradigm can be applied to almost any type of human behaviour, and in either very general or very narrow terms. Textbooks make a point of this range, listing examples of roles ranging from the breadth of 'speaker of a language' to the narrowness of 'astronaut' (cases given in Bruce Biddle's *Role Theory*). Accordingly the role paradigm can be applied to gender relations in various ways. In one direction the 'roles' can be very specific. Mirra Komarovsky's work on the family for instance attempts detailed descriptions of role behaviour in courtship or marriage. In a more recent text called *Role Structure and the Analysis of the Family* a group of American sociologists list a remarkable number of roles they have discovered inside the American family, including the 'childcare role', the 'kinship role', the 'sexual role', the 'recreational role', not to mention the 'provider and housekeeper roles' (which are, happily, complementary). What such lists mainly demonstrate is the vagueness of the role paradigm.

Most applications of role concepts to gender are of a different kind. Their basic idea is that being a man or a woman means enacting a general role definitive of one's sex – the 'sex role'. There are, accordingly, always two sex roles in a given context, the 'male role' and the 'female role'; less commonly but equivalently called 'man's role' or 'woman's role', the 'masculine' or 'feminine role', etc.

This way of talking about gender is attractive in several ways. First, it allows a shift away from biological assumptions about sex differences, emphasizing that women's and men's behaviours are different because they respond to different social expectations. Some of the most fruitful research stimulated by role ideas has looked at the way these expectations are defined in the mass media. The constricted character of media images of women is striking, a point noted in the 1960s by Betty Friedan as part of 'the feminine mystique' and repeatedly confirmed in media studies since.

Second, sex role theory connects social structure to the formation of personality, an important and difficult theoretical task. Proponents of general role theory such as Ralf Dahrendorf claim that the concept 'falls on the borderline of sociology and psychology'.

More exactly it offers a simple framework for describing the insertion of individuals into social relations. The basic idea is that this occurs by 'role learning', 'socialization' or 'internalization'. Thus feminine character is produced by socialization into the female role, masculine character by socialization into the male role – and deviants by some kind of failure in socialization.

This argument leads to an interest in the people and institutions responsible for the learning, the so-called 'agencies of socialization': mother, family, teachers, peers, media. Another large body of research inspired by sex role ideas has explored the different treatment of girls and boys by these 'agencies', the ways models of femininity and masculinity are conveyed to children, and (in a few cases) what happens when the messages are mixed. In the most sophisticated versions of sex role theory, such as Talcott Parsons's, the concept of socialization is linked to psychoanalytic ideas about the structuring of the unconscious. Usually, however, sex role theory is seen as an alternative to psychodynamic explanations such as Freud's, and the focus is firmly on overt influences and overt behaviour.

Third, sex role theory offers principles for a politics of reform. If the subordination of women is largely a result of role expectations that define them as helpmates or subordinates, their characters as passive or expressive (rather than instrumental), then the obvious path forward is to change the expectations. A great deal of energy in contemporary feminism has gone into just this kind of enterprise. It is formalized in counter-sexist curricula in schools, antidiscrimination laws, equal opportunity policies in the labour market and 'affirmative action' campaigns. Though broadly the territory of liberal feminism, this goes beyond the classical liberal focus on the individual, as the sex role concept points to the collective dimension of social stereotyping. As Alison Ziller, the Director of Equal Employment Opportunity for the NSW government, observed: 'an affirmative action plan ... means that remedy for discrimination does not rely on grievance procedures initiated by individuals'.

These virtues are substantial. Accordingly, sex role theory must be taken seriously as an intrinsic theory of gender for reasons beyond the sheer volume of its literature. Yet these virtues are bought at the price of very serious conceptual difficulties.

The problems begin with what many role theorists see as their greatest strength, the emphasis on the social via the concept of 'expectations'. Role theory is often seen by psychologists as a form of social determinism, stressing the way individuals are trapped in stereotypes. Stereotyped interpersonal expectations are indeed social facts. They are made effective, in role theory, by the idea that other people reward conformity to them and punish departures from them. In role jargon, the occupants of counter-positions sanction role performance. Little boys are praised for being assertive, ridiculed for being girlish, and so on. But why do the second parties apply the sanctions? This cannot be explained by *their* role expectations; if so, role theory reduces to an infinite regress. It quickly comes down to a question of individual will and agency, revolving around choices to apply sanctions. The social dimension of role theory thus ironically dissolves into voluntarism, into a general assumption that people choose to maintain existing customs.

Ultimately, then, role theory is not a social theory at all. It comes right up to the problem where social theory logically begins, the relationship between personal agency and social structure; but evades it by dissolving structure into agency.

What happens in sex role theory is that the missing element of structure is covertly supplied by the biological category of sex. The very terms 'female role' and 'male role', hitching a biological term to a dramaturgical one, suggest what is going on. The underlying image is an invariant biological base and a malleable social superstructure. This is why discussion of sex roles constantly slides into discussion of sex differences. The implicit question in sex role analysis is what particular superstructure has been created in such-and-such circumstances, and how far the biological dichotomy still shows through.

The result of using the role framework, then, is an abstract view of the differences between the sexes, and between their situations, not a concrete account of the relations between them. As Suzanne Franzway and Jan Lowe observe in their critique of sex role theory in feminism, the role literature focuses on attitudes and misses the realities that the attitudes are about. The political effect is to highlight the pressures that create an artificially rigid distinction between women and men, and to play down the economic, domestic and political power that men exercise over women.

As some critics have observed, we do not speak of 'race roles' or 'class roles' because the exercise of power in these areas of social life is more obvious to sociologists. With 'sex roles', the underlying biological dichotomy seems to have persuaded many theorists that there is no power relationship here at all. The 'female role' and the 'male role' are tacitly treated as equal. They are of course different in content, but reciprocally dependent on each other ('complementary'), made of the same ingredients, and (in the eyes of the mid-1970s liberals who created a critical literature on the 'male role') equally oppressive of the human being within.

For an account of power, role analysis substitutes a theory of norms. Anne Edwards has observed how drastically sex role theory simplifies the complexities of gender: reducing all masculinities and femininities to one dualism; sweeping all women into one feminine role, which in turn is equated to being a housewife and located in the family. Most sex role theory is not constructed around problems raised by field observation, but as analysis of a normative standard case.

This standard case is, typically, an abstract model of a nuclear family with a conventional sexual division of labour. It is 'standard' in the sense that most people's lives are presumed to be like it, with a minority being deviant. It is 'normative' in two senses. First, it is presumed that people in general regard it as the proper way to live – so it defines actual role expectations. Second, theorists regard it as the proper (or socially functional or biologically appropriate) way to live. Much of the intuitive, common-sense appeal of sex role literature arises from the blurring of these ideas. Thus when the sexologist John Money writes of the 'proper' path of psychosexual development, the effect is to stigmatize any departure from it (including homosexual choice) as pathological, and to reinforce the idea that conventional heterosexuality is a good thing both for the person and the society.

A crucial difficulty is that what is *normative*, i.e., expected or approved, is not necessarily *standard*, i.e., actually the way things usually happen. Perhaps especially not in the case of sexuality. Research has produced a series of upsets. The Kinsey studies are the most celebrated, finding frequencies of homosexual behaviour in the American population that normative sex role theory has never come to terms with. Data on premarital and extramarital heterosexuality make further trouble. Data on intra-family violence are also difficult to absorb: sober estimates by Straus and others that more than 50 per cent of American families have experienced domestic violence suggest a very large gap between what is morally approved and what actually happens. Statistics on household composition show that the mother-father-two-kids-cat-and-dog nuclear family routinely invoked by priests, presidents and advertising copy-writers, is not the majority form of household now and perhaps never was. The normative pattern of husband-as-breadwinner and wife-as-home-maker, still powerful in ideology, has been undermined in fact by economics: as shown in chapter 1, around a third of the world's paid workers are women, while a good many men are not in the labour force. Role theorists who do close-up field research, like Komarovsky, have to push the data very hard to get anything like the theoretical model of 'roles' out of it.

If we distinguish what is normative from what is common, instead of blending them together, new and important questions emerge. It becomes possible to see what is 'normative' not as a definition of normality but as a definition of what the holders of social power wish to have accepted. This raises questions about whose interests are embodied in the 'norms'; how far the daily life of other people represents resistance to those interests; and what potentially normative principles might emerge from currently non-normative but widespread practices.

Sex role theory has a way of accommodating departures from the normative standard case, through the concept of deviance. This term is out of favour as a result of sharp criticisms of 'labelling' in welfare practice, but it persists in role theory because it is logically required by the normative concept of 'role'. Euphemisms are available – inadequate self-concept, non-conformity – but it is no surprise when a role theorist like Biddle roundly talks of 'deviant behaviour', 'deviant identities', 'causes of maladjustment', and contrasts them with 'successful role learning'.

The dominance of the normative standard case in sex-role literature, plus the concept of deviance, have a distinct effect. They create the impression that the conventional sex role is the majority case, and that departures from it are socially marginal and likely to be the result of some personal eccentricity, produced by imperfect or inappropriate socialization. Lesbianism, men's homosexuality, chastity, prostitution, marital violence and transvestism are all liable to this treatment. Again the role framework eliminates the element of power from gender relations. It also eliminates the element of resistance to power and social pressure, the fact of social struggles – open or covert – going on around definitions of sexuality and gender.

Here, in thinking about the conflict of interests, the use of sex-role theory in feminism is most limiting. The conceptualization of sexual politics as role reform – as updating, liberalizing, or expanding the 'female role' (and in the men's movement version the 'male role' also) – means that there is no social theory of the reforming movement as such, no conception of the constitution of collective interests within gender relations. The motive of role reform is individual discomfort in the existing version of the sex role. When comfort is achieved, there is nothing to carry either the politics or the analysis forward.

The lack of a theory of movement and social struggle reflects, at a deeper level, the lack of a way of grasping social contradiction and formulating a social dynamic. The sex role framework is fundamentally static as social theory. This is not to say that role analysts ignore change. Far from it. Modernization of the female role was a leading theme in one of the first important statements of sex role theory, by Talcott Parsons in 1942. Shifting expectations have been a leading issue in North American discussions of the male sex role in recent decades. Changing definitions of the female role are the central theme in academic social science's response to feminism.

The point is that sex role theory cannot grasp change as history, as transformation generated in the interplay of social practice and social structure. Structure is given to sex role theory in the form of biological dichotomy. And the ultimate voluntarism of the practical side of role concepts prevents the formulation of a concept of social determination. As a result, change is always something that happens to sex roles, that impinges on them. It comes from outside, from society at large, as in discussions of how technological and economic changes demand a shift to a 'modern' male role. Or it comes from inside the person, from the 'real self' demanding a relaxation of the constricting sex role. The role itself is always being pushed. Sex role theory has no way of grasping change as a dialectic arising within gender relations themselves. As an intrinsic theory of gender it is therefore limited in a fundamental way.

To sum up, four basic considerations oblige us to abandon sex role theory as a framework for the social analysis of gender: its voluntarism and inability to theorize power and social interest; its dependence on biological dichotomy and its consequently non-social conception of structure; its dependence on a normative standard case and systematic misrepresentation of resistance; and the absence of a way of theorizing the historicity of gender.

To recognize these weaknesses, as Edwards notes, does not prevent fruitful research on stereotypes of femininity and masculinity, that is, on sex roles as social constructs, cultural ideals, media contents and so forth. (I will take up these questions in chapter 11.) But as Edwards also argues, it is necessary to look for ways of theorizing the domain of sex and gender that give more attention to social institutions and social structures.

The critique of sex roles has nevertheless given some useful pointers towards what such a theory should be. Plainly one of the issues it must be able to grasp is the formation and conflict of social interests that occur in gender relations. I will now turn to approaches that make this their central concern.

Categorical Theory

Accounts of gender that do give a major place to power and conflicts of interest have generally expressed this awareness through a particular form of theory. It has no familiar name, partly because its logic cuts across such familiar divides as the conflict between cultural feminism and socialist feminism. I will call the approach 'categorical'.

Its major features are, first, a close identification of opposed interests in sexual politics with specific categories of people. Jill Johnston's definition of men as 'the natural enemy of women' is a pungent example. Second, the focus of argument is on the category as a unit, rather than on the processes by which the category is constituted, or on its elements or constituents. Third, the social order as a whole is pictured in terms of a few major categories – usually two – related to each other by power and conflict of interest. If sex role theory tends to dissolve into individualism, categoricalism resolutely stays with the big picture and paints it with a broad brush.

In sex-role theory a common terminology blurs logically distinct concepts; here the same basic idea is expressed in many different terms. Early women's liberation theorists borrowed from political economy and anthropology. Roxanne Dunbar argued that women were a lower 'caste', while Shulamith Firestone wrote of 'sex class', modelling her argument self-consciously on Marx. Academic feminists borrowed terminology from academic social science. Alice Schlegel and Janet Chafetz wrote of 'sexual stratification', while Myra Strober registered 'the birth of a new science, dimorphics'. The term seems to have been coined as a joke; the fact that it was taken seriously shows how desperate was the need for a theoretical framework. Similarly the discussion of 'patriarchy' in radical feminism from the mid-1970s was commonly based on a categorical theory of gender, as in Susan Brownmiller's well-known argument that rape is 'a conscious process of intimidation by which *all men* keep *all women* in a state of fear'.

Chafetz, who has gone furthest in formalizing this approach as social theory, is particularly clear about its major presupposition. Women and men can be treated as 'internally undifferentiated general categories'. Analysis takes the categories for granted while it explores the relationship between them. Categorical theories of gender differ from each other mainly in the accounts they give of this relationship.

In one line of thought it is essentially a relation of direct domination. Dunbar and Firestone were among the pioneers of this approach. Newer versions such as Mary Daly's picture of global patriarchy have focused on men's violence towards women as its essence. The treatment of pornography and rape in cultural-feminist analyses by authors like Susan Griffin and Andrea Dworkin is closely connected. Pornography is regarded as an expression of the violence in male sexuality and a means of domination over women; rape as an act of patriarchal violence rather than sexual desire.

The academic literature on 'sexual stratification' generally takes a more abstract and open-ended approach, assuming no more than that the relationship between the categories is unequal. This has been the framework of a great deal of empirical research (some cited in chapter 1) mapping the unequal material resources of women and men and their unequal life-chances. As theory this is slender. But it has raised questions about the correlates or conditions of different levels of inequality between the sexes. Chafetz for instance conducted a cross-cultural survey to see what general conditions (economic development, environment, religion, etc.) were linked to high or low levels of inequality in 'the overall status of women and men'.

Here Chafetz verges on an extrinsic approach to gender. Categoricalism in fact provides the model of gender for most of the extrinsic theories discussed above. Analyses of the sexual division of labour, for instance, have usually set up the gender categories as a simple line of demarcation in economic life, adding complexity by mapping the twists and turns of this line in different societies. Only a minority have concerned themselves with what Margaret Power called 'the *making* of a woman's occupation' (my italics), a question which, by making the process of constructing categories a central issue, leads away from the abstract logic of categoricalism.

Similarly, much of the discussion of 'relations of production' has little to say about practice at the point of production. Notionally about social relations, actually it uses such concepts mainly to demarcate categories. Ultimately the person and personal practice can be eliminated from the equation altogether, as happened in French structuralism. Theoretical attention is focused on the social place or category into which the individual is inserted. Along these lines one can arrive at a strongly categorical theory of gender which is not biological-determinist. The 'places' in Juliet Mitchell's and Gayle Rubin's structuralist models are socially defined and the male–female opposition they stress is socially constructed. Much the same is true of the semiotic analyses of gender that appeared from the late 1970s on.

In other cases the social basis of categoricalism is a simplified normative model of the family. This is true of most of the Marxist-feminist literature on 'domestic labour'. It is also true of Christine Delphy's more original analysis of patriarchy as an economic system. Here the categories are constructed by the social institution of marriage, and the core of the relation between them is the husbands' appropriation of a surplus from the wives' unpaid labour. Yet another example is Chodorow's psychology of femininity, consciously based on an attempt to find a social rather than a biological underpinning for the psychoanalytic account of children's emotional development. Here the sexual division of labour in childcare is the core of the relationship between the categories.

For all the sophistication these authors show in developing social frameworks, the overall map of gender they produce is not too different from one based on a simple biological dichotomy. Categorical thinking about gender is most obvious when the categories can be presumed to be biological and the relationship between them a collective or standardized one. Thus Brownmiller's 'rape . . . all men . . . all women', or Dworkin's 'pornography: men possessing women'. It is worth noting that biological reductionism does not necessarily produce categoricalism. In some of the literature on transsexualism, for instance, researchers are interested in biological bases for deviance from conventional categories. But theories of biological bases or 'biogrammars' usually lead to categoricalism in one of its strongest forms. For most authors assume (wrongly) that reproductive biology divides humans neatly into two distinct categories.

Categoricalism came from a number of sources: structuralism, biologism and the sheer rhetorical appeal of large plain categories for mobilizing political action. It has remained important because it met the need for a clear-cut alternative to liberal feminism and role theory. For some problems, treating gender in terms of 'internally undifferentiated general categories' is perfectly adequate as a first approximation. The descriptive literature on sex inequalities in income, education, occupation and health is certainly successful in these terms.

The trouble starts when the first approximation becomes the end of the analysis; when the categories 'women' and 'men' are taken as absolutes, in no need of further examination or finer differentiation. For there are problem areas where this will not work at all, and others where the approach rapidly becomes misleading. Analysis couched in terms of a normative standard family is perhaps the commonest example. A good deal of feminist research on welfare has gone towards exploding the assumptions that underpin so much official welfare and economic policy: that everyone (or nearly everyone) lives in a nuclear family, that all women have (or should have) a man supporting them, that having children presupposes having a husband.

Another form of categoricalism focuses on a representative individual. The treatment of 'male sexuality' in much of the literature on violence against women is a case in point. So is the argument that explains pollution, indiscriminate exploitation of resources and the threat of nuclear war, by the personal aggressiveness and ruthlessness of the typical man.

The insight underlying this argument is certainly correct. A power-hungry and emotionally blunted masculinity is part of the social machine that is wrecking the environment, that has for instance devastated half of the beautiful island of Tasmania by wood-chipping and hydroelectric development. Historical research like that of Brian Easlea has traced the themes of masculinity, control and power in the growth of the sciences and technologies that culminated in the nuclear bomb. But to theorize this as the direct outcome of masculinity is to miss the point of the social machinery that makes a given form of masculinity environmentally destructive. (In other periods of history aggressive masculinity did not result in a radically degraded environment.) It misses the social arrangements that give a particular kind of masculinity a hegemonic position in sexual politics and that marginalize others. And in many arguments it misses the social processes that construct this kind of masculinity in the first place.

The analysis of gender through a representative individual is one case of what Hester Eisenstein calls 'false universalism'. She poses the issue in these terms:

> To some extent, this habit of thought grew inevitably from the need to establish gender as a legitimate intellectual category. But too often it gave rise to analysis that, in spite of its narrow base of white, middle-class experience, purported to speak about and on behalf of all women, black or white, poor or rich.

Theory framed in this way has a strong tendency to lump together different periods of history and different parts of the world. Texts like Mary Daly's *Gyn/Ecology* and Kathleen Barry's *Female Sexual Slavery* recite patriarchal atrocities from wife-burning in India, genital mutilation in Africa, foot-binding in China, to pornography in the United States. These are offered on the assumption that each is an example of the same underlying structure. In such theories the world-wide dimension of gender becomes a universal common structure of patriarchy.

The conviction that every country and every period shows the same structure has led Western feminists arguing on these lines into classically ethnocentric positions. As critics like Kalpana Ram have pointed out, an account of suttee based on racist Western sources that present Indian women as passively suffering atrocity, and which takes no account of their resistances, mobilization, or purposes, does justice neither to the issue nor to Indian women. It is possible to combine a clear recognition of the exploitation and subordination of women, and the fundamental character of the social changes needed to correct it, with an equally strong recognition of the specific ways in which subordination is embedded in different cultures, the different forms it takes and the different strategies therefore required. Such a case is argued for instance by the *Draft Report* of the 1979 workshop on feminist ideology and structures held in Bangkok by the United Nations Asian and Pacific Centre for Women and Development. But this leads away from categorical theory.

It is possible to incorporate class, race or nationality into a categorical theory of gender, if these structures are treated in a categorical way too. It involves cross-classification on several variables at once – a very familiar move in quantitative social science. The basic operation is logical multiplication, and the result is a grid on which people can be located. A simple two dimensional cross-classification is central to Tolson's work on masculinity, for instance:

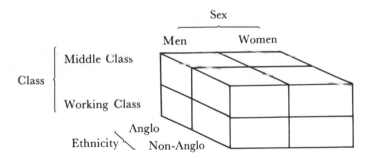

A three dimensional cross-classification underlies recent discussions of the triple oppression of non-Anglo working women:

Any number of dimensions can be added. They become harder to picture on paper, but can easily be handled by computers.

Yet the more sophisticated the cross-classification becomes, the more firmly is the analysis embedded in a static logic of categories. And this intensifies the difficulty categorical theory has in dealing with divisions that arise within the field of gender itself; that is, divisions that have to do with the constitution of the gender categories.

The most notable problem is the politics of sexual object-choice. Heterosexism and homophobia must be regarded as one of the key patterns in gender relations. It is very difficult to come to grips with heterosexual dominance while using a categorical model of gender. One might set up a new cross-classification, with 'homo/ hetero' crossing 'female/male'. But there is no obvious reason in categorical analysis why this division should matter in the first place. Cross-classification confuses the issue, since that operation logically equates women's homosexuality with men's homosexuality. There is every reason to think there are important differences between them, not only in the forms of their expression but in the ways they are initially constituted. As the chequered experience of lesbians in the gay liberation movement shows, the solidarity of women and men against oppression from straight society cannot be taken for granted. That is to say, the logical cross-classification does not correspond in any simple way to the constitution of a social interest.

Categorical theory often stresses conflict of interest, but has difficulty with the way interests are constituted and the ways people contest the structures that define interests. Its recognition of social conflict is highly schematized. Over a range of issues, categoricalism underplays the turbulence and contradictoriness within the social process of gender.

The political consequences are important. Of the two main varieties of categorical theory, the academic or stratificationist leads to a politics of access, for instance trying to raise the number of women in political leadership positions, in the law or in business management. It does not generate any particular reasons to question the social arrangements that create those positions. To this extent its practical consequences are little different from the strategy of role reform in liberal feminism.

The women's liberation movement certainly has called conventional power arrangements into question, and so do the more radical categorical theories of gender. Their tendency, however, is to pose this as an all-or-nothing issue. Rather like the 'big bang' theory of revolution implicit in Marxist structuralism, categoricalism projects a distant future and a distant past where there is no oppression, but tends to assimilate everything in the grim present to manifestations of male power and female subordination. The effect is to offer women a metaphysical solidarity ('all women ...'), an omnipresent enemy ('all men ...'), and a strong implication that struggle in existing relationships is pointless, since the structure and the categories are universal. Since most women do not have the conditions in their own lives for substantial withdrawal from relationships with men, the practical result is an unresolvable dilemma within feminism. Tension around themes of purity and guilt has been tangible in the movement for a number of years.

Towards a Practice-based Theory

In the final analysis, categoricalism can recognize power but deletes from its analysis the element of practical politics: choice, doubt, strategy, planning, error and transformation. The 'battle of the sexes' comedy in traditional popular culture is a vision of sexual politics with just this kind of deletion. From one year to the next husbands err, wives nag, mothers-in-law carp, girls flirt, boys will be boys and so on for ever amen. Whatever people attempt, nothing ever changes. In more sophisticated categoricalism practical politics is marginalized by logic rather than by humour. In texts like *Gyn/Ecology* a particular line in sexual politics is seen as a logical necessity springing from the inner nature of patriarchy, rather than as a choice of strategy.

Choice always implies doubt, and the possibility of going wrong. To give full weight to the practical character of politics, while holding to the recognition of power that is categoricalism's advance over role theory, is the most general requirement of the next steps in the theory of gender.

This requires a form of social theory that gives some grip on the interweaving of personal life and social structure without collapsing towards voluntarism and pluralism on one side, or categoricalism and biological determinism on the other. In modern writing about gender this has been done best in fiction and autobiography. In books like Doris Lessing's *The Golden Notebook*, Anja Meulenbelt's *The Shame is Over*, Patrick White's *The Twyborn Affair*, Nadine Gordimer's *Burger's Daughter*, there is a strong sense of the constraining power of gender relations (and other structures like class and race), a sense of something that people fetch up against. Yet this 'something' is neither abstract nor simple, being real in other people and their actions, with all their complexities, ambiguities and contradictions. And this reality is constantly being worked on and – in ways pleasant and unpleasant – transformed.

In very general terms, we know how to build this kind of understanding into social theory, since parallel problems have arisen in other fields. In class analysis they arose in a debate between 'structure' *à la* Althusser and 'history' *à la* Thompson. In theoretical sociology they arose in the polemic of symbolic interactionism and ethnomethodology against systems theory and functionalism *à la* Parsons; and more recently in the debates about Lévi-Strauss and structuralism. The outlines of a solution can be found in the work of Sartre, Kosík, Bourdieu, Giddens and other theorists who have focused on the interconnections of structure and practice. In principle, categoricalism can be resolved by a theory of practice, focusing on what people do by way of constituting the social relations they live in. In principle, voluntarism can be overcome by an attention to the structure of social relations as a condition of all practices.

Though no theory of gender has been formally couched in these terms, some feminist and gay liberation theorists, and a larger number of field researchers, have made a beginning with this kind of analysis. Their work is not recognized as a 'school', and their politics are very diverse. So it is worth reciting some examples to indicate the kinds of bases that already exist for a development of theory in this direction.

One of the first was Juliet Mitchell. The second section of her now somewhat neglected book *Woman's Estate* described the social position of women in terms of four 'structures', in each of which a particular form of oppression is generated. This idea has important implications for the concept of structure that will be discussed in chapter 5. Partly influenced by Mitchell's work, the American anthropologist Gayle Rubin developed a formal comparative analysis of the 'system of relationships' by which women are subordinated to men. Though her discussion of the 'sex-gender system' leans toward an abstract structuralism, her 1975 paper 'The Traffic in Women' shows more clearly than any other study what a systematic social theory of gender might be like.

In another famous essay, 'Compulsory Heterosexuality and Lesbian Existence', Adrienne Rich points to the importance of the social relationships constructed by women among themselves in

contradistinction to their connections with men. Her concept of a
'lesbian continuum' drifts towards categorical theory but can be
approached historically. This is one of the issues taken up by Jill
Matthews in her study of 'the historical construction of femininity'
in twentieth-century Australia. *Good and Mad Women* uses the
records of psychiatric incarceration to study the impact of changing
ideals of femininity in the lives of particular women. She stresses
the historicity of femininity (and by implication of masculinity) as
lived experience, not just imposed regulation; and links face-
to-face household relationships to the large-scale patterns of
demographic, economic and cultural change. On a larger scale
again, David Fernbach in *The Spiral Path* offers a social and
relational analysis of what is commonly seen as pre-social desire
(or antisocial behaviour). Focusing on homosexual relationships
among men, he sets the modern emergence of homosexual identity
in the context of the history of gender relations stretching back to
the neolithic age. This is speculative in many ways, but certainly
a good deal more like a real history than the myth-making about
ultimate 'origins'.

Instead of unanswerable questions about ultimate origins, root
causes or final analyses, these studies pose the question of how
gender relations are organized as a going concern. They imply
that structure is not pre-given but historically composed. That
implies the possibility of different ways of structuring gender,
reflecting the dominance of different social interests. It also implies
different degrees to which the structuring is coherent or consistent,
reflecting changing levels of contestation and resistance. Sexual
politics is embedded in the structure of gender relations at the
most basic level. Structures develop crisis tendencies which
materialize in radical sexual politics. These questions are the point
of departure for the chapters of Part II, which attempts to develop
a practice-based approach to the structure of gender relations.

But this is not the whole scope of the theory of practice, which
also points to the historicity of gender at the level of personal life.
The idea that forms of sexuality are socially constructed has
emerged in the work of radical historians and in discourse analysis
and interactionist sociology, not to mention the work of Marcuse.
Femininity and masculinity as character structures have to be
seen as historically mutable. There is nothing to prevent several
forms of sexual character emerging in the same society at the same
time. Multiple femininities and masculinities are, I would suggest,

a central fact about gender and the way its structures are lived. These questions are taken up in Part III, which develops from several starting-points a practice-based approach to personality.

Before launching out, however, there is one more issue to address. The main reason why it has been difficult to grasp the historicity of gender relations is the persistent assumption that a transhistorical structure is built into gender by the sexual dichotomy of bodies. This is the assumption that sex role theory finally falls back on, and most kinds of categoricalism too. A *social* theory is pointless, or at best peripheral, if it is true that the basic determinants are biological. The relationship between the body and social practice is thus a crucial issue for the theory of gender, which needs to be clarified before the structure of social relations can be addressed.

NOTES

Extrinsic Theories

(pp. 41–7). Delphy (1977) p. 25 issued an unanswerable challenge to 'class-first' dogmatism; which rolls on regardless. On Chinese family policy see Stacey (1979) and Croll (1983). The major statements of social reproduction theories of gender are Mitchell (1975); Kuhn and Wolpe (1978); Centre for Contemporary Cultural Studies Women's Studies Group (1978) and Burton (1985). My criticisms here are partly based on a general critique of reproduction theory, reprinted in Connell (1983), chapter 8. The difficulties in British Marxist-feminist theory are carefully set out by Barrett (1980). For the practical campaigns of socialist feminists in that country see Coote and Campbell (1982), and in Australia Court (1986) and Stevens (forthcoming). The most thoughtful criticism of 'dual systems' concepts I have seen is by I. Young (1981). I have written in more detail on the link between patriarchy and capitalism in Connell (1983), chapters 3, 4 and 5.

Sex Role Theory

(pp. 47–54). Bem (1974) and Steinmann and Fox (1974) illustrate the blurring of sex role and sexual character; Wesley and Wesley (1977) the blurring with sex differences. Carrigan, Connell and Lee (1985) sketch the history of sex role ideas. My argument in this section is based on a general critique of role theory in Connell (1983) chapter 10, and its application to sex roles in Carrigan, Connell and Lee; and the analyses of sex role concepts by Franzway and Lowe (1978) and Edwards (1983). Nye et al. (1976) is the source of the list of family roles quoted. The 'agencies of socialization' argument is discussed in more detail in chapter 9 below. Pleck (1981) sees role theory as alternative to psychodynamics. David and Brannon (1976) illustrate the tacit equation of male and female roles. Edwards (1983) provides a comprehensive criticism of 'deviance' notions in sex role theory. For the theme of change in sex roles see Lipman-Blumen and Tickamyer (1975) and Pleck (1976). One outgrowth was a curious literature purporting to be a history of sex roles, e.g. Branca (1978). My argument on role theory's failure to meet real criteria of historicity was formulated in discussions with Tim Carrigan and John Lee.

Categorical Theory

(pp. 54–61). Johnston's (1973) witty argument for separatism helped establish lesbianism as a political question; the quote is on p. 276. Willis (1984) gives an excellent history of the emergence of categorical views of gender in the women's liberation movement. The categorical treatment of 'relations of production' reaches a peak in Bland et al. (1978). Money (1970) is an example of biological-determinist investigation of deviance. Raymond (1979) is a notable example of theory being pushed towards biological essentialism by a categorical political logic. Categoricalism as rhetoric is well illustrated in the work of Spender (1982). Baldock and Cass (1983) and Campbell (1984) are among many feminist studies undermining the normative model of the family. On masculinity and aggression see Farrell (1974); Dinnerstein (1976) and Kelly (1984); Connell (1985a) expands the argument here. Quotation on false universalism from Eisenstein (1984) p. 132. On the complexity of interests in gay liberation see Gay Left Collective (1980) and Thompson (1985), chapter 3.

Practice-based Theory

(p. 61–4). On images of the 'battle of the sexes' see Orwell's famous 1941 essay on the picture postcards of Donald McGill. The connection between strategy and doubt is clearer in grass-roots radical politics than in radical theory: compare Alinsky (1972). Thompson's history (1968) is more valuable as a model than his polemic against structuralism (1978), though that has some fine moments. I have attempted a critical evaluation of Sartre's and Bourdieu's theories of practice in Connell (1983), chapters 5 and 8. Lefebvre's (1976) pp. 73–91 criticism of the search for a 'generative nucleus' is important in opening up a fully historical perspective on structures of power.

4

The Body and Social Practice

The Knot of Natural Difference

'Female' and 'male' are biological categories arising in a specific system of reproduction. Humans share this division with a vast array of animal and plant species. Non-sexual reproduction is characteristic of simpler life forms, and some relatively complex ones up to the fungi, algae and sponges. Some more complex species, like strawberries and orchids, alternate between sexual and non-sexual reproduction. On the whole, however, the more advanced species reproduce sexually. It seems that the sexual division of function in reproduction has been a major feature in the evolution of life.

In our culture the reproductive dichotomy is assumed to be the absolute basis of gender and sexuality in everyday life. This is not true of all cultures. But it is so strongly marked in ours that biological or pseudo-biological accounts of gender relations have wide popular credibility. Books like *The Naked Ape*, *The Imperial Animal* and *The Selfish Gene* carry rival versions of this message to a very large public. For many people the notion of natural sex difference forms a limit beyond which thought cannot go. Debates about sexual politics often end with the assertion that men and women are ultimately different, as a self-evident proposition that closes off further discussion. It is seen as a knock-out argument by many opponents of feminism.

So powerful is this assumption that it has been able to co-opt intellectual currents initially unsympathetic to biologism, such as role theory, psychoanalysis and feminism itself. For instance, in Maccoby and Jacklin's *The Psychology of Sex Differences* it is striking how different are the authors' attitudes to biological and social explanations of observed differences in traits like aggressiveness. Biological explanations clearly have priority, when they are available, and social explanations are residual. Freud's method pointed the way to one of the most radically social analyses of sex and gender yet proposed. Yet Freud believed in ultimate biological determinism and his followers have repeatedly drifted towards that view. Theodore Reik, for instance, rests a very long essay on 'the emotional differences of the sexes' on a simple biological determination; while Robert May in *Sex and Fantasy* can think of no other organizing principle for his studies of schizophrenia, imagination and myth than the natural difference between women and men.

Early second-wave feminism often implied that all sex differences are socially produced. During the 1970s, as shown in Hester Eisenstein and Alice Jardine's *The Future of Difference*, a good many Western feminists again began emphasizing difference and celebrating what was specifically feminine. And a significant number abandoned the idea that what was 'specifically feminine' was socially produced. Notions of ineradicable difference have proliferated: the idea that men are mutants from the true (female) stock; the idea that men are 'biological aggressors' or 'natural rapists'; the idea of 'metaphysical difference'; the idea that women as nurturers must save the world from male wars and technology.

In this chapter I will argue that doctrines of natural difference, whatever their political complexion, are fundamentally mistaken. This is not to contest the facts of reproductive biology, nor to deny their interest and importance for understanding human life. What I will challenge is the assumption that the biological make-up of our bodies is the 'basis', 'foundation', 'framework', 'essence', or 'mould' of the social relations of gender. The argument accepts that there is a strong relation between social practice and biology; indeed 'gender' would be inconceivable without it. I will propose that this relation has a very different character from that assumed by theorists of natural difference.

There are two main versions of the doctrine of natural difference. The first takes society to be epiphenomenal to nature, the second sees the two as additive.

In the first type of theory, biology (or ontology as its surrogate) *determines* gender. Society registers what nature decrees – or becomes sick if it doesn't. The best-known examples are the

pseudo-evolutionary accounts of masculinity and femininity in
texts like Desmond Morris's *The Naked Ape,* Lionel Tiger's *Men in
Groups* and *The Imperial Animal,* George Gilder's *Sexual Suicide* – the
literature dubbed by Marshall Sahlins 'vulgar sociobiology'. The
basic point of view is neatly summarized by Morris:

> Behind the facade of modern city life there is the same old naked
> ape. Only the names have been changed: for 'hunting' read
> 'working', for 'hunting grounds' read 'place of business', for 'home
> base' read 'house', for 'pair-bond' read 'marriage', for 'mate' read
> 'wife', and so on. ... It is the biological nature of the beast that has
> moulded the social structure of civilisation, rather than the other
> way around.

Tiger and Fox's imagery is different but the idea is the same:

> Natural selection has produced an animal that has to behave
> culturally, that has to invent roles, make myths, speak languages
> and form men's clubs. ... Agricultural and industrial civilizations
> have put nothing into the basic wiring of the human animal. We
> are wired for hunting. ... And we are wired basically on a primate
> model.

I have called this literature 'pseudo-biological' because it does
not in fact rest on serious biological investigation of human social
life, as for instance ecological studies of industry do. Rather it
rests on a series of loose analogies, which, as Marie de Lepervanche
notes, are changed by logical slides into taken-for-granted facts.
The basic logic is exactly the reverse of what it is claimed to be.
The argument starts with an interpretation of current social life
(in Morris's case an interpretation that is sexist, ethnocentric and
often factually wrong) and reads this back into a speculative
prehistory. 'Evolution' is called in to justify the social patterns
these authors advocate, under the guise of explanation. Tiger, for
instance, ends up talking about which social arrangements are
and are not 'biologically healthy' – by which he means that they
conform to his view of human evolution as a hunting species.

It is difficult to take this literature seriously as science. The
social analysis is crude in the extreme. The understanding
of 'evolution' itself is obsolete. The fundamental problem of
understanding the shift from organic evolution to history is
obliterated by the biological reduction. Yet these arguments are

extremely popular. This is partly to do with a touch of salacious humour (breasts as buttocks, the corporate executive as anthropoid ape). More fundamentally it comes from their mirror construction. They reflect what is familiar back as 'science', and justify what many readers wish to believe.

A serious attempt to repair these deficiencies has been made by the 'scientific sociobiologists' led by E. O. Wilson. In a chapter of *On Human Nature* Wilson applies the calculus of genetic advantage to show how 'human sexuality can be much more precisely defined with the aid of the new advances in evolutionary theory'. It is curious how traditional the 'new advances' turn out to be. Wilson's argument recites differences in athletic performance, studies of twins and the like to reject a 'totally environmental explanation' of sex differences, proffers the universality of the family, and tries to show that homosexuality has a genetic explanation – thus assuming that homosexuality is a unitary trait and reverting to concepts that became obsolete in sexology seventy years ago.

The conceptual confusions underlying 'sociobiology' as a school of thought are now reasonably well understood. An impoverished understanding of biology, and of the process of evolution itself, underlies the slides between social institutions and biological advantage. As Sahlins shows for Wilson's general argument, and Janet Sayers shows in *Biological Politics* for gender specifically, the sociobiologists' arguments ignore the fact that human action is highly structured in a collective sense; it is constituted interactively, not by context-free individual predispositions. A war, for instance, is a social and institutional process within history, not the sum total of several hundred thousand genetic predispositions towards aggressiveness. Most strikingly, sociobiology for all its claims to scientific explanation cannot produce for inspection the mechanisms of biological causation. Wilson, for instance, in his essay on sex, is reduced to speculations like this: 'Sexual love and the emotional satisfaction of family life can be reasonably postulated to be based on enabling mechanisms in the physiology of the brain that have been programmed to some extent through the genetic hardening of this compromise.' The triple caution ('reasonably postulated' – 'enabling' – 'to some extent') shows, as clearly as language can, that Wilson here is simply guessing. And guesswork is what this literature mostly offers on the actual determination of social life.

This gives a particular interest to Steven Goldberg's version of biological determination in *The Inevitability of Patriarchy*. Though somewhat dated, it is a serious attempt to do what Wilson and others avoid, providing a detailed account of the mechanisms linking biological difference and social inequality. It is worth examining as a type of argument.

From physiological research Goldberg takes the finding of differences in average blood concentrations of particular hormones, especially testosterone, between men and women. From psychopharmacological research he takes the findings of some differences in average performance, on certain tests, of animals and people with differing levels of these (or other) hormones in their bloodstream. He deduces that these hormones cause differences in social behaviour which give an 'aggression advantage' to men over women. This explains both the sexual division of labour and patriarchal power structure. In competition for jobs of any importance, men have the edge in assertiveness. It is rational for women to accept a subordinated position rather than exhaust themselves in a competition for power where they are constantly dragged down by their hormones. Therefore we have social arrangements that allocate home-making to women, competitive striving in the world of business to men.

The logical error in the later stage of this argument is easy to see. Goldberg postulates a situation of open competition in order to explain institutional arrangements that prevent open competition. In fact, as far as real historical evidence goes, a situation of free competition between women and men – or among men – has never existed; it is a rhetorical device constructed by social-contract theorists in the seventeenth century. A more complex slide occurs earlier in the argument. Goldberg's argument moves from *average* differences in hormone concentrations to *categorical* differences in social behaviour.

A difference between two groups on average is compatible with a great overlap in distributions. So far as mainstream psychologists have succeeded in measuring traits like aggressiveness, a great deal of overlap between women and men is exactly what they do find (see chapter 8). It is not credible to start from a-small-average-difference-within-a-large-overlap and deduce the institutional exclusion of *women as a group* from major political authority or economic power that is evident in the data on state and business elites in chapter 1. This problem is sufficiently serious to lead sociobiologists sometimes to speak of society 'amplifying' natural sex differences, and thus to move towards the additive framework to be discussed shortly.

The biological-reductionist argument, then, is too weak for at least some of the social phenomena it tries to explain. In other respects it is too strong. The idea that differences in hormone levels reach out through the complex situational, personal and collective determinants of individual behaviour to remain the ultimate determinants of its social consequences, supposes a mechanism of hormonal control far more powerful than physiological research has actually found. A typical conclusion by the physiologists is stated by Anke Erhardt and Heino Meyer-Bahlburg in a recent review of research on the 'effects of prenatal sex hormones on gender-related behaviour' – an area where hormonal effects might reasonably be expected. Some hormonal influence is probable, they conclude, but the effects are subtle. The social events of a child's upbringing are plainly the major influence: 'the development of gender identity seems to depend largely on the sex of rearing', not on hormonal determination.

This might lead to a doctrine of *weak* biological determination of social patterns; but even that would be speculative. It is worth noting that over the last century a whole series of attempts has been mounted to prove the biological determination of various forms of social inequality. Arguments for racial differences in courage and intelligence, the heritability of IQ, the heritability of mental disorder, parallel the arguments for innate sex differences in temperament and ability. In none of these cases has a mechanism been discovered that would translate the proposed biological cause into complex patterns of individual behaviour, let alone social institutions. In all of them, serious questions have been raised about the validity of the data used to establish a significant biological effect at all.

It is possible that there are some innate differences in temperament or ability between women and men. The hypothesis cannot be ruled out entirely. But if they exist, we can say quite confidently that they are not the basis of major social institutions. We can also say that in terms of human evolution they pale into insignificance beside the common capacities of women and men. These are the human 'species characteristics' of capacity for language, intellect and imagination, upright stance, thumb opposition and manipulation, tool-making and tool-using and extended childhood and parenting, that mark us off from other species and are constituents of the evolutionary jump to human society. These characteristics are shared between the sexes, and there is no good reason to doubt that the shift from biological evolution to history was also a shared accomplishment.

Once this shift was accomplished – and it would seem we are talking about a process taking two or three million years – the basis existed for a relationship between the body and behaviour that was radically different from relationships governed by organic evolution. Biological reductionism, in essence, is two or three million years out of date.

A variant of reductionism sees biology not as fixing individual characteristics, but as setting limits within which social arrangements may vary. All societies, a familiar argument runs, must reproduce themselves and their members, and therefore must accommodate and sustain the sexual and social relationships that produce new people. All societies, therefore, must accommodate themselves to the biological facts of sex. It is usually inferred that all societies must be based on the nuclear family or some variant of it. The functionalist tone of this argument is not hard to detect, and its classics are found in American social science in the heyday of functionalism, such as the work of Talcott Parsons and Margaret Mead. It is textbook orthodoxy (a) that the nuclear family is universal, (b) because it is the social form that responds to universal biological demands for sex and reproduction. A society that wanders beyond these limits will collapse, or come under terrible strain. Therefore – according to Parsons – every society has sanctions against homosexuality, so as to reinforce the differentiation of sex roles and protect the family.

This version of reductionism may sound more plausible than sociobiology; at least it sounds more social. Its difficulty is that the biological constraints proposed are so feeble that they explain almost nothing. An enormous range of social arrangements are consistent with the occurrence of enough heterosexual intercourse to reproduce the species. An enormous range of economic arrangements are consistent with giving children enough care for them to survive and grow. On the issue of sexual object-choice it is simply not true that all societies prohibit homosexuality. In quite a number of societies homosexuality is institutionalized as part of the social and religious order, for example in the New Guinea culture studied by Gilbert Herdt. The real force of the limits-to-variation version of biological reductionism is that, like sociobiology, it is a mirror structure, reflecting familiar social arrangements back to the reader as what is required by nature.

The second major type of natural-difference theory drops the notion of constraint in favour of an *additive* conception of society and nature. Biology, in this line of thought, establishes a certain difference between human females and males, but this is insufficient for the complexity of social life. It must be added to, built upon. Society therefore *culturally elaborates* the distinction between the sexes. Clothing is a familiar example. There are modest differences in average physique between men and women. Society exaggerates them, for instance with garments that emphasize women's breasts or men's penises and makes them categorical, for instance by putting women in skirts and men in trousers. Different societies elaborate the distinction of sex in different ways. Research into the variations produces the ethnography of exotic clothing, kinship and sexual customs that has titillated Western readers since anthropology began.

Sociobiology sometimes tilts towards an additive conception, as in Wilson's remark that 'the physical and temperamental differences between men and women have been amplified by culture into universal male dominance'. Most commonly, however, additive conceptions of gender are found in sex-role theory and liberal feminism. The now very large literature on sex-role socialization proceeds with impressive unanimity along additive lines, tracing out the ways society improves on nature's handiwork in shaping little girls and little boys. The very term 'sex/role' sums up the additive approach.

This may be turned in a critical direction, because some room for social choice is implied. Liberal-feminist sex-role theory condemns the way the addition is currently done, especially the imposition of derogatory stereotypes and submissive behaviour on women. Maccoby and Jacklin put this critical view with particular clarity:

> We suggest that societies have the option of minimizing, rather than maximizing, sex differences through their socialization practices. A society could for example, devote its energies more toward moderating male aggression than toward preparing women to submit to male aggression, or toward encouraging rather than discouraging.

male nurturance activities. In our view, social institutions and
social practices are not merely reflections of the biologically
inevitable. A variety of social institutions are viable within the
framework set by biology. It is up to human beings to select those
that foster the life styles they most value.

The most striking thing about this passage is the contradiction
between the notion of 'a society' as a freely choosing agent and
the underlying sense of biological constraint. If social arrangements
are 'not merely reflections' of biological inevitability it is still clear
that Maccoby and Jacklin think they are substantially so. This
passage comes from an argument against Goldberg's hormonal
version of biological reductionism. But the difference at this point
is slight: it is mainly that Goldberg thinks social training should
reinforce natural difference while Maccoby and Jacklin think it
should not. The framework is not greatly different. Indeed Wilson,
the high priest of sociobiology, reproduces almost exactly Maccoby
and Jacklin's argument about societal choice on a basis of natural
difference; he professes neutrality.

The critical content of liberal feminism, then, is consistent with
the concept of natural difference. It presumes that a kind of base-
level gender distinction is left when we strip away the pancake
make-up or the *Playboy* philosophy. This basal difference is taken
to be unoppressive because it is natural. So, for instance, Betty
Friedan in *The Second Stage* can look to a post-feminist future which
takes the comforting shape of the family. For her and many others
the underlying reality includes an unchallenged heterosexuality as
the taken-for-granted shape of sexual attraction. It begins to look
as if we are in the land of mirrors again.

Objections to the idea of natural difference usually take the form
of extra emphasis on the social end of an additive conception of
gender. This is what happens when sex-role theory is used to
combat crude nativism. A notable example is the 1970s literature
on masculinity, where ape-man reductionism was challenged by
role theorists.

This line of argument runs into two main difficulties. Because
the underlying conception of gender is additive, the effect of this
extra emphasis on the social is to minimize the importance of the
body. Therefore the argument loses its grip on what people do
find central in their experience of sex and gender: pleasure, pain,

body-image, arousal, youth and ageing, bodily contact, childbirth and suckling. Second, the correct relative weighting of social versus biological determinations is never accurately established in practice. The 'addition' remains an aspiration. And the weighting cannot be assumed equal in all departments of life. So this objection always remains a statement of opinion with no logical force.

There are, nevertheless, two arguments against the doctrine of natural difference that cut deeper and apply to all its forms. The first is developed in a brilliant though little-recognized book by the American sociologists Suzanne Kessler and Wendy McKenna. In *Gender: An Ethnomethodological Approach* they demonstrate that the scientific as well as the popular literature on sexuality and gender works within a cultural framework in which the 'natural attitude' (in the technical sense of ethnomethodology – i.e. the everyday stance) is to take gender as strictly dichotomous and unchanging. What they call 'gender attribution', the social process 'by which we construct our world of two genders', is sustained despite the failure of human reality on almost any count to be strictly dimorphic. Perhaps the most striking part of their argument is where they examine the biological literature on gender, which so much social analysis takes to be holy writ, and show that this research too is founded on the social process of gender attribution. And following this social logic, biological research continues to create new dichotomies as old ones become untenable. A striking example is the effort to reconstitute athletics as a strict dichotomy. Chromosome testing was introduced to international athletics in 1967 and used on a large scale at the 1968 Mexico Olympics. The International Olympic Committee defines people with intermediate chromosomal patterns as *men*, disqualifying them from women's events.

So far the argument is negative, simply pointing out that our taken-for-granted assumptions about gender dichotomy are not forced upon us by nature. The positive side of the argument is about the social process itself. Kessler and McKenna re-examine the anthropological literature on *berdache*, institutionalized transvestism among American Indian societies particularly. They show that when the anthropologists' perceptions based on dichotomous gender attribution are allowed for, the research reveals cultural worlds where gender is not dichotomous and is not necessarily assigned on biological criteria. It can, for instance, be chosen.

Michel Foucault makes the same point in his essay on the case of Herculine Barbin. At an earlier period in the history of Western European culture, a strict dichotomy of sex and a lifelong commitment to membership of one, was not presupposed in the way it is now.

Studies of transvestism and transsexualism in contemporary Western societies provide an exceptional insight into the social construction of gender in everyday life. Harold Garfinkel, one of the first to explore this issue, in his case study of 'Agnes' stressed the amount of work that had to be done to sustain an identity as a woman by someone starting out as a boy. Much of this is also done by people who start out as girls, but in that case it is hardly noticed as work – it is taken for granted, or as being natural.

Kessler and McKenna argue that transsexualism is itself based on the natural attitude that assumes dichotomy; what transsexuals claim is that they are 'really' members of the other sex, and seek ways of correcting the anomaly. The studies of Sydney transsexuals by Roberta Perkins show that the situation is more complex than this. For some that is true; but others are much more uncertain about where they belong and why. Further, the growth of a commercial subculture of transsexual prostitution and show business has created a new option. 'Drag queens' can make a living *as transsexuals*. In effect a new gender category is being constructed. Its history, some case studies indicate, has roots in the ambiguous situation of homosexual men in the 1950s and 1960s. This in turn points back to a tradition of thinking about homosexuality as an intersex status – the 'third sex' in one version. Even in modern Western culture, it seems, the cultural construction of gender has repeatedly failed to produce consistent dichotomies.

To sum up, our conception of what is natural and what natural differences consist of, is itself a cultural construct, part of our specific way of thinking about gender. Gender is, in Kessler and McKenna's term, a practical accomplishment – something accomplished by social practice. (We might add, not a completely consistent one.) This is not a matter of some bias or error in our ideas that might in principle be corrected by future biological research. It is a fundamental feature of the way we have knowledge of human beings.

The second basic criticism of the concept of natural difference can be stated more briefly, as it is a general point about the character of human life. The idea of natural difference is that of a passively suffered condition, like being subject to gravity. If human life were in its major internal structures – gender being one – so conditioned, human history would be inconceivable. For history depends on the transcendence of the natural through social practice.

This point holds good without the bland optimism about progress that has usually accompanied it. In a period of rising awareness of environmental disaster and nuclear threat, it is easier to see the negative side of the human rupture from the non-human. It is also possible to see an expanded meaning in the idea central to the work of Gordon Childe, the pioneer of global history as a science, that the relation between nature and history is one of practical transformation. This means both the transformations of the natural world by human practice (domestication of plants and animals, smelting of metal ores, invention of steam engines, etc.) that have sustained each stage of historical development; and the changes of practice itself that have made great shifts of social structure possible. Practical transformations open up new possibilities, which are the tissue of human life. But they do this by creating new social pressures and risks.

As shown by the title of one of his books, *Man Makes Himself*, Childe was not exactly sensitive to issues of gender. Nor is gender much registered in the recent reworking of these themes by Jürgen Habermas. But this is, I would argue, more a consequence of the influence of sexual ideology on social theorists, than any logical sense in which the social processes of gender are exceptions to the principles that apply to other social processes. There is no reason to make this exception. The body is implicated in the processes of gender, certainly; but then the body is involved in *every* kind of social practice. The natural world is implicated in class relations, for instance through the labour process and the function of the body as tool. This does not prevent class relations from being historical. No more should the implication of the body in gender relations through sexuality prevent us from seeing the historicity of gender.

To make these points is already to imply a relation between the social and the natural that is different from biological determination in any form. I will now try to spell out how this relation might be understood.

Transcendence and Negation

To speak of 'transcendence' is to imply the production of something qualitatively different. The social is radically unnatural. ('Non-natural' might be a more neutral term but I think the stronger overtones are correct.) Its structure can never be deduced from natural structures. What undergoes transformation is genuinely trans-formed.

But this unnaturalness does not mean disconnection, a radical *separation* from nature. On the contrary, the unnaturalness of society is sustained by a particular kind of connection with nature – a connection through practice. In the practice of labour, the natural world is appropriated by human beings and transformed, both physically and in terms of meaning. In the practices of sexuality and power, as well as certain kinds of labour (for example nursing), the human body itself is an object of practice.

The natural or pre-social qualities of objects are of course important to the practices that deal with them. We do not offer coffee to a tree, nor try to paint with sawdust. Nor should we expect someone who is chromosomally male to give birth to a child. Where reductionism goes wrong is in taking these qualities as determinants of the practice. This gets things precisely the wrong way round. Practice issues from the human and social side of the transaction; it *deals with* the natural qualities of its objects, including the biological characteristics of bodies. It gives them a social determination. The connection between social and natural structures is one of *practical relevance*, not of causation.

Thus a person with a chromosomally male body can be treated as a woman in social practice, and sometimes is. The person concerned will still not give birth to a child. Kessler and McKenna's demonstration of the primacy of 'gender attribution' can be seen as a particular case of the concept of practical relevance. It describes specifically the incorporation and transformation of certain aspects of bodies by cognitive and interpretive practices.

'Dealing with' is not a neutral term. What practice produces is not what it began with. The qualities of objects are changed, whether they are bits of wood or human beings. The bits of wood become a chair; the human being becomes a lover, or angry, or better educated. A transforming practice in a basic sense *negates* what it starts with in order to produce something new. This negation and supersession is the basis of historicity. For the outcomes of practice do not sit around outside time, but themselves become the grounds of new practice. As the Czech philosopher Karel Kosík puts it, practice has durability through its products and effects.

We are now in a position to formulate the non-reductionist strong connection between biology and the social. The social practices that construct gender relations do not express natural patterns, nor do they ignore natural patterns; rather, they negate them in a practical transformation. This practical transformation is a continuing historical process. Its materials are the social as well as the biological products of previous practice – new situations and new people.

We might say that reproductive biology is historicized in gender. This is true so far as it goes, but is a weak formulation suggesting an additive conception. More precisely, reproductive biology is socially dealt with in the historical process we call gender; a history that negates its biological materials as well as its social ones.

This is not an exotic or original idea. Gayle Rubin, for instance, observes of the kinship structures which are taken by reductionists to express biological imperatives: 'A kinship system is not a list of biological relatives. It is a system of categories and statuses which often contradict actual genetic relationships.' She observes of the cultural emphasis on difference between the sexes:

> Men and women are, of course, different. But they are not as different as day and night, earth and sky, yin and yang, life and death. In fact, from the standpoint of nature, men and women are closer to each other than either is to anything else – for instance, mountains, kangaroos, or coconut palms. Far from being an expression of natural differences, exclusive gender identity is the suppression of natural similarities.

The same goes for gender relations in our society. Texts on sex roles almost always contain a party-piece on sex-typed adornment – make-up, clothing, hair-style and accessories. Erving Goffman's *Gender Advertisements* adds positioning and posture to the catalogue. In the additive framework of sex role theory this is interpreted as a social marking of the natural difference: we put girls in frilly dresses, boys in running shorts and so on. But there is something odd about this. If the difference is natural why does it need to be marked so heavily? For the sex-typing of clothes and adornment really is obsessive. At some moments it reaches quite fantastic levels. No one is likely to doubt the femaleness of a nursing mother. Yet the front-opening dresses and dressing-gowns marketed to nursing mothers (in shops like the British 'Mothercare' chain) are an absolute mass of 'feminine' frills, tucks, bows, lace, ribbons and such like. When you think of the mess created by a nursing baby, it is clear there is nothing functional about this.

In fact the social practices are not reflecting natural differences with these diacritical marks of gender. They are weaving a structure of symbol and interpretation around them, and often vastly exaggerating or distorting them. As Rubin observes, social emphasis on difference negates natural similarity. When we push further into the detail of the social arrangements about gender, it is striking how regularly denials, transformations and contradictions appear. Homosexual men are socially defined as effeminate, homosexual women as mannish; in fact there are no physical or physiological differences between homosexual and heterosexual people. Employment practices that discriminate against women because of presumed childcare obligations define all women as mothers of young children; in fact most are not. Girls in early adolescence are on average bigger and stronger than the boys in their own school classes; yet it is just at this age that enormous pressure is applied to make them dependent and fearful in relation to males. To sustain patriarchal power on the large scale requires the construction of a hypermasculine ideal of toughness and dominance; the physical image of masculinity this produces is grotesquely unlike the actual physique of most men. The corresponding point has often been made about images of physical beauty in women.

At the same time another negation is taking place. The members of either sex vary tremendously in height, strength, endurance, dexterity and so on. As noted already, the distributions in the two sexes overlap to a great extent. Social practices that construct women and men as distinct categories by converting an average difference into a categorical difference – 'men are stronger than women' – negate the major pattern of difference that occurs within sexes rather than between them.

In grasping these apparently paradoxical processes, the kind of distinction between levels of practice that Jean-Paul Sartre makes in the *Critique of Dialectical Reason* is helpful. The biological differentiation of sex in reproduction is a passively suffered condition: men cannot bear children, infants require suckling and so on. To these conditions correspond a limited range of practices and consequences (of a type Sartre calls the 'practico-inert'). People can be lumped together in logically primitive categories through an external logic, a logic imposed on them that places them in parallel situations (Sartre calls this 'seriality') – like a queue of people waiting for a bus, or the audience for a radio broadcast.

These however are not the gender categories as we encounter them in social life. Indeed the practices of sexual reproduction are often quite remote aspects of the social encounters in which gender is constructed and sustained. This is obvious in the key case of children, who have gender forms vehemently imposed on them long before they are capable of reproducing, or even have much understanding of the business of reproduction. There are other, more sophisticated, levels of practice involved. To move to these levels requires negation of the previous level of practice. Thus to construct the social category of 'man' or 'woman', with a common identity and interest, requires negation of the serial dispersion characteristic of the array of parallel situations constructed by the biological categories. This is done in practices that create and assert the solidarity of the sex (or group within it).

This social solidarity is a *new fact*, in no way implied by the biological category. It can therefore be constructed, historically, in a variety of ways. Thus it is possible for a new type of solidarity, a new organization of the gender, to emerge. Masculinities and femininities can be re-constructed historically, new forms can become dominant. It is even possible for a whole new gender category to be constructed, as with the emergence of 'the homosexual' in the late nineteenth century, and perhaps 'the transsexual' now. Such a development does not make sense in any theory of natural difference as the basis of gender. It does make sense when the significance of contradiction is grasped.

There is, therefore, a logic to such paradoxes as the gross exaggeration of difference by the social practices of dress, adornment and the like. They are part of a continuing effort to sustain the social definition of gender, an effort that is necessary precisely *because the biological logic*, and the inert practice that responds to it, *cannot sustain the gender categories*.

The shift to a second level of practice is also found in the

psychodynamics of gender, according to some classical formulations. Alfred Adler's account of the 'masculine protest' as a key
structure of motivation, for instance, is based on the small child's
discovery of a physical fact about its body, its organic inferiority
to others. This perception of the body is, however, transcended in
the psychological process that constructs, in over-compensation, a
desire to dominate, a striving for power. That a real transcendence
has occurred is shown by the fact that as the child grows up the
psychological structure outlives the physical conditions in which
it was produced. The same is true for 'castration anxiety' in Freud's
psychodynamic theory, which outlives the originally extreme
disparity of force between child and parent.

The creation of the 'new fact' in transcendent practice in no
sense excludes the body, the biology of reproduction, bodily
difference or physical experience. To lose this connection would
be to make the kind of suppression made by patriarchal ideology
when it defines menstruation as embarrassing and unmentionable,
and thus eliminates part of women's experience from the language.
The point is that we do not need to fall back on reductionism to
keep the body and its ways in view. In practical transcendence
the body is carried forward, so to speak, into the next transaction.
It remains a presence, indeed a ferment, in the order of things
constructed by more complex social processes. Even when the
physical conditions of some social process change – as when the
psychoanalytic baby grows up – the body remains the screen on
which the well-launched dramas of power and anxiety are projected.
'Hysterical' symptoms like the paralyzed limb are the classic case,
but depression and dissociation are also experienced in the flesh.

Contradiction between the body and a developing practice is a
continuing fact in sexuality itself. In sexual intercourse, nobody
but the most inexperienced, insensitive or frightened person always
follows the simple bodily logic of arousal to climax. There is
tension and pleasure in working *against* immediate bodily demand,
holding back, creating rhythms, exploring. You can communicate
pleasure to a partner by working against your own desire in favour
of hers or his; you learn the ways of another body which does not
contain your own desire or need. In this way the immensely
complex practical edifice of a sexual relationship is built as a
structure of tensions and contradictions. That is the meaning of a
union of two people as distinct from a rubbing-together of two
bodies.

Practical Transformations of the Body

Even to speak of contradiction between social process and the body is not to have moved far enough from doctrines of natural difference and biological determination. For this is still to treat the body as unmoved mover, as what is fixed in relation to what is fluid, as what gives meaning and does not receive it. The body in relation to the social system still seems like the monster looming outside the bright lights of the space station, alien and immovable, compelling by its sheer presence.

That the body is intractable and recalcitrant is important. More than one radical theorist has found in a kind of biological intransigence an ultimate grounding for human freedom in the face of overwhelming social powers: Herbert Marcuse on the bodily basis of Eros, Noam Chomsky on the biological basis of speech. This may be valid as a speculation on ultimate limits to social control; I am not sure. But it should not imply that in general the body becomes a social agent as if from pure nature, from some standpoint outside society. The body-as-used, the body I am, is a social body that has taken meanings rather than conferred them. My male body does not confer masculinity on me; it receives masculinity (or some fragment thereof) as its social definition. Nor is my sexuality the irruption of the natural; it too is part of a social process. In the most extraordinary detail my body's responses reflect back, like the little mirrors on an Indian dress, a kaleidoscope of social meanings.

The body, without ceasing to be the body, is taken in hand and transformed in social practice. I do not have a systematic analysis of this process to offer, but it may be helpful to illustrate the point. What follows are brief notes on three examples: symbolic eroticism, the physical sense of masculinity and the history of body politics.

> Whenas in silks my Julia goes
> Then, then (methinks) how sweetly flows
> That liquefaction of her clothes

Commenting on Herrick's remarkable poem, Judy Barbour notes that the force of its eroticism depends a good deal on the connotations of silk as a sexual and status fetish, operating within a closed system of social thought (which she calls 'mythical') about men's and women's sexuality. Maureen Duffy makes a similar observation on Spenser's *Faerie Queen*, an erotic dream-poem in which some typical problems of Renaissance sexuality and culture are explored and resolved in violence. Jean Genet's *Our Lady of the Flowers* is equally striking as a document of the link between imagination and eroticism. Genet creates here a world of erotic objects in whose ritual dances masculinity and femininity dissolve and coagulate, now taking on sharp edges in the form of the hard youth who combines criminality and desirability, now ambiguous in the shape of Divine.

The importance of ritual in sexuality is familiar. In some forms of sexuality it becomes the matrix for an amplification of the tension set up by working against the body. Using pain, fear and humiliation, sado-masochistic rituals with 'forbidden symbols and ... disowned emotions', in the words of Pat Califia, practically turn the body against itself in the pursuit of pleasure. In the milder fetishisms where pleasure comes with rubberized raincoats or white kid gloves, the role of the imagination and the centrality of socially constructed meaning – here non-verbal and built into tactile response – is very obvious. (Even here, however, the ideological 'naturalization' of the social is under way. The standard fantasy in fetish pornography is about the unpremeditated discovery of an uncontrollable 'natural' response to the fetish, whatever it is.)

Fetishism and fetish pornography work to a large extent by playing with and recombining elements of the symbolism of gender. As sexuality, they presuppose a connection between this symbolism and the body – social definitions of the *feel* of femininity and masculinity. This physical sense of genderedness (to coin a horrible word) needs exploration. I will take the case of masculinity, as femininity has been analysed more extensively.

The physical sense of maleness is not a simple thing. It involves size and shape, habits of posture and movement, particular physical skills and the lack of others, the image of one's own body, the way it is presented to other people and the ways they respond to it, the way it operates at work and in sexual relations. In no sense is all this a consequence of XY chromosomes, or even of the possession on which discussions of masculinity have so lovingly dwelt, the penis. The physical sense of maleness grows through a personal history of social practice, a life-history-in-society.

In Western countries, for instance, images of ideal masculinity

are constructed and promoted most systematically through competitive sport. Though adults are spectators more often than
participants, schoolchildren do play sport a great deal and are
taught to regard sporting success as a matter of deep importance.
The combination of force and skill that is involved in playing well
at games like football, cricket and baseball, and which is central
even in highly individualized sports like surfing, becomes a strongly
cathected aspect of an adolescent boy's life. Though rejected by
some (a point that will be explored in chapter 8), for most it
becomes a model of bodily action that has a much wider relevance
than the particular game. Prowess of this kind becomes a means
of judging one's degree of masculinity.

So the concern with force and skill becomes a statement
embedded in the body, embedded through years of participation
in social practices like organized sport. And it is not a 'statement'
that comes from the void. Its meaning condenses some crucial
features of the social structures that environ, and participate in,
those masculinizing practices. One of these is the structure of class
relations. The system of individual competition in sport has taken
on a particular form in advanced capitalism, as recent analyses of
the Olympics and the culture of sport have shown. More directly
important is the structure of power in gender relations. The
meanings in the bodily sense of masculinity concern, above all
else, the superiority of men to women, and the exaltation of
hegemonic masculinity over other groups of men which is essential
to the domination of women.

The social definition of men as holders of power is translated
not only into mental body-images and fantasies, but into muscle
tensions, posture, the feel and texture of the body. This is one of
the main ways in which the power of men becomes 'naturalized',
i.e. seen as part of the order of nature. It is very important in
allowing belief in the superiority of men, and the oppressive
practices that flow from it, to be sustained by men who in other
respects have very little power. The importance of physical
aggression in some of the major forms of working-class masculinity
is familiar. A vignette: among a peer group of South London boys
in a particular club (where a youth worker interested in the issue
of masculinity works), the mark of friendship is hitting each other
– playfully, but hard. No one who is not a friend is admitted to
this intimacy.

The violence implicit in the physical construction of hegemonic masculinity points directly to the social distribution of violence outlined in chapter 1. It was noted there that at least some features of this distribution change historically. This is one facet of a much larger politics of the body.

Our bodies grow and work, flourish and decay, in social situations that produce bodily effects. For instance the class system that we live in produces malnutrition for the children of poor people, obesity from overeating and overdrinking among the affluent. The institutionalized racism of the Australian social order means massively higher levels of eye disease among Aborigines than among whites: in a national study of rural areas 38 per cent of Aborigines had trachoma compared with 1 per cent of whites.

The politics of the body has a gender dimension as well – which is to say, physical effects that follow from the gender structuring of social relations. Alcoholism provides a clear example. In an Australian national study of 1980 it was found that 14 per cent of men and 6 per cent of women were at intermediate to very high risk levels. Another kind of physical effect is lucidly documented in studies of the material circumstances of working-class family life. Margery Spring Rice's classic *Working-class Wives*, for instance, traced the physical effects on women of the division of labour that assigned them to back-breaking daily labour in 'the small dark unorganized workshop of the home'.

That was in Britain in the 1930s. A number of social processes gradually altered those physical effects. One was the spread of effective and reliable contraception. The history of contraception shows that the term 'politics of the body' is no metaphor. Marie Stopes, leader of the contraception movement in early twentieth-century Britain, was a political organizer and propagandist of genius – though not, it seems from Ruth Hall's biography, much of a technical expert on her subject. From World War I through the 1920s and 1930s she fought a long and sometimes bitter campaign to establish openly available contraceptive services. The story in Australia shows more clearly the other side of the struggle: that is, the mobilization of political resources *against* contraception in the early years of the century by propagandists like Octavius Beale. Fear of the 'yellow peril' from Asia overwhelming the white settlements, imperial patriotism seeking to bolster the British 'race' against the German, fear of working-class depravity, combined with medical mythology and a rational distrust of available methods of contraception to fuel a widespread pro-natalist campaign. The state was, for a while, swung to pro-natalist positions.

Concern about imperial and racial decline fed into another kind of body politics, the attempt to cultivate physique by education. As an organized practice in the schools, general physical education (distinct from sport and from military drill) developed in capitalist countries in the late nineteenth century. Some key innovations came from Sweden and the scheme for a 'scientific' physical education was known elsewhere as 'Swedish drill'. It spread through the mass schooling system in the twentieth century, with particular vigour where interventionist states developed a concern with the military or industrial efficiency of their populations. Nazi schooling, in consequence, was a model of physical education for its time. In somewhat less militarized but still ideologically loaded forms physical education continues to be an essential part of contemporary mass schooling.

We may say, then, that the practical transformation of the body in the social structure of gender is not only accomplished at the level of symbolism. It has physical effects on the body; the incorporation is a material one. The forms and consequences of this incorporation change in time, and change as a result of social purposes and social struggle. That is to say they are fully historical. Symbolically, 'nature' may be opposed to 'culture', the body (fixed) opposed to history (moving). But in the reality of practice the body is never outside history, and history never free of bodily presence and effects on the body. The traditional dichotomies underlying reductionism now have to be replaced by a more adequate and complex account of the social relations in which this incorporation and interplay occur.

NOTES

Natural Difference

(pp. 66–77). A charming short introduction to the evolutionary history of sex is Stevens (1984). On Maccoby and Jacklin's privileging of biology, note that even on the trait of aggressiveness the biological predisposition thesis is disputable: see Tieger (1980). Vulgar sociobiology quotations from Morris (1979), pp. 74–5 and Tiger and Fox (1971), pp. 20, 22; scientific sociobiology from Wilson (1978), pp. 139–40, 128. Parallels between sociobiology on natural sex difference and the pseudo-sciences of IQ and mental disease are noted in the

useful critique of genetic determination by Lewontin, Rose and Kamin
(1984). Additive quotation, Maccoby and Jacklin (1975), p. 374.

Transcendence and Negation

(pp. 78–82). The discussion of practical transcendence draws extensively
on Sartre (1976), with some assistance from Kosík (1976), whose
theory of praxis is outlined by Schmidt (1977). Kovel (1981), pp.
234–6 offers an analysis of negation between praxis and desire that
has some similarity to the argument here, but almost entirely misses
the issue of gender – quite a feat for a psychoanalyst. Quotations from
Rubin (1975), pp. 169, 179–80.

Practical Transformations

(pp. 83–7). The social meanings in eroticism are extensively explored in
the fiction of Angela Carter (e.g. 1974). On sado-masochism see
Greene and Greene (1974) and Califia (1983), pp. 118–32; the
quotation is from another of Califia's writings cited in *Smart* 3 (1984),
p. 8. The social meanings in the physical sense of masculinity are
explored in Willis (1979); Connell (1983) and Corrigan (1984). On
sport and capitalism see Brohm (1978). Data on trachoma from House
of Representatives Standing Committee on Aboriginal Affairs (1979);
on alcoholism from Department of Health (1984). Marie Stopes's
political struggles are surveyed by her biographer Hall (1978); and
Australian pro-natalism by Pringle (1973) and Hicks (1978).

Part II

The Structure of Gender Relations

5

Main Structures: Labour, Power, Cathexis

The argument so far has traced the domain of the social theory of gender and its gradual emergence in Western social thought. I have argued that this theory is autonomous: it cannot derive its logic from a source outside itself, whether natural difference, biological reproduction, the functional needs of society or the imperatives of social reproduction. An adequate theory of gender requires a theory of social structure much stronger than the implicit voluntarism of role theory. But it also needs a concept of structure that can recognize the complexities bulldozed by categoricalism, and give some grip on the historical dynamic of gender.

Chapter 3 proposed that such a theory has already begun to emerge. Chapter 4 showed how it might deal with the lion in the path of social theories of gender, the question of natural difference. The next three chapters attempt to show what the heartland of such a theory, the account of gender as a social structure, might look like.

There is no need to search for new a priori bases. The starting-points are at hand in the intuitive notions of social structure found in role theory and categoricalism. To develop them in a way that meets the criteria just stated requires three steps. First, it is necessary to modify the underlying concept of 'structure' in the light of recent developments in the theory of practice. Second, the concept of a single structure of gender relations must be broken down into component structures or substructures. Third, it is necessary to distinguish between the kind of structural analysis that produces concepts like the 'sexual division of labour' (which I will call structural models) and the kind that produces concepts like the 'gender order' (which I will call structural inventories).

The rest of this chapter explains these steps and sketches a three-part structural model of gender relations. Chapter 6 discusses structural inventories at two levels: the gender order of the whole society and the gender regimes of particular institutions. Chapter 7 explores the historical dynamic of gender relations and the crisis tendencies of the contemporary gender order.

Structure and Structural Analysis

The concept of 'social structure', though fundamental to the social sciences, is ambiguous. Its usages range from the tight and sophisticated models of Piaget, Lévi-Strauss and Althusser to the much more numerous cases where anything that shows a detectable pattern at all is called a 'structure'. Most writing about gender is well towards the latter end of the spectrum. Authors commonly get by with a rough idea that there is some large-scale order in gender relations, but little clarity beyond that.

To short-circuit what could be a very long discussion about definitions, I will assume that the concept of structure is more than another term for 'pattern' and refers to the intractability of the social world. It reflects the experience of being up against something, of limits on freedom; and also the experience of being able to operate by proxy, to produce results one's own capacities would not allow. The concept of *social* structure expresses the constraints that lie in a given form of social organization (rather than, say, physical facts about the world). 'Constraints' may be as crude as the presence of an occupying army. But in most cases the constraints on social practice operate through a more complex interplay of powers and through an array of social institutions. Accordingly, attempts to decode a social structure generally begin by analyzing institutions.

The most sophisticated accounts of gender relations as a social structure, those offered by Juliet Mitchell and Gayle Rubin, focus on the institution of kinship as the cross-cultural basis of sex inequality. Their account of the structure underlying kinship is derived from Claude Lévi-Strauss's classic *The Elementary Structures of Kinship*, which boiled down the enormous variety collected by ethnographers and historians into variants of a universal basic system of exchange. Lévi-Strauss described this as the exchange of women among groups of men and took it to be what constituted society itself. To Mitchell and Rubin this exchange founded the subjection of women.

The notion of 'structure' as a fundamental relationship that is not immediately present in social life but underlies the surface complexity of interactions and institutions, is shared by all varieties of structuralism in the social sciences. It is a major advance over simple descriptive notions of structure. But it has considerable problems, in forms like Lévi-Strauss's theory of kinship. The central difficulty that has emerged from two decades of criticism is that structuralism is based on a logic that is incompatible with the concept of practice as the substance of social process, and hence with a thoroughgoing historicity in social analysis. (For this concept see chapter 7 below.) Without historicity, a politics of transformation becomes irrational.

Mitchell tries to reintroduce practice and history and thus save the rationality of feminist politics. She does this by arguing that the underlying structure (the exchange of women), and the patriarchal social order it gives rise to, have been cultural universals up to the era of capitalism but no longer need be. Mitchell's argument was important in the mid-1970s in providing a theoretical rationale for an autonomous women's movement. But it also implies that struggle against patriarchy was irrational in all previous periods of history. This seems arbitrary, to put it mildly. To avoid drawing such a line across history, we need to overcome structuralism's sharp separation between underlying structure and surface practice.

An illustration of how a more active connection can be made is found in another classic on kinship. Michael Young and Peter Willmott's *Family and Kinship in East London* describes the matrifocal kinship structure of the working-class community of Bethnal Green, with Mum as the core figure and mother–daughter relations as the axis of the family. This structure is shown in its process of constitution, constantly being made and remade in a very active social practice. Daughters and mothers pop in and out of each others' houses up to twelve times a day; they exchange services like care in sickness, and negotiate about other family relationships – including the daughter's marriage. The notion of 'structure' here is not abstracted from practice, though it is also not given in experience. The Bethnal Greeners have no concept of 'matrifocality'. Being present in everyday practice, structure is vulnerable to major changes of practice. This is shown in Young and Willmott's famous description of the migration to an outer-suburban housing estate, which produced an unwanted and unintended nuclear family pattern. As one of the migrants remarked, 'It's like being in a box to die out here'.

The idea of an active presence of structure in practice, and an active constitution of structure by practice, has now been formalized theoretically. It is particularly clear in the 'dualist' accounts of structure developed by Pierre Bourdieu and Anthony Giddens. Bourdieu's *Outline of a Theory of Practice* ties structure and practice together mainly by an ironic emphasis on the unintended consequences of the strategies social actors pursue. The pursuit of individual or family strategies results in the reproduction of the social order from which those strategies took off. Bourdieu's approach has the great merit of recognizing the inventiveness and energy with which people pursue their lives – an unusual feat in theoretical sociology. But his image of social structure depends so heavily on the idea of social 'reproduction' that it is difficult to reconcile with any idea of a historical dynamic, except something that happens behind the backs of the actors. History does happen in Bourdieu's world, but it is not produced.

Giddens's 'theory of structuration' locks structure and practice even more tightly together. Human practice always presupposes social structure, in the sense that practice necessarily calls into play social rules or resources. Structure is always emergent from practice and is constituted by it. Neither is conceivable without the other.

The balance formulated by Giddens as the 'duality of structure' is, of all current frameworks for social theory, the closest to the requirements of a theory of gender. Yet it leaves two outstanding problems. By making the link of structure and practice a *logical* matter, a requirement of social analysis in general, Giddens closes off the possibility that its form might change in history. This is the possibility raised implicitly by Mitchell and explicitly by the practical politics of liberation movements; its significance for the analysis of gender is evident. And in attempting to convey the impact of a structure as a whole, Giddens moves sharply back towards classical structuralism. His paradigmatic example here is the structure of language, and this is deeply misleading for structures like gender or class. Stressing the 'virtuality' of structure, an argument that sees the context of an event as the alternatives allowed by given structural principles, rather than seeing its context as being its history, Giddens is back with the logic of reversible transformations that characterizes structuralism.

Dualist models, then, need an opening towards history. The crucial point is that practice, while presupposing structure in much the sense Bourdieu and Giddens explain, is always responding to a *situation*. Practice is the transformation of that situation in a particular direction. To describe structure is to specify what it is in the situation that constrains the play of practice. Since the consequence of practice is a transformed situation which is the object of new practice, 'structure' specifies the way practice (over time) constrains practice.

Since human action involves free invention (if 'invention within limits', to use Bourdieu's phrase) and human knowledge is reflexive, practice can be turned against what constrains it; so structure can be deliberately the object of practice. But practice cannot escape structure, cannot float free from its circumstances (any more than social actors are simply 'bearers' of the structure). It is always obliged to reckon with the constraints that are the precipitate of history. For example, Victorian women rejecting marriage were not free to adopt any other sexual life they pleased. Often the only practicable alternative was chastity.

Most treatments of the social relations of gender make no subdivision of structure. Texts like Michèle Barrett's *Women's Oppression Today* certainly distinguish topics such as ideology, education, production and the state. But the strong tendency in feminist thought has been to see all such fields as manifestations of a single structure, the subordination of women and superordination of men. Sex role theory, for once, is in agreement.

That there might be some problem here is suggested by the remarkable proliferation of 'ultimate causes' proposed for that single structure. Evolutionary imperatives, hormonal aggression advantage, the physical strength of men, the demands of childbearing, the universality of the family, the functional imperatives of capitalism, the sexual division of labour in childcare, and others, jostle each other as explanations. Since none can be decisively established, the rival root causes cancel each other out. So in the feminist theorizing of the later 1970s and the 1980s there is a tendency for subordination/superordination to float free as pure phenomenon with no roots at all.

But this impasse could also suggest that the treatment of structure is too simplified. A fundamentally different approach was proposed by Juliet Mitchell in her first book, *Woman's Estate*; indeed it was outlined in her famous article 'Women: The Longest Revolution' as early as 1966. Following the method though not the letter of Althusser's revision of Marxism, Mitchell divided gender relations into four 'structures': production, reproduction, socialization and sexuality. Each of them, she argued, generates its own form of the oppression of women. Each has its own historical trajectory, and at different times may be changing at a faster or slower pace than the others. Though Mitchell does not emphasize the point, it is implicit in her argument that the patterns of relationship in the different structures may come into conflict with each other. That is, the structure of gender relations may be internally contradictory.

I would argue that the concepts of internal differentiation, historical unevenness and internal contradiction are essential for understanding the structure of gender relations. This aspect of Mitchell's thought has been remarkably neglected by later theorists, though the fourfold model has been used to good effect in social history by Kerreen Reiger and Michael Gilding.

One reason why the model has not been taken up in theory is that Mitchell's version of it was inconsistent. Production, reproduction, etc. are not, strictly speaking, structures at all. They are types of practice, and they overlap each other. Sexuality is implicated in reproduction, clearly enough. Socialization – if we accept feminist analyses of childcare as work – is a form of production. Certainly there are structures to be discovered in these practices, but there is nothing in Mitchell's argument to imply that the structures active in these domains of practice are separate ones. So Mitchell has pointed towards a new form of structural analysis, but has not produced it.

The detailed research on women's subordination since *Woman's Estate* has nevertheless fulfilled its promise. Studies over the past decade have traced the outline of two substantially different structures of relationship between women and men. One has to do with the division of labour: the organization of housework and childcare, the division between unpaid and paid work, the segregation of labour markets and creation of 'men's jobs' and 'women's jobs', discrimination in training and promotion, unequal wages and unequal exchange. The second has to do with authority, control and coercion: the hierarchies of the state and business, institutional and interpersonal violence, sexual regulation and surveillance, domestic authority and its contestation.

To say these structures are substantially different is not to imply they are generally *separate*. Indeed they interweave all the time. It is to point to some basic differences in the ordering of the social relations involved. As a first approximation one might say that the major organizational principle of the former is separation or division, and of the latter, unequal integration. The accumulation of wealth through the production of goods and services follows a different historical trajectory from the institutionalization of power, and has different effects in the shaping of femininity and masculinity.

Many of the institutional and psychological issues about gender can be understood in terms of the structures of labour and power, but not all. The ways people create emotional links between each other, and the daily conduct of emotional relationships, seem to follow a different, though undoubtedly social, logic. The issues raised by gay liberation, by psychoanalysis and by feminist arguments on sexuality, are not accounted for by labour and power alone. In short, there seems to be a third major structure. It has to do with the patterning of object-choice, desire and desirability; with the production of heterosexuality and homosexuality and the relationship between them; with the socially structured antagonisms of gender (woman-hating, man-hating, self-hatred); with trust and distrust, jealousy and solidarity in marriages and other relationships; and with the emotional relationships involved in rearing children.

The argument of this chapter now proceeds on the assumption that these three structures are empirically the major structures of the field of gender relations. That is to say they (a) are discoverable in current gender research and sexual politics, and (b) account for most of the structural dynamics currently understood. The argument does not assume that they are the only discoverable structures, that they exhaust the field. Nor does it claim that they are necessary structures (a claim which in any case might land us back with the metaphysics of ultimate causes). The argument rests on the gentler, more pragmatic but perhaps more demonstrable claim that with a framework like this we can come to a serviceable understanding of current history.

The general conception of social structure as the pattern of constraint on practice inherent in a set of social relations can be made specific in a number of different ways. The structures just outlined – the division of labour, the structure of power and the structure of cathexis – are examples of what I will call 'structural models'. They operate at a particular level of logical complexity and implicitly make comparisons across historical situations at this level. They lead to questions like what changed in the sexual division of labour as a result of capitalist industrialization; or whether there is a difference in sexual power structure between communist and non-communist states.

In the long debate about structuralism, structural modelling became the be-all and end-all of structural analysis. There was an understandable intoxication with structural models based on virtual transformation, such as Lévi-Strauss's theories of kinship and myth, Piaget's theory of intelligence, Chomsky's theory of syntax. They are intellectually powerful, and they gave order and precision to social science at a time when it was dominated by a mixture of functionalism and muddy empiricism. Yet they drew attention away from other possibilities for structural analysis; and especially from the connection with history.

These possibilities have been indicated, in a rather programmatic way, by Lucien Goldmann. His theory of 'genetic structuralism' never got beyond a methodological sketch, though he gave classic practical demonstrations of the structural analysis of culture. Goldmann showed that it is possible to study the transformations of a complex structure over real time as opposed to the 'virtual' time of structuralism – an approach adopted in the rest of this chapter. His method in *The Hidden God* also indicates the importance of a second kind of structural analysis, the compiling of what might be called an inventory of the structural features of a given situation.

Where structural models push towards comparisons across situations at a given logical level, structural inventories push towards a more complete exploration of a given situation, addressing all its levels and dimensions. There is nothing arcane about this. Any historian reviewing the background to a particular event, any politician scrutinizing the current state of play or balance of forces, is compiling a structural inventory. Any attempt to grasp the current moment in sexual politics, to define where we have got to, any attempt to characterize the gender relations of another culture or another time, likewise involves a structural inventory.

Two useful concepts have been developed for this procedure. Jill Matthews speaks of the 'gender order', a historically constructed pattern of power relations between men and women and definitions of femininity and masculinity. Following Matthews I will use this term for the structural inventory of an entire society. The concept of the 'gender regime' developed in our educational research to describe the state of play in sexual politics within a school involves the same kind of logic on a smaller stage. I will use this term for the structural inventory of a particular institution.

Recognizing the procedure of structural inventory does not introduce a separate set of issues or topics. The division of labour, the structure of power, the structure of cathexis are the major elements of any gender order or gender regime. Structural models and structural inventories are in principle complementary ways of looking at the same facts. In practice they are constantly done together, with shifting emphases. This chapter and the next discuss them separately to emphasize the logic of analysis, but the separation is far from absolute.

Labour

The sexual division of labour at its simplest is an allocation of particular types of work to particular categories of people. It is a social structure to the extent that this allocation becomes a constraint on further practice. This happens in several interrelated ways. First, the prior division of work among people becomes a social rule allocating people to work. An employee entering a firm is given job X if a woman, job Y if a man. The working of such rules is found in almost every study of paid employment that has considered the issue of gender, and this is no primitive hangover found only in low-technology industries. The superb ethnography of a British motor vehicle component assembly plant by Ruth Cavendish, *Women on the Line*, shows an almost absolute separation between jobs allocated to women and to men. 'It was obvious', the author remarks, 'that the only qualification you needed for a better job was to be a man'. Motor vehicles are not the cutting edge of technology any more, but computers certainly are. Game and Pringle in *Gender at Work* show that the growth of computing has resulted in job markets as segregated as any in the work-force. Women are hired as data entry key-punchers; men predominate as operators, salesmen, systems analysts and managers.

A segregation rule in operation becomes the basis of new forms of constraint on practice, such as differential skilling. Where women and men have been skilled or trained differentially, discriminatory employment becomes rational from the employer's point of view. As Carol O'Donnell shows in *The Basis of the Bargain,* differential skilling and training by sex is a very general feature of the interface between the education system and labour markets. Through such mechanisms the sexual division of labour is transformed into an apparently technical division of labour, resistant to the more obvious antidiscrimination strategies. Where men are usually better prepared or trained than women for a given job, choosing 'the best applicant' will normally mean choosing a man. The almost complete dominance of the upper echelons of universities by men is a striking example of this indirect discrimination.

Skilling and training is one of the mechanisms by which the sexual division of labour is made a powerful system of social constraint. Just how powerful is revealed when a conscious attempt is made to change it. The experience of antidiscrimination and affirmative action programs is relevant here, and the slow progress they have made is familiar. Less well known, but equally important, is the evidence that has begun to accumulate about attempts to alter the sexual division of labour in unpaid work, notably housework and childcare. This has become, as Lynne Segal notes, an important focus of the personal politics that grew out of the New Left in the 1970s in Britain. Paul Amato, reflecting on two years experience house-husbanding in Melbourne, notes that the reversal was never accepted by most men he dealt with, who felt that men should work (i.e., housework was not work) and men should not be economically dependent on women. One solution to the dilemma was to regard him as successfully exploiting his wife. Clearly the conventional sexual division of labour has strong cultural supports. A recent survey in southern England by R. E. Pahl shows no tendency for unemployed men to take on more housework; and the Australian study of domestic 'role reversal' by Graeme Russell shows shared childcare arrangements between husband and wife to be highly unstable.

Nevertheless the fact that there are some attempts to reverse it, together with the creation of a new sexual division of labour in industries like computing, indicate that the structure is not only a constraint but also an object of practice. The research that documents division in workplaces also documents the activity, the social labour, that sustains it. In Ruth Cavendish's factory, management was in the hands of men, so was the union, and it is no accident that both hierarchies resisted the attempt of women workers (eventually by a wildcat strike) to alter their situation. Another British workplace study, by David Collinson and David Knights, vividly shows the methods that sustain the sexual division of labour in a white-collar workplace, in this case an insurance firm. Women who look for promotion above routine clerical work are talked out of it by men in management, appealing to anxieties that the men themselves have done much to create. What amounts to a complete miniature ideology of women's psychological unsuitability for insurance work is sustained; and the real prejudice of managers against women is rationalized by appeal to the presumed prejudices of customers.

The gender regimes of these two workplaces are, however, significantly different, and it is possible that the mechanisms by which the sexual division of labour is sustained are quite specific. Michael Korda's *Male Chauvinism*, an early American account of sexual politics in the workplace, presents the oppression of women mainly as a consequence of individual discrimination by bosses. This cannot be true for a situation of collective exploitation like Cavendish's factory. But in the New York corporate office world from which Korda writes, where hiring and firing, salary determination and promotion are all highly individualized, the exclusion of women perhaps does mainly operate through the individual sexism of corporate executives.

Beyond the individual workplace there is a wider social process that constitutes the sexual division of labour in terms of whole categories of workers. Margaret Power speaks of 'the making of a woman's occupation' as a historical process in which new categories of work and workers are formed. It is by no means a matter of an existing division being mechanically reproduced. We now have case studies of individual occupations that document this. One of the best is Eve Gamarnikow's study which shows how the modern occupation of trained nurse was constructed by entrepreneurs such as Florence Nightingale. Its basis was a trade-off that accepted the control of medical practice by men (i.e., doctors) in order to open a semi-professional career path to middle-class women.

As this case shows, the construction of the sexual division of labour is not just a matter of the allocation of work to people. It also involves the design of the work. The argument about 'appropriate technology' – machinery or techniques that are less environmentally destructive, or cheaper, or particularly suited to Third World needs – has made it obvious that there is never just one technique for doing a job. There are even alternative ways of building a nuclear bomb. A socio-technical system, such as industrial manufacturing or domestic work, can be set up in various ways. The particular designs and practices current at a given time therefore represent a social choice of some kind. The current labour practice gets embodied in technology designed with given social arrangements in mind – among them the sexual division of labour. For instance the waterframes in the cotton mills of north-western England and southern Scotland in the early Industrial Revolution were designed to be operated by women and children. As T. C. Smout notes, women and children were preferred as workers for the new factories because they were presumed more docile in the face of unprecedented demands for labour discipline. The factory owners faced the interesting problem of what to do with the husbands in order to attract their preferred labour force.

A more complex example is the technology of housework. Machines like vacuum cleaners or washing machines are equally suited to be operated by women or by men. The models widely sold are however designed to be used by just one household and presuppose one permanent domestic worker per household. This arrangement happens to be provided by the conventional sexual division of labour and not by any other likely or practicable arrangement. Accordingly they are always advertised with pictures of smiling women operating them, not smiling men. It is quite possible to design equipment for doing the same work under other social arrangements. For instance the communal laundries operated by British local government provided a practical alternative way of mechanizing laundry in the 1930s and 1940s. They were squeezed out by post-war privatization. The consumer-goods boom of the 1950s was, among other things, a reconstitution of the domestic sexual division of labour by new means.

These considerations imply that the idea of a 'division of labour' is itself too narrow. We are dealing not just with the allocation of work, but with the nature and organization of that work. It is impossible to separate either fact from the distribution of the products of work – that is, the distribution of services and income. Coming back to Cavendish's factory, the fierce insistence on the sexual division of labour by the men makes more sense when we learn that the men's jobs were much better paid. Some of the men in the plant were paid twice what the women got, for doing easier jobs. The women got 'married women's wages' whether married or not. This is far from being an isolated case. As shown in chapter 1 for a country which has theoretically had 'equal pay' for men and women for fifteen years, the actual average income of women in Australia is still less than half the average income of men.

So the 'sexual division of labour' can no longer be seen as a structure in its own right. It must be seen as part of a larger pattern, a gender-structured system of production, consumption and distribution.

To think of a gender structuring of production, not just a sexual division, allows a clearer recognition of differentiations within the work-force that have to do with sexual politics but which operate *within* the broad categories of sex. Some have to do with the marketing of sex itself, in prostitution or the entertainment industry. But the issue is much broader. Cases include the making of jobs like receptionist, air hostess and secretary as a combination of particular technical skills with a particular femininity. Particular industries, notably clothing and theatre, are associated with homosexual masculinity. On the other hand business management is integrated with forms of masculinity organized around interpersonal dominance: 'tough' stances towards labour are admired in business, and phrases like 'aggressive marketing' are terms of approval in management jargon.

This extension of the concept, however, runs up against the concept of the 'mode of production', or its near equivalent the 'social division of labour', in Marxist theory. There is a good deal of literature attempting to link the position of women to these concepts; as noted in chapter 3, this has been the most important extrinsic theory of gender. The barrenness of this theoretical enterprise is largely because the theorizing has not been bold enough. Almost all this literature has accepted the traditional definition of the 'capitalist mode of production' in Marxism as a production system fundamentally defined by *class* relations. Even the attempt to define a 'domestic mode of production' located in the household has left the class analysis of capitalism undisturbed.

It must now be accepted that gender divisions are not an ideological addendum to a class-structured mode of production. They are a deep-seated feature of production itself. They are not confined to domestic work, or even to the division between unpaid domestic work and paid work in industry. They are a central feature of industrial organization too. They are not a hangover from pre-capitalist modes of production. As the cases of computing and world-market factories show, they are being vigorously created in the most advanced sectors of the capitalist world economy.

A series of arguments lead firmly to the conclusion proposed by Game and Pringle. Gender divisions are a fundamental and essential feature of the capitalist system; arguably as fundamental as class divisions. Socialist theory cannot any longer evade the fact that capitalism is run by, and mainly to the advantage of, men.

This is one of the grounds for a wider rethinking of the socialist analysis of capitalism. For the feminist argument has an interesting parallel with the view from Third World radical movements, which have seen capitalism mainly as a system of global inequality and imperialism. Together they suggest a new view of capitalism, as a system for the concentration and regulation of profits extracted by a number of qualitatively different mechanisms of exploitation, rather than the basically homogeneous structure implied by the concept of a 'mode of production'. If that is broadly correct, we no longer need the kind of sideways skip performed by Eli Zaretsky in *Capitalism, the Family and Personal Life*, proposing that capitalism took over the existing patriarchal organization of gender or domestic life and used it for its own reproduction. The connection is more direct. Capitalism was partly constituted out of the opportunities for power and profit created by gender relations. It continues to be.

Given this understanding of gender relations in production and consumption, what are their main principles of organization? What kind of 'system' are we dealing with? At this point my argument becomes more speculative and uncertain. I offer the following as an organizing hypothesis rather than a firm conclusion. It is, nevertheless, based on the research on domestic and industrial labour already referred to, as well as some practical experiences of reform. Five points in particular seem important:

1   the sheer scale and insistence of demarcations between women's and men's work, despite their technical irrationality and the impossibility of making them complete;
2   the connection of many demarcations with issues of profitability

or labour control, or both, in the workplace;

3 the way they function to exclude virtually all women from opportunities for the accumulation of wealth on a scale usable as capital, or from career paths that would lead to the control of significant capitals;
4 the importance of practices promoting the solidarity of men – often across class lines – in maintaining these demarcations;
5 the consistency with which divisions of labour and differences of income operate to allocate childcare to women, especially younger women.

Much of this can be understood in terms of two major principles. One might be called the gendered logic of accumulation. The overall gender organization of labour concentrates economic benefits in one direction, economic losses in another, and on a scale sufficient to produce a dynamic of accumulation in its own right. Christine Delphy identified such a mechanism in her study of French marriages, but by confining the issue to the household and the one-to-one marriage relation, missed the larger possibilities of accumulation in industry. The benefits and costs are not distributed in an all-or-nothing manner between the sexes as blocks. The printing tradesmen studied by Cynthia Cockburn are minor beneficiaries; the media capitalists who employ them are major beneficiaries. Not all women are major losers, a fact of strategic importance to feminism. Overall the benefits, opportunities and costs are large enough to be worth fighting for, and motivate the active practice of demarcation and exclusion by many groups of men.

There are two internal limits to the pace and scale of gender-based accumulation. One is the fact that the division of labour, while marked, is far from absolute. Very few women are sailors and very few men are secretaries, but quite a lot of both are clerks, shopkeepers, sales personnel, programmers and teachers. Much of the labour in peasant agriculture is shared. The second is the fact that marriage is a one-to-one relationship. There is limited scope to extract material advantages from the labour of just one other person. So the scale of economic inequalities resulting from labour organized through marriage is severely limited, when compared with the economic inequalities that can be produced by accumulation in industry. In this respect the nuclear family form must be seen as an important restraint on sex inequality. The current commercialization of domestic work, for instance in the growth of 'fast food' outlets, is likely to increase the economic inequalities of gender.

The second principle might be called, perhaps less happily, the political economy of masculinity. A number of important practices have to do with the definition of masculinity and its mobilization as an economic resource. Ann Curthoys has argued that childcare is the basis of the sexual division of labour and that the childcare issue is the structural basis of feminism. This overstates the case, but the general importance of the issue is undeniable. Curthoys acutely observes that childcare is not just an issue for women but an issue about men: 'the notion that caring for young children is not a fit occupation for men is extraordinarily deepseated'. Since men have more control over the division of labour than women, their collective choice *not* to do childcare, as Margaret Polatnick has argued, reflects the dominant definition of men's interests, and in fact helps them keep predominant power. The ability of management, in many industrial conflicts, to mobilize men workers and their unions in tacit alliances against women workers confirms the strength of these definitions of interest. How particular definitions of masculinity are interrelated will be discussed later. Here I will simply note that a hegemonic pattern of masculinity, in organizing the solidarity of men, becomes an economic as well as a cultural force.

This force does not operate without resistance. The sexual division of labour itself creates bases for solidarity among women. In industrial employment the widespread exclusion of women from career grades has the effect of giving them shared work experiences and little structural reason to be in competition with each other. The routines of commuting make women the daytime majority in dormitory suburbs; and studies of new suburbs by sociologists such as Lyn Richards emphasize how important, how carefully sought and monitored, are their relationships with each other. Beatrix Campbell, discussing the current recession in Britain, notes how the division of labour in childcare means that young single mothers on state welfare benefits enter a community of women that links very different age-groups. While none of these are blanket effects, they do indicate a potential for self-definition or resistance.

Power

Particular transactions involving power are easy enough to observe. Mr Barrett the Victorian patriarch forbids his daughter to marry; parliament makes homosexual intercourse a crime; a bank manager refuses a loan to an unmarried woman; a group of youths rape a girl of their acquaintance. It is often difficult to see beyond individual acts of force or oppression to a *structure* of power, a set of social relations with some scope and permanence. Yet actions like the ones just listed are not intelligible without the structure. Rape, for instance, routinely presented in the media as individual deviance, is a form of person-to-person violence deeply embedded in power inequalities and ideologies of male supremacy. Far from being a deviation from the social order, it is in a significant sense an enforcement of it.

This connection of violence with ideology points to the multiple character of social power. Force is one important component. It is no accident that the means of organized violence – weapons and knowledge of military technique – are almost entirely in the hands of men, as shown in chapter 1. Yet 'naked force' is rare. Much more often violence appears as part of a complex that also involves institutions and the ways they are organized. Power may be a balance of advantage or an inequality of resources in a workplace, a household, or a larger institution. By and large the people who run the corporations, the government departments and the universities are men, who so arrange things that it is extremely difficult for women to get access to top positions. Organizational control is no more naked than force usually is. Both secrete, and depend on, ideologies. The ability to impose a definition of the situation, to set the terms in which events are understood and issues discussed, to formulate ideals and define morality, in short to assert hegemony, is also an essential part of social power. Much of the critical work of feminism and gay liberation has necessarily been devoted to contesting cultural power: for instance cultural definitions of women as weak, or of homosexuals as mentally ill.

That relations of power function as a social structure, as a pattern of constraint on social practice, is in one sense all too obvious. The constraint on practice extends to the elemental question of staying alive. Helen Ware, in *Women, Demography and*

Development, notes that in rich countries, where basic nutrition is
not a problem, women live longer than men; in the poorest
countries women die earlier than men. Here, it appears, discrimination against women in forms like less food and less medical
attention is operating at a level where life is at stake. Differential
infant mortality, including infanticide of girls, is another case in
point.

It is less obvious, but also important, that the practice of those
who hold power is constrained as well. Men are empowered in
gender relations, but in specific ways which produce their own
limits. For instance, in a patriarchal gender order emphasizing
monogamous marriage there is serious tension between men about
issues of adultery; a structure that defines women as a kind of
property makes men liable to reprisals for theft. Sustaining
hegemonic definitions of masculinity is often an issue of importance,
and homosexual men attract hostility partly because they undermine these definitions.

As with labour, the structure of power is an object of practice
as well as a condition. Many accounts of patriarchy give the
impression of a simple, orderly structure like a suburban war
memorial. Behind the facade is likely to be a mass of disorder and
anomaly. Imposing order requires a mobilization of resources and
expenditure of energy. What Donzelot calls the 'policing of families'
is just a part of this. Research on the welfare state, such as Sheila
Shaver's study of Australian taxation and benefit payments, shows
an apparatus of social policy that assumes women's dependence
on men and reinforces it.

Imposing order in and through culture is a large part of this
effort. One notes, for instance, the enthusiasm with which the
Catholic hierarchy – all men – emphasize an ideal of purity,
meekness and obedience for women. Its effectiveness has just been
demonstrated in Ireland where the Church has succeeded in
defeating a referendum to permit divorce. Elsewhere in the
capitalist world priests are becoming less important as ideologists
of gender, journalists more so. Though 'quality' newspapers like
The Guardian in Britain are liberal in sexual politics, most mass-
circulation journalism is unrelievedly sexist and homophobic. The
people doing this cultural and material 'policing' are not necessarily
the main beneficiaries as individuals. They are, rather, participants
in a collective project in which the power of men and subordination
of women is sustained.

If authority is defined as legitimate power, then we can say that the main axis of the power structure of gender is the general connection of authority with masculinity. But this is immediately complicated, and partly contradicted, by a second axis: the denial of authority to some groups of men, or more generally the construction of hierarchies of authority and centrality within the major gender categories.

The authority of men is not spread in an even blanket across every department of social life. In some circumstances women have authority; in some others the power of men is diffuse, confused or contested. Research by American feminists such as Carroll Smith-Rosenberg has traced the history of institutions and practices which have been controlled by women, among them girls' education, friendship networks, and non-market production. This insight can also be inverted. We can identify a complex of institutions and milieux where the power of men and the authority of masculinity are relatively concentrated. There is a 'core' in the power structure of gender, contrasted with the more diffuse or contested patterns of power in the periphery.

In the advanced capitalist countries, four components of this core are reasonably clear: (a) the hierarchies and work-forces of institutionalized violence – military and paramilitary forces, police, prison systems; (b) the hierarchy and labour force of heavy industry (for example, steel and oil companies) and the hierarchy of high-technology industry (computers, aerospace); (c) the planning and control machinery of the central state; and (d) working-class milieux that emphasize physical toughness and men's association with machinery.

The connections between (a), (b) and (c) are familiar. President Eisenhower, not a noted feminist, warned of the power of the 'military–industrial complex' in the United States. There is a close analogue in the Soviet Union. In both countries, as Joel Moses observes of the latter, there is an 'almost complete exclusion of women from the major policy-making centres'. These parts of the complex are tied together by an ideology linking masculinity, authority and technological violence, which has slowly become a focus of research. But it is their connection with (d) that is crucial in sexual politics as a whole. This connection gives a mass base to militarist beliefs and practices that might otherwise be so repellent as to destabilize the governments that rest on them. Perhaps the most striking feature of this connection is the extent to which it is mediated by machinery, especially motor vehicles. The gradual displacement of other transport systems by this uniquely violent and environmentally destructive technology is both a means and a measure of the tacit alliance between the state and corporate elite and working-class hegemonic masculinity.

It was often pointed out by 'men's movement' writers in the 1970s that most men do not really fit the image of tough, dominant and combative masculinity that the ideologists of patriarchy sell. That image is not intended to fit. The celluloid heroism of a John Wayne or Sylvester Stallone is heroic only by contrast with the mass of men who are not. The 'justifying' ideology for the patriarchal core complex and the overall subordination of women requires the creation of a gender-based hierarchy among men. (I stress 'gender-based' because discussions of power relations between men have commonly stopped after identifying divisions of class and race.) As gay liberation points out, an essential part of this process has been the creation of a negative symbol of masculinity in the form of stigmatized outgroups, especially homosexual men. In general, then, a hierarchy is created with at least three elements: hegemonic masculinity, conservative masculinities (complicit in the collective project but not its shock troops) and subordinated masculinities.

Feminist thought around 1970 commonly identified the family as the strategic site, the key to the oppression of women. If anything the pendulum has now swung too far the other way. It has become clear that household and kinship relations are not a test-tube case of pure patriarchy. The family as an institution might best be regarded now as part of the periphery rather than the core complex. Colin Bell and Howard Newby remark that the authority of husbands requires a good deal of bargaining and negotiation for it to be maintained in working order. The importance of bargaining and the tensions around marital authority are confirmed by a considerable body of close-up research on families, from Mirra Komarovsky's classic *Blue-Collar Marriage* to more recent studies like Lillian Rubin's *Worlds of Pain* in the United States, Pauline Hunt's *Gender and Class Consciousness* in Britain, Claire Williams's *Open Cut* and Jan Harper and Lyn Richards's *Mothers and Working Mothers* in Australia. These studies also suggest a recent historical shift, with husbands now finding it more difficult to impose an openly patriarchal regime in the home.

The contestation of domestic patriarchy is so widespread in

some settings that it makes sense to talk of a working-class feminism, rooted in these struggles as much as in paid employment. Marital power struggles are often won by the wives. The research that produced the case study of the Princes in chapter 1 also showed a number of families where the father's control was eroded or simply non-existent. Komarovsky noted this in the 1950s too. I think it is important to acknowledge that there are genuine reversals of power here. It is not a question of women being conceded an apparent power which can then be revoked, but of the hard relational outcomes of domestic conflicts and negotiations over years or even decades.

It is also important to acknowledge that these local victories do not overthrow patriarchy. Komarovsky observed among her American working-class couples that where the wife was the controlling member of the marriage, this could not be acknowledged publicly; a facade of men's authority was maintained. The general implication is that we must distinguish the *global* or macro-relationship of power, in which women are subordinated to men in the society as a whole, from the *local* or micro-situation in particular households, particular workplaces, particular settings. It is possible for the local pattern to depart from the global pattern, even to contradict it. Such departures may provoke 'policing', i.e., attempts to establish the global pattern locally as a norm. They may also signify structural tension that leads to large-scale change in the longer run.

Cathexis

To recognize a social structure in sexuality it is necessary first to see sexuality as social. The following analysis therefore presupposes the argument, made in Gagnon and Simon's *Sexual Conduct*, Foucault's *History of Sexuality* and Weeks's *Sexuality and its Discontents*, that sexuality is socially constructed. Its bodily dimension does not exist before, or outside, the social practices in which relationships between people are formed and carried on. Sexuality is enacted or conducted, it is not 'expressed'.

There is an emotional dimension, and perhaps an erotic dimension, to all social relationships. However the focus here will be on what are called 'sexual social relationships' by the Red Collective in *The Politics of Sexuality in Capitalism*: relationships organized around one person's emotional attachment to another. The structure that organizes these attachments I will call the 'structure of cathexis'.

Freud used the term 'cathexis' to refer to a psychic charge or instinctual energy being attached to a mental object, i.e., an idea or image. Here I am generalizing it to the construction of emotionally charged social relations with 'objects' (i.e., other people) in the real world. As with Freud's usage, it is important to note that the emotional attachment may be hostile, not only affectionate. It may also be hostile and affectionate at the same time, i.e., ambivalent. Most close relationships have this degree of complexity.

Of course sexual practices are governed by other structures as well. Emma Goldman put this pungently when trying to deromanticize 'the traffic in women': 'It is merely a question of degree whether she sells herself to one man, in or out of marriage, or to many men. Whether our reformers admit it or not, the economic and social inferiority of women is responsible for prostitution.' Yet psychoanalysis and the sexual liberation movements both point to the constraining power of patterns of emotional attachment in their own right. It should be possible to analyse them without falling into romanticism.

The social patterning of desire is most obvious as a set of prohibitions. The incest taboo, and specific laws about rape, age of consent and homosexuality, all prohibit sexual relationships between certain people. (Strictly speaking the laws prohibit particular actions, but the intention is to destroy the relationships.) Psychoanalytic theories of the Oedipal crisis and the super-ego interpret the impact of society on emotions mainly in terms of the internalization of prohibitions. Yet the prohibitions would be pointless without injunctions to love and marry the right kind of person, to find such-and-such a kind of masculinity or femininity desirable. The social pattern of desire is a joint system of prohibition and incitement.

Two principles of organization are very obvious in our culture. Objects of desire are generally defined by the dichotomy and opposition of feminine and masculine; and sexual practice is mainly organized in couple relationships.

Historically and cross-culturally, sexual attachment has not always been organized in terms of a dichotomy. Nevertheless in the rich capitalist countries at present sexuality is firmly organized as either heterosexual or homosexual. If it is not, we actually label it as mixed: 'bisexual'. Though coupling is often seen as the basic structure of attachment, the gender dichotomy of desire seems to have some priority. When couples break up and their members form new attachments, it is almost universal practice for the new companion to be of the same sex as the old one, whichever that was.

In the pattern of desire that is socially hegemonic, cathexis presupposes sexual difference. 'Woman needs man and man must have his mate', as time goes by. The solidarity of the heterosexual couple is formed on the basis of some kind of reciprocity, rather than a basis of common situation or experience. This is in marked contrast to solidarities generated by the structures of labour and power. The latent contradiction here has often been noticed, indeed is a theme of romantic literature, as well as a political issue of some importance in feminism in the last decade. More, the sexual difference is a large part of what gives erotic flavour to the relationship. Hence it can be emphasized as a means of intensifying pleasure. This goes some way to explaining the systematic exaggeration of gender differences discussed in chapters 4 and 8.

But 'difference' is a logical term, and social relationships are more loaded. The members of a heterosexual couple are not just different, they are specifically unequal. A heterosexual woman is sexualized as an object in a way that a heterosexual man is not. The fashion industry, the cosmetics industry, and the content of mass media are tangible proof of this. For instance, the glamour shots on the covers of women's magazines and men's magazines are pictures of women in both cases; the difference is in the way the models are dressed and posed. Broadly speaking, the erotic reciprocity in hegemonic heterosexuality is based on unequal exchange. There are, as Emma Goldman noted, material reasons why women participate in unequal relationships. The 'double standard', permitting promiscuous sexuality to men and forbidding it to women, has nothing to do with greater desire on the part of men; it has everything to do with greater power.

The process of sexualizing women as objects of heterosexual desire involves standardizing feminine appeal, as the term 'fashion' itself implies. There is a complex of tensions and contradictions around this. Though hostility can be and often is directed at a whole gender category (misogyny, misandry, homophobia), attraction is not. Rather, heterosexuality and homosexuality as structural principles are definitions of the social category *within* which a partner can be chosen. Perhaps the implication is that both are constructed mainly by blocking out the category from which the partner is *not* to be drawn.

At the psychological level this implies repression and at the social level prohibition. Both imply some attraction to the negated object. Classical psychoanalysis made us familiar with this under the name of 'ambivalence'. Its significance in understanding the construction of masculinity will be discussed in chapter 9; here I want to raise its structural implications. In *The Ego and the Id* Freud noted that the 'complete Oedipus complex' is twofold. Underneath the familiar triangle of love and jealousy is another set of emotional relations where the attachments run the other way: 'A boy has not merely an ambivalent attitude towards his father and an affectionate object-choice towards his mother, but at the same time he also behaves like a girl and displays an affectionate feminine attitude to his father and a corresponding jealousy and hostility towards his mother.' Carl Jung proposed as a general rule that what is repressed is emotion that cannot be expressed in social practice, with the result that the unconscious comes to be a negative of the conscious mind and public life.

If we take these ideas seriously, it can be argued that the visible structure of emotional relationships coexists with a shadow structure whose sense is very different. It is a familiar fact that public affection in a married couple often coexists with private hostility. The Red Collective has suggested a great difference between the 'inside' and 'outside' of couple relations in general. Gay men have often suspected that the hostility they receive is sharpened by unconscious desire. Bringing up small children is virtually guaranteed to produce both love and hostility on both sides and to a strong degree. Since most of this parenting is done by women, relationships involving mothers are likely to be highly ambivalent, a theme stressed by Nancy Friday in *My Mother/My Self*.

There is so little research that gives depth-psychological information and has a sense of social context that it is difficult to do more than speculate on how this shadow structure is organized. All that is clear is that the structure of cathexis must be regarded as multilevelled, and major relationships as ambivalent, in the general case. The old cliches about how easily love and hatred turn into each other, and the power of fables on this theme like

Puccini's *Turandot*, make better sense if sexual practices are generally based on structural relationships in which both love and hatred are already present.

Nancy Friday's argument points towards another principle of organization. She remarks that when girls develop a desire for men, it is more security than sexuality that they want. It is often said of teenage sex that the girls want affection and the boys want sex. Gabrielle Carey and Kathy Lette in *Puberty Blues* add that in teenage peer-group life, the sex is as much for symbolic purposes as for physical pleasure. This is probably true of adults too. The argument connects with Herbert Marcuse's observations in *Eros and Civilization* about the development of genital primacy and the de-erotization of the rest of the body under the rule of the performance principle. It appears that a broad opposition has been constructed between genital performance and diffuse sensuality. In contemporary hegemonic heterosexuality these forms of eroticism are defined as masculine and feminine respectively. But they need not be. In other cultures they certainly are not, as the *Kama Sutra* of Vatsyayana illustrates. It is wonderfully ironic that this compendium of mannered and leisured sensuality is now (in the West) mainly sold in porn shops dedicated to the mighty erection and the quick climax.

With labour and power, the structure can be the object of practice; with cathexis, it commonly is. One of the striking things about sexuality is that the structure itself can be cathected. Hence, for instance, the erotic value of gender difference already noted. Hence the gender element in narcissism, the extent to which cathexis of the self is focused on the diacritical marks of gender. Hence, most strikingly, the erotic circularities of sexual fetishism, where the symbolic markers of social categories (lace handkerchiefs, high-heeled shoes, leather jackets) or structural principles (for example, dominance) get detached from their contexts and themselves become primary objects of arousal.

This kind of practice can be captured for profit-making or repression, as it is by the advertising industry. But another practice directed towards structure is possible, the attempt to rework patterns of attachment in an egalitarian direction. Autobiographies of this practice, like the Red Collective's book, or Anja Meulenbelt's account of personal life, feminism and the Dutch Left in *The Shame is Over*, show the difficulties more readily than the potentials. David Fernbach, who argues in *The Spiral Path* that there is an inherent egalitarianism in gay relationships because of their transitive structure (my lover's lover can also be my lover), is more sanguine.

A Note on 'System' and Composition

Setting out this account of multiple structures risks a new kind of reductionism, implying a coherence and completeness in each which earlier was denied to gender relations as a whole. Certainly the exercise of separating structures is pointless unless there is some gain in coherence. But it is important that none of the three structures is or can be independent of the others. The structure of cathexis in some respects reflects inequalities of power; the division of labour partly reflects patterns of cathexis, and so on. In none is there an ultimate determinant, a 'generative nucleus' to use Henri Lefebvre's term, from which the rest of the pattern of gender relations springs.

There is, however, a unity in the field, an orderliness, which needs to be understood. People do not walk around all day with an ache in their shoulders from the sociological cross-pressures. A gay man can be beaten up in the streets of Sydney in a way that somehow fits with the experience of being beaten up in New York. There is some coherence between the division of labour in childcare, the psychodynamics of femininity and the possibilities of women's liberation.

My argument, briefly, is that this unity is not the unity of a *system*, as functionalist analysis would imply. Nor is it the expressive unity that would be provided by the existence of a generative nucleus. It is a unity – always imperfect and under construction – of historical composition. I mean 'composition' as in music: a tangible, active and often difficult process of bringing elements into connection with each other and thrashing out their relationships. It is a matter of the real historical process of interaction and group formation. The difference from music is not that the process lacks a composer, but that it has a whole stack of them; and that all are inside the piece being composed, since what is being composed is their own lives. The product of the process is not a logical unity but an empirical unification. It happens on particular terms in particular circumstances. At the level of a whole society it produces the gender order to be discussed in the next chapter.

The idea of 'composition' implies that a structure may be less than perfectly formed, and a field of practice less than completely governed by a particular structure. In short, the level of systematic-ity in gender relations varies. It is possible for the processes I have called 'empirical unification' to work powerfully and achieve a high degree of order, as seems to be the case for the core complex within the structure of power. But if this is achieved, it is not the consequence of an inherent or categorical logic, and never justifies functionalist analysis. It is the outcome of strategy in the historical process of group formation and interaction.

A high degree of systematicity is likely to reflect the dominance of a group whose interests are served by a particular gender order. For instance, the extent to which housing, finance, education and other spheres of life are all organized around the model of the heterosexual couple reflects the dominance of heterosexual interests and the subordination of homosexual people. The extent to which homosexual experience itself has been organized in heterosexual terms ('butch' and 'femme' for instance) is a striking proof of subordination. A major task of gay-liberation politics has logically been to contest this way of organizing homosexual experience – to 'desystematize' or 'de-compose' gender, so to speak.

It is historically possible to have a low degree of systematicity, a good deal of incoherence and contestation. And it is possible to have the combination of structured conflict of interest and potential for de-composition that can be recognized as a crisis tendency. This will be explored in chapter 7.

NOTES

Structure and Structural Analysis

(pp. 92–9). The critique of structuralism and of Bourdieu draws on several essays in Connell (1983). The account of 'dualist' theory follows discussions in a seminar course on 'Practice, Self and Social Structure' held at Macquarie University in 1985; my thanks to Sue Kippax in particular. On the logic of structuralism I find Piaget (1971) illuminating. Giddens rejects the definition of structure as 'constraint' but I would argue that this can be formulated in ways that make it simpler and at least as powerful as his model. My definition of 'structural models' is entirely distinct from the concept of 'structural modelling' in business-oriented operations research: see e.g. Linstone et al. (1979) and other papers in the same issue of *Technological Forecasting and Social Change*, where 'structure' has the extremely weak sense noted in the text and 'modelling' means feeding vague ideas into a computer to make them look precise. Quotation from Young and Willmott (1962, p. 133).

Labour

(pp. 99–106). Quotation from Cavendish (1982), p. 79. Segal et al. (1979–80) provide a rare analysis of a sustained attempt to change childcare in a politicized environment. Quotation from Curthoys (1976, p. 3).

Power

(pp. 107–11). The argument here assumes the points established by Lukes (1974) about the different forms of social power. For American historical research tracing women's fields of power see Du Bois et al. (1980). Quotation from Moses (1978, p. 334).

Cathexis

(pp. 111–16). Quotations from Goldman (1972a, p. 145) and Freud (1923, p. 33).

6

Gender Regimes and the Gender Order

Institutions

Theories of gender, with hardly an exception, focus either on one-to-one relationships between people or on the society as a whole. Apart from discussions of the family, the intermediate level of social organization is skipped. Yet in some ways this is the most important level to understand. We live most of our daily lives in settings like the household, the workplace and the bus queue, rather than stretched out in a relation to society at large or bundled up in a one-to-one. The practice of sexual politics bears mostly on institutions: discriminatory hiring in companies, non-sexist curricula in schools and so on. Much of the research that is changing current views of gender is about institutions like workplaces, markets and media.

When the social sciences have made the connection, it has usually been by picking out a particular institution as the bearer of gender and sexuality. The family and kinship have usually been elected to this honour. Accordingly the structure of the family is the centre-piece of the sociological analysis of sex roles stemming from Parsons and Mead. The flip side of this election was that it allowed other institutions to be analysed as if gender were of no account at all. In text after text on the classic themes of social science – the state, economic policy, urbanism, migration, modernization – sex and gender fail to get a mention or are marginalized.

One of the most important effects of the new feminism on the social sciences has been a comprehensive proof that this approach is untenable. Murray Goot and Elizabeth Reid's classic demon-

stration of the mixture of gender-blindness and patriarchal prejudice in mainstream political science is one example of a series of
critiques. They range from electoral sociology through the welfare
state to class analysis, showing not just that gender relations are
present in major institutions but also that they are systematically
important to them.

I will not repeat the details of this research, simply taking the
general conclusion now firmly established. We cannot understand
the place of gender in social process by drawing a line around a
set of 'gender institutions'. Gender relations are present in *all* types
of institutions. They may not be the most important structure in
a particular case, but they are certainly a major structure of most.

The state of play in gender relations in a given institution is its
'gender regime'. An example may help to clarify the idea. In
the research project in which Delia Prince was interviewed (chapter
1), we found an active though not always articulate politics of
gender in every school. Among both students and staff there are
practices that construct various kinds of femininity and masculinity:
sport, dancing, choice of subject, class-room discipline, administration and others. Especially clearly among the students, some
gender patterns are hegemonic – an aggressively heterosexual
masculinity most commonly – and others are subordinated. There
is a distinct, though not absolute, sexual division of labour among
the staff, and sex differences in tastes and leisure activities among
the students. There is an ideology, often more than one, about
sexual behaviour and sexual character. There are sometimes
conflicts going on over sexism in the curriculum or over promotion
among the staff, over prestige and leadership among the kids. The
pattern formed by all this varies from school to school, though
within limits that reflect the balances of sexual politics in Australian
society generally. No school, for instance, permits open homosexual
relationships.

Compact formal organizations like schools perhaps have particularly clear gender regimes, but others have them too. Diffuse
institutions like markets, large and sprawling ones like the state,
and informal milieux like street-corner peer-group life, also are
structured in terms of gender and can be characterized by their
gender regimes. In this chapter I will take up three cases. The
discussions are very condensed, and represent no more than a
start with each case. I hope they will still be enough to get some
bearings on the institutionalization of gender.

The Family

Conservative ideology speaks of the family as the 'foundation of society' and traditional sociology has often seen it as the simplest of institutions, the building-block of more elaborate structures. Far from being the basis of society, the family is one of its most complex products. There is nothing simple about it. The interior of the family is a scene of multilayered relationships folded over on each other like geological strata. In no other institution are relationships so extended in time, so intensive in contact, so dense in their interweaving of economics, emotion, power and resistance.

This is often missed in theorizing because of a concentration on the normative standard case. Enough has been said already about how little we can rely on that concept; but it is worth noting that even families which match it to a reasonable degree are internally complex. The emotional undercurrents in the Prince household have been suggested in chapter 1. Lillian Rubin's *Worlds of Pain* documents the ambivalences and complexities of conventional working-class families in the United States. Laing and Esterson's *Sanity, Madness and the Family*, dealing with the more combustible materials of schizophrenia, shows the extraordinary tangles that can be produced in British families by the pursuit of respectable normality.

To understand gender and the family, then, it is necessary to unpack the family. The three structures outlined in chapter 5 provide a framework for the attempt.

The sexual division of labour within families and households has a specific literature and is well recognized. Both broad types of work and very fine details are subject to this division. In the English village studied by Pauline Hunt, for instance, wives clean the insides of window panes and husbands clean the outsides. The division of tasks is not absolute, and does change with time. There are now fewer wives than in the 1920s of whom it could be said: 'Her husband was a steady man, but the same as other men – went out and left her to it [i.e. to bring up the children and run the home] to do as she liked.'

Yet not all the changes reduce sexual divisions. The autobiography of a shepherd's son notes that as the eldest surviving child he had 'to be mother's help, to nurse the baby, clean the house, and do sewing like a girl'. That was in England in the 1830s. There are few households now that depend on children's labour to such an extent and hence give boys experience in mothering. Studies of the changing sexual division of labour over more recent periods, like Michael Gilding's research on the family in Sydney up to 1940, suggest that the main effects have been redistribution of housework among women rather than from women to men.

It is equally well recognized that the contemporary urban family/ household is constituted by a division of labour that defines certain kinds of work as domestic, unpaid and usually women's, and other kinds as public, paid and usually men's. The interplay of the structure of production inside and outside the family changes character in different class settings. In Mirra Komarovsky's American working-class families this revolves around the husband's *wage*. In a study of American bourgeois 'lives in progress' done at much the same time by Robert White, the connection revolves around the husband's *career*. The latter case is an important qualification to Delphy's picture of domestic labour as a form of appropriation by the husband. A professional's or businessman's wife may well maximise her own lifetime income by integration into a successful husband's career.

Most households include children for a considerable part of their history, and this affects the division of labour in two ways. Childrearing is itself work, and bulks large in the sexual division of labour as a whole. Since in rich capitalist countries most care of young children is done unpaid and in the home by their mothers, this has particular prominence in the domestic division of labour. So it is not surprising that R. E. Pahl's recent study in southern England finds the most clear-cut and conservative sexual division of labour in those households which currently have children under five to care for. The second point is made by the shepherd's son already quoted: children themselves work, both in the home and at school. This work too is structured on gender lines. Given the points already made, it is not surprising that the study of Sydney adolescents by W. F. Connell and others found housework to be done by girls about twice as often as by boys.

The sexual division of labour reflects ideas about 'a woman's place'; but who defines that? As Colin Bell and Howard Newby observe, the way families work is partly a consequence of the husbands' power to define their wives' situation. The underlying interest appears to be consistent and strong. The patriarchal pattern, with young people subordinated to old and women subordinated to men, reappears in a long series of sociological researches on families in different countries, together with the ideologies of masculine authority that support it.

Research into family power-structure, by and large, has taken a conventional approach to the definition of 'power' as influence in decision-making. Other kinds of evidence suggest this is not enough. The work on domestic violence shows that force is important in many families. On the other hand the research on 'schizophrenia' by Gregory Bateson, R. D. Laing and others indicates the fierce emotional pressures that can be brought to bear on family members without any open command or display of power. These cases often concern the power of mothers over their children; but the prohibition on escape in Bateson's double-bind theory of schizophrenia is also reminiscent of the 'factors preventing women leaving violent relationships' in domestic violence research. In more ways than one the family can be a trap. Finally the marital sexual relationship can itself embody power. The topic is not very thoroughly studied but it seems likely, from evidence such as Lillian Rubin's, that in most cases it is the husbands who hold the initiative in defining sexual practice.

Given some awareness of this, it is understandable that critics of marriage like Emma Goldman should declare the husbands' 'protection' of their wives a farce. It is also understandable that one way of handling a strong power imbalance is to build a praxis of compliance. Marabel Morgan's stunning *The Total Woman*, a Florida dream of being totally subordinate and loving it, is at the same time a shrewd how-to-do-it manual for this kind of practice. It is notable that her right-wing religion and social outlook are strongly flavoured with eroticism. In getting the husband to stay home, it is the wife's business to titillate:

> 'For an experiment I put on pink baby-doll pyjamas and white boots after my bubble bath. ... When I opened the door that night to greet Charlie, I was unprepared for his reaction. My quiet, reserved, nonexcitable husband took one look, dropped his briefcase on the doorstep, and chased me around the dining-room table.'

The power of husbands shows in the family, but it is certainly not based in the family alone. Studies of the erosion of patriarchal authority by migration, such as Gillian Bottomley's research on Greek families in Australia, show that domestic patriarchy is dependent on support from its environment. Even without the drastic upheaval of migration, this support has not always been consistent or sufficient. The family sociologies, even in the 1950s, found some power-sharing between husbands and wives. As noted in chapter 5 some families show a pattern of eroded patriarchy, where a claim to authority is made by the husband but is not successful – where wives control the household in reality. Under the impact of the New Left and feminism in the 1970s, conscious attempts have been made in some families and households to dismantle power relations altogether. This has not been easy, but a certain amount of experience about egalitarian households has now accumulated.

Marabel Morgan's white boots point daintily towards the connection between domestic power and the structure of cathexis. Of all aspects of the family this is perhaps the most researched, since it is the main subject-matter of psychoanalysis. The theory of the Oedipus complex is a map of the emotional interior of the family. However the yield for social theory from some eighty years of psychoanalytic investigation is much less than the volume of evidence would suggest. This is partly because what psychoanalysts publish in their journals is so strongly framed by questions about therapy. But part also is a result of the influence of the normative standard case as a presupposition in Freud's own writings and in most psychoanalytic thinking since.

When a psychoanalyst is led to question this norm the results can be striking. A notable example is Anne Parsons's study of a non-Oedipal 'nuclear complex' in Naples. Cultural and psychological evidence here shows a family pattern where the mother is central, the father has little real domestic authority and the mother–son and father–daughter relationships are emphasized more than same-sex identifications. This highlights the importance of cross-sex relationships in the formation of femininity and masculinity, and suggests a kind of discontinuity in the history of gender that bears thinking about in other contexts. The evidence on sexual abuse similarly indicates the charged character of cross-sex relationships within the family.

The shadow structure of cathexis suggested in chapter 5 is clearer for the family than for any other case, again because of the concentration of psychoanalytic research. Phyllis Chesler in *About Men* suggests its importance when noting the degree of hostility between fathers and sons that persists despite identifications. She speculates about a connection with larger patterns of violence between men. Repressed fear and hatred is a possible though certainly incomplete way of explaining how large numbers of men are motivated to staff the institutions of violence. It is not, of course, any explanation of how those institutions work on the large scale.

At several points already the interplay between structures within the family has been evident. Wage and career affect domestic power; domestic power affects the definition of the division of labour; Marabel Morgan eroticizes powerlessness. The very ideas of 'the housewife' and 'the husband' are fusions of emotional relations, power and the division of labour. The gender regime of a particular family represents a continuing synthesis of relations governed by the three structures.

This synthesis is not trouble-free: the components of a family gender regime may contradict each other. In the traditional patriarchal houschold, a marked sexual division of labour actually places some limits on the patriarch's ability to exercise power, since women monopolize certain kinds of skill and knowledge. Vanessa Mahler describes a considerable degree of psychological independence for women in Moroccan culture, where patriarchal domination is massive and the division of labour strong. A very sharp division of labour may produce a degree of segregation of daily life that makes it difficult to sustain patriarchal power as a routine. This is suggested, for instance, by Annette Hamilton about Australian Aboriginal societies.

Such contradictions mean potential for change within the family as an institution, most likely to be realized when its context changes markedly. The case of migration has been mentioned. Another powerful pressure is the arrival of capitalist market relations in a non-capitalist setting. The pressure is not all in the one direction. A study of peasant households in Mexico by Kate Young shows a splitting of family patterns as class stratification develops, with gender regimes moving in different directions.

The State

Theoretical literature on the state is at the other pole from the family: almost no one has seen it as an institutionalization of gender. Even in feminist thought the state is only just coming into focus as a theoretical question.

Yet reasons to address it are easy to find. The personnel of the state, as noted in chapter 1, are divided by sex in quite visible, even spectacular, ways. State elites are the preserve of men, with a very few exceptions. The state arms men and disarms women. President Carter, though supporting the Equal Rights Amendment, still announced that he would not give women a combat role in the military. The diplomatic, colonial and military policy of major states is formed, as noted in chapter 5, in the context of ideologies of masculinity that put a premium on toughness and force. The South Pacific is at present having a textbook demonstration of this from the French, with atomic testing at Muroroa Atoll, the bombing of the *Rainbow Warrior* in New Zealand in 1985, and anti-independence violence by French settlers in Kanaky (New Caledonia).

The state engages in considerable ideological activity on issues of sex and gender; this very diverse activity ranges from birth-control in India and China, through the reimposition of the *chador* on women in Iran, to the Soviet efforts to increase the number of women in paid work. States attempt to control sexuality: criminalizing homosexuality, legislating on age of consent, venereal disease, AIDS and so on. The state intervenes in the sexual division of labour in ways ranging from subsidized immigration to equal opportunity policies. It regulates workplaces and families, provides schools, builds houses.

Given all this, control of the state is a major stake in sexual politics. Accordingly the state has been a major object of strategy. From the Seneca Falls convention of 1848 to the Equal Rights Amendment (ERA) campaign of the 1970s, American feminism has placed demands on the state and tried to guarantee women's access to it. Australian feminism has put considerable energy into gaining a presence inside the state bureaucracy, through welfare funding and the 'femocrats'. The main focus of groups like the Campaign for Homosexual Equality in Britain has been legal reform through lobbying of parliamentarians and bureaucrats. The American New Right in its turn has attempted to roll back feminism through control of courts and legislatures.

It can hardly be denied that the state is deeply implicated in the social relations of gender. Alain Touraine remarks that 'the state is not the one who represents the metasocial guarantees of social order ... but rather the agent of a concrete historical collectivity, situated in relation to other communities and to its own transformation.' Yes; but that 'historical collectivity' has to be defined in gender as well as class terms. The question is how to understand the connections.

There are four arguments in the theoretical literature on the state that might do the job. The first is the liberal theory that thinks the state in principle a neutral arbiter, which in practice can be captured by interest groups, in this case men. The institutional sexism of the state is therefore a matter of the imperfect citizenship of the excluded group, women. This approach can make sense of the main concerns of liberal feminism, both in terms of legal equality (suffrage, Equal Rights Amendment, equal employment opportunity) and specific welfare needs. But it does not give any grip on the sexual division of labour among state personnel, or on the gender structuring of state violence. On the face of it, the approach is contradicted by the fact of state oppression of groups of men, notably homosexual men, and by the heavier criminalization of men's sexuality than women's.

This is consistent with a second approach which sees the state mainly as an apparatus of regulation and soft domination. Jacques Donzelot's *The Policing of Families* and Michel Foucault's *History of Sexuality* are the classics of an approach now also adopted by some theorists of gay liberation such as Jeffrey Weeks. They picture the state as part of a dispersed apparatus of social control working through dominant discourses as much as through force. This is useful in getting beyond the state as an organization to its sphere of operation, making the connection with everyday life. It also allows a recognition of the multiple and sometimes contradictory apparatuses at work. But it is not at all clear in this approach why the state regulates to the extent that it does, unless it is simply prurient. Foucault and Donzelot do not account for the constitution of *interests* in sexual politics.

A third approach certainly does. It defines the state as a class state producing effects on sex and gender in pursuit of class interests. The 'Freudian Left' from Wilhelm Reich to Herbert Marcuse conceived of state action in these terms, with sexuality either repressed or carefully ventilated according to the needs of capitalism. Marxist feminism has generally seen the state's motivation in class terms, though seeing its effects as maintaining men's subordination of women. Discussions of state action on wage

levels, welfare provision and welfare ideology by theorists like
Mary McIntosh have succeeded in getting the dimension of
political economy into the argument. But, as the discussion of
extrinsic theories in chapter 3 noted, it is not clear why *gender*
effects are essential for the reproduction of capitalism or the
maintenance of profit.

A fourth group of theorists tackle this head-on by arguing that
the state is from the start a patriarchal institution. David
Fernbach proposes that the state was historically created as the
institutionalization of masculine violence. Catherine MacKinnon
looks at the form of state action, in particular legal 'objectivity',
as the institutionalization of a male point of view, and shows how
it impinges on sexual politics in the management of cases of rape.
Zillah Eisenstein's dual systems model sees the central state as an
agent in sexual politics at the same time as class politics, showing
for instance how Carter's support of the ERA made tactical sense
in terms of factional divisions in the American elite. Carole
Pateman proposes that the development of the liberal state was
itself underpinned by a new form of patriarchy in civil society
developing in the seventeenth and eighteenth centuries.

These lines of work have the potential to deal with the full
range of issues about gender. But before they can converge there
are some difficulties, or at least complexities, to be dealt with.

When the state is considered as a repressive apparatus, it is
clear that the main objects of physical repression are men. The
evidence is clear enough in statistics like those on arrest and
imprisonment in chapter 1. There are cases where state violence
is directed mainly against women, such as the European witch
craze that peaked in the seventeenth century, and the mass rape
by the Pakistani army in Bangladesh in 1971; but the most
persisting and general uses of state force are by men against men.

Yet this does not mean that state repression has nothing to do
with gender. There is a very active gender process here, a
politics of masculinity. The state both institutionalizes hegemonic
masculinity and expends great energy in controlling it. The objects
of repression, e.g. 'criminals', are generally younger men themselves
involved in the practice of violence, with a social profile quite like
that of the immediate agents of repression, the police or the
soldiers. However the state is not all of a piece. The military and
coercive apparatus has to be understood in terms of relationships
between masculinities: the physical aggression of front-line troops

or police, the authoritative masculinity of commanders, the calculative rationality of technicians, planners and scientists.

The internal complexity of the state is now well recognized in class theory and is equally important in relation to gender. Actual states are by no means consistent in their processing of gender issues. The political leadership in New South Wales has introduced a broad equal-opportunity program mainly directed at women; much of the bureaucracy, which is of course run by men, has quietly resisted it. Recent policy in a number of Western countries has been to hand more welfare functions from the state to 'the community', i.e. to the unpaid work of women; but at the same time the training of girls for paid work has been expanded, with rising retention rates in school and new occupational preparation programs. Equal employment opportunity programs have been expanding in Australia at the same time that funds for childcare, which would make them effective, have been cut. The gradual extension of the civil rights of homosexual men via decriminaliz-ation and antidiscrimination laws is contradicted by continued exclusion from state employment and now by official scaremonger-ing over AIDS. The Canadian state has got itself into serious difficulty with the contradiction between strong antidiscrimination provisions in the Charter of Rights and Freedoms, which came into effect in 1985, and the formal exclusion of homosexuals from the military and Mounted Police. The patriarchal state even finds itself funding feminism, across a considerable spectrum from rape crisis centres through women's units in the bureaucracy to grants for feminist academic research. Some of this is mere incoherence, to be expected from the sheer complexity of the state as a set of instrumentalities. But some is real contradiction.

How can these points be built into a gender analysis of the state? They suggest that the state is not inherently patriarchal, but is historically constructed as patriarchal in a political process whose outcome is open. The process of bureaucratization is central here, as conventional bureaucracy is a tight fusion of the structure of power and the division of labour. Together with selective recruitment and promotion, these structures form an integrated mechanism of gender relations that results in the exclusion of women from positions of authority and the subordination of the areas of work in which most women are concentrated. But conventional bureaucracy is itself under pressure, as the huge contemporary output of management-theory repair manuals testifies. Demands for more efficiency, for decentralization, even for more democracy, can unhinge parts of this mechanism. It is largely in the spaces where gender politics and organizational reform intersect that feminists in the state have gained ground.

Power in the state is strategic because there is more at issue than a simple distribution of benefits. The state has a constitutive role in forming and re-forming social patterns. For instance the state at a superficial level supports marriage through taxation incentives, housing and so on. At a more fundamental level marriage is itself a legal action and a legal relationship, defined, regulated and to some extent enforced by the state. Another notable state enterprise is in the field of fertility. Pro-natalist and anti-natalist policies have been debated and contraceptives accordingly banned or distributed. How far state policy has actually been successful in controlling this aspect of women's bodies is debatable, but there have certainly been vehement attempts, from antiquity to the present, to do so.

In managing institutions and relations like marriage and motherhood the state is doing more than regulating them. It is playing a major part in the constitution of the social categories of the gender order. Categories like 'husbands', 'wives', 'mothers', 'homosexuals', are created as groups with certain characteristics and relationships. Through them the state plays a part in the constitution of the interests at play in sexual politics. They in turn react on the state through political mobilization. The classic example is the state repression and regulation of sexuality that played a central part in the creation of 'the homosexual' as a social category and personal identity. This in turn became the basis of a politics of civil rights for homosexuals. The same kind of cycle is very general.

The patriarchal state can be seen, then, not as the manifestation of a patriarchal essence, but as the centre of a reverberating set of power relations and political processes in which patriarchy is both constructed and contested. If this perspective is sound, it makes the historical trajectory of the state vital to an understanding of its place and effects in sexual politics. I will finish this discussion with a couple of hypotheses about this trajectory.

The growth of the modern state depends, as Pateman proposes, on a change in patterns of gender relations. A key part of this is a change in patterns of masculinity. The tradition-centered patriarchal authority that was criticized at the level of public politics by liberal rationalists such as Locke represented the hegemony of a particular kind of masculinity in domestic life too. Over the period in which both the modern state and the industrial economy were produced, the hegemony of this form of masculinity was challenged and displaced by masculinities organized much more around technical rationality and calculation. The system of industrial capitalism was constructed by this shift as well as by class dynamics; and so was the characteristic form of state bureaucracy sketched above.

This did not eliminate other masculinities. What it did was marginalize them: and this created conditions for new versions of masculinity that rested on impulses or practices excluded from the increasingly rationalized and integrated world of business and bureaucracy. Such 'wild' masculinities emerged through the nineteenth and twentieth centuries. In one direction, the forbidden sexual affection between men became the basis of a homosexual masculinity labelled and stigmatized by the state. In another direction, the forbidden violence between men became the basis for aggressive masculinities that – given the conditions that followed World War I – were mobilized in fascism. The importance of front-line soldiers in the fascist movements is familiar. Less familiar but equally significant is Hitler's contempt for the 'gentlemen with diplomas' who ran the bourgeois world he despised.

The condition of women was also implicated in the process of rationalization. There was a deepening contradiction between their subjection to individual men in domestic patriarchy and the powerful eighteenth and nineteenth century trend to universalize citizen rights, closely connected with the rationalization of the state and of markets. This contradiction was picked up in the feminisms of Mary Wollstonecraft in England and Susan B. Anthony in the United States and pithily expressed by John Stuart Mill. The early woman suffrage campaign was not a diversion from 'social' issues (though it later came to be a means of ignoring them); it seized on the major contradiction that the development of the state at that point had exposed.

The winning of citizen rights by women did have profound effects on politics, though not in reshaping party politics. Women's organizations have been important in some conservative parties, but women's parties as such have had no impact. Much more generally women were constituted as direct consumers of state services. Through the twentieth century a complex network of services and benefits has grown around the widows' pensions and maternity allowances that were first provided: baby health centres, women's health centres, supporting mothers' benefits, taxation allowances and so on. As is well known, women are now the major consumers of welfare services *in toto*, partly because they live longer but also because of the ways in which state support is designed to substitute for husbands' wages, presupposing women's exclusion from the labour market. Kerreen Reiger notes how such welfare developments provided vehicles for intervention by professional experts (doctors, nurses, psychologists, social workers) in households, reshaping women's domestic work. Sheila Shaver notes that when welfare and taxation policies are taken together as a system of transfers, the state is in effect taking from women as individuals and redistributing to them as someone's mother, wife or widow. Putting these points together we can see the state as being deeply involved in the growth of much more mediated and abstract relations between women and men through the twentieth century. It is tempting to link this with the growth of a mere mediated and alienated sexuality, with commercial standardization in advertising, pornography and mass entertainment.

The Street

The street is not often thought of as an institution. It is something we walk and drive along, or that chickens cross. Yet a famous sociological text is called, with only mild irony, *Street Corner Society*, and we speak of 'street-wise' kids. It is at least a definite social milieu, with particular social relations.

A good deal of work goes on in the street. Jobs that concern children, like pushing them around in strollers, are almost all done by women. So is most shopping and most prostitution. Selling of newspapers, food and other small objects is mixed. Driving cars, trucks and buses, petty crime and policing, repairing vehicles and the street itself are mainly done by men. Though women have been working as bus drivers more often, heavy trucks are still a masculine speciality.

The street is the setting for much intimidation of women, from low-level harassment like wolf-whistling to physical manhandling and rape. Since it is not always predictable when the escalation will stop, in many parts of the city women rarely walk, especially after dark. The street then is a zone of occupation by men. Concentrations of young adult men are the most intimidating and dangerous.

Such concentrations are commonest in areas where there is high unemployment and ethnic exclusion to go with it, like Brixton in London, Redfern in Sydney, the South Side in Chicago. Contests of daring, talk about sport and cars, drugs (mainly alcohol) and sexism provide entertainment in a bleak environment. Women generally avoid this; but since there are no women's streets and few welcoming public buildings, the effective alternative is the home: 'A woman's place ...'. In outer suburbs this effect is not as strong, but threat still occurs.

The young men who offer this threat are also subject to it. The street is a scene of intermittent but routine conflict between different groups, which the media call 'gangs', and between them and the police. It is in fact young men who are the main victims of street violence, not elderly people, though the elderly are kept in a chronic state of fear about it. The police are the Great Power in street life, though in a few cases like the Watts insurrection of August 1965 in Los Angeles they may vanish as an authority. The reserve power of the state is still great enough to 'restore order' by military means if the political leadership is willing to pay the price, as in Belfast.

In some ways the street is a battleground; in others it is a theatre. In an urban shopping centre the street is full of advertising displays: shop windows, billboards, posters. Their content is heavily sex-typed and has become more heavily eroticized over recent decades. Some particularly crude appeals to masculine violence, like the London poster in 1984 showing a car fired from a pistol and captioned 'The trigger is under your right foot', have been forced off the street. But the cigarette and beer ads continue in the same merry way.

The pavement is equally full of displays, though more varied. People convey messages about themselves by dress, jewellery, posture, movement, speech. The street is one of the great theatres of sexuality and styles of masculinity and femininity. A bus queue or shopping crowd will show a wide range of styles and manners, some extroverted and attention-seeking, some dowdy or uncaring. During the cycle of a day or week the dominant styles turn over as the population changes: shift-workers, commuting business men, shopping mothers, after-school teenagers, late-night lads hanging out.

The street as a milieu thus shows the same structures of gender relations as the family and state. It has a division of labour, a structure of power and a structure of cathexis. Similarly the local patterning of these relationships is linked to the structure of gender relations outside. As Emma Goldman observed, women working the street as prostitutes are not in it for the fun; they are there because women's wages are low. 'Opportunist submission' (the phrase is Jan Morris's) to patriarchy may be obligatory, given the different resources that people bring to it. Gay relationships are rarely displayed on the street outside tightly defined areas; it could be very dangerous to do so.

At the same time there is something specific to a loosely structured milieu like a street that distinguishes it from deeply sedimented institutions like family and state. It gives room not only to diversity but also to quick turnover of styles. The theatre of the street may be experimental theatre. A recent example is young women appropriating and making-over an aggressive style of sexuality, in punk fashions with a good deal of black and leather about them. Something of a negotiation goes on about new forms in gender. There are even attempts to turn this into a conscious political practice, through feminist street theatre or events like the gay Mardi Gras in Sydney. I suspect the dominance of the car now prevents any full-blown new development of the street as festival. But it is still an extremely interesting register of sexual politics.

The Gender Order

At several points in this analysis of institutions the importance of context has become obvious, especially the context provided by other institutions. To compile a complete structural inventory it is therefore necessary to go beyond a collation of gender regimes to the relationships between them.

In some cases this relationship is additive or complementary. The patterns surrounding women's part-time employment are a familiar example. The conventional division of labour in working-class families in Western cities assigns most childcare and house-work to the wife-and-mother; and femininity is constructed in a way that defines the work of caring for other family members as womanly. The labour market constructed by capitalist industry and the state offers some low-paid, low-status part-time jobs; and curiously enough most of the people recruited to these part-time jobs are married women. This pattern of recruitment is justified by employers on the grounds that married women only want part-time work because of their domestic responsibilities and only need low pay because theirs is a 'second wage'. At home the much heavier domestic work of women is justified by husbands because their wives can only get part-time jobs.

The dovetailing is neat, and it is anything but accidental. The pattern has developed particularly in the 1970s and 1980s, and in the context of the recession represents a practical accommodation between the institutions involved. The dovetailing of structures is produced by a meeting of strategies: the profit-maximizing strategies of employers in a slack labour market and the household work strategies (as Pahl calls them) of the employees.

If this kind of fit were the normal case, we would indeed have the tightly integrated system presupposed by categoricalism. But the gender regimes of interacting institutions are rarely so harmonious. I know of no starker example than 'The Blood Vote', a famous poem and poster used in the World War I campaign against conscription in Australia. Two stanzas run:

> Why is your face so white, Mother?
> Why do you choke for breath?
> O I have dreamt in the night, my son,
> That I doomed a man to death.

> I hear his widow cry in the night,
> I hear his children weep;
> And always within my sight, O God!
> The dead man's blood doth leap.

The conflict dramatized here, between the emotional relationships of the family and the demands of a state at war, is a common theme in pacifist campaigns, including the current campaign against nuclear weapons. A well-known poster reads: 'What to do in the event of nuclear war: Kiss your children goodbye.'

A more complicated pattern of institutional abrasion surrounds the reversals of state policy about welfare. There has long been a conflict between the goal of redistribution implicit in welfare policy and the goal of stabilization implicit in the machinery of repression and ideological control. Once internal to the state, a classic 'steering problem' in the language of Jürgen Habermas, this has been externalized by the recession as a conflict over the terms of the relationship among state, family and labour market. The welfare conservatism of the post-war boom, predicated on full employment, managed class and gender tensions with a gradual extension of welfare measures. But the state was never accepted as wholly benign. A constituency developed for the New Right swing towards welfare cuts, labour market discipline and selective direct repression.

Given the feminization of poverty the welfare cuts have deepened the economic disadvantages of women, while, as we have seen, the military and police are the preserves of men. The changing balance of advantage in gender relations is perhaps reflected in opinion-poll data showing a much heavier support for Reagan among men than women in the United States presidential election of 1980. But there is no simple translation of sexual politics into votes. One of the first governments to use the New Right rhetoric, the Fraser government in Australia, was elected in 1975 with heavier support from women than men; and even in the 1983 election that ousted it, women stayed with the conservative parties more than men did.

A third pattern of connection between institutions sets them in parallel, so to speak, as the domain of a common strategy or movement. For instance the Equal Employment Opportunity campaigns have moved from one organization to another, attempting to bring them into line with the policy, using experience gained in one to move things along in the next. At another level, 'coming out' as gay has to be done in a whole series of settings: workplace, family, friendship networks, etc. As Wendy Clark observes, the emotional patterns to be dealt with vary: coming out to your parents is different. But the logic of the process still links the institutions.

What is common to the three patterns is the fact of politics, the social struggle around the terms of relationship between institutions. The state/family connection has been particularly inflamed. It has given rise to political programs that range from Alexandra Kollontai's desire to use the revolutionary state in the Soviet Union to dismantle the patriarchal family, to the Vatican strategy of using the Italian and Irish states to prop it up. The more generalized programs we see here are a sign of the formation of more generalized interests than the analysis of any one institution could account for. Here we come to a second major step in the constitution of the gender order.

The basic point is that the groupings which are the major actors in sexual politics on the large scale are constructed historically. It may still sound strange to say this of categories like 'women' and 'men'. But it makes sense when the 'construction' itself is more closely defined. It means giving a particular content to a social category, establishing particular contrasts with and distances from other social categories, and constituting an interest around which identity and action can be organized. To recall the argument of chapter 4, the biological categories of female and male determine only a limited range of practices (bearing, suckling, etc.) which define the participants as occupants of a range of parallel situations – in Sartre's technical term, 'a series'. Groups which are actors in sexual politics are constituted by moves in which seriality is negated and a collective practice undertaken. Such moves are necessarily social processes, action in history.

That is very abstract, but cases in point have already been discussed. The categories 'male' and 'female' are not categories of social life and sexual politics; the categories 'men' and 'women' are. The two pairs overlap but the second pair is far richer and more complexly determined than the first. The category 'men' for instance has a specific cultural content in a given time and place. Its meaning in social action is not the same in Bali in the 1980s, London in the 1980s and London in the 1680s. One of the key differences between these two dates in London was the expulsion of homosexual practice from the conventional definition of masculinity. The creation of a social category of 'homosexuals' has been mentioned several times; less noticed is the simultaneous creation of a category of 'heterosexuals'. Since heterosexuality only has meaning through a gender opposition, this actually requires two categories, heterosexual men and heterosexual women. Their newly purged polarity became the major axis of gender relations in the twentieth century.

The construction of a social category is not quite the same thing as the constitution of a social interest. 'Twins', for instance, is a well-recognized category, but it is not easy to define any interest that all or most twins share. An interest is defined by the possibility of advantage or disadvantage in some collective practice. The groupings of sexual politics are constituted as interests by the facts of inequality and oppression. The interests are articulated by processes of mobilization that define collective goals and strategies. Interests are not necessarily articulated. For instance it is clear from David Lane and Felicity O'Dell's *The Soviet Industrial Worker* that it is politically impossible for women workers in the Soviet Union to mobilize as a distinct group outside the Party and the unions, both of which are controlled by men. Yet their unequal social and economic situation provides a good motive for collective action.

Interests can be constituted on very different bases, which may cut across each other. Marriage and kinship involve collective practices in which advantage may be gained for one family over another family, and people may well see this as the primary definition of their interests. On the other hand 'men' and 'women' are collectivities of a more generalized kind which have conflicting interests defined by the inequalities of income, power and so on already documented.

Both of these cross-cutting sets of interests are real, and both can become the basis of a very active politics. Feminism is a mobilization on the latter basis. Mobilization on the former is illustrated by Pierre Bourdieu's account of Kabyle society in Algeria, with lineages manoeuvering for advantage through marriages as much as through land deals. The tendency in social theory has been to pick one basis of interest and regard the rest as secondary. Thus Bourdieu simply subsumes the interests of Kabyle women in those of their menfolks' lineages. Conversely Christine Delphy ignores the material interest ruling-class wives have in their husband's careers by assimilating their situation to that of peasant and working-class women. This is not a point to be settled by postulation. The way of defining interest that is ascendant at a given time and place is an empirical question. Indeed a great deal of sexual politics is precisely about trying to make a latent interest salient in practice.

Interests are immediately defined by existing inequalities, but they can also be defined in a longer-term sense. Gender relations are historical, they can be remade in new patterns, and the new patterns will advantage and disadvantage particular groups. So there are interests in historical transformations. Barbara Ehrenreich's *The Hearts of Men* is a notable attempt to define the interest heterosexual men had in the remaking of sexuality and the family in postwar North American society. It is not easy to do this, since the public articulation of sexual issues reflects interests only in oblique and censored ways. But it is clear that a pattern of interest can be found.

The conflict of interest on this society-wide scale, the formation and dissolution of general categories and the ordering of relationships between institutions, together amount to a macro-politics of gender. This is analytically distinct from, though at all points linked to, the face-to-face issues that are the usual sense of 'sexual politics'. The 'gender order', defined abstractly at the end of chapter 5, can be defined dynamically as the current state of play in this macro-politics.

Its processes include the creation and contestation of hegemony in definitions of sexuality and sexual character (see chapter 8) and the articulation of interests and organization of political forces around them (see chapter 12). At stake are the institutional resources that bear on gender relations, such as the state powers discussed earlier in this chapter; cultural definitions of gender (see chapter 11); and through both of them, the definition of historical possibilities in gender relations. The historical dynamic in this macro-politics is the crux of the social analysis of gender, and the most difficult of all issues to grasp. It will be addressed, in a preliminary way, in the following chapter.

A Note on the Definition and Institutionalization of Gender

In common-sense understanding gender is a property of individual people. When biological determinism is abandoned, gender is still usually seen in terms of socially produced individual character. It is a considerable leap to think of gender as being also a property of collectivities, institutions and historical processes. This view is nevertheless required by evidence and experience of the kind just traversed. There are gender phenomena of major importance which simply cannot be grasped as properties of individuals, however much properties of individuals are implicated in them. It may be useful to get clearer the exact sense in which we can speak of gender as collective, and social practices as gender-structured.

Chapter 4 argued that the social relations of gender are not determined by biological difference but deal with it; there is a practical engagement rather than a reduction. It is this engagement that defines gender at the social level, demarcating gender-structured practice from other practice. 'Gender' means practice organized in terms of, or in relation to, the reproductive division of people into male and female. It should immediately be clear that this does not demand an overriding social dichotomy. Gender practice might be organized in terms of three, or twenty, social categories. Indeed our society recognizes a fair variety – girls, old men, lesbians, husbands and so on. It should also be clear why a dichotomy of women and men is likely to be an important part of any gender order.

Gender then, is a linking concept. It is about the linking of other fields of social practice to the nodal practices of engendering, childbirth and parenting. The definition just offered leaves wholly open the question of how extensive and how tight those links are, and what their social geometry is. There are times and places where the links are more extensive and compelling, where (to change the metaphor) a greater percentage of the social landscape is covered by gender relations; and times and places where they are less. This is a basic reason why Gayle Rubin's concept of a 'sex/gender system' in all societies cannot be sustained.

Gender in this conception is a process rather than a thing. Our language, especially its general categories, invites us to reify. But it should be clear that the 'linking concept' is about the making of the links, the process of organizing social life in a particular way. If we could use the word 'gender' as a verb (I gender, you gender, she genders ...) it would be better for our understanding. The Marxist-feminist literature of the late 1970s that talked awkwardly about 'gendered subjectivity' was groping in this direction, and discussions of 'gendered language' are already there.

The 'process' here is strictly social, and gender a phenomenon within sociality. It has its own weight and solidity, on a quite different basis from that of biological process, and it is that weight and solidity that sociology attempts to capture in the concept of 'institution'.

The notion of institution classically signifies custom, routine and repetition. Anthony Giddens in *The Constitution of Society* follows this by defining institutions as practices with 'the greatest space-time extension' within societies, or 'the more enduring features of social life'. But practice does not have the long duration Giddens attributes to institutions; practice is of the moment. What persists is the organization or structure of practice, its effects on subsequent practice. This can either depart from, or reproduce, the initial situation; that is to say, practice can be divergent or cyclical. As argued in chapter 3, it is not a logical requirement that social reproduction occurs; that is simply a possible empirical outcome. But it is an important one, and the cyclical practice that produces it is what is meant by an 'institution'. The process of 'institutionalization' then is the creation of conditions that make cyclical practice probable.

Speaking of a 'cycle' is intended as an alternative to the notion of a continuum of practice, the idea that structure is a matter of sameness in practice. This is implicit in Giddens, explicit in Adrienne Rich's concept of the 'lesbian continuum' as a transhistorical reality. Structure may involve a cycle of opposites. Anne Parsons's psychoanalytic study of the non-Oedipal 'nuclear complex' in Naples is a particularly clear example, where a particular pattern of masculinity is socially reproduced through the relation with the mother, and femininity through the relation with the father. The opposites may also be at the collective level. The discussion of power earlier in this chapter noted situations where a local power pattern is out of kilter with the more global one, for instance women having authority within a household. This does not undermine the conception of a power structure, merely the idea that a structure must be homogeneous.

Putting these bits together, gender is institutionalized to the extent that the network of links to the reproduction system is formed by cyclical practices. It is stabilized to the extent that the groups constituted in the network have interests in the conditions for cyclical rather than divergent practice.

NOTES

Institutions

(pp. 119–120). For good critiques of gender-blindness in mainstream social science see Goot and Reid (1975); Wilson (1977) and West (1978). The analysis of gender regimes in schools is based on Kessler et al. (1985).

The Family

(pp. 121–5). Quotations on English families from Davies (1977) p. 62 and Burnett (1982) p. 72, and on Florida eroticism from Morgan (1975) p. 94.

The State

(pp. 125–32). On feminism and the bureaucracy see Eisenstein (1985) and Pringle (1979). Quotation from Touraine (1981), p. 108. The argument on relationships between masculinities in armies is developed in Connell (1985a). On Hitler's social consciousness see Bullock (1962).

The Street

(pp. 132–4). This section is mainly based on observation and impressions in Brixton during 1984.

The Gender Order

(pp. 134–9). Full text of 'The Blood Vote' is in Harris (1970), p. 239. Poll figures from 1980 United States elections in Friedan (1982), p. 210; from 1975 and 1983 Australian federal elections from Morgan Gallup Polls, 102 and 499A.

7

Historical Dynamic

Historicity and 'Origins'

In 1984 the British government's program of coal-pit closures provoked a national strike by mine workers, one of the bitterest industrial confrontations in recent times. As the struggle got under way with miners' leaders and National Coal Board shaping up in best macho style, the media ran stories about how the miners' wives were opposed to the strike. Since industrial disputes in mining are very much a community affair, these claims provoked a good deal of anger. Some miners' wives organized a demonstration to show their support for the strike, and to the surprise of the mineworkers' union as well as the government a solidarity movement among women developed quite rapidly on a national scale.

One of the initiating groups, from the town of Barnsley, brought out a booklet about their experience called *Women Against Pit Closures*. Its main theme is how the women of the district are part of the class solidarity of the miners. But the booklet also criticizes the union for excluding or ignoring women. It conveys a strong sense that now the women have taken public action, gained a political voice and among other things have been harassed by police and some arrested, things can never be the same in the mining towns again: relations between the women and the men have changed decisively.

This sense that things 'can never be the same again', that new possibilities have opened and old patterns closed off, is exactly what the *historicity* of gender relations is about. The concept of historicity is stronger than the concept of 'social change', which may be mechanical and external, something that happens to people, like a comet, a fire or a plague. The idea of historicity is about change produced by human practice, about people being inside the process.

The idea that gender relations have a history is more than a century old. As noted in chapter 2 it was a basic element in the creation of a social science of gender. Its early formulations, in best nineteenth-century style, revolved around the problem of 'origins'. This is at best a half-way house to the concept of historicity. The concept of 'origins' implies that something is already formed, though not fully developed, in its earliest appearance, and that what follows is the unfolding of a nature already settled.

Of the origin theories that dot the landscape, by far the most influential has been Friedrich Engels's *Origin of the Family, Private Property and the State*, which appeared in 1884. Engels's view of primitive social structure was, in its day, a reasonable piece of armchair research. It was based mainly on Greek and Roman literary sources enlivened by a little early ethnography. But it was not state-of-the-art prehistory even then. The Assyrian civilization had been revealed a generation before; the Egyptian hieroglyphs had been deciphered in the 1820s; and while Engels wrote, major excavations were showing the outlines of a yet more ancient civilization in Sumer. In the decades that followed, Engels's limited sources were overwhelmed by an explosion of archaeological information. In the Mediterranean region, which his main sources dealt with, archaeology brought to light the Minoan, Mycenaean, Hittite and Etruscan cultures, to mention only the most spectacular. By the 1920s prehistory had become a sophisticated science with well-developed field methods. Technically detailed regional syntheses like Gordon Childe's *Dawn of European Civilization* were appearing; and speculative library essays like Engels' *Origin* were simply obsolete.

One reason it has remained the focus of argument is that the prehistorians have not done their job. There is no literature that debates and synthesizes the field evidence, now vast, that bears on the early history of gender relations. The secondary literature on prehistory, with very few exceptions, takes the sexual division of labour and the subordination of women for granted.

Here, for instance, are two famous prehistorians discussing the early family:

Since hunting put a premium on masculine qualities, this activity became a special province of males, and a sexual division of labour was instituted under which women continued to gather plant, insect and comparable foods while men developed the skills required for tracking down and killing game. This heightened the need for a partnership of the sexes.

No evidence is offered for this; the sexual division of labour from later societies is simply read back. It is difficult to think of any other topic on which such a colossal anachronism would get past a professional historian's self-censorship. This example is from two decades ago, but little has changed in the archaeological literature since. With modern historiography sunk in patriarchal ideology, even an obsolete essay that asks some of the right questions looks good.

Of course Engels is more than the author of an obsolete essay. With the founding fathers' texts canonical (or nearly so) for orthodox Marxists, his *Origin* has inevitably become the focus of argument over Marxist explanations of women's oppression now. Opponents of Marxism have found it easy to carry on the combat by inventing an alternative prehistory. As Homeric warriors battled for possession of a hero's corpse wherever the hero fell, struggle has raged over the true origin of patriarchy without much thought about the choice of battlefield. The most bizarre results were a completely speculative debate about whether there was a primitive matriarchy, a prehistoric world ruled by women, and if so how it was overthrown by men; and a completely speculative theory of evolution that found the origins of patriarchy in palaeolithic hunting, the 'master pattern' of the human species according to Lionel Tiger.

Christine Delphy, whose splendid demolition of Origin myths deserves to be better known, observes the drift of this debate away from the insight that began it. 'In fact, under cover of putting an historical question, an ahistorical one has actually been posed: "What are the *natural* reasons which caused male supremacy?"' Since there are no natural reasons for a social relationship, this debate cannot ever be resolved. It is basically symbolic, a way of making declarations about the present; one of those really satisfying arguments that exclude all evidence that might tend to settle them.

The ultimate weakness of the Origin debate is that to have any force, either strategically or symbolically, it must assume that nothing much changes *after* the Origin. Like the Elephant's Child in the *Just So Stories* having its nose stretched, once you get it you are stuck with it. In all essentials, the argument assumes, 'male bonding' is the same now as it was among the mammoth-hunters, patriarchy as it was when Moses came down from the mountain.

Alongside the mythography of the Origin there is a hybrid literature that presents itself as a scientific search for origins; the participants include Kathleen Gough, Rayna Reiter and Maurice Godelier. Its basis is an attempt to synthesize data from archaeology with contemporary studies of the behaviour of apes and monkeys and the ethnography of small-scale societies, preferably hunter-gatherers. The latter two are supposed to cast light by analogy on what things were like in early human evolution. Clare Burton's critique of this literature is apt. The analogical evidence fails to establish anything significant about the remote past, and the origins argument establishes absolutely nothing about the present. Reiter's paper 'The Search for Origins', perhaps the most interesting in this literature, shows the stress by falling apart into two quite incompatible arguments. One is a sketch of major transitions in the world history of gender relations – a novel and important exercise. But this is framed by the quite spurious claim that knowing the origins of gender hierarchy gives the strategic clue to how it may be abolished now.

The origin literature's assumption of the homogeneity of history, to put it formally, is important as a mechanism of ideology. As a basis of theory it is less compelling. It either denies historical change, or allows just one model of change, the natural unfolding of a fixed logic. This is incompatible with the view that social structures are constituted by practice. It is inconsistent with any conception of internal contradictions in gender relations, since they must give rise to historical discontinuities. It is also inconsistent with the subdivision of structures proposed in chapter 5, since a consequence of recognizing different logics of relationship is recognizing contradictions that emerge between them. If the arguments and evidence assembled in chapters 3, 5 and 6 have any weight, the notions of a homogeneous history and a formative origin are ruled out absolutely.

We must also reject the conventional 'history of sex' and the more recent history of 'sex roles', both of which are based on a similar premiss of homogeneity. Such familiar texts as Rattray Taylor's *Sex in History* conceive their subject-matter as the varying expressions of an underlying essence. The history is the story of how these expressions modulate under different circumstances: changing religious ideas, heavier or lighter censorship and so forth. But sexuality itself is not understood as formed in history, indeed as changing at all. Vern Bullough, a historian of homosexuality in this vein, puts it succinctly: 'In sum, homosexuality has always been with us; it has been a constant in history'. As R. A. Padgug argues in an essay on conceptualizing sexuality in history, the idea of an unchanging essence misses the connection of sexuality with practice, the historical formation of the categories and relations that I have called the structure of cathexis.

The same is true of the history of 'sex roles' that emerged in the late 1970s. Patricia Branca's *Women in Europe Since 1750*, Peter Stearns's *Be a Man!* and Elizabeth and Joseph Pleck's *The American Man* may serve as respectable examples. The 'role' framework declares a concern with social definitions. Stearns's book, for example, opens with an essay on 'manhood as a social construct'. But as the analysis in chapter 3 showed, 'sex role' theory is only notionally social. It actually rests on a pre-social sex dichotomy, which supplies the missing structure to the analyses of attitudes and interactions. Exactly the same is true of sex-role history. These texts rest on the fixed dichotomy of sex – women's history plus men's history – and concern themselves mainly with mapping changes in attitudes and expectations about the dichotomy.

A much more profound grasp of the historicity of gender is shown in the new gay history that has superseded work like Bullough's. Homosexuality is a historically specific thing, and the fact that it is socially organized becomes clear once we distinguish between homosexual behaviour and a homosexual identity. While homosexual behaviour of some kind may be universal, this docs not automatically entail the existence of self-identified or publicly labelled 'homosexuals'. In fact, the latter are unusual enough to require a historical explanation. Jeffrey Weeks argues in *Coming Out* that in Western Europe, male homosexuality did not gain its characteristically modern meaning and social organization until the late nineteenth century. That period witnessed the advent of new medical categorizations, homosexuality being defined as a pathology by the German psychiatrist Westphal in 1870. There were also new legal proscriptions. All male homosexual behaviour was subject to legal sanctions in Britain by the end of the century.

Such medical and legal discourses underlined a new conception of the homosexual as a specific type of person. Alan Bray in *Homosexuality in Renaissance England* shows that while homosexual encounters certainly occurred in the sixteenth and early seventeenth centuries, the participants did not have a clear social definition. They were therefore not persecuted systematically, though treated with extreme brutality on occasion. Homosexual behaviour was seen as a potential in the lustful nature of all men, or indeed a potential for disorder in the cosmos. When men with same-sex preferences began to be defined as a group, in the milieu associated with the 'Molly houses' of London in the early eighteenth century, they were characterized by a high degree of effeminacy and what is now known as transvestism.

Thus the emergence of both the medical discourse on homosexuality, and the corresponding self-conception of homosexuals, need to be related to particular social conceptions of femininity and masculinity and to the social reorganization of gender. Just as 'the housewife', 'the prostitute' and 'the child' are historically specific social types that must be understood in the context of gender relations of the time, so 'the homosexual' represents the modern definition of a new type of adult male. It was a man who was classified as an invert, and who, frequently at least, understood himself to possess a 'woman's soul in a man's body'.

These developments in gay history move decisively beyond the concept of modulations to a radical view of sexuality and gender identity as constructed within the history of a changing social structure, by processes of social struggle.

There are some connections with the work of Jacques Donzelot and Michel Foucault. Foucault's *History of Sexuality* argues forcefully that an emphasis on sexuality as a motivating force in life is not only distinctively modern but is part of a process of social control. He is very clear about the social construction of sexual ideology and gender identities. As he observes in an essay on the transsexual Herculine Barbin, the demand that everyone should have a clear-cut and fixed identity as a member of one sex is historically recent.

But the focus of this work on the apparatuses of power – the professions and the state – and the forms of knowledge they generate, gives no grip on the grass-roots reality that was the *object* of the strategies of control. This theoretical problem has become a strategic dilemma in gay liberation. When identity as a homosexual is seen as an effect of 'regulation', of the discourses and strategies used by the powerful to fix, study and label the dissident, the logical response is to deregulate or deconstruct. But deconstructing homosexual identity means dismantling the political power that has been gained by a mobilization stressing that identity, proclaiming gay pride. So the theoretical advances generated by gay liberation seem to require the end of gay liberation.

The roots of this paradox are in a lopsided conception of social process endemic in theories of discourse and regulation. The practical side of the problem will be discussed in chapter 10 below. At the level of theory it can be corrected from feminist history. The approach pioneered by Sheila Rowbotham in *Hidden from History* and *Women, Resistance and Revolution* holds the focus on social relations, especially structures of power. But it gives a central place to the practice of the oppressed. The uses of power meet strategies of resistance, with varying results. Such an approach acknowledges the reality of power without presenting woman as eternal victim; and insists on the agency of the oppressed without denying the reality of oppression.

Thus the *historicity* of gender defined at the beginning of this section is not a completely abstract concept. Change is produced by human agency; conversely all practice occurs in specific settings and has a particular place in the sequence of events. The idea of historicity implies a concrete *history*, some of whose features are now clear. Its subject matter is a structure of social relations and the form of life constituted in them, including sexual and political life. This history is not homogeneous. As Juliet Mitchell emphasized, the different structures of relationship may develop in different rhythms and come into contradiction. Real social struggles do not have predictable or standard outcomes, and sometimes change the conditions that gave rise to them. There is a long-term historical dynamic of practice and structural transformation.

The study of the historical dynamic of gender relations is still in its early days, but it is clear that its shape is nothing like the smooth unfolding of a predetermined logic. Gender history is lumpy. There are moments of transition, when the conditions of practice alter fast; there are periods of more or less steady shift in a given direction; and there are periods when a particular balance of forces is stabilized.

The concrete focus of this history (as distinct from the abstract definition of its subject-matter and scope) is the composition of the gender order of a given time and place, and the collective projects that compose it. To make sense of these projects requires a history of the formation of groups and categories, and of the types of personalities, motives and capacities drawn upon in sexual politics.

In those terms, the following section is not even the sketch of a history. But it is important at least to move the argument as far as posing concrete historical problems. What follows is an attempt to state some of the questions that need answering about the dynamics of gender on the scale of world history.

The Course of History

The early development of gender relations is a matter of deep interest, regardless of the origins debate. In fact it hardly matters whether we can define an origin or not. The history begins when the archaeological evidence becomes full enough to throw some real light on the structure of gender relations.

There is no evidence of any weight before the upper palaeolithic, nor is it likely to appear. The earliest stages of human tool-making and food production have left material traces like tools, bone deposits and hearths, but there is nothing in such objects to indicate the gender relations in which they were produced. There is no basis of evidence for the conventional assumption, made alike by archaeologists, sociobiologists and many feminists, that there was a sharp sexual division of labour with men making tools and going hunting while women gathered or stayed at home. That is simply guesswork.

By the upper palaeolithic some evidence is accumulating in the form of paintings, bone carvings and burials. While these are as uncertain a representation of social reality as a single page of *Playboy* would be, they are at least pointers. For instance a sexual division of labour is suggested by rock paintings in eastern Spain, where genitals and breasts are distinguishable and women and men are associated with different forest scenes. A burial and other objects at a settlement of mammoth-hunters at Dolní Věstonice in Czechoslovakia imply some association of a woman with ritual power.

To assemble such fragments into a historical argument will require a lot of work; isolated examples like these may be quite misleading. I mention them simply to show that this is the stage in the story where a reconstruction becomes just possible. The evidence becomes very much richer with the development of the first agricultural societies in south-western Asia – the lands around Mesopotamia – around 10,000 years ago.

Some speculation about the history of gender identifies a matriarchal, or at least egalitarian, stage in neolithic village society based on domestication of plants and animals and the invention of cloth and pottery. This is followed at a considerable interval by a patriarchal stage associated with cities or nomadic herders, warfare and kingship. Unfortunately for this scheme the results of post-war excavation have broken down the once clear distinction between an 'agricultural revolution' and an 'urban revolution'. It now appears that towns like Jericho in Palestine, Çatal Hüyük in Anatolia and Abu Hureyra on the middle Euphrates developed long before the plains civilizations of Mesopotamia and Egypt, close to the time when agriculture and animal husbandry emerged. If city walls are an indication of warfare, then at Jericho war came before pottery. There is no evidence whether it was a male monopoly or not.

Two conclusions about this era seem clear, nevertheless. One is that the cultural elaboration of gender had begun. At Çatal Hüyük for instance women's graves included jewellery more often than men's, and there were differences in the types of tools and features of clothing. In some respects women and men were being treated differently in ritual and religion. The second is the absence of a sharp sex difference in access to social goods. Women's graves and ritual objects are not reported as poorer than men's. Argument from a negative is notoriously weak, but so far as this goes it suggests that the cultural marking of gender differences in early settlements did not require an economic subordination of women. The excavator of Çatal Hüyük, James Mellaart, cautiously remarks that 'the position of women was obviously an important one'.

With the invention of writing in Sumer around 5,000 years ago the history of gender relations takes on new detail and immediacy, and a history of the structure of cathexis becomes possible. The surviving records include myths that show patterns of emotion, commercial and legal documents that evidence divisions of labour and household arrangements, and state archives that cast light on the organization of power. Some of this is stunningly familiar. Stories of jealousy, disputes about paternity, idylls of love and loyalty, are found in the earliest surviving literatures. Yet it is also very alien. Early epics from the Gilgamesh tablets to the *Iliad* show structures of emotion very different from ours. A good part of the dynastic history of Egypt revolves around planned incest on a scale that should have turned Freud's beard prematurely white. There is no clearer case of the need to treat gender history rigorously as history, not as a reading-back. The reconstructed patterns are likely to be unfamiliar, perhaps shockingly so.

Writing is not only a source of evidence, it was itself a major social technique, closely bound up with the centralized states and commercial networks that were knitting whole regions into the provinces of an urban culture. By perhaps 5,000 years ago in south-west Asia and the eastern Mediterranean, 3,000 years ago in India and China, 1,500 years ago in Central America, a new social order was entrenched beyond the power of wars or famines to destroy. It was characterized by state structures that linked cities to agricultural hinterlands, with large populations integrated by exchange of services and goods as well as religion and power. Its history has been continuous from then until the advent of industrial capitalism.

Historians' accounts of this transition, in so far as they have addressed social dynamics, have focused on the class issues by which Gordon Childe originally characterized the 'urban revolution'. We can now pose the question of a gender dynamic at a more fundamental level than the traditional question of the effects of this transition on the status of women. If the argument of chapter 6 is broadly correct, the creation of the state is itself a reorganization of gender relations, particularly the structure of gender power. The sexual division of labour is implicated in the production processes that generate the surplus of goods and services which makes urban populations possible. It is important to know to what extent the surplus is appropriated through sexual politics and on gender lines, and to what extent the increased specialization of workers is a gendered one. It seems likely that the changed population densities, opportunities and demographic structure of urban populations were accompanied by changes in the structure of cathexis.

The construction of the state is a particularly interesting and important aspect of these issues. One of its key features was the invention of armies. As far as the written and visual record goes, the armies of Sumer, Egypt and their successors were composed wholly (or nearly so) of men. David Fernbach proposes that the 'masculine specialization in violence' is a key both to the development of the state as an instrument of class and patriarchal power, and to the history of masculinity. The point is important, but this overstates it. Ancient armies were small, so it is likely that organized violence could determine the character only of a minority of men. Nor did the masculine personnel of the machinery of violence immediately determine a subordination of women in other spheres of life. Both in Sumer and in Egypt there is a good deal of evidence of women's prestige and authority. In Sumer for instance women owned property, engaged in trade and so on, while the myths have goddesses active and powerful, notably the cycle of legends around the goddess Inanna (Ishtar). In Egypt much the same is true, with women's prestige perhaps rising in the period of the Empire, when Egyptian military power was at its height.

Yet the control of the means of violence by some men rather than by any women remains a central fact. So does the concentration of supreme political authority in the hands of a man or group of men. The implication is that early states were a vehicle of the differentiation of masculinities and a site of contestation between them. The conflict between the priests of Amon and the reforming Pharaoh Akh-en-Aton at the height of the Egyptian Empire is a striking example. The stake of these struggles was still limited because the exclusion of women from supreme power did not mean their overall subordination in other spheres.

There seems to be some confirmation of this in the structure of emotion in the world's first (surviving) literary masterpiece, the Sumero–Akkadian Epic of Gilgamesh. The story centres on the conflict and passionate attachment of Gilgamesh, King of Uruk, and Enkidu, a hero from the wild; the two men turn out to be mirror images of each other. The sexuality in the epic seems to involve ritual more than emotional relationships. The strongest feelings and personal attachments are connected with war and rulership rather than sex.

These bits of evidence suggest societies that were controlled by men but not 'patriarchal' in the sense usually understood today. That is to say, the patterns of emotional relationship, production and consumption were not closely integrated with the relations of gender subordination and exclusion that had developed in the state. The culture was not completely 'gendered'. If that is true, the subsequent history of agricultural/commercial civilization in western Asia and the Mediterranean involves a deepening institutionalization of patriarchy to the point we are familiar with in classical Greece (for example the exclusion of women from the public sphere in Athens) and the Roman Empire. There is a major transition in gender relations here which does not obviously correspond to a major change in technology, demography or class relations.

However it is important not to presume a single sequence of events, for two strong reasons. One is the diversification of urban civilizations, including their gender orders. The connection of hegemonic masculinity with militarism and violence that developed in the Mediterranean world and Europe seems not to have developed in China, at least to the same degree. In Confucian culture soldiers had much less prestige, scholars and administrators more. It seems likely that the social surplus produced in agricultural/commercial society allowed new options, more potential diversity of social structure. With no global dynamic to constrain them, the result was likely to be divergent gender histories in the major world provinces of urban culture.

The other reason is that in the five millennia of its ascendancy, agricultural/commercial civilization never controlled, let alone covered, the greater part of the inhabited world. Because of their density urban cultures probably included the majority of the world's human population, but left vast tracts where settlement was organized on different bases. Lower-density economies were pastoral (central Asia), hunter–gatherer (northern North America, Amazonia, Australia), agricultural but not urban (Mississippi–Great Lakes, western Africa) and an infinite range of combinations. It is a gross historical error to treat these societies as primitive survivals (much of the literature on 'origins' does), as static, or as just peripheral to the real human story. Synthetic works like Basil Davidson's *Africa in History* show dramatically how active and intricate was the history of societies beyond the pale of the major empires.

It is difficult to get bearings on the gender orders of such a range of situations, and I will make only a few suggestions. The most promising sources are written decriptions of these societies by travellers from literate cultures. Roman and Chinese descriptions of the barbarians across the frontier have an understandable emphasis on what was perceived as the main threat, the hypermasculinity of undisciplined warriors. The account of gender relations from such sources, then, is likely to be systematically biased; the reality may be very different. The mutual dependence of women and men in subsistence agriculture is likely to give considerable power resources to women. High rates of fertility plus high rates of infant mortality mean that close mother–child relations are unlikely, as Philippe Ariès has argued for mediaeval Europe, and femininity cannot be constructed around dependence and nurturance. It is a cliche that peasant women are 'hard' in terms of urban sensibilities; there are hard reasons for it. Finally it is notable that the heroic literatures of societies on the fringes of urban culture, while stressing masculine violence, do not picture women as simply subordinate. In the pre-Christian mythology of the Anglo-Saxons, for instance, when Beowulf had triumphed over the monster Grendel he faced an even fiercer struggle with Grendel's Mum. Meanwhile the Vikings imagined the Valkyries, war goddesses more bloody and terrifying in the original than in the sanitized modern versions.

Over the last 500 years the world order just sketched has been replaced by something very different. This era sees the first global empires, controlled from western Europe; the first global economy, centered on the North Atlantic; a new system of production and exchange, with rationalized agriculture, industrial manufacturing and capitalist control; a revolutionary development of transport, medical technique and nutrition resulting in a spectacular increase of world population; bureaucratized and powerful state structures, which have developed not only an unprecedented capacity to educate and control, but also an unprecedented capacity for mass killing. As with the 'urban revolution', the node of this transition has long been taken to be the class dynamic. As in that case, we can now pose questions not only about the effects on gender relations but about the gender dynamic of the transition itself. Three issues emerge most clearly, centering on the three main structures.

The first has to do with the reconstruction of the state and of masculinity. On the argument of chapter 6, the bureaucratized state is in fundamental respects a pattern of gender relations. The previous exclusion of women from the state apparatus cannot be sustained. More and more women are now drawn into employment in the state; exclusion is replaced by various forms of segregation and direct subordination. The rationalization of administration is incompatible with forms of masculinity that were hegemonic in the aristocratic ruling classes of the old regime. Even in the military branch of the state, heroic personal leadership is steadily displaced by the calculating masculinity of General Staffs and logistics experts. Napoleon appealed to '*la gloire*'; Admiral Nimitz, the architect of the American defeat of Japan in World War II, hung a sign in his office that read: 'IS IT IN THE REALM OF PRACTICABILITY OF MATERIALS AND SUPPLIES?' Commercial capitalism calls on a calculative masculinity and the class struggles of industrialization call on a combative one. Their combination, competitiveness, is institutionalized in 'business' and becomes a central theme in the new form of hegemonic masculinity.

The second issue has to do with the wedge that is driven between money economy and domestic economy, between wage work and house work. As Elizabeth Janeway remarks, the notion of 'the home' as a distinct sphere of life, the stronghold of family and leisure, did not exist before the eighteenth century in Europe. The notion that women were or ought to be *dependent* on men would have seemed absurd in the context of the reciprocities of village agriculture and commercial towns. In fact women's extensive involvement in production, and in earning cash, continued through the period of industrialization. As Joan Scott and Louise Tilly have shown, the percentage of European women in paid jobs remained impressively stable in the nineteenth century. It was the location and social meaning of the work that changed. A combination of technology and industrial politics gradually levered women out of the core industries of the Industrial Revolution, creating the segregated occupations and low wage structures now familiar. The 'family wage' model of male breadwinner and dependent wife, never a reality for much of the working class, nevertheless became a criterion both of union activity and state policy. The construction of the gender division between 'breadwinner' and 'housewife' was formative not only for modern definitions of masculinity and femininity but also for the character and direction of working-class politics.

The third issue has to do with a new structure of cathexis centering on what might be called hegemonic heterosexuality. The shift here is complex and subtle. Heterosexual relationships had been predominant in the previous European agricultural/ commercial civilization, but were not exactly hegemonic, given the importance of asceticism in the Christian tradition before Protestantism. The married heterosexual couple now came to be defined as a cultural ideal, and this involved a splitting-off of kinds of sexuality that came to be seen as deviant. More, they come to be identified with types of people: the homosexual, the pederast, the whore-master, the Don Juan, appear as social types. It seems that this typification is reflected in the internal organization of emotions. There is a marked growth in the tendency to form fixations, both on people and objects, a tendency essential to the construction of the family as a tightly knit emotional unit but which ultimately breaks its bounds. One result is the cult of sexual fetishes – high heels, corsets and so on – which is in full swing by Krafft-Ebing's day. The partial reification of emotional relationships here is surpassed by the development of a completely externalized sexuality in twentieth-century mass media, starting with the cult of movie sex goddesses and moving on to the pin-up and the eroticization of advertising. The reorganization of emotions that allows this externalization of cathexis is perhaps the truth behind Foucault's claim of an increasing incitement rather than repression of sexuality.

These are issues about the nature of the transformation in the core countries of the new world order. Another set of issues arises about the global spread of these relations. There is now considerable research on the effects of imperialism on the position of women in the colonized world. The impact is plainly uneven. We can nevertheless say that for the first time in history since early urbanization there is a strong dynamic tending to standardize gender relations in different parts of the world. The spread of wage relationships is one part of this; the labour market segmentation strategies of international businesses another; the cultural prestige of the 'Western' family, especially among urban people, a third.

At the same time the creation of the imperialist world order involves a global *differentiation* of gender patterns, or inserts a global dimension into their definition. The frontier of trade, conquest or settlement exalted forms of masculinity different from those becoming dominant in the core countries. The formula of the Davy Crockett story – the frontiersman elected to Congress at odds with the urban elite – is classic. So is the formula of normalization: the white women arrive to raise families. An Australian history of women's work in the colonies is called *Gentle Invaders*, and the point is well made. The expansion of white settlement involves a dialectic of masculinities and femininities as well as race and class; the women were invading white men's realms as well as the lands of the blacks.

More broadly than the process of settlement, imperialism involves reconstruction of the sexual division of labour on a global scale. Agricultural communities are systematically disrupted. New industries commonly involve a stark sexual division of labour: men in mines and copra plantations, women picking cotton, etc. More recently a strong sexual division of labour has been created in Third World manufacturing, in industries such as garment-making and microprocessor assembly. Yet women have also gained access to education on an unprecedented scale, and with it entry to expanding occupations like clerical work and some semi-professions such as teaching.

Though the evidence is much more difficult to come by, it seems that there might also be differentiation in the structure of cathexis. The psychoanalytic arguments of Octave Mannoni in *Prospero and Caliban* and Frantz Fanon in *The Wretched of the Earth* and *Black Skin, White Masks*, suggest that colonialism disrupts existing forms of masculinity and femininity and produces on both sides a distinctive organization of the unconscious. Episodes like the Port Moresby (Papua) race/rape panic of 1925, documented by Amirah Inglis in *Not a White Woman Safe*, suggest that this dynamic can have drastic effects in colonial politics.

Crisis Tendencies

The 'crisis of the family' has not ushered in Armageddon, despite the confident predictions made a decade ago. Indeed with the current conservative ascendancy in Western politics it is easy to feel that the cultural and sexual radicalism of the 1960s and 1970s has gone for nothing. Yet rhetoric about threats to the family and the decline of family values is not to be dismissed as a tactical ploy. It is a pointer to real changes, real tensions and fears. Nor have the sexual liberation movements been dispersed, however far short their accomplishments have fallen of the hopes of 1968–75. A political force was created then which is still active and in some situations effective. If the idea of a full-blown crisis of the gender order is exaggerated, it is undeniable that we are in the presence of powerful *tendencies* towards crisis. The political conflict over issues of gender and sexuality is structured around those tendencies and the historical possibilities they open up.

In *Legitimation Crisis* Jürgen Habermas analyses the concept of 'crisis tendencies' in relation to the class dynamics of late capitalist societies. The details of his analysis assume a generative nucleus (or 'principle of organization'), which I have argued in chapter 3 and 5 is not applicable to gender relations, and may be misleading for class relations too. Yet the concept of crisis need not depend on a postulate of systematicity. It can be applied to a historically composed gender order, or to the gender regime of a particular institution, provided it is possible to distinguish historical developments that call into question the properties of the gender order as a whole from those that can be contained locally. For instance the political processes that allow an Indira Gandhi or a Margaret Thatcher entry to power are not crisis tendencies in terms of the overall structure of men's dominance. They do not imply an improvement in the conditions of practice for women generally; in fact with Thatcher it has been the reverse.

The following discussion explores possible crisis tendencies in the gender order of the rich capitalist countries. I take the major structural features of this gender order, produced by the history sketched in the last section, to be (a) the gendered separation of domestic life from the money economy and the political world; (b) heavily masculinized core institutions and a more open-textured periphery; (c) institutionalized heterosexuality and the invalidation or repression of homosexuality. These patterns sustain (d) the major pattern of sexual politics, the overall subordination of women by men. If this is broadly correct, the analysis of crisis tendencies is a question of identifying dynamics which have the potential to transform these four features, and thus change in fundamental ways the conditions of future social practice.

The debate on the 'crisis of the family' provides a useful starting-point on the assumption that it provides evidence of real crisis tendencies, though misunderstood because conservative sexual ideology reifies the family as *the* basis of society. The discussion in chapter 6 of the dynamics constructing the family raised two points highly relevant here: the dependence of the family form on other institutional structures, notably the state; and the weakening of legitimate patriarchy as the form of authority within the family. There is an obvious parallel between the latter and developments within the state connected with women's gaining citizenship rights.

On these bases we may define a tendency towards a *crisis of institutionalization*, a weakening in the ability of the institutional order of family-plus-state to sustain the legitimacy of men's power.

The long-term political source is the importance of generalizable claims to equality as the basis of legitimacy of the state. This claim has operated in class relations (as argued by T. H. Marshall), race relations (the civil rights campaign for American blacks being an immediate source of the New Left and the new feminism) and global politics (decolonization). Nothing has prevented it having an impact on gender relations. Responding to challenges to the legitimacy of the political order, or even to the government of the day, involves the state in strategies that inevitably disrupt the legitimacy of domestic patriarchy.

Some are quite direct: funding women's education on a scale comparable with men's, providing machinery for no-fault divorce, funding women's refuges and training police for intervention in domestic violence, and so on. Others are more indirect, such as the changing provisions about property, taxation and pensions that treat a married woman as a person in her own right. There need be no intention to undermine domestic patriarchy. The machinery of these policies – divorce courts, the police, etc. – become the sites of a political struggle in which masculine prerogatives are defended, often successfully. An example is divorce proceedings involving lesbian mothers, in some of which attacks on lesbianism are made and influence decisions on the custody of the children. Nevertheless the whole process destroys the taken-for-grantedness of patriarchal authority on which the simple reproduction of power inequalities rests.

The result is not an automatic disruption of the institutional order of power, but must be an increasing vulnerability to challenge. Whether and how challenges develop is a further question. Conditions for the challenge that did develop in rich capitalist countries in the 1960s and 1970s include, at a minimum, the fact that women had easier and more reliable contraception (the Pill, intra-uterine devices, etc.); the growth of women's higher education to a mass scale; and the sharpening contradiction, for groups of younger women radicalized in the anti-war, civil rights and campus struggles of the 1960s, between the rhetoric of equality and the practice of sexual oppression in the radical movement itself.

The advent of the Pill in the late 1950s was denounced as a giant step towards a general breakdown of morality, a theme still pursued by the Pope. Once again the rhetoric of the Right is a useful guide to underlying tensions. We may define a complex but powerful tendency towards a *crisis of sexuality*, in which hegemonic heterosexuality comes unstuck as a stable resolution of the issues of cathexis and motivation.

In the previous section and in chapter 6 I argued that heterosexual masculinity was historically constructed by the exclusion of particular forms of desire and relationship, which were split off into marginalized masculinities, most significantly homosexual. It can be argued that a comparable process has operated in the construction of modern femininity, though the resulting patterns are not symmetrical because of the structure of power (see chapter 8).

In the ideal couple relationship defined by hegemonic hetero-sexuality, and theorized as 'the family' by Talcott Parsons, a stable reciprocity of cathexis is achieved. But it is achieved only by a process of repression, both internal and external, which creates resistances and oppositions. Externally these include the 'wild' masculinities discussed above, and the bonds among women theorized by Adrienne Rich as the 'lesbian continuum'. Internally the opposition includes a range of forbidden impulses and attachments, evidence on which has emerged mainly in psychoanalytic research (see chapter 9 on the 'layering' of gender in personality).

Hegemonic heterosexuality, then, is not a natural fact but a state of play in a field of power and cathexis; at best an ongoing accomplishment. The accomplishment may cease, the state of play alter. The resistances and oppositions amount to a crisis tendency if the social supports of the process of repression prove inadequate, are weakened or altered in ways that allow the emergence of alternative patterns of sexuality on a significant scale.

Several arguments point to this possibility being realized. As suggested in the previous section, the logic of fixation involved in the creation of hegemonic heterosexuality is not obliged to stop within the relationships making up the family. It can and does go on to create an increasingly externalized and alienated sexuality which, while admirably suited to commercial exploitation, corrodes reciprocity at a personal level. Barbara Ehrenreich picks up an important dimension of this in her argument about the 'flight from commitment' among heterosexual men in the United States.

There are also arguments that suggest a dismantling of hetero-sexuality itself. Herbert Marcuse's well-known thesis that genital primacy in sexuality was a product of a level of repression now superseded in advanced capitalism suggests the emergence of a polymorphous sexuality. Theorists such as Mario Mieli have argued that gay relationships are the key to emergent forms of liberated sexuality. One current of feminist theory from Jill Johnston on has seen the centre of feminism as coinciding with the development of lesbian sexuality.

The economic trend most often seen as evidence of a crisis of the family is the rising proportion of married women who are in 'the workforce': 42 per cent at the beginning of the 1980s in Australia. This need not represent a breakdown at all. Much of it is produced by the need for a second income to *sustain* conventional family patterns. The very high proportion of employed women who are part-time workers underlines the point.

Yet the effects of large-scale and long-term employment of married women are more subversive than the statistic itself. On the one hand a wife's wage – even if firmly defined as a 'second income' – is a power resource in domestic politics and feeds into the crisis of domestic patriarchy noted above. On the other hand the fact that large numbers of women are now employed for long periods of their lives in the largely segregated labour market documented in chapter 5, creates a new political situation in the workplace.

It is often remarked that domestic labour in suburban houses separates women from each other physically. It is also remarked that heterosexuality separates women from each other emotionally. The concentration of large numbers of women at the point of production in industry is one of the strongest tendencies working in the opposite direction. A parallel development in relation to consumption has been important in gay men's politics, with the growth of commercial venues. The gay liberation movement in New York sprang directly from a mobilization in defence of such venues against the police, the 'Stonewall riots'.

What these points imply is a tendency towards a *crisis of interest formation*, the emergence of bases for the social constitution of interests that cut across patterns of interests compatible with the existing gender order. The definition of a married woman's interests as being essentially those of her husband and children is the hegemonic pattern; the definition of her interests as those of a group of exploited women in a factory is subversive. As with institutionalization, it is a further question whether these possibilities are realized, whether new interest groupings are formed. Ruth Cavendish's *Women on the Line* provides a fascinating case where this did happen. The general issue of working-class feminism will be taken up in chapter 12.

The three tendencies defined here are certainly not a complete map of the structural tensions of the current gender order. A fuller account would address the interactions of structures, such as the contradictions surrounding childcare, women's employment and fathering; and the problems of the hegemonic definition of sexual character, femininity and masculinity. This may, however, be enough to establish how an account of crisis tendencies can provide the rational link between structural analysis and liberation politics that is missing from sex-role theory and categoricalism. The emergence of women's liberation and gay liberation movements did reflect crisis tendencies of a general kind, though not a general crisis. Crisis tendencies are uneven in their impact; while acting generally, they are likely to come to a head in quite specific milieux. In this case the milieu most affected was the younger intelligentsia of large Western cities. Some of the reasons and consequences will be discussed in Part IV after the constitution of sexual character has been considered.

NOTES

Historicity and 'Origins'

(pp. 141–50). Discussions of Engels almost always ignore the historical context of his own research. For Mesopotamian archaeology in the nineteenth century see Lloyd (1955). Quotation on prehistoric hunting from Clark and Piggott (1965), p. 40; criticism of origin-hunting from Delphy (1977) pp. 53–60, at p. 59. Homosexuality always with us, Bullough (1979), p. 62. My argument on homosexual history is taken from Carrigan et al. (1985). For the transformation of homosexuality in England see, besides work noted in the text, the pioneering work of McIntosh (1968). For the paradox of gay liberation theory see Johnston (1982) and Sargent (1983).

My argument on historicity has some parallels with Touraine (1981). His understanding of structural change however is basically confined to class dynamics and it is difficult to extend his rather specific definition of historicity to gender relations. My approach is derived from Collingwood (1946) and Carr (1961). I depart sharply from Collingwood's argument that feelings and emotions are incapable of rational reconstruction from evidence, which draws a thick line between history and psychology. I would argue that both the practice of psychotherapy and modern social history refute Collingwood, and that psychology is a branch of history. The historicity of the structure of cathexis depends on this.

The treatment of patriarchy as a transhistorical fact or 'cultural universal' in much feminist writing is incompatible with the historicity of gender relations as formulated here. This is not to say that a historical approach portrays gender as always in flux. Rather, what does not change is as much in need of historical evidence, analysis and explanation as what does.

The Course of History

(pp. 150–8). On gender in palaeolithic art see Pericot (1962) and Cucchiari (1981); on the Dolní Věstonice burial see Klíma (1962). My sketch of prehistoric western Asia draws on Burney (1977). For Jericho see Kenyon (1960–83); for Çatal Hüyük see Mellaart (1967), quotation at p. 225. On the position of women in Sumer and Egypt see Kramer (1963), pp. 153–63; Wilson (1951), pp. 202–3; 206–35 on Akh-en-Aton; and Trigger et al. (1983), pp. 79, 312. The Gilgamesh epic is translated in Pritchard (1950), pp. 72–99 with other relevant myths. Admiral Nimitz's wall quoted from Costello (1985), pp. 366. *Gentle Invaders* is by Ryan and Conlon (1978).

Crisis Tendencies

(pp. 158–63). For social meanings of New Right sexual ideology see Poole (1982). The varying significance of antihomosexual prejudice in divorce proceedings is carefully analysed by the Anti-Discrimination Board of NSW (1982), pp. 252–87. Statistics on married women in the work-force from Edgar and Ochiltree (1982).

Part III
Femininity and Masculinity

8

Sexual Character

Unitary Models and Sex Difference Research

The most common conception of the psychology of gender is that women and men as groups have different traits: different temperaments, characters, outlooks and opinions, abilities, even whole structures of personality. There is no accepted term for this concept; I will call it 'sexual character'. The analogy is with David Riesman's term 'social character'; 'sexual' is more apt than 'gender' since in most usages the idea is specifically linked with sex.

Often it is assumed that there is just one set of traits that characterizes men in general and thus defines masculinity. Likewise there is one set of traits for women, which defines femininity. This unitary model of sexual character is a familiar part of sexual ideology. It can be quite explicit: 'just like a woman', 'just like a man'. More often it is implicit. Jokes against 'women drivers', or the 'Mere Male' column in the women's magazine *New Idea*, work by calling into play shared assumptions of this kind: that women are hopeless with cars, that men are hopeless around the house.

More sophisticated, but logically similar, ideas appear in academic writing. In Talcott Parson's classic work 'instrumental' versus 'expressive' traits are supposed to mark the two sexual characters that correspond to the male and female roles. A unitary model of sexual character underlies Nancy Chodorow's feminist reworking of the same themes. Here the focus is on how women's sexual character prepares them for mothering and men's does not. Notions of unitary sexual character have also emerged in cultural feminism in the last ten years. The antipornography campaigns, for instance, have often presented a lust for domination as the core of male sexuality, and as being more or less undifferentiated among men.

Freud's writings implied rather different conceptions of femininity and masculinity, but most of Freud's followers returned to convention. Prominent in the psychoanalytic shift towards conservatism was the Austrian/American Theodor Reik. His long essay 'The Emotional Differences of the Sexes' is a classic statement of the unitary model. It takes for granted that women and men have sharply different emotional characteristics, and postulates that these are based on their different functions in biological reproduction. Reik draws from this, mainly by speculation, complacent explanations of an extraordinary range of matters, from the double standard to cooking, cattiness, premenstrual tension, and why women are concerned about furniture.

In more recent psychoanalytic literature such conceptions of gender remain active. The American Robert May, for instance, makes the difference between 'the male and the female fantasy patterns' the central theme of his book *Sex and Fantasy*. He pursues a general distinction between 'pride' and 'caring' – compare Parson's 'instrumental' and 'expressive' – through ancient myths and modern personality tests and clinical case histories.

It is clear that unitary conceptions of sexual character have a wide appeal and can give comfort to people of very different political persuasions. This is partly because having a unitary conception of feminine or masculine character does not in itself settle what the content of the two opposed characters might be. Speculation, assertion and inference from biology are the order of the day.

Yet there is a large research literature closely related to this problem: the psychological 'sex difference' research mentioned in chapter 2, which as Viola Klein and Rosalind Rosenberg show has been flowing since the turn of the century.

The facts at issue in this research are what might be called the block differences between women and men – for instance, differences between the average reaction times or tactile sensitivity of women and men; or between average scores on tests of verbal ability, anxiety, or extraversion. There are well-established conventions of method. Comparable samples of women and men are needed, together with a reliable measure of some sort. A test is always made for the statistical significance of whatever difference turns up between average scores, or between the proportions of women and men who meet a given criterion.

'Significance testing' itself presses the research towards a focus on block differences, since what is tested is not its size or psychological importance, but simply the probability that there exists some difference which is not the result of chance. The kind of conclusion that passes from the journal articles into the textbooks and popular-psychology best sellers is that 'women have higher verbal ability' or 'men are more aggressive'. If a statistically significant block difference does *not* emerge, the researcher is likely to be disappointed and the research may not get published, since it seems to have nothing to say. I have written this kind of data-dredging paper, about adolescents in Sydney, and, as usual in this genre, paid a lot of attention to items where sex differences did appear and much less attention to the larger number of items where they did not.

When block differences do appear they are conventionally explained by appeal to some underlying traits which distinguish women from men – in other words by a unitary conception of sexual character. Often sex role notions are brought in to provide a common-sense explanation of how sexual character is formed. Thus women are said to be less achievement–oriented than men because they have been socialized to dependency, and so on. Often sex differences are hardly distinguished from sex roles at all; the two blur together in a single concept.

A vast compendium of this kind of research was made in the mid-1970s by Eleanor Maccoby and Carol Jacklin. *The Psychology of Sex Differences* reported that block differences between women and men (generally white, affluent, North American college students) did appear fairly consistently in studies of some traits: verbal ability, visual/spatial ability, mathematical ability, aggressiveness. A finding of no block difference fairly consistently appeared in studies of rather more traits: sociability, suggestibility, self esteem, types of learning, cognitive styles, achievement motivation, sensory modality. The authors entered an 'open finding' – i.e., no consistent pattern – on another range of traits: tactile sensitivity, timidity, activity level, competitiveness, dominance, compliance, nurturance. The research has flowed on since Maccoby and Jacklin wrote. Its results have been mixed, but if it has had any trend it has been to close some of the gaps between women and men that they left open. Robert Plomin and Terry Foch, for instance, find sex differences accounting for only 1 per cent of the variance in a study of children's verbal and quantitative abilities. Olive Johnson and Carolyn Harley report that being right- or left-handed is a better predictor of cognitive abilities than is sex. Of course these are only two examples from a mass of studies, and there are others which suggest stronger sex differences. Nevertheless one can be very confident of a negative point. Recent research has *not* shown that Maccoby and Jacklin systematically underestimated sex differences.

A striking conclusion emerges. The logic of the genre focuses on 'difference' and its explanation. In fact the main finding, from about eighty years of research, is a massive psychological *similarity* between women and men in the populations studied by psychologists. Clear-cut block differences are few, and confined to restricted topics. Small differences-on-average, in the context of a very large overlapping of the distributions of men and women, are usual even with traits where differences appear fairly consistently. If it were not for the cultural bias of both writers and readers, we might long ago have been talking about this as 'sex similarity' research.

In so far as these scales and measures can be trusted, the notion of distinct unitary sexual characters for women and men has been decisively refuted. With it, much of the common-sense understanding of sex and gender, together with most functionalist sex role theorizing, should collapse.

This has not happened. There is too much invested in the notion of sexual character for a simple factual refutation to destroy it. Yet there has been serious pressure to modify it. The simplest modification is to abandon the idea of categorical differences and interpret the results of data-dredging sex difference research through the formula of variation about a norm.

Overlapping distributions now matter less. Differences between means suffice to establish difference between a male and a female norm. Role theory provides a gloss. Variation about each norm reflects role distance, vagueness or conflict in the expectations, or even deviance. Those studies which fail to find mean differences are interpreted as evidence of overlapping expectations or the convergence of traditional sex roles.

As argued in chapter 3, role theory is infinitely plastic. There is no great interest in its exercises in retrieval. But there is something of more note here: the shift to a focus on variation. Concern with variation in the traits for which feminine and masculine sexual character are explanations is only a step from concern with variation in femininity or masculinity themselves.

This path leads to non-unitary conceptions of sexual character.

The need to take this path is now clear in the research literature; all interesting conceptions of sexual character from here on are non-unitary. Both femininity and masculinity vary, and understanding their variety is central to the psychology of gender. How is that variety to be understood? There are several possible approaches.

Masculinity/Femininity Scales

The most popular way of grasping diversity in sexual character is to think of people as being arrayed along a dimension that represents differences in some gender-related trait. This is the basis of most paper-and-pencil tests of masculinity/femininity (hereafter M/F). The problem is how to specify where, on the imaginary line representing the dimension, any given person's shadow falls. This is called 'measuring' the trait, and M/F scales differ in the solutions they offer.

Some tests have used projective methods, such as the 'IT' scale which shows children a sexually ambiguous figure and invites them to make up a story about it. But since the 1940s, when the Minnesota Multiphasic Personality Inventory (MMPI) came into use, a different form has been usual. This most famous of all psychiatric screening tests contained a masculinity–femininity subscale, and set the pattern of a self-report inventory with many short items. The respondents describe themselves on each item separately, and a count is made of how often a certain kind of response is made. This count, sometimes transformed statistically, becomes the respondent's femininity or masculinity score.

The form of the self-description varies a little. Janet Spence and Robert Helmreich in *Masculinity and Femininity* use a questionnaire which invites people to rate themselves on where they fall between two specified extremes, for example:

very rough . . . . . . *very gentle*
goes to pieces under pressure . . . *stands up well under pressure*

Sandra Bem, author of the famous 'androgyny' scale, dispenses with the polar opposites. Each item simply names a trait and asks respondents to rate how often it is true of them:

ambitious ...
forceful ...
affectionate ...
child-like ...

How is it known that these scales measure femininity and masculinity? The usual test has been that each item discriminates statistically between women and men. As Anne Constantinople points out in her excellent review of M/F scales, this results in a systematic confusion between 'sex difference' and 'masculinity/ femininity'. In principle any item that shows a sex difference can figure in M/F scales. In practice almost anything does. Items range from generalized self-descriptions like those quoted above, to job preferences, word associations, neurotic symptoms, information and aesthetic interests. Constantinople remarks that while some items reflect an intuitive notion of what 'masculinity' and 'femininity' mean, in many cases the content seems 'irrelevant to any identifiable definition of the concept'.

Once a point of departure has been established another psychometric criterion takes over, the scale's internal consistency. Candidate items are kept in the scale, or dropped, according to their correlation with other items. Spence and Helmreich's scales illustrate this. The correlation of each item with the total (i.e., the sum of scores on all items) is presented as justification of the coherence of each trait and scale; and those items which have high item–total correlations are chosen for the 'short form' of the scale.

This criterion is likely to whittle down the heterogeneity of content, as it is familiar in questionnaire research that the highest correlations are between items which ask the same kind of question in slightly different language. More important, it eliminates any possibility of recognizing tension or incoherence within the trait being measured.

The reason for using a scale score is that individual items are not very reliable, and can only be presumed to carry a small drop of the trait being measured, mixed up with various impurities. By combining the answers to a number of questions, the impurities tend to cancel each other out. The way this combining is done is the key to the kind of psychology that quantitative personality research produces. In adding together the item scores, the specific meaning of each question is ignored. In old-fashioned hand-scoring of questionnaires it was usual to lay a cardboard sheet which masked the questions over the page, with the ticks or crosses of answers appearing through small windows cut in the cardboard. In modern machine-scoring only the number of the question is needed – its wording does not enter the machine or the processing at all. Semantics, in short, is abandoned.

Gutting answers of their particular meaning in order to treat them as partial measures of a dimensional whole is taken for granted in the psychometric literature. What a person thinks she is saying to the researcher is set aside. The tick or cross is treated not as an answer to a question but as a 'response' providing a clue to an underlying entity. The researcher knows about this entity but the 'subject' does not.

Nearly thirty years ago, in *The Person in Psychology*, Paul Lafitte mounted a sustained critique of what he called 'substantive abstraction' in psychological measurement. Other criticisms of the dubious assumptions and attenuation of reality in paper-and-pencil surveys have come from quarters as diverse as psychoanalysis, anthropology and ethnomethodology. The problem is not that the technique was rough in its early days. Recent research commonly takes less account of such problems than the pioneering studies did. The problem is about the bases of the method. Gender scaling, like other forms of personality and attitude scaling, involves a radical desemanticization of human practice. It is a case of what R. D. Laing in another context called 'transpersonal invalidation'. The chances of a sound understanding of human beings coming out of such research are infinitesimal.

But the approach does have important ideological effects. Desemanticization allows research to recognize variation without having to deal with contradiction. If a person's answers to related items conflict, this does not register as a problem, for instance a question of ambivalence. It simply lowers the total score. If some items do not fit with the others, there is no requirement to investigate why. They are simply dropped from the item pool as a normal step in producing the final instrument.

Femininity and masculinity are thus implicitly theorized as homogeneous dimensions of temperament, which can be measured in all people. In a roundabout way this allows scalar research to recognize a point that unitary conceptions of sexual character could not, the coexistence of masculinity and femininity in the same person. Not in the way Freud saw them, as desires and identifications in conflict with each other, but through the notion of multiple dimensions of variation. Femininity and masculinity need not be treated as polar opposites, i.e., as ends of the same dimension. Each might be treated as a separate scale, and the same person might get high scores on both. This idea occurred to a number of American psychologists in the early 1970s, with Bem's version, 'androgyny', gaining most attention. Spence and Helmreich performed a kind of *reductio ad absurdum* by constructing a femininity scale, a masculinity scale and a M/F scale and showing they were all statistically unconnected when administered to the same people.

The muddle in interpretation that follows from the desemanticization of human communications is obvious enough. Constantinople's summing-up on masculinity and femininity scales a decade ago is still sound: 'both theoretically and empirically they seem to be among the muddiest concepts in the psychologist's vocabulary.' The scalar approach has produced very little new understanding of the psychosocial processes involved.

The reasons for its popularity perhaps have more to do with the politics of academic psychology. Scalar M/F research offers a way of treating an important social question in terms acceptable to a psychological establishment very much concerned with scientificity, formal measurement and statistical proof. It is quick and straightforward, since the conventions of scaling are well established; the professional journals like it, and no one is threatened by it. At this level scalar research is part of the domestication of sexual politics in the name of science. It is an important political fact that a great deal of it has been done by women.

At a deeper level this kind of psychology participates in the process of reification. Turning a process, an action, or a relationship into an object, or treating it as if it were an object, is one of the fundamental dynamics of modern culture. Gender scaling involves a drastic reification of the process of self-expression or accounting for oneself. Even the stylized self-description called for by the scale items is converted, by the operations that produce 'scores' and then statistically manipulate them, into location in the abstract space of a personality dimension.

If this research has been popular, and people feel they recognize themselves in dimensional accounts (or in the unitary accounts of sexual character discussed previously), it is not because people *are* dots on a computer-generated graph in N dimensions. It is, perhaps, because the process of reification is so far advanced as to make recognition of qualitative diversity threatening. Fear, not of 'otherness' so much as of the riotous exuberance of motive and imagination that is a possibility in sexual life, can be a powerful motive in a world partly reified already.

Multiple Models: From Typology to Relationship

Scalar models of personality have often stemmed from theories of personality 'types'. Extraversion–introversion scales and the famous 'F scale' of authoritarianism both derive from such typologies, devised by Jung and the Frankfurt school respectively. M/F scales similarly derive from unitary models of sexual character, in effect 'dimensionalizing' them by adding a range of possibilities in between. But this is not the only way diversity can be recognized in a theory of types. One may hold to the conception of a whole personality rather than a dimension, and subdivide or multiply the types.

In the case of sexual character the classic of this approach is Simone de Beauvoir's account of femininity in Book Two of *The Second Sex*. Starting with a general difference in the social situation and ontological status of women and men, she goes on to develop a subtle account of half-a-dozen types of femininity in literature and French social life: the lesbian, the married woman, the prostitute, the independent woman, etc. Her types are partly based on social circumstances, partly on the patterns of inner dynamics that will be discussed in the following chapter.

In principle the same kind of thing can be done for types of masculinity, though no Simon de Beauvoir has appeared to do it. Andrew Tolson's *The Limits of Masculinity* makes a beginning. Going through the (mostly British) research in community studies and industrial sociology, Tolson draws out connections between economic circumstance, life cycle and sexual identity in a broad distinction between a working-class type and a middle-class type of masculinity.

Both de Beauvoir and Tolson assume a one-to-one correspondence between character type and milieu. This is a step forward from unitary models of sexual character, but not a long one. Character is still treated as unitary within a given setting. The logic is the same as in 'national character' or culture-and-personality research that described the 'modal personalities' supposed to characterize Germany, Japan, Samoa. The same treatment of sexual character is found in the cross-cultural contrasts made by Margaret Mead in *Male and Female*.

The next step is to recognize that qualitatively different types are produced within the same social setting. Evidence for this is not difficult to find. Here is an example taken from the collection of working-class autobiographies already quoted. The author, Bim Andrews, is talking about growing up and going to work at Cambridge in the 1920s:

> In the mid-twenties, I learned how to become a clerk at the Co-op, and after evening classes in shorthand and typing, a higher grade office worker. A dutiful, heads-down-all-day, worker, with no ideas at all about my rights. Not even my basic rights as a human being, never mind my rights as part of a deal involving my work and their money. True, there was some talk of a Trades Union, but no girl or woman ever thought it applied to her. Some of my work kept me standing up all day, and when I had bad menstrual cramps, as I often did, I would slink off to the lavatory to sit down for as long as I dared. No rest room, not even a chair in our crowded cloakroom.
>
> Some new ideas did take root – the Co-op was quite an evangelical movement then, and it was their evening classes which I joined. But my emotions and understanding were still at sixes and sevens. Which was the right way to live? Like Nellie, with her placid face and her engagement ring, and her pieces of linen and underclothes in tissue paper, brought for display to the girls before settling in her bottom drawer? Or like Jessie, coy and nudging – what we would now call sexy – surrounded by men, single and married? Or like Miss Marshall, the General Manager's secretary and our immediate boss. Composed, and sharp with us, the owner of a little car, involved in a sly relationship with the Manager of the Grocery Dept?

Nellie, Jessie, Miss Marshall and indeed the earnest Bim herself, are present in her mind as types – real types, not ideal or abstracted types – standing for different 'ways to live'. Yet they do not float free from each other. Bim experiences a relationship between them. It is a kind of rivalry between alternatives, confronting her with an existential and to some extent moral choice. She can become a certain kind of woman, enter a certain kind of femininity, by throwing herself forward along one path in life.

I will return to the idea of a life path in chapters 9 and 10; here the important point is that the types exist in a relationship with each other. In the research which first raised this question for me, in an Australian ruling-class boys' school, the connections take the definite form of a hierarchy. A teacher whom we call Angus Barr described to us an episode, some details of which we could confirm from other sources, of what he thought of as 'bullying' between two groups of boys:

> There are a group ['the Bloods'] which I suppose you can say is a traditional one, the sporting group, they are more active physically ... And sometimes they ride a bit rough over another group who have been called, and now call themselves, 'the Cyrils', the conshies. [From 'conscientious'.] Who are the ones who don't play any games. Who have this year [had] a particularly bad time from the Blood group ... And about the middle of the year I had to – it hasn't arisen in past years, I've taken the form for a number of years so I think I know – had to intervene. And say, Well now, what is being done by some of you to some others has reached limits where it has got to stop, it is going too far ... [The Cyrils] were these quite clever little boys who are socially totally inadequate, and yet who have got very good brains. They've all got glasses, short, very fat and that sort of thing ... I think I was reasonably successful in stopping it. I tried to ask discreetly some of the Cyrils how things had been getting on, and they said, Well it had been better. And I spoke to one or two of the Bloods, said that it's got to stop.

In contrast to Bim Andrews's perceptions, the difference between these masculinities is not a matter of free choice by the boys: an unathletic way of life may for instance be imposed by a boy's understanding of his physique. Larger cultural dynamics can be detected here. But the crucial point is that entering one group does not make the other irrelevant. Far from it: an active relationship is constructed. The Bloods persecute the Cyrils, because being a Blood *involves* an active rejection of what they see as effeminacy.

This particular pattern of conflict does not arise by chance. The school in question is noted for its attachment to a fiercely competitive body-contact sport, football. Both official school policy, and the ethos among staff, parents and Old Boys, encourage activities in which the kind of aggressive, physically dominant masculinity represented by the Bloods is at a premium. The boys are obliged to define their attitude to this demand, either for or against. Hence they polarize along the axis described by Mr Barr. Yet those boys who react against the model embraced by the Bloods are not simply pushed into limbo. For the school not only wants football glory, it also must have academic success. A high rate of performance in matriculation examinations is necessary if the school is to hold its position in the now strongly competitive secondary-education market. In short, the school needs the Cyrils too. Within their own sphere it gives them honour: acknowledging examination success by means of prizes, giving awards to the chess club as well as the football team. And it protects their interests, as Mr Barr's intervention to stop the 'bullying' neatly shows.

The production of multiple masculinities and femininities can be seen in studies of other schools. In one of the earlier school ethnographies, *Social Relations in a Secondary School*, David Hargreaves portrayed the production of a semi-delinquent 'subculture' in the lower streams of a British secondary modern school. One of its components was a rough, aggressive masculinity, strongly and no doubt deliberately contrasted with the more compliant behaviour of boys in the upper streams. A similar pattern in a similar school a decade later is traced by Paul Willis in *Learning to Labour*, a contrast between 'the lads' and 'the ear'oles'. Willis is more explicit about the construction of masculinity and its connection with class fate, as the two groups of boys head for factory jobs on the one hand and white-collar jobs on the other.

In the Australian girls' private school we call Auburn College, there is not only a differentiation between several kinds of femininity, but also a recent change in the pattern of hegemony among them. An academic renovation of the school, undertaken by a new headmistress and new staff, has altered the context of the girls' peer-group life. The prestige formerly enjoyed by a 'social' set of girls has been broken and their place in the sun taken by academically successful girls headed for university and professional careers.

The pattern of differentiation and relation appears in other institutions besides schools. The fashion industry is an important case, given the significance of clothes and cosmetics as markers of gender. Here there is a constant interplay between the economic need for a turnover of styles – the basis of 'fashion' itself – and the need to sustain the structures of motive that constitute their markets.

In the aftermath of the new feminism, the promotion of a 'liberated' femininity became the basis of many marketing strategies. 'Charlie' perfumes and cosmetics (introduced by Revlon in 1973) and 'Virginia Slims' cigarettes were among the most heavily promoted examples. Yet a femininity that gets 'liberated' too completely loses the need to present itself through cosmetics and fashionable clothes. Thus an oscillation: on one poster 'Charlie' strides out boldly in trousers; on another, 'Pretty Polly' advertises its fragile pantihose with the caption 'For girls who don't want to wear the trousers'. Some marketers take the contradiction inside the one promotion: thus 'natural look' *cosmetics*; or a magazine that uses a feminist name, *Ms London*, as a vehicle for wholly stereotyped advertising.

The fashion industry works through competition of images, but also on the assumption that the competition is always being resolved. A leading designer emerges; a 'look' is settled on; a particular presentation of femininity made normative. In cases such as Dior and the 'New Look' of 1947, a trend lasting over a number of seasons may be set. Moreover, the brilliantly lit centre stage of high fashion is only a small part of the clothing industry's sales. The bulk of the business concerns cheap, drab, and poorly made clothing for the mass market in styles that change slowly. Two centuries ago this was called bluntly 'slop cloathing'; it is now called in the rag trade 'dumb fashion'. So the currently exalted style does not eliminate all other styles. Rather it subordinates them.

There need not be any psychological traits which all femininities have in common and which distinguish them from all masculinities, or vice versa. The character structure of the academic high-flyers at Auburn College is probably closer to that of Milton's 'Cyrils' than to socialite femininities. What unites the femininities of a given social milieu is the double *context* in which they are formed: on the one hand in relation to the image and experience of a female body, on the other to the social definitions of a woman's place and the cultural oppositions of masculinity and femininity. Femininity and masculinity are not essences: they are ways of living certain relationships. It follows that static typologies of sexual character have to be replaced by histories, analyses of the joint production of sets of psychological forms.

The Effect of Structures

To this point I have discussed the production of sexual character as if each milieu were independent of all others. It is time to bring into the analysis the structures that interrelate milieux (chapter 6) and their historical composition into a gender order for the society as a whole (chapter 7).

To start with the structure of power, workplace studies like those discussed in chapter 5 show that face-to-face relations are strongly conditioned by the general power situation between employers and employees and its materialization in particular labour processes. A notable case is the job of personal 'secretary' in business. An apparently very individualized relationship of mutual dependence and trust between the executive (generally a man) and the personal secretary (almost always a woman) in fact rests on sharp differences of income, the industrial vulnerability of the employee, and the overall social power and authority of men. A specific version of femininity is called for, in which technical competence and the social presentation of attractiveness, social skill and interpersonal compliance are fused. This kind of femininity has to be produced, and is by the informal training documented in Chris Griffin's study of British girls moving from school into office work.

The power hierarchy among men in the industrial enterprise is clear enough, from managers and professionals at the top to unqualified manual workers at the bottom. In sharp contrast to the situation of personal secretaries, the men in manual industrial work are often in situations that allow a countervailing solidarity (one of the bases of unionism) and with it a rejection of the masculinity of the dominant group. John Lippert provides a striking description of the aggressive, sometimes violent, heterosexual masculinity produced among motor manufacturing workers in Detroit. The description can be matched in other countries: Meredith Burgmann's account of 'machismo' among radical builders' labourers in Sydney and Paul Willis's account of masculine 'shop-floor culture' among metal workers in Birmingham. The common elements are a cult of masculinity centring on physical prowess, and sexual contempt directed at managers, and men in office work generally, as being effete.

These examples also point to the gender structuring of production. Elements of sexual character are embedded in the distinctive sets of practices sometimes called 'occupational cultures'. Professionalism is a case in point. The combination of theoretical knowledge with technical expertise is central to a profession's claim to competence and to a monopoly of practice. This has been constructed historically as a form of masculinity: emotionally flat, centred on a specialized skill, insistent on professional esteem and technically based dominance over other workers, and requiring for its highest (specialist) development the complete freedom from childcare and domestic work provided by having wives and maids to do it. The masculine character of professionalism has been supported by the simplest possible mechanism, the exclusion of women. Women have had a long struggle even to get the basic training, and are still effectively excluded from professions like accountancy and engineering.

In manual trades, and manual work more broadly, the claim to competence is rather different. Here the most competent are not the most specialized but the most versatile – those with a range of skills, able to tackle any job that offers. This too is often constructed as a form of masculinity dependent on a domestic division of labour. Tradesmen have often been prepared to move around from place to place, even from country to country, to increase their range of experience, the wife's willingness to stay or go being assumed. Fathers have taken care to provide their sons with a range of skills as insurance against economic fluctuations. To quote another British working-class autobiography, from a miner's son called Fred Broughton who grew up in the years before World War I, 'Father used to say, "I shall not leave you much money, but I will teach you every job, then you can always get work". He showed us every job in the garden and on the farm, including how to get stone in the quarry and trim it and build stone walls.'

The construction of nursing as an element of the sexual division of labour, an occupation blending a particular version of femininity with the technical requirements of the job, has already been discussed.

Finally the structure of cathexis is involved. This is the most obvious of structural determinations of sexual character because of the prominence of heterosexual couple relationships in everyday life. It is folklore that 'opposites attract'. One of the most familiar features of sexual display is behaviour and clothing that emphasizes stereotyped sex differences. Studs display their biceps and pectorals, suave charmers grow their pencil moustaches; 'girls' emphasize their vulnerability in tight skirts and high-heeled shoes, sheer stockings and make-up that is constantly in need of repair. So much emotion is adrift around these marks of difference that they can get cathected in their own right, as argued in chapter 5. These stereotypes are so familiar that it is necessary to stress that they are not the whole story. Alongside the Errol Flynns and John Waynes are figures like Cary Grant, whose appeal is specially as a model of sympathetic (though not effeminate) masculinity. In a study of images of masculinity in Australian television, Glen Lewis has pointed to the prominence of 'soft' men as presenters, especially in daytime programs directed at women.

Desire may be organized around identification and similarity rather than around difference. Homosexual love is the obvious case. The attempt to reduce this to attraction-of-opposites by assuming it is based on a butch/femme pattern is now generally discredited. Gay liberation theory lays emphasis instead on the *solidarity* created by love between women or between men. The point is that there are many more possibilities than the standard dichotomy or complete structurelessness. Works like Pat Califia's *Sapphistry* explore a variety of erotic constructions of femininity (homosexuality still presupposes gender division) based on identification and shared experience; the same can be done for masculinity.

There is a related possibility among heterosexual people, for powerful desire can exist between those whose character structure is similar. An *interplay* between identification and reciprocity, and a literal playing with similarity and difference, becomes possible as a basis of eroticism. On such a basis heterosexual masculinity and femininity might be recomposed as various kinds of psychological hermaphroditism, a possibility I will return to in chapter 13.

To sum up: it is possible to see how each of the major structures impinges on the way femininity and masculinity are formed in particular milieux. Conversely, these structures must be seen as the vehicles for the constitution of femininity and masculinity as collective patterns on a scale far beyond that of an individual setting. In the terms proposed in Part II, we have moved from particular gender regimes to the society-wide gender order. The question now to be faced is how, at the level of a whole society, the elements are composed, interrelated and ordered.

Hegemonic Masculinity and Emphasized Femininity

The central argument can be put in a few paragraphs. There is an ordering of versions of femininity and masculinity at the level of the whole society, in some ways analogous to the patterns of face-to-face relationship within institutions. The possibilities of variation, of course, are vastly greater. The sheer complexity of relationships involving millions of people guarantees that ethnic differences and generational differences as well as class patterns come into play. But in key respects the organization of gender on the very large scale must be more skeletal and simplified than the human relationships in face-to-face milieux. The forms of femininity and masculinity constituted at this level are stylized and impoverished. Their interrelation is centred on a single structural fact, the global dominance of men over women.

This structural fact provides the main basis for relationships among men that define a hegemonic form of masculinity in the society as a whole. 'Hegemonic masculinity' is always constructed in relation to various subordinated masculinities as well as in relation to women. The interplay between different forms of masculinity is an important part of how a patriarchal social order works.

There is no femininity that is hegemonic in the sense that the dominant form of masculinity is hegemonic among men. This is not a new observation. Viola Klein's historical study of conceptions of 'the feminine character' noted wryly how little the leading theorists could agree on what it was: 'we find not only contradiction on particular points but a bewildering variety of traits considered characteristic of women by the various authorities'. More recently the French analyst Luce Irigaray, in a celebrated essay 'This Sex Which Is Not One', has emphasized the absence of any clear-cut definition for women's eroticism and imagination in a patriarchal society.

At the level of mass social relations, however, forms of femininity are defined clearly enough. It is the global subordination of women to men that provides an essential basis for differentiation. One form is defined around compliance with this subordination and is oriented to accommodating the interests and desires of men. I will call this 'emphasized femininity'. Others are defined centrally by strategies of resistance or forms of non-compliance. Others again are defined by complex strategic combinations of compliance, resistance and co-operation. The interplay among them is a major part of the dynamics of change in the gender order as a whole.

The rest of this section will examine more closely the cases of hegemonic masculinity and emphasized femininity, making brief comments on subordinated and marginalized forms. The latter will come back into focus in chapters 10 and 12.

In the concept of hegemonic masculinity, 'hegemony' means (as in Gramsci's analyses of class relations in Italy from which the term is borrowed) a social ascendancy achieved in a play of social forces that extends beyond contests of brute power into the organization of private life and cultural processes. Ascendancy of one group of men over another achieved at the point of a gun, or by the threat of unemployment, is not hegemony. Ascendancy which is embedded in religious doctrine and practice, mass media content, wage structures, the design of housing, welfare/taxation policies and so forth, is.

Two common misunderstandings of the concept should be cleared up immediately. First, though 'hegemony' does not refer to ascendancy based on force, it is not incompatible with ascendancy based on force. Indeed it is common for the two to go together. Physical or economic violence backs up a dominant cultural pattern (for example beating up 'perverts'), or ideologies justify the holders of physical power ('law and order'). The connection between hegemonic masculinity and patriarchal violence is close, though not simple.

Second, 'hegemony' does not mean total cultural dominance, the obliteration of alternatives. It means ascendancy achieved within a balance of forces, that is, a state of play. Other patterns and groups are subordinated rather than eliminated. If we do not recognize this it would be impossible to account for the everyday contestation that actually occurs in social life, let alone for historical changes in definitions of gender patterns on the grand scale.

Hegemonic masculinity, then, is very different from the notion of a general 'male sex role', though the concept allows us to formulate more precisely some of the sound points made in the sex-role literature. First, the cultural ideal (or ideals) of masculinity need not correspond at all closely to the actual personalities of the majority of men. Indeed the winning of hegemony often involves the creation of models of masculinity which are quite specifically fantasy figures, such as the film characters played by Humphrey

Bogart, John Wayne and Sylvester Stallone. Or real models may be publicized who are so remote from everyday achievement that they have the effect of an unattainable ideal, like the Australian Rules footballer Ron Barassi or the boxer Muhammed Ali.

As we move from face-to-face settings to structures involving millions of people, the easily symbolized aspects of interaction become more prominent. Hegemonic masculinity is very public. In a society of mass communications it is tempting to think that it exists only as publicity. Hence the focus on media images and media discussions of masculinity in the 'Books About Men' of the 1970s and 1980s, from Warren Farrell's *The Liberated Man* to Barbara Ehrenreich's *The Hearts of Men*.

To focus on the media images alone would be a mistake. They need not correspond to the actual characters of the men who hold most social power – in contemporary societies the corporate and state elites. Indeed a ruling class may allow a good deal of sexual dissent. A minor but dramatic instance is the tolerance for homosexuality that the British diplomat Guy Burgess could assume from other men of his class during his career as a Soviet spy. The public face of hegemonic masculinity is not necessarily what powerful men are, but what sustains their power and what large numbers of men are motivated to support. The notion of 'hegemony' generally implies a large measure of consent. Few men are Bogarts or Stallones, many collaborate in sustaining those images.

There are various reasons for complicity, and a thorough study of them would go far to illuminate the whole system of sexual politics. Fantasy gratification is one – nicely satirized in Woody Allen's Bogart take-off, *Play it Again, Sam*. Displaced aggression might be another – and the popularity of very violent movies from *Dirty Harry* to *Rambo* suggest that a great deal of this is floating around. But it seems likely that the major reason is that most men benefit from the subordination of women, and hegemonic masculinity is the cultural expression of this ascendancy.

This needs careful formulation. It does not imply that hegemonic masculinity means being particularly nasty to women. Women may feel as oppressed by non-hegemonic masculinities, may even find the hegemonic pattern more familiar and manageable. There is likely to be a kind of 'fit' between hegemonic masculinity and emphasized femininity. What it does imply is the maintenance of practices that institutionalize men's dominance over women. In this sense hegemonic masculinity must embody a successful collective strategy in relation to women. Given the complexity of gender relations no simple or uniform strategy is possible: a 'mix' is necessary. So hegemonic masculinity can contain at the same time, quite consistently, openings towards domesticity and openings towards violence, towards misogyny and towards heterosexual attraction.

Hegemonic masculinity is constructed in relation to women and to subordinated masculinities. These other masculinities need not be as clearly defined – indeed, achieving hegemony may consist precisely in preventing alternatives gaining cultural definition and recognition as alternatives, confining them to ghettos, to privacy, to unconsciousness.

The most important feature of contemporary hegemonic masculinity is that it is heterosexual, being closely connected to the institution of marriage; and a key form of subordinated masculinity is homosexual. This subordination involves both direct interactions and a kind of ideological warfare. Some of the interactions were described in chapter 1: police and legal harassment, street violence, economic discrimination. These transactions are tied together by the contempt for homosexuality and homosexual men that is part of the ideological package of hegemonic masculinity. The AIDS scare has been marked less by sympathy for gays as its main victims than by hostility to them as the bearers of a new threat. The key point of media concern is whether the 'gay plague' will spread to 'innocent', i.e., straight, victims.

In other cases of subordinated masculinity the condition is temporary. Cynthia Cockburn's splendid study of printing workers in London portrays a version of hegemonic masculinity that involved ascendancy over young men as well as over women. The workers recalled their apprenticeships in terms of drudgery and humiliation, a ritual of induction into trade and masculinity at the same time. But once they were in, they were 'brothers'.

Several general points about masculinity also apply to the analysis of femininity at the mass level. These patterns too are historical: relationships change, new forms of femininity emerge and others disappear. The ideological representations of femininity draw on, but do not necessarily correspond to, actual femininities as they are lived. What most women support is not necessarily what they are.

There is however a fundamental difference. All forms of femininity in this society are constructed in the context of the overall subordination of women to men. For this reason there is no femininity that holds among women the position held by hegemonic masculinity among men.

This fundamental asymmetry has two main aspects. First, the concentration of social power in the hands of men leaves limited scope for women to construct institutionalized power relationships over other women. It does happen on a face-to-face basis, notably in mother–daughter relationships. Institutionalized power hierarchies have also existed in contexts like the girls' schools pictured in *Mädchen in Uniform* and *Frost in May*. But the note of domination that is so important in relations between kinds of masculinity is muted. The much lower level of violence between women than violence between men is a fair indication of this. Second, the organization of a hegemonic form around dominance over the other sex is absent from the social construction of femininity. Power, authority, aggression, technology are not thematized in femininity at large as they are in masculinity. Equally important, no pressure is set up to negate or subordinate other forms of femininity in the way hegemonic masculinity must negate other masculinities. It is likely therefore that actual femininities in our society are more diverse than actual masculinities.

The dominance structure which the construction of femininity cannot avoid is the global dominance of heterosexual men. The process is likely to polarize around compliance or resistance to this dominance.

The option of compliance is central to the pattern of femininity which is given most cultural and ideological support at present, called here 'emphasized femininity'. This is the translation to the large scale of patterns already discussed in particular institutions and milieux, such as the display of sociability rather than technical competence, fragility in mating scenes, compliance with men's desire for titillation and ego-stroking in office relationships, acceptance of marriage and childcare as a response to labour-market discrimination against women. At the mass level these are organized around themes of sexual receptivity in relation to younger women and motherhood in relation to older women.

Like hegemonic masculinity, emphasized femininity as a cultural construction is very public, though its content is specifically linked with the private realm of the home and the bedroom. Indeed it is promoted in mass media and marketing with an insistence and on a scale far beyond that found for any form of masculinity.

The articles and advertisements in mass-circulation women's magazines, the 'women's pages' of mass-circulation newspapers and the soap operas and 'games' of daytime television, are familiar cases. Most of this promotion, it might be noted, is organized, financed and supervised by men.

To call this pattern 'emphasized femininity' is also to make a point about how the cultural package is used in interpersonal relationships. This kind of femininity is performed, and performed especially to men. There is a great deal of folklore about how to sustain the performance. It is a major concern of women's magazines from *Women's Weekly* to *Vogue*. It is even taken up and turned into highly ambivalent comedy by Hollywood (*How to Marry a Millionaire*; *Tootsie*). Marilyn Monroe was both archetype and satirist of emphasized femininity. Marabel Morgan's 'total woman', an image that somehow mixes sexpot and Jesus Christ, uses the same tactics and has the same ambivalences.

Femininity organized as an adaptation to men's power, and emphasizing compliance, nurturance and empathy as womanly virtues, is not in much of a state to establish hegemony over other kinds of femininity. There is a familiar paradox about antifeminist women's groups like 'Women Who Want to be Women' who exalt the *Kinder, Kirche und Küche* version of femininity: they can only become politically active by subverting their own prescriptions. They must rely heavily on religious ideology and on political backing from conservative men. The relations they establish with other kinds of femininity are not so much domination as attempted marginalization.

Central to the maintenance of emphasized femininity is practice that prevents other models of femininity gaining cultural articulation. When feminist historiography describes women's experience as 'hidden from history', in Sheila Rowbotham's phrase, it is responding partly to this fact. Conventional historiography recognizes, indeed presupposes, conventional femininity. What is hidden from it is the experience of spinsters, lesbians, unionists, prostitutes, madwomen, rebels and maiden aunts, manual workers, midwives and witches. And what is involved in radical sexual politics, in one of its dimensions, is precisely a reassertion and recovery of marginalized forms of femininity in the experience of groups like these.

NOTES

Unitary Models and Sex-difference Research

(pp. 167–71). Research since Maccoby and Jacklin is large and life is short; one example must do. The text cited two studies of cognition, an area where Maccoby and Jacklin thought sex differences were well established. Fairweather (1976) argued that these differences were trivial. Hyde (1981) concluded they were consistent but small. Rosenthal and Rubin (1982) concluded they were not so small, but probably declining. Lest this seem like a trend, Fendrich-Salowey et al. (1982) and Denno (1982) agree with Fairweather. An outside observer may reasonably suspend judgement between these views, but all must agree that if there are systematic sex differences here, they are not very large in terms of overall variance on the measures.

Masculinity/Femininity Scales

(pp. 171–5). For classic critiques of reified measurement in attitude and personality research see Goldhamer (1949), Williams (1959) and Cicourel (1964). Lafitte's critique (1957) remains the most penetrating on technical grounds.

Multiple Models

(pp. 175–9). Bim Andrews' quotation from Burnett (1982), pp. 130–1. Angus Barr quoted from original interview transcript. For the story of 'Auburn College' see Connell et al. (1981). The argument at the end of this section leaves open the sense in which we can speak of 'femininity' in a man and 'masculinity' in a woman. The psychoanalytic evidence to come in chapter 9 implies that these are meaningful expressions, but since they involve a psychological structure that works *against* bodily experience it can hardly be the same kind of structure as women's femininity or men's masculinity. The pressures set up can be ferocious enough to change the body-image itself, as with those transsexuals who experience their penises or their breasts as not being part of their bodies.

The Effect of Structures

(pp. 180–2). Fred Broughton quotation from Burnett (1982), p. 299.

Hegemonic Masculinity and Emphasized Femininity

(p. 183–8). Quotation from Klein (1946) p. 164. On Burgess's remarkable immunity see Seale and McConville (1978). The concepts discussed in this section are both important and underdeveloped; my argument is more tentative than usual here. The mother–daughter relationship might modify the argument about femininity significantly.

9

The Mystery in Broad Daylight

Gender Formation and Psychoanalysis

How are the structures of personal life discussed in the last chapter formed? There are two main approaches to this question that are compatible with a social analysis of gender. Socialization theory treats gender formation as the acquisition and internalization of social norms. It stresses continuity between social context and personality, and the homogeneity of personality itself. Psychoanalysis treats gender formation as the effect of an encounter with power and necessity rather than normative prescriptions. It emphasizes discontinuity between social context and personality, and points to radical division within personality. I will make only a brief examination of socialization theory as it quickly appears inadequate to the problem; then turn to the two main branches of psychoanalysis that offer some grip on the question.

Socialization

In both academic social science and the popular literature on gender in the last two decades the commonest approach has been through concepts of social moulding or 'socialization'.

Schematically, the main argument runs like this. The new-born child has a biological sex but no social gender. As it grows older society provides a string of prescriptions, templates, or models of behaviour appropriate to the one sex or the other. Certain agencies of socialization – notably the family, the media, the peer group and the school – make these expectations and models concrete and provide the settings in which they are appropriated by the child. The sequence of agencies may be important and distinctions between primary and secondary socialization are often made. Various mechanisms of learning come into play: conditioning, instruction, modelling, identification, rule learning. There is much debate in the gender-socialization literature about the relative importance of these mechanisms. Whatever the details, the social models or prescriptions are internalized to a greater or lesser degree. The result is a gender identity that in the usual case corresponds to the social expectations for that sex. Some cases will 'deviate' because of the abnormal functioning of an agency of socialization (for example, a father-absent family), or because of exceptional biology. The products of these deviations are homosexuals, transsexuals, intersexes and others whose gender identity fails to correspond in the usual way to their sex.

A close affinity between socialization concepts and sex role theory is obvious. The social prescriptions are often called 'norms' and the process of social learning is often called 'role learning', 'role acquisition', or 'sex role socialization'. To this extent the critique of role theory stated in chapter 3 applies in full force. Role-learning theory is internally incoherent, and incapable of providing a genuinely social analysis of social process. But though they are commonly phrased in sex role terms, strictly speaking the main elements of socialization analyses can be separated from the role framework and need to be considered in their own right.

The notion of a school, family, peer group or television network as an 'agency of socialization' implies a definite script, a charter under which the agency acts on behalf of the society, and a degree of consensus about what it is to do and how to do it. Such smooth pictures of socializing agencies are given by most of the literature on sex-role socialization, including the writings of liberal feminism.

Both historical evidence about the institutions involved, and close-up studies of their contemporary working, oblige us to reject this picture of consensual agencies acting on behalf of the social order as a whole. Social history shows schools and families often in conflict with each other and with larger social structures. Examples are Richard Sennett's Chicago study *Families Against the City*, and Pavla Miller's *Long Division* which shows how the mass school system in South Australia was imposed as an intervention into working-class families and in the teeth of considerable resistance from them.

Nor are these institutions internally homogeneous, consensual, or even roughly consistent in their dealings with the people being 'socialized'. Psychoanalytic studies of families such as Laing and Esterson's *Sanity, Madness and the Family* and Françoise Dolto's *Dominique* show intolerable contradictions in the pressures and demands placed on children. These cases are, by definition, exceptional in the intensity of the pressures they generate. But other evidence goes far to show that internal conflict and cross-pressure is quite normal. Examples are American research on families like Mirra Komarovsky's *Blue-Collar Marriage* and Lillian Rubin's *Worlds of Pain*, and the British research on working-class schools cited earlier. The classic of liberal feminism, Betty Friedan's *The Feminine Mystique*, was precisely an exploration of contradiction within the American bourgeois family. When institutions appear consensual and consistent, closer examination is likely to show this is because a great deal of energy has been put into overriding conflicts of interest to create a front of harmony and good order. This is shown for ruling-class schools in *Teachers' Work*, and is evident in case studies of families like the Princes in chapter 1.

These data have considerable implications for our understanding of the way institutions shape people. The notion of 'socialization' rests on the idea of internalization through one or other of the mechanisms described by the psychology of learning. What is produced inside the person is a psychological structure that reproduces or reflects the characteristics of the socializing agency. The notion of 'modelling', taking on the attributes of the socializer, encapsulates this feature of socialization theory.

This becomes untenable as a general conception of gender formation once we recognize the fact of contradiction within the process. This eliminates the possibility of mechanical causation: the only mechanical outcome of contradiction would be random-ness, and the evidence will not support that. Instead it introduces two possibilities, both of which lead away from 'socialization' notions to something radically different. One is the production within the person of psychological structures qualitatively different from the properties of the institution or milieu. This is the basis of classical psychoanalysis. The other is the possibility of constitutive choice in a field opened up by contradiction. This is the basis of existential psychoanalysis.

The popularity of socialization notions in academic research has been supported by two occupational blindnesses, the inability of sociologists to recognize the complexities of the person, and the unwillingness of psychologists to recognize the dimension of social power. Both groups have been willing to settle for a consensual model of intergenerational transfer – playing down conflict and ignoring violence – and for a consensual model of the psychological structure produced.

The notion of a 'gender identity' at the core of femininity and masculinity is the psychological counterpart of the notion of a 'sex role' into which one is socialized. Indeed its basis seems to be the act of recognizing oneself as the kind of person that conventional images of femininity and masculinity define. Accordingly investigators like Robert Stoller trace the foundations of gender identity back to the first years of life, when the child is introduced to definitions of femaleness and maleness. Likewise the origins of aberrant gender identity, in Stoller's case studies of transsexuals, are traced to aberrant family constellations at that stage of life.

The notion of identity as a coherent core to personality or sexual character was popularized in the 1940s and 1950s by Erik Erikson in *Childhood and Society* and by the culture-and-personality school of anthropology. It is not accidental that this happened at the same time as the rise of role theory in sociology. Identity theory traded on the psychoanalytic idea of different levels in personality, but gutted it by removing the idea of fundamental conflict between the levels. Surface levels of personality became the more or less straightforward expression of the core.

A full critique of such models of personality would involve a long detour. I will state the main points briefly. A homogeneous or consensual model of gender identity loses the ability to account for creativity and resistance. It recognizes the production of different gender practices only as deviance resulting from inadequate or aberrant socialization. Its homogeneous picture of the core misses or marginalizes that mixing of elements of gender which classical psychoanalysis referred to as normal bisexuality and which even scalar conceptions of personality have now acknowledged as important (androgyny etc.). And it makes a cognitive act – recognizing oneself as male or female – central to the structuring of emotion without acknowledging either the social structuring of such cognition (gender involves social categories presented to the child in the practices of adults) or its dependence on emotional processes that are not cognitively organized (what the Freudians call 'primary process').

Socialization theory, supposing a mechanism of transmission

and a consensual model of what is produced, has been credible only to the extent that social scientists have been willing to ignore both choice and force in social life. I would argue, with Sartre and Laing, for seeing them as constitutive. 'Agencies of socialization' cannot produce mechanical effects in a growing person. What they do is invite the child to participate in social practice on given terms. The invitation may be, and often is, coercive – accompanied by heavy pressure to accept and no mention of an alternative. The emotional pressure involved has been well brought out in autobiographical writings from the American antisexist men's movement, such as those by Seymour M. Miller and Michael Silverstein. Yet children do decline, or more exactly start making their own moves on the terrain of gender. They may refuse heterosexuality, though gay autobiographies show it often takes a long time to construct a positive alternative as homosexual. They may set about blending masculine and feminine elements, for example girls insisting on competitive sport at school. They may start a split in their own lives, for example boys dressing in drag when by themselves. They may construct a fantasy life at odds with their actual practice, which is perhaps the commonest move of all.

If socialization were as smooth and successful as socialization theory presupposes, it would be difficult to account for the degree of violence that has existed historically in relations between adults and children. It seems that its level has declined a great deal in capitalist core countries over the last hundred years – one of the few senses in which this really has turned out to be, as Ellen Key predicted, 'the century of the child'. Yet even here the decline has been very selective. In a Sydney survey of 1969, over 70 per cent of adolescent boys aged eleven to fourteen reported being caned or strapped at school in the current year. Observation in any supermarket will indicate that hitting young children is still a commonplace of daily life.

The imbalance of power makes it possible for adults to put very heavy pressure on children if they set out to. Adults too respond to contradiction in the 'socialization' process, and their response may take the form of attempting to impose order and direction on it, creating vehement regimes of character formation and indoctrination. A classic description of such a regime in an Irish Jesuit school was provided by James Joyce in *Portrait of the Artist as a Young Man*. In many cases vehement regimes do work as intended: the novitiate produces the nun, the school produces scholars, the boy grows up to be the image of his father. Suddenly the socialization paradigm seems apt. Yet notions of 'role learning' are all too mild for the fierce pressures generated in such settings. And even here the response may be rather different from what was intended; then we get not a good Catholic Civil Servant but a James Joyce.

An adequate account of gender formation must be able to understand such events as something more than random exceptions or social deviance. That is only possible if the analysis of the successful case of 'socialization' is in terms that also allow us to understand the unsuccessful.

Several criteria for a theory of gender formation are implicit in what has just been said. It must be able to reckon with social contradiction and contradiction within personality. It must be able to reckon with power and its effects without turning people into automata (for instance recognizing motives for compliance like the child's need for love). It must be able to recognize different levels in personality without depending on the notion that one level simply expresses the characteristics of another. Most important – and in a sense subsuming the others – it must be historical, both in the sense of seeing the person in terms of a trajectory through time and situations, and in recognizing the constant historical reconfiguration of the social forces impinging on personal growth.

Those are reasonably strong criteria. There are, I think, only two approaches that come close to meeting them, classical psychoanalysis and existential psychoanalysis. Their accounts of gender formation are the subject of the rest of this chapter. For different reasons, neither fully meets the criteria just outlined. Considering these reasons points towards a reformation of personality concepts, which is attempted in the following chapter.

Classical Psychoanalysis: The Dynamic Unconscious

Freud wrote voluminously on sexuality and gender. My purpose here is not to give a summary or a history of his ideas and those of his followers, but to explore the contribution they make to a social theory of gender. Accordingly I will start not with the Oedipus complex and Freud's discussions of femininity and masculinity but with his general theorizing about the relationship between the psychic and the social.

On this theme Freud developed two main lines of thought. One made sweeping and mostly fanciful analogies between the psychic life of children and neurotics on the one hand, and 'savages', crowds and groups on the other. The other, much more profound, was concerned with the social repression of sexuality in European culture. This led him in 1908 to a remarkable psychological critique of marriage and the double standard as institutions that hinge on the suppression of women's sexuality. The social pressure that denied women sexual happiness was the major force behind the growth of neurosis. In later writing, culminating in *Civilization and its Discontents* (1930), Freud generalized this argument about repression and laid more stress on its historical dynamic.

A conflict between civilization and nature is of course a traditional theme of Western thought. But Freud is not merely doing the rounds of antique philosophy. The clinical tools of psychoanalysis, especially the concept of repression, enable him to formulate the issue in a much more precise and complex way and move it in a new direction. In 'Civilization and its Discontents' he argues a similarity 'between the process of civilization and the libidinal development of the individual', which is not just an analogy but a relation: 'civilization is built upon a renunciation of instinct'. The 'renunciation' is not projected into a mythical past or a philosophical heaven, as in Rousseau's *Social Contract* (and indeed Freud's *Totem and Taboo*). It is something that operates in every person's life in the process of psychosexual development, and takes effect at the level of the individual unconscious through the mechanism of repression. Neurosis is a material, not a metaphorical, consequence of the social pressures on the person required by the advance of civilization. The structure of the adult personality is formed by this pressure, principally by the way it is experienced by the young child in the family. The formation of the super-ego as part of the person's psychic equipment is itself a social mechanism. In Freud's striking simile: 'Civilization, therefore, obtains mastery over the individual's dangerous desire for aggression by weakening and disarming it and by setting up an agency within him to watch over it, like a garrison in a conquered city.'

But if 'nature' is thereby rendered partly social, so, conversely, the social is brought within the sphere of nature. Civilization is not seen as something external to the events and processes of psychic life: it is seen as a product and extension of them. Its achievements represent a sublimation of the impulses that would, but for repression, find expression in a more raw and bloody fashion. In these later and more complex formulations Freud has shifted from a position that makes civilization the cause of neurosis, to one – admittedly not clearly stated but certainly implied – that sees civilization as continuous with neurosis, as part of the same structure. At this point he expounds the important concept of a historical dynamic in repression:

> This conflict [of Eros and Thanatos] is set going as soon as men are faced with the task of living together. So long as the community assumes no other form than that of the family, the conflict is bound to express itself in the Oedipus complex, to establish the conscience and to create the first sense of guilt. When an attempt is made to widen the community, the same conflict is continued in forms which are dependent on the past; and it is strengthened and results in a further intensification of the sense of guilt ... If civilization is a necessary course of development from the family to humanity as a whole, then ... there is inextricably bound up with it an increase of the sense of guilt, which will perhaps reach heights that the individual finds hard to tolerate.

Which brings back the problem of unhappiness and closes the circle, for him – but is precisely the point of departure for others.

With the technical concepts of psychoanalysis Freud thus dismantled the traditional antinomy of nature and culture. He replaced it, most unexpectedly – it is certain that he did not himself see the theoretical significance of this – by the concept of a historical process. This process operates simultaneously at the macro-social and the individual levels. In it both human personalities and their troubles, and collective social achievements, are integrally produced.

As Marcuse saw, this conception makes it possible to sociologize psychoanalytic concepts. The Oedipus complex can be seen as a product of a definite historical type of the family. Repression itself is no abstract consequence of human relation in general, but takes definite form and intensity in specifiable historical contexts. This does not reduce psychoanalysis to sociology, any more than it can be reduced to biology. But the concept of a historical process allows a much more powerful connection between the social and the unconscious and those theories which, for instance, have simply tacked psychodynamic notions such as 'identification' onto a sociology of social control. It makes possible a socially critical use of psychoanalysis, which is no longer the theory of an eternal contest between instinct and reality.

In the early years of Freudian theory its potential for social criticism was developed mainly by Alfred Adler, a socialist whose original and fertile psychoanalytic writings on power, masculinity, war and motivation are now mostly forgotten. (Adler later became the father-figure of a small cult based on a bland 'individual psychology' which had no use for his early radicalism. The parallel with the fate of Wilhelm Reich's socialist writings is close.) Adler emphasized the social shaping of motives and criticized Freud's persistent attempts to derive them from biology. He had a clear view of the importance of power relations in social structure, and attempted to develop a 'psychology of power', a psychoanalytic account of responses to powerlessness in childhood and social insecurity in adulthood. Most notably he focused part of this argument on the power relations of gender.

Perhaps influenced by the socialist feminism of the day, Adler noted that femininity was devalued in European culture, and argued that this devaluation shaped the psychological patterns of childhood. Children's weakness *vis-à-vis* adults was interpreted by them as femininity, 'childish value-judgements' crystallizing around the cultural polarity of masculine and feminine. Submission and striving for independence coexisted in the child's life, setting up a contradiction between masculine and feminine tendencies. Usually this led to some kind of compromise, the tendencies balancing, if under tension, in the adult personality. But the compromise was not always reached. Anxiety about weakness could lead to overcompensation in the direction of aggression and compulsiveness, which Adler dubbed, in a famous phrase, 'the masculine protest' (applicable to both sexes). He saw this as the key structure in neurosis, but also generalized it as a forcible critique of hegemonic masculinity: 'To this [children's uncertainties about sexuality] is added the arch evil of our culture, the excessive pre-eminence of manliness. All children who have been in doubt about their sexual role exaggerate the traits which they consider masculine, above all defiance.'

Adler's sketch of a critical psychology of gender, unfortunately, bore little fruit. After the break between Adler and Freud in 1911, and another radical wave in the 1920s which included a debate on Freud's theories of femininity, psychoanalysis evolved in much more conservative directions. A continuing interest in the psychology of women by a few analysts such as Karen Horney moved away from the social grounds on which Adler had attempted to locate gender issues. By the 1940s and 1950s, in the writings of John Bowlby, Theodor Reik, Erik Erikson and their contemporaries, mainstream psychoanalysis had become a powerful ideological support of the patriarchal family and conventional definitions of gender. The subsequent feminist criticisms of psychoanalysis were thus well warranted, though much of the fire was misdirected at Freud rather than his interpreters. A striking indication of the political shift is the attitude to homosexuality. Freud had scrupulously refused to define this as an illness, and had cautioned against attempts to 'cure' a homosexual orientation. By the 1950s psychoanalysts freely defined homosexuality as pathological in itself, and proposed and undertook psychoanalytic treatment. They had a singular lack of success.

It was theoreticians outside the clinical world of official psychoanalysis who pushed on with the social dimension of Freud's thought. For various reasons, including the fact that most were men and few had practised analysis, the question of gender dropped gradually out of focus. The interest rather was in the psychological underpinnings of capitalism.

In the 1930s and 1940s the focus was on the emergence of fascism out of liberal capitalism. Karl Mannheim, trying to understand the popular success of fascist movements, brought psychoanalytic arguments into sociology in his *Man and Society in an Age of Reconstruction*. Wilhelm Reich did something similar from further left in *The Mass Psychology of Fascism*. A whole programme of research attempting to weld psychoanalysis to a reconstructed Marxism came from the Frankfurt school: the Horkheimer collection *Studien über Autorität und Familie*, Erich Fromm's *Fear of Freedom*, and most famous of all, Adorno et al.'s *The Authoritarian Personality*. This work moved in the direction of characterology, and inadvertently began producing a typology of masculinity. 'Mack' and 'Larry', the celebrated case studies of high and low authoritarianism, can equally well be read as studies in the formation of contrasting masculinities.

In another line of development Herbert Marcuse took up Freud's argument about the rising level of repression with the advance of civilization. *Eros and Civilization* argued that some of this was the 'surplus repression' required to sustain an exploitative class society, and that this bore down mainly on non-genital sexuality, narrowing spontaneous eroticism. In *One Dimensional Man* Marcuse turned back on his own tracks and argued that advanced capitalism now allowed a controlled release of repressions. This was, however, in forms that stabilized the social order rather than disrupted it. The result was a socially repressive 'desublimation' of instinctual urges.

Both these lines of argument have the same goal, which I will call a theory of embedding. Their purpose is to explain how a social movement like fascism or a social system like advanced capitalism can establish links with unconscious mental processes and thus gain mass support regardless of its irrationality and destructiveness.

The two psychoanalytic concepts central to theories of embedding were the displacement of cathexis and the constitutive role of repression. Most social applications of psychoanalysis postulate a displacement of emotions originally formed in childhood and attached to family members, onto objects or relations in the larger social world in adulthood. The energy of the displaced emotions is largely due to the blocking of original impulses in the process of repression, the pattern of which is decisive in the formation of adult character. The same formative encounters thus shape personality and generate macro-social effects, by dividing conscious from unconscious and determining a particular content for each level.

When in the 1970s a new generation of feminist theorists roped in psychoanalysis to supply part of a critical theory of gender, it was largely as a theory of embedding. The social structure whose stability was at issue here was patriarchy, especially the sexual division of labour. What was felt surprising or in need of explanation was women's acceptance, even active endorsement, of social arrangements that oppress them. The search for explanation was partly a matter of finding the psychic gain in the social loss, and partly a matter of tracing out through psychoanalysis the forms of adaptation to necessity in the shape of men's social power.

Nancy Chodorow's argument in *The Reproduction of Mothering*, though its details derive from the object-relations school of psychoanalysis, follows the basic logic of Fromm and Adorno. What comes out of the analysis is a character typology, in this case a fundamental distinction between femininity and masculinity.

The typology is used to provide a psychodynamic explanation of the acceptance of a social structure, in this case the sexual division of labour in childcare. Because of the different patterns of attachment to the mother, girls grow up with less sharply defined boundaries of the self and a greater need for emotional completion in relationships, boys with more clear-cut ego boundaries and a greater need for separateness. Women both want to mother, and are psychologically adapted for mothering, more than men.

Juliet Mitchell's *Psychoanalysis and Feminism* is also concerned with character structure, though in her case the focus is a reconstruction and correction of Freud's account of femininity. The scope of Mitchell's social theory is considerably wider than Chodorow's, as she construes Lacanian psychoanalysis in terms of an Althusserian theory of ideology, and patriarchy in terms of Lévi-Strauss's theory of kinship and culture. It is, however, less dynamic.

Like most of the structuralist theorists on whom she draws, the tendency of Mitchell's argument is ahistorical. Embedding is construed as the insertion of people into places already laid out for them in a structure whose characteristics are predetermined. This is a common feature of feminist arguments based on Lacan's reworking of psychoanalysis, for instance by Luce Irigaray. In Irigaray's work, for all its psychological subtlety, there is a thoroughly categorical social analysis of gender. This is partly because of the structuralist style, partly because the focus is not on the division of labour but on the symbolic aspect of social process. 'Patriarchy', or the 'law of the father', in these writings is less the structure of social relations than the structure of how the world is imagined.

History is more fundamental in the most complex and original work of feminist psychoanalysis, Dorothy Dinnerstein's *The Mermaid and the Minotaur*. This is to an extent in spite of her own theory, as she takes the sexual division of labour to be an evolutionary constant in human society before the present. Dinnerstein focuses on women's work as mothers – 'the female monopoly of early childcare' – as the main determinant of the adult emotional patterns that sustain patriarchy. In explaining this she depends much of the time on a normative standard case.

She departs from the formula, however, in a series of brilliant sketches of emotional interactions. Here she catches, as no other social analysts and only a few novelists (Nadine Gordimer, Patrick

White) have done, the ambivalences of women and men towards each other, and the ways childhood resonances in their interactions lock the participants into patterns they would not rationally choose. Dinnerstein teases out the tendrils of the pre-Oedipal emotional relationship to the mother in explanations of adult women's sexuality, men's hatred for women, women's acceptance of exclusion from 'world-making' in the public sphere, and, ultimately, the ecological crisis of contemporary civilization. Unlike structuralist appropriations of psychoanalysis, Dinnerstein's does lead to a conception of a historical dynamic and a historical appreciation of the present moment. The book ends, in fact, with a remarkable psychodynamic account of the emergence of the New Left and the new feminism in the United States.

The crucial difference from structuralism is Dinnerstein's focus on routine practice: the practice of childrearing on the one hand, the practices of interaction among adults on the other. This allows her to see the emotional patterns as structurally based but not structurally fixed, and to give a central place to emotional contradiction (in the Freudian tradition called 'ambivalence'). The approach allows a recognition of the development of practice, of its historical cumulativeness. Habermas, in a moment of optimism, spoke of this capacity to form new structures as the 'evolutionary learning process' of societies. In Dinnerstein's view the cumulation is rather in the direction of global disaster: 'the prevailing symbiosis between women and men has something deadly wrong with it ... It supports a growingly perilous societal posture; it helps lock us, as a species, into a suicidal stance toward the realities on which our collective survival hinges.'

Here we reach the limits of 'embedding' arguments, where the consequences of embedding bid fair to destroy the social order being embedded. We are also left with two theoretical difficulties. First, Dinnerstein's argument is built around a normative standard case, though it carries conviction mainly when it complicates or departs from it. Can those complications and departures be made more systematic? Second, Dinnerstein's argument, like Chodorow's and Mitchell's, assumes a fairly straightforward displacement of affect from individual family figures in childhood to whole categories of people in adulthood, most notably by undifferentiated use of 'woman' for both. But this displacement is not straightforward, as psychoanalytic studies abundantly show. A classic example is the enormous difficulty and complexity of a young boy's attempts to construct a stable pattern of attachment documented in Freud's 'Wolf Man' case history. As in Freud's theoretical writings about femininity and masculinity, Dinnerstein leaves us unclear why the displacement must happen, and what agency or choice the growing child/adult has in the matter.

Theories of embedding state the effects of gender formation; psychoanalysis also offers maps of the route towards those effects. They centre on the Oedipus complex, 'the fateful combination of love for one parent and simultaneous hatred for the other as a rival' as Freud summarized it, that emerges with the maturing of the child's erotic life around four to six years old. This appeared in Freud's psychiatric casework as the nucleus of the neuroses, and mainly on this evidence became the key moment in psychoanalytic theories of human development. It was, Freud assumed, structured differently for girls and boys. The basis of this assumption was the different places of the mother and the father in family dynamics. Some feminist reworkings of the Oedipal theory have stressed the power dimension of this relation (Firestone), others the division of labour (Chodorow, Dinnerstein); they are not clearly distinguished in Freud.

The outcomes of the differently structured Oedipal crises are the bases of Freudian accounts of femininity and masculinity. With girls the process involved a messy and incomplete abandonment of the desire for a penis, eventually transformed into desire for a baby and the man who could give one. With boys the mother was retained as erotic object, a cathexis eventually displaced onto other women; but this desire was repressed by fear of the castrating father, itself provoking identification with him, the internalization of prohibitions, and formation of a strong super-ego. No such process stimulated super-ego formation in women. These were, so to speak, standard resolutions. They could and often did go wrong. Further, closer analysis would show underneath these patterns traces of contradictory ones. The 'complete' Oedipus complex, Freud insisted, involved ambivalent feelings of desire and hatred towards both parents.

The main modification of this argument within the psychoanalytic tradition has been a greater attention to the pre-Oedipal period. Freud himself began it. In the 'Wolf Man' case history, his most extensive study of the problem of masculinity, Freud noted that in the crisis of the boy's relation to his father, the feminine aim in relation to the father was repressed because of the fear of castration: 'In short, a clear protest on the part of his masculinity!' This argument clearly presumes a pre-Oedipal masculinity, which was important enough to the little boy to force the repression of the strongest attachment in his sexual life. Freud never spelt out the nature of this early 'narcissistic masculinity', but it is clear that it cannot be identified with the 'activity' end of the activity/passivity polarity that plagues psychoanalytic discussion of gender, including Freud's earlier writings. It probably does not have much to do with sex of object-choice either; 'narcissistic' is an apt adjective. It is difficult to escape the conclusion that it is the cultural value placed on maleness in a patriarchal society that is at issue here, and is a decisive presupposition of the classic Oedipus complex. In this context the emphasis in the French analytic tradition on the symbolic valorization of the phallus seems justified.

The pre-Oedipal years also emerge as crucial in Chodorow's and Dinnerstein's arguments. What Chodorow calls mothers' 'Oedipally toned' responses to little boys push them along the path to the Oedipus complex, while the closer identification of mothers with their young girls leads to more permeable boundaries of the self. Chodorow and Dinnerstein both emphasize the sexual division of labour as the crucial condition of these pre-Oedipal effects. This suggests that the psychoanalytic sequence might be interpreted in terms of the structures defined in chapter 5. The structures interact in different ways as the child grows older. The dominant interaction affecting the emotional life of the child changes.

Period	*Major structural interaction*
Pre-Oedipal	Cathexis x division of labour
Oedipal	Cathexis x power

If this is correct, we may conclude that the emotional dilemmas of the encounter with power in the Oedipal stage depend on the outcome of the earlier interaction of cathexis and the division of labour.

The psychoanalytic theory of the normative standard case can be revised sociologically along these lines. But this still leaves unclear what Freud left unclear, just how 'standard' this case is supposed to be. The long controversy about the supposed 'universality of the Oedipus complex' across cultures has not been particularly helpful. Those combatants who were sympathetic to

Freud usually took for granted that Oedipus was standard
equipment in European families and debated whether he could be
found in 'primitive' cultures. Nor are we helped by Dinnerstein's
honest confession that none of the five people to whom she is
closest matches at all well 'the composite portraits of "normal"
masculinity and femininity' presented in her book.

The roots of this difficulty are connected to the unitary
conceptions of gender discussed at the start of chapter 8. It is
assumed that the systematic character of gender and sexual
relations requires one central pattern of personality, plus deviations.
The argument of the later part of chapter 8 may help sort out the
place of the Oedipus complex as well. More than one major
pattern of childhood emotional development is produced; and they
are produced in relation to each other.

Freud succeeded in isolating and analysing one important
pattern of psychosexual development in European families. For
masculinity this was quite probably, in the social context of
upper-middle-class Vienna, the hegemonic pattern. Some of his
descriptions of femininity imply the 'emphasized' pattern sketched
in chapter 8, though his confusions and hesitations about femininity
show he found this harder to pin down. That too is consistent
with the argument about the absence of a 'hegemonic' femininity
in patriarchal society.

The crucial point is that no one pattern of development can be
taken as universal even within the specifical social context Freud
studied. Researches like Anne Parsons's work on southern Italy
have documented alternative 'nuclear complexes', and this point
has to be applied within cultures as well as between them. The
Oedipal drama is constructed in quite specific situations. Not only
are there multiple pathways through childhood, the routes can
and do change as gender relations change in history. Erikson's
suggestion that the focus of neurotic conflict has changed during
the twentieth century – formerly about sexuality, now about
identity – is a useful warning, though greatly overgeneralized. The
now familiar research by Philippe Ariès and others on the history
of the family implies longer-term changes in the psychodynamics
of child development.

In this light, the formulations of femininity and masculinity by
dissident psychoanalysts like Adler and Jung acquire a new
interest. Instead of seeing them as displacing Freud's theory of
the Oedipus complex (which Adler and Jung certainly intended),

we can see them as accounts of other paths of psychosexual development that were available to be discovered through the research method that all schools of psychoanalysis share, the reconstructed clinical case history. The alternatives include Adler's notion of the compulsive 'masculine protest', already described; Jung's somewhat similar notion of a strong, authoritative masculine 'persona' based on the repression of weakness and dependency which then coexists as the unconscious 'anima'; the Frankfurt school's models of 'authoritarian character'. These can be brought together as elements of the psychoanalysis of a historically constructed range of masculinities. *The Authoritarian Personality*, sketching the 'democratic personality' and the social and political conditions for resistance to fascism, even made a beginning on the immensely difficult problem of the relations between these different dynamics.

This is as far as I can take this problem at the moment. The next step, clearly enough, is the empirical investigation of the range of developmental paths and psychodynamic patterns in a given milieu, and their interconnections. The methods of such a study cannot be formulated without a closer examination of the idea of life histories, which I will attempt later in this chapter and in the next. Before doing so it is necessary to take a closer look at the concepts shared by all schools of classical psychoanalysis, repression and the unconscious.

In Freud's original and most influential version, repression is applied to libido, to erotic impulses, and the whole theory of the formation of personality thus rests on an account of libidinal development. As Mitchell points out this is what revisers of Freud have found hardest to handle, and have most commonly dropped, in particular the theory of children's sexuality. With a few exceptions, the libido theory was preserved only by the most orthodox school of psychoanalysts, whose increasing social and political conservatism blanked out its subversiveness.

The attempt to recover the erotic dimension, and to bring out the social criticism implicit in the theory of repression, has been central to radical reworkings of psychoanalysis which have seen Freud as a theorist of liberation more than a theorist of embedding. Norman Brown in *Life Against Death*, Marcuse in *Eros and Civilization* and *An Essay on Liberation*, and Reimut Reiche in *Sexuality and Class Struggle* present versions that largely ignore gender. But the same themes have been applied to women's liberation by Dorothy

Dinnerstein, and to gay liberation by Dennis Altman in *Homosexual: Oppression and Liberation* and Mario Mieli in *Homosexuality and Liberation*.

The concept of repression, then, points to an erotic dimension of liberation, though it does not fully specify it. All the works just cited are forced to go outside the psychoanalytic framework to formulate the process of liberation. A purely psychic liberation is rather hard to sustain. Freud's own therapeutic purposes were deliberately limited, given his acceptance of the established social order and family structure.

If patterns of femininity and masculinity are composed as patterns of repression, the reconstruction of gender does involve a reworking of erotic attachment and expression. Mieli sees this optimistically and expansively, as early gay liberation generally did. Dinnerstein is rather more sombre about the 'project of sexual liberty', though she sees it as central to whatever chance humans have of surviving. An important tendency in feminism sees the path forward as a withdrawal of women's emotional attachments and energies from men to focus them on other women. Though there is a long way to go with any of these strategies, the political experience of the last twenty years is already consistent with psychoanalytic theory in at least two respects. Patterns of erotic attachment have proved deep-seated and difficult to change. The attempt to change them provokes strong and complex resistances at the personal level as much as the political.

The concept of repression is central to the main complication that psychoanalysis introduces to the concept of sexual character, since repression constitutes the unconscious. The conceptions of sexual character discussed in chapter 8, for all their differences, mostly share the assumption that personality is homogeneous – expressed in gender scaling by the requirement of statistical consistency, in humanistic psychology by the notion of a core 'gender identity', and so on.

Classical psychoanalysis violates this assumption comprehensively, and this is one of its most important contributions to the analysis of gender. The notion of 'primary process' thinking in the id and 'secondary process' in the ego; the idea of unconscious impulses which cannot be directly expressed in consciousness; the notion of the dream or symptom as a 'condensation'; and the structural model of personality (id, ego, super-ego) – all were ways in which Freud tried to formulate the idea that repression marks out qualitatively different parts of the human psyche. They not only can contradict each other, they normally are in contradiction. Repression itself is a mechanism of contradiction.

We do not need to accept Freud's particular formulations to appreciate the importance of the idea. It implies that femininity and masculinity are normally internally fissured and in tension. To use a rather static model, they are normally layered. (To correct the image one must bear in mind that the relationships between the layers are as important as their content, and the layers themselves writhe around, so to speak, as the person moves on a life trajectory.)

This can be accepted without the libido theory on which Freud based it. Indeed its most clear-cut application to gender is not by Freud but by Jung in his essay 'Anima and Animus'. Here Jung suggests that sexual character is systematically layered in the sense that the public face of femininity and masculinity, compatible with the conventional social role, is always constructed by a repression of their opposites. A kind of unconscious personality (the 'anima' for men, 'animus' for women) develops as a negative of the socially acceptable one, and their incompatible demands underlie many of the tortured emotional dynamics of marriages.

Freud's case histories present more complex layerings again. The 'Wolf Man' is the classic example, Freud peeling off in turn an inhibited adult heterosexuality, a promiscuous but emotionally shallow adolescent heterosexuality, a passive and highly ambivalent homosexual attachment to the father, arriving at last at the pre-Oedipal narcissistic masculinity that has already been mentioned. Dinnerstein's argument likewise revolves around the idea of layering, with the pre-Oedipal attachments as hidden determinants in the most complex adult emotional relationships.

Jung's argument dramatizes the most problematic aspect of this: that femininity and masculinity can coexist in the same personality. Freud wrestled with this idea endlessly, talking variously of bisexuality, of activity/passivity, and so on; he was never very satisfied with his answers and we need not be either. Jung's analysis is better since not reductionist – the starting-point is social role rather than biology – but is too schematic to carry us far.

The evidence for layering is convincing, and requires us to see the tension between different layers or tendencies in personality as a constitutive force in gender relations. Yet its theorizing seems fragile, vulnerable to any criticism of the concepts of repression and the unconscious.

Two critiques are of particular importance. The one formulated by Sartre depends on an account of consciousness and motivation which will be discussed in the next section. The other mounts an essentially political critique of the concept of the unconscious. Its clearest statement is in *The Politics of Sexuality in Capitalism* by a London radical group of the early 1970s. The 'Red Collective' argue that what Freud took to be effects of the unconscious are in fact effects of power, both class power and patriarchal power, their causes being invisible only so long as these structures are not brought into question by political practice. Psychoanalysis is an emanation of the establishment, and the concept of the unconscious is a mystification justifying dominance of the therapeutic situation by the therapist.

The Red Collective is right to point to the social practices in which psychological concepts are formulated. The book is theoretically interesting, as well as moving, in reporting the group's own attempts to work through the personal politics of sexual relationships. Its criticism of the notion of the unconscious is apt as far as the unconscious is thought of as a place where certain mysterious things happen, comprehensible only to the expert. Freud has to bear some responsibility for this, as much of the time he used spatial metaphors in talking of the unconscious.

But fundamentally Freud's concept was processual, based on the dialectic of impulse, repression and symbolization. Even more, it was strategic, a concept arising in connection with practices of transformation. As Freud insisted at boring length, he did not discover the unconscious mind; that had been known to poets and philosophers for centuries. He was simply one of the first to try to do something about it, in the sense of working out therapies for people who had got it badly snarled. All Freudian theory developed in relation to a practice of attempting to transform lives. The concepts of repression and the unconscious mark both obstacles and potentials encountered in this practice. And that is, I think, the fundamental sense in which they are important to other practices of sexual politics.

Structuralist and poststructuralist 'readings' of Freud have been misreadings exactly so far as they separate the concepts from their context in practice. That separation is central to the pessimism these readings have led to. To bear a different fruit, analytic concepts have to be reconnected to practice. The Red Collective rightly argues that this will have to be based on different social foundations from the doctor/patient format. The medical model of psychoanalysis proved easy to absorb into conventional medicine, and to turn into a politics of 'adjustment' and non-violent social control.

Existential Psychoanalysis: The Project

It has long been objected that Freud's theory results in too mechanical a view of personality and too limited a view of human possibility. Adler was one of the first to raise these points, though he did not take them far. Much more radical was the critique developed by Jean-Paul Sartre in *Being and Nothingness* and applied to the theory of gender by Simone de Beauvoir in *The Second Sex*. The argument started with the theory of libido and moved on to the concept of the unconscious.

The problem with 'empirical psychoanalysis', as Sartre called Freudian thought, is that it takes as a necessary structure of the person what should be regarded as the product of choice. For one's psychic life to be determined by libido is certainly a possible form of human existence, but it is not the only one. It is a way of being that a person may take up, may choose. What is human is precisely the process of constructing oneself by choices that transcend given circumstances. This is far from the easy-going voluntarism of 1970s 'growth movement' psychology. To Sartre, being in a position to choose also means having to take responsibility – in a famous phrase, 'we are condemned to be free'. The act of choice also means the fact of commitment. We are stuck with what we do; what's done cannot be undone. To make a choice is to walk into a future defined by the consequences of that choice.

Humans project themselves into their future by their choices, by the way they negate and transcend the circumstances that are given to them to start with. The person is constructed as a 'project' of realizing oneself in a particular way. This is certainly intentional, but it involves more than the concept of purposive behaviour. The project is, to use a term coined later by the Czech philosopher Karel Kosík, 'onto-formative', constitutive of social reality. The process itself appears as a complex unification, a constant bringing-into-relation, of actions that are uncaused (because always choices) but intelligible in relation to each other. Looking back, the process can be decoded by a reconstruction of the life history that relates later parts of the trajectory to the original, constitutive choices. This decoding is 'existential psychoanalysis'. Sartre himself did this job only in the form of literary biographies, notably of Genet and Flaubert. There is now also a body of case histories by two British psychiatrists influenced by Sartre, R. D. Laing and Aaron Esterson, which show what the approach looks like in a clinical setting.

One of the most impressive parts of Sartre's argument, given his lack of clinical experience, was his intuitive acceptance of Freud's insistence on the difficulty of self-knowledge. The concept of the unconscious was built around the practical difficulty that some important facts about the person were not accessible to conscious inspection. Sartre vehemently rejects the metaphor of regions in the mind, and the concept of a system of mental processes that we do not know about. To him the process of choice and transcendence, i.e., what is specifically human in human life, is necessarily conscious. But this does not imply that everything about a person is immediately accessible. There is mystery: a 'mystery in broad daylight'. Human self-consciousness can have different structures. The unreflective structure of being-for-itself is very different from self-knowledge with the structure of being-for-others. The latter can be very difficult to produce, as the practice of psychoanalysis shows. But its production is, in a sense, the psychoanalytic cure itself, the famous 'talking cure'. Psychoanalysis is not a process of 'bringing to consciousness' material that always was an aspect of consciousness. Rather it is a question of attaining knowledge of what one is, instead of just being what one is.

This argument yields a rather different image of cathexis. Freud's hydraulic model of the libido suggests a stream of affect flowing here, being blocked up there, bursting through somewhere else. Sartre's treatment suggests cathexis is a kind of commitment, a throwing-oneself-into a particular emotional involvement. The intractability of attachment, the stickiness of cathexes dramatized by hopeless love, is a fact of our emotional lives not because we cannot choose other attachments but because we cannot walk away from the consequences of past ones. An emotional commitment of any force comes to structure not only our social interactions but also our fantasy life, our self-concepts, our hopes and aspirations.

One can only switch them off at a cost that for many people is intolerable, the cost of making a great void in every aspect of our life. We know what this feels like for people who have suffered it involuntarily – the abandoned lover, the bereaved. Few people would choose to be in that position.

There are various ways of denying freedom and refusing responsibility, which give existential psychoanalysis an armoury of concepts for analysing the rigidities of social interaction. De Beauvoir, for instance, connects the valorization of the penis in masculinity with the near-universal tendency towards alienation:

> The anxiety that his liberty induces in the subject leads him to search for himself in things, which is a kind of flight from himself ... Here is to be found the primary temptation to inauthenticity, to fail to be genuinely oneself. The penis is singularly adapted for playing this role of 'double' for the little boy.

From the 'incarnation of transcendence in the phallus' flows, naturally enough, the fear of castration in the Oedipus complex. Here the psychoanalytic theory of gender appears as a special case. It presupposes, as de Beauvoir forcibly argues, a specific set of social and historical circumstances which it cannot itself explain.

Sartre's treatment of 'bad faith', situations where people refuse responsibility for what they do and claim that their decisions are made for them by external forces, suggests a different kind of connection with Freudian theory. The concepts of libidinal determination and the unconscious offer psychoanalytic patients a tremendous temptation to assign their actions to uncontrollable mental forces. From another starting-point Thomas Szasz in *The Myth of Mental Illness* convincingly argues that the concept of 'mental illness' invites collusion among patient, family and doctor. The hysterical 'symptom' is a claim for the sympathy and care due to the sick, made by someone who will not speak out about what is intolerable in their lives or personal relations. The 'layering' of sexual character appears as a form of bad faith, of refusal of responsibility for one's own conduct in sexual politics.

The existentialist argument does not imply that the world described by classical psychoanalysis is non-existent. It is real, but real as a world of alienation. Its obscurity is the darkness of escape and refusal. It is always capable of being transcended; as de Beauvoir argues:

> The psychoanalyst describes the female child, the young girl, as
> incited to identification with the mother and the father, torn
> between 'viriloid' and 'feminine' tendencies; whereas I conceive her
> as hesitating between the role of *object, Other* which is offered her,
> and the assertion of her liberty.

The concept of sexual liberation, if it can be formulated at all, is
not a matter of unshackling native eroticism but of dismantling
alienations (including erotic ones) and realizing native freedom.

Sartre presents existential psychoanalysis as the decoding of a
way of being in search of original, constitutive choices. In his
study of Genet, for instance, he traces a great deal back to Genet's
childhood choice to be what his foster parents regarded him as, a
thief. This procedure runs a considerable risk of homogenizing the
person, as do de Beauvoir's pictures of 'the avenues of inauthentic
flight open to women', the basis of her character typology discussed
in chapter 8. The risk is that the intelligibility of a life will be
found only in its consistency, in the bits that hang together. The
Freudian idea that the intelligibility of a life might lie in its
contradictions is too valuable to lose.

The problem can, however, be corrected. There is nothing in
Being and Nothingness, nor in Sartre's later reworking of existential
psychoanalysis as 'the progressive-regressive method' in *The Question
of Method*, that requires constitutive choices to be always singular,
or always consistent with each other. The practical applications
by Laing and Esterson have not found this assumption necessary.
For instance Laing's case study of the flamboyant student 'David'
in *The Divided Self* shows contradiction developing between the
boy's choice to be his dead mother and his choice to be a man.

'David' was driven towards psychosis by the fact that these two
choices or commitments had incompatible consequences. The
choice to be a man involved fear and hatred of femininity, and
thus of 'the woman who was inside him, and always seemed to
be coming out of him' – that is, the consequences of his choice to
be the mother. It might have been possible not to fear that
femininity, had the masculinity in question been differently
organized. Laing's case history gives a few hints of a father whose
masculinity was highly conventional, at least in relation to issues
like the household division of labour, but does not give enough
detail to be sure.

This case study suggests a distinction between hegemonic

masculinity and forms of masculinity that are heterosexual without being directly organized around domination – conventional masculinities, loosely. Both are founded on a claim to power, which the one carries through in all its consequences and the other does not. Conventional masculinity is, to an extent, hegemonic masculinity in bad faith. Men can enjoy patriarchal power, but accept it as if it were given to them by an external force, by nature or convention or even by women themselves, rather than by an active social subordination of women going on here and now. They do not care to take responsibility for the actions that given them their power. Hence their often slightly shamefaced admiration for the heroes of hegemonic masculinity, the footballers, jet pilots, wife-beaters and poofter-bashers, who do.

The claim to masculinity here embeds social structure in sexual character in a sense almost exactly the reverse of 'embedding' in psychoanalytic sociology. The power relations of the society become a constitutive principle of personality dynamics through being adopted as personal project, whether acknowledged or not. At the social level, what this produces is not the stabilization of a social order, but what could be called a *collective project of oppression*. The subordination of women and the marginalization of homosexual and effeminate men are sustained neither by chance nor by the mechanical reproduction of a social system, but by the commitments implicit in conventional and hegemonic masculinity and the strategies pursued in the attempt to realize them.

The notion of a collective project is not easy to get clear, except in the all-too-easy form of a conspiracy. There certainly are conspiracies among men, for instance to exclude women from most positions of power in business and the state. There are conscious individual actions to protect men's privileges, such as a senior bureaucrat blocking the appointment of a feminist to a particular government job. Such things not only do occur, they occur quite commonly, and are well known to insiders. But as the argument of Part II has shown, this cannot be taken as the fundamental structure of patriarchal power, for this also rests on institutionalization. The collective project of oppression is materialized not only in individual actions but in the building up, sustaining and defence of an institutional order that generates inequalities impersonally.

Sartre's own attempt to do this analysis for the case of class dynamics shows the enormous complexity of the problem and I don't propose to match his effort here. I do want to register, first, the conceptual importance of the question and second, the fact that practical beginnings have been made with it. Aaron Esterson's case study and theoretical formulations in *The Leaves of Spring* illustrate the dialectical intelligibility of collective practice in the family. Cynthia Cockburn's *Brothers*, though not conceived on a psychoanalytic paradigm, still documents very clearly some of the structures of a collective project of sexual politics in the workplace.

The notion of a collective project, like that of an individual project, implies both freedom and responsibility. At the minimum it implies freedom to participate or not, and responsibility for the choice made. This has proved difficult for men influenced by feminism to get straight. Accepting the feminist critique of patriarchy has often led to overwhelming guilt and desire for redemption. Hence the 'effeminist' tendency that repeatedly emerges in counter-sexist politics among men. In its own appealing way, this is just as inauthentic as any 'masculinist' denial of the facts of inequality. It makes no sense for me to take responsibility for what other grown-up people do, or have done in the past. I take responsibility for what I do and for its consequences. A clear view of what I do – as the whole argument of this book goes to show – includes the way my actions interact with those of other people and either sustain or subvert the collective project of oppression. But to take responsibility for, and hence feel guilt about, that collective project as a whole is at one level paranoid, at another paralyzing. It has certainly not led to any practically effective form of politics over the last dozen years.

More hopefully, relations between men and women also include the project of love. This is a project in the strict sense, a commitment of selves, a relation around which practice becomes organized. It is a formative commitment, whose consequences ramify and develop through a life history, often changing the complexion of the original relationship very deeply.

It is commonly assumed that love is incompatible with hatred or oppression. This is one reason why women may reject feminism, because they have experienced love from men (and towards them) and take feminism to be a doctrine that denies or rejects that fact – despite the passionate writings of heterosexual feminists like Sheila Rowbotham, Dorothy Dinnerstein and Barbara Sichtermann. In reality love is a project that can be interwoven with the project of oppression. Psychoanalysis has shown the importance of ambivalence, the coexistence of strong but opposed feelings towards the same object. Shulamith Firestone analysed 'romantic love' as the corrupted version of love that develops when the parties are unequal. This is debatable, but there are other ways heterosexual attachment and subordination can be connected. De Beauvoir and Dinnerstein both analyse in some detail the incorporation of a loving woman into the loved man's projects as an important mechanism sustaining the exclusion of women from 'world-making' in public life.

Yet love is also, notoriously, a destroyer of conventions, a force difficult to channel and control. Héloïse and Abélard, Guinevere and Lancelot, Paolo and Francesca, Romeo and Juliet, Tristan and Isolde, are not exactly marginal figures in the European imagination. The myths generally kill them off before they get to old age, but the images live on with compelling emotional force. The contradiction between the project of erotic love and the requirements of patriarchal institutions – marriage, property and kinship relations – also has to be recognized as a permanent tension in patriarchal society.

To transform tension into structural change, actually to start dismantling structures of domination, is the collective project of liberation. It has proved no easier to get its personal and structural dimensions together in practice than it is in theory. The New Left of the 1960s criticized mainstream Stalinists and labourites for trying to change society without changing themselves. The New Left was criticized by feminists and gay liberationists for macho public politics and domestic sexism. The growing visibility of 'communities' of gay men has sparked criticism from feminists, especially since the reassertion of masculine styles in the late 1970s. Feminism in turn has been criticized for dogmatism, power plays, elitism and jobs-for-the girls since it won a thin slice of power in education, welfare and the bureaucracy.

There is some truth in each of these criticisms. We are living in the real world and not on a drawing-board. But none of them invalidates the premiss of the project, that social and personal change are essentially connected. The next task is to take a closer look at the object of the politics of everyday life, and consider how personality can be understood in terms consistent both with the psychodynamic arguments just traversed and the structural analysis of Part II.

NOTES

Socialization

(pp. 191–6). Debate in the 'sex role socialization' literature has mainly concerned the different mechanisms or paradigms of acquisition: useful reviews are by Constantinople (1979) and Cahill (1983). Though Cahill's 'social interactionist' paradigm is helpful in stressing the child's agency more than usual, this whole literature is contained within the framework criticized in the text. For Ellen Key's phrase and its context see W. F. Connell (1980), pp. 92 ff., and for the corporal punishment figures quoted, W. F. Connell et al. (1975).

Classical Psychoanalysis

(pp. 196–211). Quotations from Freud (1930), pp. 123–4, 132–3; Adler (1956), p. 55; Dinnerstein (1976), pp. 230–1; Freud (1918), p. 47. For the debate on the universality of the Oedipus complex see Parsons (1964), whose solution is incomplete but certainly along the right lines, and unfortunately neglected in the feminist psychoanalytic literature. The problem of the politics of psychoanalytic treatment raised by the Red Collective has recently been explored in great detail by Kovel (1981) who is more committed to therapy but also rather insensitive to gender.

Existential Psychoanalysis

(pp. 211–17). For the 'mystery in broad daylight' see Sartre (1958), p. 571. Other quotations: de Beauvoir (1972), pp. 79, 83. The notion of a 'collective project' is all too simple for the intricate analyses in Sartre's *Critique of Dialectical Reason* but is perhaps an allowable condensation for present purposes. Its full development would embrace the subject-matter of Part II of this book.

10

Personality as Practice

Personality, Society and Life History

Chapters 8 and 9 have described how structures of gender relations enter into personal life and shape personalities. The fact is clear, but how to understand it is more difficult. 'Enter into' is a metaphor, and we might ask just what is being 'entered'. Has personality some distinctive substance, as implied by the other familiar metaphor for these relationships, that personality is 'moulded' or 'shaped' by social pressure, like clay under a potter's hands?

The critique of socialization theory and the discussion of the 'project' in chapter 9 both imply that the answer is no. The components of personality traditionally discussed in psychology – attitudes, abilities, drives, repressions, fantasies and so on – are not separate from social interactions. On the one hand practices have a 'personality' dimension. It makes good sense, for instance, to talk of the characteristic emotional problems of particular social practices, such as teaching. (Indeed this is a theme in recent research on teachers.) On the other hand personality needs a social field for its realization. People can, of course, hide some aspect of themselves. (Teenage girls have often been advised to make sure they do not seem more clever than the boys they want to date.) But personality in general is not hidden; nor is deliberate hiding usually very successful. As Freud remarked about sexual motives in 'symptomatic acts', 'He that has eyes to see and ears to hear may convince himself that no mortal can keep a secret. If his lips are silent, he chatters with his finger-tips; betrayal oozes out of him at every pore.'

Here the argument on gender converges with the current rethinking of social psychology in texts like Rom Harré's *Social*

Being and *Personal Being*, Paul Secord and co-workers' *Explaining Human Behavior*, Edmund Sullivan's *A Critical Psychology* and the joint work by Julian Henriques and others, *Changing the Subject*. These theorists have tried to move beyond the approach that founds psychology on the category of the 'individual', beyond the belief that laboratory experiment is the paragon of methods, and beyond the conceptualization of social context as a 'variable' to be correlated with 'behaviour'. Instead this work implies a historical conception of the person. As Harré observes, the very idea of individual character and the self is the product of collectives, of particular societies. The approach emphasizes the situational meanings of action and explores how personal life is constructed through the play of social relations. In Sullivan's phrase, 'the person is person only as I-and-you'; the personal world *is* relational.

In the terms used in this book, personality has to be seen as social practice and not as an entity distinct from 'society'. Personality is what people do, just as social relations are what people do, and the doings are the same. Yet there is a difference which makes personality a coherent object of study. Personality is practice seen from a particular angle, which I will call the perspective of the life history. Psychologies of personality that have stressed the case study as the basic form of understanding are thus an important resource for social analysis. John Dollard's nearly forgotten *Criteria for the Life History* is a brilliant summary of early versions that demonstrates this point.

There is a strain of individualism in much case-history research, where dynamics are treated as wholly internal to the case. This amounts to seeing the life history as the only form in which practice can be understood. The structural and institutional analyses in Part II above show this is untenable for the analysis of gender. The most penetrating case-study research, including Dollard's own *Caste and Class in a Southern Town*, combines the logic of the life history with the logic of institutional analysis.

At least in our society, people experience themselves and their practice most readily in terms of a life trajectory, a personal past and a personal future. Personal time can also be conceived in terms of a 'life cycle', and a good deal of academic research on the family, growth and ageing is done in that framework. But history is not cyclical, and a personal history is not an unfolding. It is a construction, something made.

What is 'made', specifically, is the coherence, intelligibility, and liveability of one's social relationships through time. Sartre's notion of personal life as a 'unification', a making-into-a-unity, is important here. Without it, social analysis reduces a life to a collection of roles learnt, expectations enacted or structural locations occupied: Ralf Dahrendorf's *Homo Sociologicus*, the man-who-is-his-roles. Some of the recent work on the construction of subjects by discourses, influenced by Althusser and Foucault, comes very close to this conception.

In *Being and Nothingness* Sartre treated the life history as a unification with a single principle, the ramifying consequences of some initial, constitutive choice. I argued in chapter 9 that such a view over-simplifies the person and misses the importance of contradiction. Even on Sartre's model, initial choices may be multiple. More importantly, complexities of personal life arise from structural contradictions that go far beyond the particular person.

However much detail is known about a given life, personal life becomes unintelligible if the structural bases of practice are not kept in view. A striking demonstration is the attempt to document 'total personality' in a study already referred to, Robert White's *Lives in Progress*. In a monumental exercise in longitudinal method White followed three 'normal' upper-class Americans from their student days well into adulthood, applying a battery of psychological tests and collecting data from interviews and essays. The detail is remarkable; the insight resulting is remarkably small. Lacking organizing questions about structure, the study runs out into the sands of eclecticism and blandness, flavoured with a faint life-cycle ideology of 'natural growth'.

The contrast with Freud's study of an upper-class Russian, the 'Wolf Man', is notable. Not that Freud had a theory of social structure worth twopence, but as a therapist he was highly sensitive to structural effects in the dynamics of personal life. The 'Wolf Man' is a howling mass of contradictions, and his personality is contradictory because the elements of an emotional life offered him were impossible to work into a smooth and consistent whole. Obviously enough the class relations between peasants and landowners in pre-revolutionary Russia were in tension. The case history shows how these relations intersected with gender dynamics – ambivalences between husband and wife, divisions of labour among servants in childcare and housework, rivalries between girls and boys – to construct a household that was an emotional minefield for the small boy.

My experience of life-history interviews suggests that the conclusion about the contradictory bases of personal life might hold very generally. The materials offered a growing person are lumpy and indigestible; 'unification' is often hard and may be impossible. The evolving pattern of a person's life often involves disjunction, incoherence or schism. Sartre does not consider that the practice of unification, like all other practices, may fail. Some theorists even suggest that participation in contemporary society requires schism in the person. Laing in *The Politics of Experience* argues this way about 'normality' in a mad society, as do some feminist critiques of the front that has to be put up by conventional femininity.

Lives are not monads closed off from others. People experience themselves as having shared pasts and sharing the present; 'for we are members one of another', as the Apostle Paul wrote. (The metaphor is stronger in seventeenth-century English: the phrase means roughly 'we are each others' limbs'.) This sharing may be as intimate as the story of a marriage or a love affair never spoken of beyond the two concerned, or as public as the proceedings of parliament.

Collective practice is not reducible to a sum of individual practices. In a strict sense there is no such thing as 'individual practice' at all; the phrase is an abstraction from a tissue of relational conduct. Even masturbation involves socially constructed fantasies, techniques of arousal and a kind of minimal society in which you are the object of your own cathexis.

So a personal life is a path through a field of practices which are following a range of collective logics, and are responding to a range of structural conditions which routinely intersect and often contradict each other. It is no wonder that theories of personal life which reify 'the individual' and his or her features – such as trait theories of personality and the scalar conceptions of gender discussed in chapter 8 – give very little grip on reality. The structure of personality is not the structure of an object. It is a particular unification of diverse and often contradictory practices.

Thus the concept of personality is logically co-ordinate with the concept of an 'institution', being another empirical unification of practices. The gender analysis of personality will explore the same menu of structures as the gender analysis of institutions in chapter 6.

To some extent it already does. Analyses in relation to the structure of cathexis are very familiar in classical psychoanalysis. An analysis in relation to the structure of power has been sketched by Shulamith Firestone, and in another context by the psychoanalysts of colonialism, Octave Mannoni and Frantz Fanon. Personality analysis in terms of the structure of labour is the least common, though it exists in embryo in the work of the German psychologist Frigga Haug and the theoretical work of Edmund Sullivan in Canada.

A pattern of practice is likely to appear frail when formulated in terms of its constitutive contradictions and dialectics, tensions and layerings and historical transformations. If it keeps one shape over a long period that is because a lot of energy has been invested in keeping it that way. The Prince family in chapter 1 shows one version of this. Another is shown by the business and professional families found in our study, and by J. M. and R. E. Pahl in *Managers and their Wives*. These are families whose personal lives are kept in order by the immense labours of a wife, who appears to have no career but whose work is the absolute condition of her husband's apparently 'individual' success.

But it is also important to register the potential resilience of a given organization of practice. Where it constitutes dominant social interests, it constructs motives to expend a great deal of energy in defence of the status quo. The depth of anti-feminism among men, discussed by William J. Goode, is a case in point. Personality does not constitute social interests, but it embodies personal relations to social interests which may act powerfully as motives: defences, identifications, commitments and fears. Where these interlock in related lives, a pattern may result that is proof against severe stresses. Stable marriages are perhaps the most familiar example.

Personality dynamics are not the secret key to society, as the first generation of Freudians like Ernest Jones supposed. Nor are they irrelevant, as sociological structuralism supposes. In the context of a theory of practice, personality appears as one of the major sites of history and politics. It is connected with other sites like institutions, but has its own configurations. The rest of this chapter will explore some of these configurations and try to map the sexual politics that happen on this site.

The Historical Dynamic in Personality

The historicity of personality has been recognized in social theory mainly by constructing historical typologies of character. A particular character type is supposed to be dominant at one period of history and then is swept aside in favour of a new type in a new epoch. The classic sequence is David Riesman's 'tradition-directed', 'inner-directed' and 'other-directed' character types in *The Lonely Crowd*. Other typologies are Charles Reich's 'Consciousness I, II and III'; John Carroll's 'puritan', 'paranoid' and 'remissive'; and countless renditions of the 'traditional' versus 'modern' theme. Paul Hoch's typology of masculinity in *White Hero, Black Beast* has an alternation instead of a sequence. His masculine character-types, 'puritan' and 'playboy', chase each other through some 3,000 years of history.

A subtler approach can be found in the work of the Frankfurt school on the psychological bases of fascism. Erich Fromm in *Fear of Freedom* argued that the authoritarian character structure was a psychological solution to problems of alienation created by the economic and cultural development of capitalism – but not the only one. In *The Authoritarian Personality*, as already noticed, the rigid and prejudiced character is contrasted with others produced in the same historical setting. The general argument in chapter 9 for the existence of multiple paths of gender formation suggests a multiple pattern of personality at the end.

The historicity of personality can be understood as the reconfiguring, by the dynamic of social relations, of the points of tension in personality development and the politics of personal life. It is not necessary to suppose a succession of dominant character types to analyze changes in motivation and personality organization. This can be done by recognizing emergent sets of pressures and possibilities within which the actual diversity of personality is composed.

The application of this approach to the analysis of sexual character is clear in principle, complicated in practice. I would like to illustrate both the complexities and possibilities with a line of thought about the recent history of femininity.

Bim Andrews, whose autobiography was quoted in chapter 8, posed the question 'which was the right way to live?'. Though the alternative femininities she perceived are interesting in themselves,

the most notable fact of all was that she saw them as a *choice*.
Bim's world did not present her with one pattern as her natural
character or inevitable fate. As the daughter of a domestic servant
and coming to adulthood in Cambridge in the 1920s, she did not
grow up in a hotbed of feminism. Nevertheless the taken-for-
grantedness of gender relations and femininity had been disrupted
in southern Britain during the previous generation. Agitation by the
women's suffrage movement was only its most visible expression.
Others were the literary debates over the 'new woman', the re-
employment of working-class women in heavy industry during
World War I and the mobilization of some groups of women
workers in unions and in the co-operative movement. Perhaps
most important, there was now a mass education system which
working-class girls had to attend at the elementary levels, and
through which a few had access to secondary schooling. One was
Bim Andrews, who 'endured the acute embarrassment of always
being top of the class' and who stayed at school till she was
fourteen and a half. This experience seems to have combined with
her mother's 'firm intention to keep me out of domestic service'
to distance Bim from the conventions of the 'embryo wives and
mothers' who were her schoolmates.

Her experience was exceptional but it was not isolated. It was
part of a historic shift in the construction of femininity in the
richer parts of the capitalist world. The same shift can be traced
in some detail in Australia as a result of recent work by sociologists
and social historians including Kerreen Reiger, Jill Matthews,
Michael Gilding, Ann Game and Rosemary Pringle. This research
documents a complex of institutional changes over the first half
of the twentieth century affecting gender relations in the family,
state, labour market and professions. Among them are exactly the
changes that affected Bim Andrews: the expansion of girls'
education and the redefinition of its content; changes in the
composition of households and the domestic division of labour
which soon obliterated 'service' as a mass occupation; and the
increasing availability of office work for women.

In combination, these institutional changes redefined the issues
in young women's lives that needed to be resolved in the
construction of femininity in adolescence and early adulthood.
Two issues appear particularly important. The first was the choice
of vocation, which now replaced the issue of resignation to women's
lot versus protest against it. 'The new woman' was essentially a

woman with a vocation outside the home. But the main issue was not a choice between jobs, rather about them. The key development was the construction in the early decades of the twentieth century of the 'housewife' as a vocation. Among other things this involved the growth of 'domestic science' as a segregated curriculum for girls in schools. Whether married women worked for wages or not had previously been an issue of respectability (to the nineteenth century labour aristocracy and small-business owners, withdrawing a wife from earning was a mark of the husband's success), or of simple need. It now became a question of rejecting the vocation of housewife.

The second issue was one of competition with men. In a sense this had been around much longer, as shown by the expulsion of women workers from mining and heavy manufacturing during the nineteenth century. Nevertheless the doctrine of 'separate spheres', which as Susan Magarey suggests had gone some way to rationalizing such moves, was under pressure at the turn of the century. Girls, for instance, were conspicuously successful in schooling. In Australia their participation rates in secondary schooling were higher than boys' at all ages from fourteen to seventeen, in the first decade of the twentieth century.

These developments did not automatically construct a new femininity. But they certainly redefined the field within which sexual character was constructed and relations between different kinds of femininity worked out. The extraordinary celebration of the normative nuclear family in mid-century, the apotheosis of the housewife described by Game and Pringle in their essay 'The Making of the Australian Family', was an attempt to resolve these issues in a new model of emphasized femininity. The issue of vocation would be resolved by conscious choice of home-making as a path in life, even as a 'career', a concept stressed by magazines like *Readers Digest* targeted on the more affluent housewives. The issue of competition could be resolved by women withdrawing from men's sphere, compensated by capital investment and cultural boosting in their own, especially in the form of new technology like electric refrigerators. Hence the media emphasized the *modern* housewife as something new. At the same time a new sphere of life was defined that was very deliberately shared, from which competition was consciously drained. The 1950s popular literature on marriage laid heavy emphasis on 'companionate' marriage, 'togetherness' and doing things 'as a family'.

At one level this was a model pushed on women by social interests which stood to gain from such a resolution, not least the domestic appliance industry, using new techniques of mass communication and persuasion. At another level it was a genuine resolution of the issues of vocation and competition which many women made their own in good faith.

It was a resolution that proved historically unstable. By the 1970s women who had grown up in the 1950s were the main force in the new feminism. In *The Mermaid and the Minotaur* Dorothy Dinnerstein offers a wonderful account of the psychodynamics of this development in the United States. She stresses the ambivalences of liberal parenting that produced the men of the 1960s New Left, able to break with the state and establishment but not with their masculine prerogatives; and the women who, once radicalized in the campus and anti-war movements, would carry the challenge through to their own exclusion from political power.

A somewhat more jaundiced view of the dialectic producing feminism is offered by Faye Taylor, an Australian teacher interviewed during our research in schools. At one point she cast her mind back over her own family history:

> My grandmother was the controlling factor in her household. She decided everything that would be done, and I think this was because she was the more intelligent of the two. Her husband worked very hard but she directed him. Which meant that she was in control. My mother from the time she married was, I suppose, controlled in that her finances were limited by what her husband gave her. But she had complete independence in what she wanted to do, how she wanted to use her time, what she could do within that. So that she always did what she wanted to, remembering that her responsibilities came first. So I wouldn't say that she was ever a second-class citizen. But from my own generation, we could do whatever we wanted to do, remembering that when we left school and got a job, there were certain jobs that were not open to girls. The ones which were open to girls were very limited in pay and promotion, simply because it was expected that when girls married they would stop work. That has opened up. But with opening it up, there's been more of a definition of roles. Instead of being individual in your own right, you are now pushed into a stereotype *inferior* model, instead of being a *different* model. And in fighting for equality, some of the so-called double standards have been accepted where they never really existed before.

This very suggestive passage implies that feminism (liberal feminism strictly, the only kind most teachers are familiar with) is a kind of 'regulation' of femininity in the Donzelot–Foucault sense. Breaking down separate spheres has meant a bringing-under-control, as women are subjected to direct comparison with men, while being disadvantaged in the comparison from the start.

Whether Faye is correct or not on this point, her family history does illustrate the emergence of competition with men as an issue in the formation of femininity. Though there is no 'feminist personality', it seems likely that the femininities formed in the historical dynamic that created contemporary feminism share a position on this issue, rejecting 'withdrawal from competition' as a formative personal strategy. It is also clear that other femininities which do accept this strategy are still produced. Gabrielle Carey and Kathy Lette's autobiographical novel *Puberty Blues* nicely captures this polarity. The book ends with the two heroines, who like other girls have spent their time on the beach looking decorative and waiting for the board-riding boyfriends to come back out of the surf, buying a cheap surfboard and heading into the waves themselves. The other girls stay on the beach.

Politics of Personality

To speak of personality as an object of politics is to tread on dangerous ground; the issue of totalitarianism is very close. Authoritarian regimes of all persuasions in the twentieth century have made sustained attempts to mould the upbringing and outlooks of their citizens. Liberal critics of 'totalitarianism' such as Hannah Arendt have their most effective moments when documenting and rejecting the invasion of personal life by the party–state.

Yet liberal regimes have done the same kind of job. In *One Dimensional Man* Marcuse described the general process of cultural and psychological manipulation in the United States. The argument can be pinned down to particular institutions, such as schools. Mass schooling in the United States, from the late twentieth century to the present, has been characterized by relentless propaganda in favour of the regime and against its opponents. As a small example I cite some chapter headings from a history textbook used in my (relatively liberal) high-school class in New York in 1959:

UNIT NINE (1920–1945): AMERICANS DEFEND DEMOC-
RACY IN A TROUBLED WORLD
28   The nation faces the threat of world depression
29   The United States becomes a friendly neighbor
30   Americans fight round the globe in World War II
UNIT TEN (1945–now): AMERICAN DEMOCRACY MEETS
THE COMMUNIST THREAT
31   Modern Russia arises to threaten the free world
32   The United States leads the free world in the West
33   The United States leads the free world in Asia
34   Americans practise and protect democracy at home
YOU ARE AMERICA

It doesn't leave much to the imagination – nor much room for unauthorized attitudes. Beyond the obvious propaganda content, mass schooling in the United States over a long period has attempted to shape attitudes and work habits, and to sort, classify and specialize its pupils, in response to the policies of the central state and business leadership.

So a politics of personality exists in the 'free world' as well. On the argument of this chapter, it must. Personality being a field of the dynamics of social relations, its construction must be affected by the formation of social interests, the functioning of institutions and the mobilization of power. The early women's liberation slogan 'the personal is political', intended mainly to validate political discussion of sexuality and domestic work, expressed a general truth.

To make this connection is not to welcome state intervention. There are good reasons for resisting the state as we now find it, and many of its policies and mechanisms for influencing people. Along with several millions of other children I was taught a pack of lies about American history. Such a practice should be rejected as noxious to growing minds and dangerous for the future – as it has proved to be, with the terrifying growth of American chauvinism in the 1980s. The point is that criticisms of such practices have to be conducted on the merits of the case. The idea that we should, or can, draw a general line between politics and personal life is logically misconceived.

The New Right doctrine of 'small government' and 'rolling back the state' does not end or seriously reduce state influence on personal life. It simply changes its direction. As Elizabeth Wilson, Lois Bryson and Martin Mowbray argue, cutting back on welfare and 'returning' care of the sick, elderly or troubled to the 'community' or 'the family', in reality means loading extra unpaid work onto women. The sexual division of labour and inequalities of gender are intensified. Cutting the 'burden' of taxation does not increase freedom for citizens in general. It increases the advantages of groups who benefit from income being distributed through the market (capitalists as against workers, employed as against unemployed, men as against women) at the expense of those whose welfare depends on distribution of income through the state.

The real question is not whether politics can be removed from personal life, but what kind of politics invests personal life and how far it can be democratic or egalitarian. Most important is the political question as to whether personality can be formed and reconstructed 'from below'.

Radical movements have, by and large, been much less interested in these questions than authoritarian movements, the state and business. But in the last twenty years the problem has come into focus in radical politics, especially in sexual politics. The methods available for working on them are complex and not well defined. They have mostly been evolved by trial and error. Still, a good deal of experience has now accumulated, which needs examination if we are to judge the prospects of a radical sexual politics.

The most widespread has been the 'consciousness-raising group' (CR group) developed in the early years of women's liberation. It was not a completely new invention; aspects can be found in the 'affinity groups' of anarchism, in sewing-circles and other traditions of women's informal organization and in American group-therapy techniques. But the combination was new, the needs it met were general and the technique spread rapidly. In the early 1970s the women's liberation movement in countries like the United States, Canada, Britain and Australia could well be regarded as a network of CR groups which coalesced in partial and often fleeting ways for public politics.

The CR group aimed at the reconstruction of femininity in two main ways. First was discussion and re-evaluation of the past and present experiences of the women in them. Doing this in a group meant that everyday relationships, with men, children and other women had to be thought through as 'being-for-others', their everyday logic no longer presupposed. It also meant that there was support for 'speaking bitterness' (to use the Chinese phrase) about men, saying and thinking hostile things that were censored or suppressed in everyday life. A CR group might set an agenda of working systematically through oppressions in different areas of life. This would call attention to the political dimension of practices and symbols that normally go without comment, such as housework, dress and habits of speech. The overall result was to disrupt the taken-for-grantedness of many of the practices that constitute conventional femininities.

The second step was to support new practices that might displace the ones thus disrupted. The CR group became a forum for talking about what to do in households, in sexual relationships, in bringing up children and in public politics. In many cases the group itself became a new friendship network, with the members going to entertainments, travelling, sometimes working together. In this way the CR group merged into the construction of feminist communities as the 1970s wore on.

As a technique for the reconstruction of femininity this had several important strengths. It was flexible, easy to start, inexpensive and easy to manage in an egalitarian way. It contrasted sharply with both traditional party politics and traditional psychotherapy. It could deal with work as well as domestic life and sexual relations. It was easy to disband if things went wrong.

It also had some significant drawbacks, which were slower to emerge. It was good at dealing with what was common in women's experiences, less good with what divided them. If serious conflicts arose there was little to prevent the CR group simply splitting up. Like the 'talking cure' of psychoanalysis, it suited the highly educated and affluent and never spread far among working-class women. The exclusion of men, which was a condition of much that the CR groups did, meant that heterosexual relationships were likely to be worked at from only one end. CR technique had little power to reach unconscious processes or constitutive commitments, and might therefore work on emotional issues only at a surface level or within narrow limits. One such limit, pointed out by lesbian feminists, was a widespread failure in CR groups to question heterosexuality.

The process of 'coming out' as gay is a form of reconstruction that contrasts sharply with CR work. In the collective coming-out at the end of the 1960s, the low-key, even covert, strategy of seeking tolerance and law reform that had characterized earlier homosexual politics was replaced by a highly visible celebration of gayness. The public demonstration of 'gay pride' went along with a playfulness about gender, a subversion and recombination of elements – radical drag, gay weddings, pink boiler suits and so on – which gave an air of carnival to many gay liberation activities. Public celebration, for instance in the Mardi Gras in Sydney, has remained an essential part of homosexual politics.

Coming out individually is less spectacular but still involves a visible break. It means repudiation of a whole history of interactions – in families, workplaces, the street – that were predicated on an assumption of heterosexuality. Nothing as drastic is implied in CR work. Two things moderate the drama of the act. First, 'coming out' is not done once and for all, like a wedding; there is no Registrar of Births, Deaths and Comings-Out. As autobiographies make clear, coming out to friends is different from coming out to workmates, and both are different from coming out to one's parents and other relations. They may be done at different times and with very different results. Second, declaring oneself gay, in whatever setting, can be only one moment in a process. It may result in major shifts in relationships, but even so has to be followed by making the new situation work. Friendship networks, political practices and sexual relationships have to be constructed on new foundations.

In this sense 'coming out' inverts the order of things in CR groups; a personal reconstruction has to occur, or at least be well advanced, before social support can be generated. The social support is variable in the extreme. Coming out in a supportive workplace may be easy and enriching. In a hostile one it probably means losing the job. In some families the result is easy acceptance, in others appalling emotional trauma, depending on the interaction with parents' masculinity and femininity.

In another respect the process is closer to CR: the extension of reconstructed personal networks into a gay 'community'. There were of course networks of homosexual people before gay liberation, whose stories are gradually being retrieved by gay historians. The 1970s saw a qualitative change in their conditions of existence and those of the discreet businesses based on them. Gay communities developed on a considerable scale in cities like San Francisco and Sydney, with a rapid growth in the number, size and visibility of the businesses servicing them. 'Gay capitalism' emerged and gay businessmen became a force in homosexual politics, with an influence comparable to that of the radicals who had launched the gay liberation movement.

This development sharpened the question implicit in 'coming out' from the start, what exactly one was claiming to be. Dilemmas about the nature of homosexual identity have been mentioned in chapter 7. For both sexes coming out as gay meant repudiating central features of one conventional sexual character. Did this mean claiming the other? Attempting to mix masculine and feminine characteristics risked dissolving the category of homosexuality itself. Where then was gay pride, and the basis of movement and community? Though theorists like David Fernbach insisted on gay men's effeminacy and Mario Mieli argued for the transsexual basis of gayness, the drift among homosexual men during the 1970s was increasingly to resolve these tensions by defining a gay masculinity. The 'clone' style of the late 1970s and early 1980s was its most visible crystallization, the moustache, T-shirt and tight jeans proclaiming a male body. This in turn produced tensions with lesbian women, some of whom have found this uncomfortably like a claim to the privileges of conventional masculinity.

In one dimension the deconstructionist argument does continue the logic of 'coming out'. To come out is to repudiate the business of keeping up a front of heterosexuality. This front is not likely to be a trivial part of personality, and may involve an elaborate 'false-self' system like those described by Laing (see the case of 'David' discussed in chapter 9). One cannot simply obliterate such a structure of personality. Nor will it be replaced by some natural gayness that wells up from the inner self. The deconstructionist argument extends the critique of the false self to the constructed selves that replace it, which equally may freeze the person in outmoded and repressive postures.

But 'coming out' was not just a gesture of personal reconstruction. It was also an attempt to reach out, to create solidarity. A thorough deconstruction of gay identity would undermine this, and risk dismantling the personal and collective resources for dealing with shared problems and combating the hostility that gay people still meet. The spread of AIDS, creating a need to support those with the disease, to work out strategies to halt its spread, and to deal with scaremongering media, shows how important these resources are. As long as the definition of homosexuality is sustained in the

larger structure of gender relations, gay people are not exactly free
to adopt or deny it as they please.

In the face of this the reconstruction of personal life is always
done under pressure and at risk. CR groups were vulnerable to
criticism that they did not go deep enough. The personality politics
of 'coming out' likewise include strong motives to limit the amount
and visibility of change.

The emergence of women's liberation and gay liberation challenged not only the power of heterosexual men but also the worth
of their masculinity. While most ignored or dismissed the challenge,
some were affected strongly, an experience particularly well
described by Vic Seidler in his essay 'Men and Feminism'. A
historic moment was reached on the American Left when one of
the authors of *Unbecoming Men* saw his girlfriend head off for one
of the early feminist conferences and realized he was no longer
where the action was. The resulting essay, 'Women Together and
Me Alone', is a classic of mixed emotions. After some early
experiments with mixed CR groups, feminism more or less told
the men to get their own house in order. The tangled public
politics of the resulting 'men's movement' will be discussed in
chapter 12; the point of interest here is the two practices it
developed for the reconstruction of masculinity at a personal level.

The first was very simple in conception. The idea of a CR group
was borrowed from feminism and applied to men. A group of men
would meet regularly over a period of months to discuss their lives
and emotions. Such 'men's groups' were central to the anti-sexist
men's movement through the 1970s and some are running now.
Documents such as *Unbecoming Men* and the narrative of a men's
group in Warren Farrell's *The Liberated Man* show that even in the
early days their focus was divided. In these and later accounts by
Paul Morrison and others, three main themes emerge: recognizing
and working on participants' sexist attitudes and behaviour towards
women; discussing their own masculinity, how it was formed in
growing up, and how it constricts the expression of their emotions
and limits the depth of their relationships; and providing emotional
support to each other.

This contained both a political project intended to support
feminism and a therapeutic project intended to repair the damage
bad gender relations did to men. They were not necessarily
consistent, and may even have been contradictory. Certainly the
political project of rooting out the sexism in masculinity has proved

intensely difficult. Work in men's groups on how one oppressed women was very different from work in women's groups on how one was oppressed. It provoked guilt rather than anger, a reaction intensified by the accusatory tone of radical feminism's interactions with men. A massive sense of guilt runs through mid-1970s literature such as Jon Snodgrass's collection *For Men Against Sexism*. It seems likely that guilt and frustration between them destroyed many of the groups set up.

Frustration was a likely outcome and is obvious in Andrew Tolson's discussion of mid-1970s men's groups in Britain. While women's CR groups fed into the construction of wider networks, counter-sexist men's groups made it more difficult to work in men's networks outside. On the one hand the routine and often vicious sexism in masculine milieux became hard to handle at a personal level. On the other hand, sticking to the task of raising issues about sexism and challenging patriarchal practices was likely to result in a drastic loss of credibility. A man pursuing issues about women's interests was easily defined as a fool, slightly mad, or a pervert.

An easier answer to the sense of guilt was to deny the oppression of women; better still, to claim that men are equally oppressed. This path was taken in the United States by authors such as Farrell and Jack Nichols, whose *Men's Liberation* presents the reform of masculinity as a simple parallel to the feminist reconstruction of femininity. The sex-role interpretation of gender relations made this very easy: if a woman's sex role was oppressive for the person in it, a man's sex role was also likely to be. The appropriate response was to try to break out of the stereotypes and repair the psychic damage they caused.

The result was a practice that might be called 'masculinity therapy', which rapidly outgrew the anti-sexist men's movement. Some was undertaken in self-directed men's groups, but more occurred in settings like encounter groups, retreats, courses, clinics and centres, and one-to-one counselling and psychotherapy. The defining feature of these settings was the presence of therapists with a message about masculinity. Their writings, such as Herb Goldberg's *The Hazards of Being Male* and Albert Ellis's *Sex and the Liberated Man*, make clear that the message is one that depoliticizes gender. Guilt is treated as irrational or obsolete. The oppression of women is treated as an illusion or an excess of role rigidity. Homosexuality is, as far as humanly possible, ignored. The main thing to be overcome is men's inhibitions and inexpressiveness which leads them into emotional binds.

I have seen no evidence whatever about the success or failure of this therapeutic program. But it is clear what its point is: not contesting inequality but modernizing heterosexual masculinity. The discontent many men feel as holders of power under challenge is to be relieved by a change of personal style – a change of tactics in dealings with women, perhaps a changed self-concept – without any challenge to the institutional arrangements that produce their power. Perhaps the most interesting thing about this business is that it often requires a therapist's assistance.

It is easy to conclude from the difficulties in these attempts at reconstructing sexual character that the politics of personality would be best left alone. The trouble is that it will not be left alone by others. The New Right, for instance, is actively constructing aggressive, dominant and violent models of masculinity for adolescents and children. *Rocky* has led to *Rambo* and *Rambo* to *Rocky IV*, nicely keyed in with Reagan's 'Star Wars' campaign. A large marketing program is currently pushing exceptionally violent toys into young boys' hands, like the 'Masters of the Universe' whose he-man models seem to be based on images from the Nazi cartoonist Mjölnir. It is difficult to justify abandoning the field of personality politics to influences like these.

More positively, the experiences sketched in this section show that there are several ways in which a self-help reconstruction of personality can at least be started. Whether it goes very far depends on other people; for this experience also suggests a strong connection between personal change and social movements in sexual politics. Chapter 12 will come back to the issue in the collective context.

NOTES

Personality, Society and Life History

(pp. 219–23). Quotations from Freud (1905), pp. 77–8; Sullivan (1984), p. 55; Paul in Ephesians 4:25. On the emotional dimension of teaching see among others Otto (1982). The approach to the life history suggested here was worked out in the research for *Making the Difference* and especially *Teachers' Work*. A recent revival of interest in the life history as social science method – see Bertaux (1981) and Plummer

(1983) – looks promising. But it stops short of the most important body of life-history research, psychoanalysis. And it has learnt nothing from the most profound theorist of the method, Sartre.

Historical Dynamic in Personality

(pp. 224–8). Girls' participation rates in schooling from Schools Commission (1975). Faye Taylor quoted from *Teachers' Work*, p. 188.

Politics of Personality

(p. 228–36). Textbook chapter headings from Casner and Gabriel (1955). For the 'hidden curriculum' and business pressures see Bowles and Gintis (1976). Accounts of CR groups can be found in Allen (1970) and Pogrebin (1973). Discussions of coming out in Wolfe and Stanley (1980), Silverstein (1982) and Clark (1983).

Part IV
Sexual Politics

11

Sexual Ideology

Discourse and Practice

When Mary Wollstonecraft wrote to vindicate the rights of women, it was mainly questions of ideology that she had in mind: morals, manners, education and religion. These topics have been constant friends in the literature of gender since, and few authors have doubted the power of ideology. Even so vigorous a materialist as Emma Goldman was content to explain the difficulty of unionizing women this way:

> The woman considers her position as worker transitory, to be thrown aside for the first bidder. That is why it is infinitely harder to organize women than men. 'Why should I join a union? I am going to get married, to have a home.' Has she not been taught from infancy to look upon that as her ultimate calling?

In contemporary theory too there is a strong tendency to make ideology *the* site of sexual politics. Julia Kristeva writes of the 'inseparable conjunction of the sexual and the symbolic' as the terrain of the new feminism. Juliet Mitchell and Roberta Hamilton treat patriarchy as the realm of ideology in contrast to a realm of production governed by class relations. A vigorous literature drawing on French semiotics and discourse theory analyses patriarchal symbolism and language as, effectively, a self-contained system.

Some notable research on the symbolization of women and men has resulted, moving beyond the familiar research on stereotypes to the implicit structure of whole discourses about gender. The most penetrating, such as Jo Spence's 'What do People do all Day?' and Wendy Hollway's 'Gender Difference and the Production of Subjectivity' go on to trace change and contradiction in the process of symbolic representation.

The results of these researches are important. But there are serious difficulties with a theoretical program that gives an absolute priority to ideology or to semiotic analysis and treats discourse as a closed system. Lynne Segal remarks on the drift towards idealism in recent feminist theory, and how an overemphasis on matters like language marginalizes grass-roots concerns of the feminist movement. From a theoretical viewpoint too, much of this writing appears startlingly one-sided. Neglecting institutions, economics and the routines of politics means that analyses of ideology are often parked on top of crude categorical assumptions about power and the relations between person and group. No matter how sophisticated the analysis of symbolization much of its value must then be lost.

The way to resolve this is not only to give due attention to institutions, economics and so forth. It is essential to recognize that discourse and symbolization are themselves practices, which are structurally connected with other practices and have a great deal in common with other forms of practice. They too have to be analysed with attention to context, institutionalization and group formation. It is important to consider what groups engage in them and how specialists in these kinds of practice are socially constituted within gender relations. This is why I have delayed the analysis of ideology, despite its prominence in current debate about gender, until after a framework for the structural and personal analysis of gender has been established.

The practical context and institutionalization of language is more than a question of 'pragmatics', the application or use of an existing syntactic and semantic structure. Practice is constitutive of syntax and semantics too, when considered over historical time. For instance, historians of language have noted the increasing sexism of the English language in the early modern period, as in the use of masculine pronouns to refer to men and women together. As Casey Miller and Kate Swift argue, this has to be seen in the context of the historical emergence of intellectuals (Dr Johnson being one) able to act as 'authorities' on language and impose sexist usage as standard. One of the major tools invented was the dictionary. It is notable that early dictionaries were in part directed to the education of women, as a substitute for schooling.

The importance of social context in the 'uptake' of culture, in the appropriation and use of elements of ideology, can be documented in a wide range of situations. Angela McRobbie's research on the 'culture of femininity' in Britain is an especially convincing example because her theory is structuralist. The field-work shows very clearly how the impoverished, constricted and oppressive situation of working-class teenage girls is made tolerable by a cultural practice exaggerating femininity and romanticizing marriage as the main goal in life.

Studies of families similarly show ideology in context among adults. Pauline Hunt's research on the division of labour in an English village shows how 'the situation itself breeds traditionalism' for wives who do full-time childcare at home. They are obliged to adapt to their husbands' timetables, are isolated from the public world and intimidated by politics, and find that childbearing has become the central experience of life. Yet in some ways ideology is able to override the logic of other practices. The belief that husbands are breadwinners is sustained in families where the wife earns a wage. Even when she earns more than he does, the ideology is not criticized but the couple's situation is – 'it's degrading for a man.'

It is, however, in studies of workplaces that the interplay of situation and ideology is clearest. Michael Korda's description of New York office life in *Male Chauvinism* shows how sexist ideology is embedded in management and supervisory practices, such as promotion of staff and the segmentation of tasks, and acts as a discursive rationalization of inequality. In this setting, Korda notes, the shift of feminist argument onto issues of sexuality (for example in Germaine Greer's *The Female Eunuch*) came as a relief to men, as it excused corporate executives from facing the issues that were the hard ones to them – about money. The study of an insurance office in Britain by Collinson and Knights, described in chapter 5, underlines the amount of work that goes into construct-ing and defending sexist ideology.

The most complex and sophisticated account of the maintenance of sexual ideology in the workplace is Cynthia Cockburn's *Brothers*. Here the analysis of ideology is set in the context of the historical development of the British printing industry, from which women were expelled some generations ago. The ideology of the 'natural' weakness of women and their unsuitability for work as compositors is thus a suppression of history as well as a rationalization of present practice. The collective practice of the compositors is now

being undermined by drastic technological change, and with it the
traditional justifications of the sexual division of labour. Cockburn
documents the passing of a particular form of sexual ideology,
traditional patriarchalism, while the institutional bases of men's
power in these workplaces, the control of management, unions
and training, remain. New rationalizations, such as the masculine
mystique of high technology, are imperfect substitutes.

Parallel evidence of process and tension in sexual ideology can
be found in research on schools. In the literature on sex roles,
schools are frequently discussed as an 'agency of socialization'
impinging on children. They are also workplaces, with a work-
force divided on gender lines. Recent research on teachers shows
a good deal of involvement in issues of sexual politics. Teachers
are one of the main occupational groups to be influenced by the
growth of the new feminism; their reactions range from strong
endorsement to bitter hostility. In many schools the result is an
active negotiation, sometimes turning into open conflict, about
issues of curriculum, promotion, sexual harassment and so on. A
school's whole policy may be made over. A case in point is the
private secondary school for girls, 'Auburn College', mentioned in
chapter 8. This school was repositioning itself towards the
professional labour market and revamping its curriculum to
emphasize maths and sciences. A changed definition of femininity
was at issue in almost every aspect of the school's educational
policy.

Such evidence does not imply that ideology can be reduced to
economics or institutional arrangements, nor that ideology is to
be contrasted with a 'material' world. It does imply that ideology
has to be seen as things people do, and that ideological practice
has to be seen as occurring in, and responding to, definite contexts.
Some ideological practice is very plainly work. The school
curriculum, for instance, is a labour process for the teachers as
well as a definition of the pupils' learning. To understand it fully
requires an investigation of the social structure of the workplace
and the political economy of the industry, as well as its connections
with patterns of ideology in other milieux.

These considerations lead to an approach to sexual ideology
that is closer to the tradition of the sociology of knowledge than
it is to contemporary theories of discourse. There are some well-
recognized difficulties with this approach. Some versions of the
'sociology of knowledge' are reductionist, presenting ideology as a

reflex of social interest. Much of the sociology of knowledge takes a rather crude approach to the internal structure of ideas and has little to say about the process of symbolization. Finally, most of the sociology of knowledge has been based on a class analysis of social structure and ignores gender completely.

None of these problems is insoluble. Reductionism can be avoided, not by claims for the autonomy of ideological practice, but by consistently seeing it as practice, ontologically on a par with any other practice and equally involved in the constitution of social interests. Some classic researches in the sociology of knowledge, such as Georg Lukács' analysis of reification and European philosophy, and Lucien Goldmann's analysis of Jansenism, are very concerned with the internal structure of ideology. And there is a notable proof that the sociology-of-knowledge approach can be effectively applied to gender: Viola Klein's *The Feminine Character*, which appeared as long ago as 1946.

The point is not to apply a precast 'sociology of knowledge' to the subject-matter of gender but to use methods generated in that tradition to expand the social theory of gender. In what follows I draw partly on analyses of discourse and symbolization to characterize ideological practice; and partly on ideology theory and the sociology of knowledge to raise questions about the contexts of the production of sexual ideology, its consequences for the gender order, and the social character of its producers.

Ideological Processes

Gender relations involve the structuring of social practice around sex and sexuality. The commonest process in sexual ideology involves collapsing that structure, merging the elements into one by 'naturalizing' social practice.

The interpretation of gender relations as natural facts is extraordinarily widespread. Sexual divisions of labour are constantly interpreted this way. Cockburn, for instance, notes how women were firmly believed to be naturally incapable of handling the machinery of printing, in the teeth of the fact that women actually had done so. In discussions of the division of labour in childcare women's natural desire to mother children is almost always taken for granted. The mechanism operates equally powerfully on the structure of cathexis. Heterosexual attraction is

constantly interpreted as natural – the 'attraction of opposites' –
and socially forbidden relationships, especially homosexual, are
interpreted as 'unnatural'. Even the structure of power is naturalized, for instance in sociobiology, though this seems less insistent
than with the other two structures.

The profoundly political character of this process becomes
apparent when quite opposite social relations are 'naturalized' in
different times and places. For instance women were treated as
naturally frail in European polite culture in the eighteenth and
nineteenth centuries, naturally tough in most peasant cultures. At
times the mechanism of naturalization is used in an argument for
social change, for instance the suffrage movement's argument that
the realm of politics needed an injection of women's natural
qualities of compassion and purity. Some contemporary eco-
feminism is very close to this. Nevertheless the main effect of
naturalization is conservative; progressive uses of it risk being
incorporated. To interpret social relations as natural is, fundamentally, to suppress their historicity. To do that is to close off the
possibility of human practice recreating humanity. Verena Stolcke's
and Marie de Lepervanche's studies of the 'naturalization' of
inequality show close connections between this process in relation
to gender and in relation to other forms of social inequality such
as racism. Indeed one becomes a condition of the other. As Stolcke
notes, biologism leads to a drive to control women's sexuality in
the name of racial purity.

Naturalization, then, is not a naive mistake about what biological
science can and cannot explain. At a collective level it is a highly
motivated ideological practice which constantly overrides the
biological facts. Nature is appealed to for justification more than
for explanation. To be able to justify, nature itself must be got in
order – simplified, schematized and moralized.

Naturalization thus implies a second basic process in sexual
ideology, the cognitive purification of the world of gender. Its
most familiar form is the stereotyping documented in media studies
such as Patricia Edgar's *Media She*. Real practices are messy and
complicated, ideological representations of them squeaky-clean.
The families in television advertisements are all happy, their
fathers are all employed, their mothers just love housework. The
'girls' dancing on the screen all have long legs, white teeth, ladder-
resistant stockings and are certainly free this evening. Children's
books, as Bob Dixon shows at length in *Catching them Young*, are

as packed with stereotyped images of gender as they are with messages about race and class.

Jo Spence's study of photographic images of women shows how the process of stereotyping goes beyond the individual item. Taken as a set, a body of advertising or photo-reportage constructs an 'implicit narrative' of a woman's life, in which individual items are embedded and to whose logic they appeal. In the British popular media studied by Spence in the 1970s this narrative was a highly traditional life cycle (though excluding death), presenting women as providers of services to men and children. Spence noted, however, an altered narrative emerging in the late 1970s with rather more acknowledgement of problems and of paid work and rather more self-gratification for women.

The purification of the ideological world by excluding items that do not fit the implicit narrative reaches a high point where the narrative concerns the public world. It is a familiar finding in media research that only a small percentage of news coverage is devoted to women. Women are also liable to be dropped from view in other forms of communication. The first human to step onto the moon announced to the waiting world: 'That's one small step for a man, one giant leap for mankind.' A highly praised book that appeared in the same year (1969) called *A History of the Scottish People* was almost entirely about men, often read as if men were the only inhabitants of Scotland, and discussed every industry except the one which had the greatest number of Scottish people working in it ('houses' appear in its index, but not 'housework'). A high-powered international conference about the 'Dialectics of Liberation' met in London; all of its speakers were men, who discussed war, madness, the environment, imperialism, race, literature, capitalism and socialism, but made no reference to the position of women or the oppression of homosexuals.

These three examples were events of the late 1960s and at least some areas of cultural practice have changed since. Formal language is less likely to be openly sexist. Even so establishment a body as the American Psychological Association introduced a policy of non-sexist language in its journals in 1977. Most big publishers now have a feminist, women's studies, or women writers' 'list'; indeed this is one of the more buoyant areas in contemporary book publishing. But the problem Sheila Rowbotham noted in *Woman's Consciousness, Man's World*, the difficulty even left-wing men have in acknowledging gender issues as serious politics,

remains – and not just on the Left. To some extent the exclusion
of women is replaced by marginalization, through such devices as
a separate publishing list, or media trivialization. The main
narrative of the public world – wars, rockets, governments falling,
profits rising – carries on as before.

The familiar public/private distinction is part of a process of
dichotomizing the world that is the most systematic form of
'purification' attempted by sexual ideology. In this simplification,
however, is a source of complexity. For if pushed to an extreme,
the qualitative distinction between men's world and women's world
requires different cultural mechanisms to operate in each. A
curious illustration of this is an obscure 1951 science-fiction novel
by Philip Wylie called *The Disappearance*. Its premiss is that women
and men disappear from each other's physical world for four years;
the results are different kinds of social breakdown, nuclear war in
one world and fire and pestilence in the other.

The drive for purification reaches its greatest emotional intensity
in the treatment of men's homosexuality as a symbol of disorder,
dirtiness and danger. There is a paradox about a patriarchal social
order being so hostile to erotic relations between members of the
dominant sex. A sense of this paradox is part of the ambivalent
feelings between women's liberation and gay liberation. The
explanation of Western culture's homophobia is complex, but part
of it must be the degree to which the fact of homosexuality
threatens the credibility of a naturalized ideology of gender and a
dichotomized sexual world.

Within the dichotomized world of sexual ideology two devices
for the representation of social life become dominant. One is
romanticism. Since this term is often associated with fantasy in
the style of Georgette Heyer or J. R. R. Tolkien, I would stress
its relevance to everyday life. The Broadway musical is a notable
illustration. Its classic subject-matter is the lives of little people:
farm workers (*Oklahoma!*); soldiers (*South Pacific*); fairground workers
(*Carousel*), small-time crooks (*Guys and Dolls*), factory workers (*The
Pyjama Game*), teenage street 'gangs' (*West Side Story*). Everyday life
is appealed to, its difficulties even emphasized. But it is transformed
by the glow of the love affair on which every plot turns, beside
which the other issues pale. True love – in the Broadway musical,
in Mills and Boon novels, in women's magazines – is a symbolic
reconnection of the dichotomized worlds. It both asserts the
rightness of the dichotomy, and claims a way for each woman as

a loved individual to escape the narrow and impoverished world the dichotomy constructs for women as a group.

On the other side, hegemonic masculinity is naturalized in the form of the hero and presented through forms that revolve around heroes: sagas, ballads, westerns, thrillers. The cultural focus on exemplary individuals is not only a way of justifying privileges which happen to be shared by the unheroic majority of men. Like romanticism it is also a way of dealing symbolically with real problems.

One of the problems about gender relations for men has long been the level of violence between men. It is no accident that the classic hero is usually a specialist in violence. 'I sing of arms and the man', announced Virgil at the start of the *Aeneid*, and one notes that the 'arms' come first. Aeneas, Achilles, Siegfried, Tristan and Lancelot hack their respective ways through quite a tonnage of flesh and bones. Tarzan, Bulldog Drummond, James Bond, Rambo and the Bruce Lee characters have different techniques but much the same regard for human life.

The figures in the first list, however, are considerably more than specialists in violence. The plot of the *Iliad*, for instance, revolves not around Achilles' superiority in war but around his refusal to use it. When he returns to the fight it is because of his grief for his dead friend Patroclus. Tristan is not only a champion duellist and dragon-slayer but also a tormented lover, an ambivalent friend, a lukewarm husband and something of a songwriter and practical joker to boot. Violence is part of the framework of these epics, but it is also posed as a moral and human issue.

By comparison, the twentieth-century killer–heroes are cardboard cut-outs, and in modern pulp fiction the questioning is gone. There is a disconnection of action from emotion – at least from emotional complexity – which relates to the historical trajectory of alienation and hegemonic masculinity sketched in chapter 7. A wonderful document of this is a 1955 thriller by Clark Smith called *The Speaking Eye*. The tough-guy hero is, of all things, an accountant, who is precipitated into a Chandler-style narrative of murders and tight-lipped beatings when sent to do an audit for a company take-over.

Cultural Dynamics

The historicity of sexual ideology is seen not only in details like the content of heroism, but in its organization on the largest scale. In pre-capitalist and early modern Europe sexual ideology was organized as part of a religious world-view. The issues of sexual politics were framed as moral questions, to be decided by appeal to revelation or to priestly authority. The massive modern secularization of European culture occurred in sexual ideology as much as elsewhere. The production of a natural science of sexuality and a social science of gender were the theoretical faces of this development.

From the viewpoint of mass practice, the key development was not the shift from a religious to a scientific form of abstraction but the shifting basis of authority. Secularization undermined the ability of ministers and bishops to arbitrate questions of gender. It was by no means a foregone conclusion who, if anyone, would succeed to the office. Scientists, bureaucrats, teachers and philosophers all had claims, and have kept some corner of the action. It was doctors, however, whose claims were most effective and who took the hegemonic position in constructing secularized discourses of gender and sexuality.

The medicalization of sexual ideology has now been traced by historians in a number of areas. Jeffrey Weeks documents the application of the 'medical model' to homosexuality in Europe; Barbara Ehrenreich and Deirdre English the medicalization of women's bodies in the United States; Kerreen Reiger the medical take-over of early childcare in Australia. In all these cases, as Foucault also argues for France, the crystallization of a medical theory of sexual life is accompanied by a practice of control. A form of social authority is constructed, which immediately reaches beyond the business of treating physical diseases.

A major consequence was the medicalization of problems of emotional life and interpersonal relations in the form of psychiatry. Under the aegis of psychiatry homosexual relationships were defined as an expression of mental illness. Resistance by women to domestic subordination became 'housewife's neurosis'. A host of conflicts in everyday life were reinterpreted as outcomes of unresolved childhood complexes. Medicalization thus had a double effect. It depoliticized gender relations directly, while building a more mediated power-structure based on the authority of a masculine profession.

Of course the creation of this authority did not put an end to conflict. The new authority is itself challenged, sometimes successfully. Gay activists have forced official psychiatry to abandon the definition of homosexuality as a pathology, though it is evidently still treated as such in some psychiatric practice. Rather than ending conflict, the growth of medical authority highlights the extent to which the dynamic of sexual ideology is a struggle for hegemony. What is at issue is the power to set the terms on which questions of gender are understood and conflicts fought out.

Hegemony, as noted in chapter 8 for relations between masculinities, does not mean total cultural control and obliteration of alternatives. Such a degree of control does not happen in practice. In sexual ideology generally, ascendant definitions of reality must be seen as accomplishments that are always partial and always to some extent contested.

Indeed we must see them as partly defined by the alternatives against which they are asserted. Medicalized ideologies of gender, for instance, are defined partly against alternative forms of authority such as the Church. Hence the need to claim scientific warrant for what are actually judgements of practical morality, like psychiatric interventions in sexual politics. The claim is often made implicitly, by the use of a technical language. Medical ideologies are also defined against attempts to take control of healing into the people's own hands. Hence the need to assert a strong distinction between the sound judgement of professionals and the ignorance and errors of 'lay' people. Here medicine has actually adopted the language of the Church.

Contestation, then, is an integral part of ideology. The forms of symbolic opposition to which it gives rise, for instance in erotica, are intricate and fascinating. Here I will consider only one pattern of contestation, the pattern that follows the lines of crisis tendencies as defined in chapter 7.

Karl Mannheim made a famous distinction between 'ideologies', world-views that are integrated with the established order, and 'Utopias' which transcend it. This is too neat a package; the argument just made about the contested position of hegemonic sexual ideology complicates the picture. It is still useful to distinguish perspectives and frameworks that are broadly compatible with the existing gender order from those that are not.

Such a distinction is implicit in the argument made in chapter 10 about masculinity therapy, which adapts hegemonic masculinity to changed conditions without risking the institutional bases of men's power. The anti-sexist men's movement represented in Jon Snodgrass's *For Men Against Sexism* and Andy Metcalfe and Martin Humphries's *The Sexuality of Men* is looking for conceptions of masculinity that transcend those power bases. It has clearly had a hard time finding them.

Feminism, by contrast, has generated Utopias both in Mannheim's broad sense and in the specific sense of imagined ideal worlds. Texts like Charlotte Perkins Gilman's *Herland* (1915), a novel about an all-woman society hidden in the highlands of the Amazon, document in a striking way both the break with hegemonic ideology and the limits of the shift. In the case of *Herland* the limit of thought is sexuality. Gilman can conceptualize an all-woman government and radical changes in education, but cannot admit mass lesbianism in her imagined world. She has to get around it by doing away with sexual impulses almost completely.

Formal Utopias are the exception, however intriguing; it is an occupational hazard of academics to overemphasize systematic ideology. Most of the cultural politics of gender is much less spectacular. Its field of action is the possibilities that open up in particular milieux and institutions: the curriculum changes possible in a particular school, the repertory possible in a particular theatre and so on.

Taken case by case, the opportunities are likely to seem limited. The objective possibilities in a particular high school, for instance, are constrained by many forces outside it: the bureaucratic organization of the state, the social composition of the school's catchment, the nature of the credentials market, as well as the strength of various ideologies of gender. Yet possibilities for contestation and movement are there, and some teachers do explore them. This goes beyond clearly labelled issues of gender. As Lyn Yates argues, the mainstream curriculum is a key field of implicit sexual politics in schools and has its possibilities for change. The sense of overwhelming constraints in a single milieu becomes less dampening when the connections between milieux come into view. Grass-roots cultural politics does cumulate, sometimes into social movements. And it provides the base on which the makers of formal ideologies build.

Recognizing the importance of cultural politics within the sphere of gender raises the reverse question, the impact of gender relations and sexual ideology on culture generally. There is every reason to agree with feminist cultural criticism that this impact is both powerful and largely unacknowledged. The 'naturalization' of gender has extended to the making of culture itself. Until recently it has not been a question why most playwrights, physicists or newspaper editors were men. It is still not a question in the majority of theatres, physics departments and media corporate offices.

The view that sexual politics is the structural basis of culture in general – that for instance our culture is patriarchal before it is anything else – is another matter. The overall analysis in this book would suggest that this view is wrong, at least as a transhistorical generalization. The scope of gender relations is historically variable, and their power to determine cultural processes in general must be variable too. But a more limited strategic claim may be right. There are likely to be historical moments where the possibilities of general change in consciousness and culture depend more crucially on the dynamic of gender relations than on any other social force. It can be argued that we are in such a moment now. The case is a long way from being proved but cannot be disregarded. I will come back to related questions in the final chapter.

Ideologists and Interests

If the strategic argument is even partly correct, it highlights the importance of the people who are engaged in remaking cultural forms. Discussions of sexual ideology have to a remarkable extent ignored the ideologists. The main exception is Viola Klein in *The Feminine Character*. Her approach from Mannheim's sociology of knowledge led to a concern with the people who formulated the knowledge, the social positions they occupied and the interests they articulated. The resulting study remains, 40 year later, one of the most significant analyses of sexual ideology.

What Klein's analysis conspicuously lacked was the concept of gender as a social structure in its own right. The same is true of more recent histories of ideas that have dealt with movements in sexual ideology: Paul Robinson's *The Sexual Radicals*; Christopher Lasch's *Haven in a Heartless World*; Michel Foucault's *History of Sexuality*. To the extent that there are structural categories in this research, they are loosely derived from class analysis. The result is a social analysis of ideas conducted with a 90-degree twist in the middle. The argument constantly has to move off the axis of class onto the subject-matter of sex and gender. It remains a shade mysterious why whole groups of intellectuals should arise who are concerned with sexual politics.

Nevertheless these studies point up the importance of the intellectuals who construct accounts of gender relations. In understanding them it should be possible to draw on existing theories of intellectuals in the traditions of Mannheim and Gramsci; and perhaps also on 'new class' theorists who have focused on intellectuals, such as Gouldner, and Konrad and Szelenyi. But there can be no simple translation of any of these ideas, for all of them are constructed within a class framework and ignore the structure of gender. New questions have to be asked about intellectuals and gender relations.

In some recent research, strongly influenced by feminism, these questions are opening up. Ehrenreich and English's *For Her Own Good* and Reiger's *The Disenchantment of the Home* are perhaps the best examples. Both trace the emergence of new forms of domination of women by men, in which groups of intellectuals are central – professionals rather than the academics who figure in Klein's story. It is not only a question of professional men justifying and exercising new powers. More strikingly, the historical process surrounding these medical interventions into women's health and childcare constitutes groups of intellectuals in terms of gender relations. An example is the category of 'medical authorities on childrearing', a social category constituted by the sexual division of labour that makes mothers primary carers for children, and by the gender structure of power that makes medical authority masculine.

This work points to a more general issue. From the perspective of a theory of gender, the question is where and how intellectuals and intellectual work fit into the structure of gender relations. From the perspective of a sociology of intellectuals, the question is how and how far they are constituted as a group by gender relations, and how far the character and impact of intellectual work is determined by gender dynamics. Once the questions are posed in these terms, the tools of ideology–theory and the sociology of intellectuals can be put to work on new bases.

A case in point is Gramsci's category of 'organic' intellectuals, meaning people who perform an intellectual function within a class, giving it self-definition and helping to mobilize it as a political and social force. There are, I would argue, people who perform that kind of task in gender relations. A notable example is Harriet Kidd, a clerk at the Women's Co-operative Guild head office in Britain in the years leading up to World War I. She was successively a mill worker, an unmarried mother after rape by her employer, a local labour and community organizer and then an administrator. The Guild, founded in the 1880s, was a mass organization of working-class women claiming over 60,000 members between the wars. The combative socialist feminism of organizers like Kidd was clearly very important in its success.

An organic intellectual of a very different stripe is Marabel Morgan, a Florida housewife and business woman of the 1970s. *The Total Woman* has already been mentioned as a classic presentation of emphasized femininity. The book grew out of a four-week course in which other wives were taught the tactics of being a 'total woman', with homework assignments about adapting to their husband's wishes. Though the authorities Morgan appeals to are men, mainly Biblical prophets and psychiatrists, they are not very prominent in the text. Her main argument is carried by dozens of little anecdotes from the 'total woman' classes. Morgan is, in effect, mediating an ideology constructed by women and circulating among women. Though it is, as Andrea Dworkin argues in *Right-Wing Women*, a response to their powerlessness in relation to their husbands, this does not alter the organic character of the intellectual work.

A more general formulation is worth attempting, even in a preliminary way. Groups active in the making of sexual ideology include priests, journalists, advertisers, politicians, psychiatrists, designers (for example, of fashion), playwrights and film-makers, actors and actresses, novelists, musicians, movement activists and academics. When the activities of these groups are considered in relation to the gender order, they fall broadly into three categories.

First is the regulation and management of gender regimes. The Catholic priesthood is a clear example, for its involvement went far beyond papal declarations on sacred motherhood and unholy contraception. Theology justified a patriarchal power structure but hardly settled how it was actually to work. The traditional village priest spent a great deal of time sorting this out, giving advice, laying down interpretations of rules and managing the domestic tensions of his parish via the confessional, visits to homes and so forth. Psychotherapists, family therapists and counsellors do a lot of the same kind of work now.

Second is the articulation of experiences, fantasies and perspectives characteristic of particular groups in gender relations. Harriet Kidd and Marabel Morgan, in different ways, did this. But in other cases the relationship is anything but organic, as the mass fantasies of Hollywood show. Clark Gable articulated fantasies for women, Raquel Welch for men. Third is the theorization of gender relations, a business that implies a degree of disconnection from daily practice and an effort at reflection and interpretation. I mean this rather more broadly than just writing treatises about the sociology of gender. As suggested in chapter 3, novelists like Nadine Gordimer and Patrick White and autobiographers like Anja Meulenbelt are engaged in 'theorization' in this sense.

Returning to the question of structural location, if a group of intellectuals is constituted as a clear-cut group in gender relations it implies a strong patterning of the sexual division of labour. Intellectual work is work, with a labour process of its own and a demand for material resources, not the least of them being time. Situations vary and groups of intellectuals vary in the degree to which they are formed around the sexual division of labour rather than around some other structural pattern (for example, class relations).

If we now integrate these two classifications the result is the grid in table 5, on which I have tentatively placed the groups mentioned above.

This is, obviously, only a beginning in thinking about these groups. It is perhaps enough to suggest that there are some systematic links between intellectuals and the structure of gender relations. If so, further exploration on these lines should yield results of importance for our understanding of both.

For the theory of gender, the potential dividend is a good deal more than the deeper understanding of the history of ideas that has been defined as the value of the sociology of knowledge. In chapter 6 a definition of 'interests' was suggested in terms of inequalities constructed by gender relations. At that level of definition the interests are inert, in the sense of Sartre's 'practico-

Table 5 Intellectuals and the gender order

Major practice in relation to gender order	Degree to which group formation is defined by gender (sexual division of labour) rather than by other structures.			
	Gender minor ———————————— Gender marked			
Management	Advertisers	Psychiatrists	Politicians	Priests
Articulation	Designers	Film-makers	Musicians	Movement activists
				Actors/actresses
Theorization	Novelists	Academics		Movement theorists

inert'. For them to become active as political forces requires a mobilization, one of whose conditions is a reflective awareness of the inequalities and the oppositions of interest they define. The creation of that awareness is intellectual work. Much of it has in practice been done by specialists, the intellectuals of the groups just discussed.

We may say, then, that intellectuals have a historic place in the translation of structural inequality into sexual politics, at least at the level of public politics. To say that, however, is not to circumscribe very much the form of politics that emerges. For the reflective awareness of inequalities may take very different forms, depending on the circumstances and character of the reflection. Marabel Morgan is articulating such an awareness just as much as Andrea Dworkin; Morgan calls the wife the 'Executive Vice-President' of the marriage, leaving no doubt about who is President.

It matters, then, how the articulation of interests is done. To put it another way, ideological struggle in gender relations is to be expected and has effects. It is easy to exaggerate the significance of the abstract clash of ideas. Some of the wars of academics have remarkably little relevance to anything in the world outside. But intellectual work and ideological struggle are scarcely confined to the academy. They occur to some degree in every institution and setting. And if academic abstraction has to be discounted from its own estimate, it is not to be ignored. Generalized formulations of ideas can be important in crystallizing consciousness, in giving names to things felt but not yet stated. When the world is ready, ideas can be a revolutionary force. The problem is to understand the readiness as well as the ideas.

NOTES

Discourse and Practice

(pp. 241–5). Quotations from Goldman (1972b), p. 163; Kristeva (1981), p. 21.

Ideological Processes

(pp. 245–9). Cancian and Ross (1981) illustrate media research showing the marginalization of women in news and how it varies over time. The case of Scottish history, Smout (1969); the case of the London conference, Cooper (1968). APA guidelines for non-sexist language published in *American Psychologist*, (June 1977).

Ideologists and Interests

(pp. 253–8). To Klein's work we can now add detailed histories of ideas like Rosenberg (1982), which are an improvement in terms of detail but still have a less sophisticated social analysis. Harriet Kidd's brief biography in Davies (1977).

12

Political Practice

The Scope of Sexual Politics

In ordinary speech 'politics' is a narrow and faintly disreputable term, meaning elections, parliaments, presidents and party antagonisms. 'Politician' can be a term of abuse, 'political' a label for distrust. Social science has found the negative overtones unnecessary and the narrow definition untenable.

In what follows 'politics' is assumed to be neither bad nor good, simply an essential part of social life and a very widespread one. The same kinds of processes occur in companies, voluntary organizations, and in stateless societies as occur in and around the state: contests for power, mechanisms of succession, debates over policy. Sociological research on families found power structures and power struggles even in that haven, as soon as it looked. R. D. Laing's *The Politics of Experience* marked another discovery made in the cultural politics of the 1960s. When Kate Millett characterized politics as 'power-structured relationships, arrangements whereby one group of persons is controlled by another' and by applying the idea to relations between men and women defined 'sexual politics', the term startled many people but her thought followed a well-marked path.

Millett's definition now appears too narrow, given the range of overt social conflicts about sex and gender over the last two decades. It is worth trying to get these conflicts in some sort of order to arrive at a definition of the scope of sexual politics.

There is, first, a political process centred on the state, some of whose dimensions were discussed in chapter 6. Its most visible moments have been attempts to commit major states to guarantees of equality for women, such as the Equal Rights Amendment in the United States, and the United Nations declaration of the International Decade for Women. Of course 'sexual politics' also include the counter-mobilization that scuppered the Equal Rights Amendment and undermined UN policy, for instance the repression of women in Pakistan and Iran. Attempts to introduce equal opportunity policies have contested the sexual division of labour in the state and provoked widespread, if muted, resistance. Issues of access have been fought out in political parties, notably in attempts to get more women endorsed as candidates, and in a few places like San Francisco and Sydney, gay men too. Resources issues have been opened with the creation of women's units in the bureaucracy, and specific welfare programmes directed towards women, gays, and even transsexuals. A new resources politics is emerging around the unequal impact of apparently gender-neutral state policies such as the form of taxation or welfare-funding cuts. The 1985 'Women's Tax Summit' which contested the Australian government's proposed shift to indirect taxes is a notable example.

Overlapping all this is a politics of workplaces and markets. Campaigns to break down prohibitions on women's employment, or restrictions on promotion, continue. In 1985, for instance, women's exclusion from the steelworks in Wollongong was declared unlawful. Sexual pressure on women employees by men, especially their bosses, is now defined as sexual harassment and cases are being taken before tribunals – not always with progressive results, as Jocelynne Scutt shows for a landmark Australian case of 1983. The long-standing exclusion of women from power in trade unions, and the corresponding lack of interest by unions in the interests of women members, is also being challenged. In 1983 Jenny George became the first woman elected to the executive of the Australian Council of Trade Unions; in 1979 the Trade Union Congress in Britain sponsored a mass demonstration in support of abortion rights. It is more difficult to get leverage on a whole labour market than a particular workplace, but the attempt is made. There are for instance programmes to get girls into apprenticeships, to break down the sharp sexual division of skilled trades; and to get more girls into professionally oriented streams in schools and colleges.

The content of schooling, and other areas of cultural work, has become a focus of struggle. The new feminism sparked the rewriting of sexist textbooks and attempts to remove discriminatory material from curricula and libraries; similar issues have been raised by gay liberation though with less result. Right-wing politicians attempt the opposite: in 1978, for instance, the Queensland government banned the use of the MACOS primary curriculum because it was thought to undermine the sanctity of the family. Mass-media content has come under fire for sexist advertising and hostile stereotypes of gays, though media-reform groups have not had much leverage. In book publishing rather more space has been gained by feminism. Attempts to gain more space in performance arts, like the 'Women and Theatre' project launched in Sydney in 1980, have provoked remarkably hostile reactions from some of the men in the same trades.

The politics of families has a public face. Official campaigns to increase or to limit the number of children are familiar, with the Catholic Church's intransigence on contraception a curious counterpoint to rising concern with world over-population. Negotiation of the relations between husbands and wives often ends in the courts for adjudication of terms of divorce and custody of children. A struggle also surrounds the courts that do this, from parliamentary conflict over divorce legislation, and feminist criticism of inadequate enforcement of maintenance payments, to murderous attacks on family court judges by embittered husbands. The use of force between family members is now a public issue, with campaigns on domestic violence, child abuse and incest. An informal political process has developed around the attempts within parts of the Left to construct egalitarian households, working through conflict-ridden issues over child-care, sexual relationships and property ownership.

The politics of contraception raises the question of control over sexuality. Some of the bitterest conflicts of the last fifteen years have concerned abortion, with right-wing mobilizations in defence of the 'unborn child'. Conservatism desires to confine sexuality to marriage, though conservatives now divide over whether marital sex should concentrate on procreation (the Pope) or pleasure (Marabel Morgan). Both versions are homophobic. The control of men's homosexuality is a well-established area of state action, with the front-line police and courts backed by security agencies, discrimination in employment and exclusion from schools. Control of erotica and pornography is also well established. In the 1960s a sudden liberalization occurred in the rich capitalist countries, marked by the 'Danish Sex Fairs' of 1969–70. The rapid growth of a mass-circulation pornography industry provoked bitter criticism from some tendencies in feminism for its exploitative content; some unexpected alliances in the politics of control have emerged in the United States especially.

Finally, the movements addressing these issues have a politics of their own presence. Quiet campaigns for legal reform on homosexuality were transformed into a highly visible Gay Liberation movement in the rich capitalist countries; these have since changed again in the context of visible gay 'communities'. The new feminism was divided early between liberal and radical currents, with radical feminism in turn dividing between socialist and cultural feminisms. New concerns with violence, disarmament and ecology have emerged. There have been internal conflicts over lesbianism, separatism, Marxism, connections with the state and a range of other issues. There have been attempts to create a counter-sexist movement among heterosexual men, which have not been very successful. Nor have the attempts at permanent mobilization of right-wing sexual politics. Organizations like the anti-feminist Women Who Want to be Women remain small; parties like the Call to Australia movement have minor electoral success. For the most part the churches and conservative parties provide the organizational framework for reaction. Their potential strength is shown by the fundamentalist mobilization in the United States over the last ten years. At the time of writing a television evangelist is making a strong bid for the Republican nomination as President in succession to Reagan.

The six fields just sketched involve overt politics, with issues publicly stated and the course of events readily accessible. This is not the entire scope of politics by any useful definition. Tacit politics, where conflicts of interest and power struggles are not publicly articulated, are equally real though less easily documented. Some examples have been given: the family and the street in chapter 6 and workplaces in chapters 5 and 11. The difference between the two kinds of politics is not just a matter of degree of publicity. It has to do with the way interests are articulated and political movements formed.

The Articulation of Interests

The crucial moment in the social dynamic of politics is the

constitution of interests. In chapter 6 interests were defined in terms of the inequalities constructed by gender relations. At that level the interests are inert, and though they structure practice it is only as the external conditions of practices which are directed to other ends. In this sense we might speak of latent interests and demobilised politics.

When practice is, however, directed to these conditions as its object, the interest is articulated in a collective project. The most obvious example is a social movement like gay liberation and women's liberation. As proposed in chapter 9 a collective project may also take an institutionalized form. It may be embodied in the functioning of a bureaucracy or the structure of a labour market, and may be pursued as a project by the defence of those institutional arrangements. Broadly the interests of heterosexual men in sexual politics are articulated in this way. There is no need for an anti-liberation movement to defend patriarchy.

The constitution of an interest as a collective project requires awareness of inequalities and the social oppositions they define. While that awareness may be aroused by any event – a police raid, a beauty contest or whatever – to clarify and sustain it requires intellectual work. In practice much of this is done by specialists, the groups discussed in chapter 11. Thus intellectuals have often played a strategic role in the constitution of social interests. The notion of the 'organic intellectual' is best understood in these terms.

The classification of intellectuals suggested in chapter 11 is related to forms of politics. Much of the interplay between social interests is what Gramsci called for class relations a 'war of position', in contrast to the 'war of manoeuvre'. The tacit politics of bureaucracies and families, for instance, seem constant though the conflicts are real. Both the repetition and the conflict are acknowledged in the folklore of the 'battle of the sexes' where drunken husbands, wives with rolling-pins, flirtatious 'girls' and dim-witted boyfriends perform their endless ballet.

In such politics the management function of intellectuals is uppermost. Priests negotiate the tensions of the village; psychotherapists talk out the tensions of the urban rich and drug or hospitalize the urban poor; social planners fine-tune the welfare system to mop up the direst effects of structural inequality. The interests of dominant groups can be represented simply by providing rationalizations of the structure as a whole. Such theory takes a degree of naturalization for granted, suppresses the question of interests and concerns itself with explaining deviations. Sex role theory is a classic solution to these requirements, and can be regarded as an organic ideology of the gender regime in the modern welfare state.

The contrast with the 'utopias' discussed in chapter 11, and the crisis tendencies underlying them, is obvious. The interests of subordinated groups are capable of articulation as collective projects which break the bounds of the existing gender order. This may be only in fantasy, as in the classic literary utopias. But the crisis tendencies discussed in chapter 7 create real conditions for transformative practice. Here the formation of a collective project involves the articulation of some group's interest in a changed gender order, defining a historical trajectory from deprivation or repression in the present to a future of equality or liberation.

In this context the function of theorization is uppermost in intellectual work. Simply to formulate such an interest requires some mental distance from the current gender order, comparing it with conceivable alternatives. In theorizing the existing order the conflict of interest moves to the centre of attention. Categorical-ism is an understandable result, as we see in radical feminism. But categoricalism creates difficulties with the need to grasp processes of transformation and the construction of political forces. So even when ascendant this kind of theory is unlikely to be under challenge or constantly modified in practice.

The broad contrast just drawn has two major qualifications. First, the interests of groups advantaged in the gender order may also be articulated in a transcendent project. A case in point is the contest for hegemony discussed in chapter 6, the displacement of authoritarian patriarchy in the eighteenth and nineteenth centuries by a masculinity oriented to technical rationality and institutionalized through bureaucracy and markets. Among other things this involved the creation of utopias – social contract theory and political economy – which articulated the interests of the ascending groups of men. Another case is masculinity therapy and the 'men's liberation' movement of the 1970s. Here transcendence was pursued because the existing gender order was felt to have become unworkable; the modernization of masculinity was required as a rescue operation.

The second qualification is that the inert interest defined by existing patterns of inequality can always be articulated in more than one way, as the history of ideological conflict shows. For instance, a common response to crisis tendencies is fear of losing what you already have. Right-wing sexual politics attempts to articulate women's interests in this way, with some success; some of the bitterest opposition to feminism has come from other women. The 'threat to the family' is a threat to the mother where femininity is defined in relation to childcare and domestic work and where 'the family' is the only sphere in which women have any power.

These possibilities mean that the pattern of sexual politics cannot be deduced mechanically from structural analysis. The line-up of political forces is always a question of how interests have been constituted, and what alliances are constructed between them. Equal opportunity programmes in the state, to take one example, developed through an alliance between technocratically oriented men pursuing efficiency and professional women pursuing women's interests as articulated in liberal feminism.

To make this abstract argument concrete, the following sections examine two patterns of political practice, one demobilized and the other highly mobilized. The choice is not arbitrary. I would argue that a combination between the two groupings discussed here is required for a general transformation of the relations between women and men; though to make it happen, both forms of politics would themselves have to change.

Working-class Feminism

In plain language, both in law and in popular morality, the wife is still the inferior in the family to the husband. She is first without economic independence, and the law therefore gives the man, whether he be good or bad, a terrible power over her. Partly for this reason, and partly because all sorts of old half-civilized beliefs still cling to the flimsy skirts of our civilization, the beginning and end of the working woman's life and duty is still regarded by many as the care of the household, the satisfaction of man's desires, and the bearing of children. We do not say that this is the case in every working-class home, or that there are not hundreds of husbands who take a higher view of married life and practise it. What we do say is that these views are widely held, often unconsciously, and are taken advantage of by hundreds of men who are neither good men nor good husbands and that even where there is no deliberate .

evil or viciousness, these views are responsible for the overwork
and physical suffering among women and for that excessive childbearing, of which more will be said later.

The author of this remarkable passage, written seventy years ago,
was Margaret Llewelyn Davies, general secretary of the Women's
Co-operative Guild in England and one of the most effective
organizers either feminism or socialism has known. Here she
sketched out both the main arena of mass sexual politics, the
working-class household, and some of its major issues: economic
dependence, ideological subordination and the physical consequences of oppression.

The inequalities in such a setting are clear enough, and therefore
the inert opposition of interests between women and men. In terms
of income, authority, leisure time, prestige, access to organizations
and public life generally, working-class husbands had privileges
to defend. Though some of the details have changed, in broad
terms they still do. This has never gone without challenge, as is
clear from the vivid autobiographies of women in the co-operative
movement collected by Davies and published in *Maternity* and *Life
As We Have Known It*. The articulation of this challenge is the
political practice I will call working-class feminism.

Power and inequality within the family are the objects of a
widespread, active, often vehement face-to-face politics. Most of
it leaves no record except in the memories of the participants. It
therefore goes undocumented, except for novels like Glen Tomasetti's *Thoroughly Decent People* and academic family research of the
scientifically disreputable kind that actually listens to people
talking about themselves. From one such study comes the following
example. The setting is the working-class Australian suburb in
which the Princes (chapter 1) also live.

Mrs Markham is very much the central person in her family, the
hub of discussions and decisions, and emotionally the source of
strength for others. She has been conscious of prejudice against
women for a long time. She recalls being 'bitterly disappointed'
when forced to leave school early, and thus miss out on her ambition
to become a journalist, because *her* mother could see no point in
education for women. Mrs Markham is determined that her girls
will not repeat her frustration, and has pushed them hard at school.

Elaine Markham, the oldest daughter, has taken over this project, internalized it, and become highly competitive at school. With success: she is in the 'A' class and indeed one of its academic stars. Like her mother she is contemptuous of 'the little housewife' and of her schoolmates who are growing up in that image. Though she will not go as far as 'Women's Libbists' burning bras and demonstrating in the street, she firmly supports 'the overall idea of women being equal'. But all this has not come easily. She sometimes comes home from school in tears from tension and frustration. She talks of the school as a 'dead' place. She is thinking about leaving early despite her academic success.

The corollary of Mrs Markham's strength is Mr Markham's marginality. He is a storeman, earning below average wages. He came from a poor family, left school at 15, has held a range of jobs. He gets pushed around a good deal at work. While antagonistic to unions he is also angry at his bosses for not giving him recognition and a better wage. He finds their pressure for profit erodes the service his unit can give, and offends his pride in workmanship. The work situation, in short, constantly erodes his self-esteem. He tried to assert patiarchal rights in the family, for instance refusing to take on a share of housework when his wife took a job. But the main result was that he became increasingly marginal in the household. The women have concluded that he has failed as a husband and father. He too, rather wistfully, now accepts that opinion of himself.

This is only the barest outline of an intricate situation; even so it is of interest. In the last few years a whole series of problems about gender relations have been at issue inside the Markham family: ideas about the proper place of women in the world, access to new resources for girls, the division of labour in the household, the authority of men, the character of masculinity.

These issues are not exactly light-years away from the concerns of organized feminism. But the Markhams have no contact with that movement. Their only knowledge of it is the media stereotype of 'Women's Libbists', with whom neither Elaine nor her mother care to identify. Their sexual politics is developed out of their own experience.

A politics mostly generated in the family and mostly conducted in the family is unlikely to make an issue of the family. The low level of women's wages, and the lack of collective provision for childcare, make it extremely difficult for women who do not have the capital to buy a house nor qualifications that would guarantee

a good job – but who usually do have children to be supported –
to survive without a husband and a husband's wage. In working-
class life, accordingly, the family as an institution is not very much
contested. The questions at issue are the terms on which family
relationships work.

Mrs Markham has a job in a factory, Elaine goes to school;
both places have their own gender regimes and surrounding
politics. The workplace is the second main site of working-class
feminism, with the inequalities of wages, power and conditions
already discussed. The assembly-line workers in the plant studied
by Ruth Cavendish respond to these inequalities in a way which
I suspect is very general. They are basically disillusioned with
men, and are familiar with feminist arguments about men's
unjustified privileges. In the daily struggles about work and
conditions in the factory they systematically support each other
against the men who are their supervisors and managers. Since
most of them have a household to run also, with a sharp sexual
division of labour and little help from their husbands, they are
chronically tired and have no leisure. Both facts make it difficult
to organize. Men control the union, which did little for them in
ordinary times and undermined them when they did go on strike.
The union, as in the Melbourne factories where the Centre for
Urban Research and Action interviewed immigrant women in the
study *But I Wouldn't Want my Wife to Work Here*, tends to be seen
as part of management.

The general picture is a consciousness of sex inequality developing in an extremely constricting situation which prevents much
expression beyond a practice of face-to-face solidarity. Within
those limits the consciousness of oppression is vivid and the
response active. Other studies have found comparable responses;
Judy Wajcman's study of a group of women in Britain who took
over their failing factory is particularly interesting. Not all women
workers have such a consciousness. Yet there is enough evidence
to say that this is an important form of articulation of women's
interests in industrial settings.

There is no platform that lists the demands of working-class
feminism. It is nevertheless possible to formulate in outline the
issues around which these family and industrial politics revolve
and the direction of movement implied.

(1)   *In relation to the division of labour and gender structuring of production.*

In the family: control of the household budget; the search for an independent wage for women and the right to spend it; sometimes, more equal sharing of housework. In the workplace: more equal wages between men and women; ending practices that keep women out of better-paid or easier jobs.

(2) *In relation to the structure of power.* In the family: control over decisions about the children, such as schooling and apprenticeship; personal independence, notably freedom from put-downs and violence by husbands or *de facto* husbands. In the workplace: freedom from arbitrary authority, such as rough treatment by bosses or headmasters; being heard by the unions that are supposed to represent women workers.

(3) *In relation to cathexis and sexuality.* In the family: adequate contraception, including the right to abortion; control of one's own sexuality. (For teenagers, the right to be a sexual being and to be active in initiating and controlling sexual adventures; for married women, the right to set terms with husbands or leave unsatisfying marriages.) In the workplace: freedom from sexual harassmemt.

Cavendish argues that the concerns of her factory workers are very distant from those of middle-class feminism, and this is a reasonably common view of the issue. I suspect the difference would have seemed less if she had been able to study the same women in equal detail in their families. Overall there seems no obvious reason why this kind of politics should not be called 'feminist'. It articulates women's interests and involves an extensive critique of the power of men. Its forms and priorities are certainly different from those of 'movement' feminism, especially cultural feminism. It is also happening on a larger scale.

That is, perhaps, the central paradox of working-class feminism. There is every reason to think it is very widespread. The same kinds of struggle bubble up in factories and families in different industries, different countries, and at different times. But in both families and factories the structures that generate this politics also localize it. The result is a vast spectrum of small-scale political processes, each disconnected from the others. They are known about, through folklore, tradition and conversation; but they do not easily feed into each other.

There have been attempts to mobilize working-class women in

a more collective and public politics. Their high point was in the early twentieth century, with movements like the Social Democratic women's organizations in Germany, the Women's Co-operative Guild in Britain, and women's organizations connected with the Socialist Party in the United States. More recently there are events like the Working Women's Charter campaign and Women Against Pit Closures in Britain; the involvement of working-class women in refuges and the radicalization of Labor Women's conferences in Australia. Most of these mobilizations have been connected with organizations constructed and dominated by men – parties, unions, cooperatives – and have therefore involved a politics of representation and access from a structurally weak position. The Labor Women's conferences, for instance, have no formal power at all; as was shown in NSW in 1986 when the dominant right-wing faction in the party, which could not control the women's conference, simply abolished it. At the national level 76 per cent of the delegates to the 1984 Labor Party federal conference were men, and among the major power-brokers there were no women at all.

To recognize the weakness of mobilizations is not to imply that working-class feminism has been ineffective. Reading the British accounts of family life in *Round About a Pound a Week*, *Life As We Have Known It*, and *Working-class Wives* creates a strong impression of the distance travelled during the twentieth century. Patriarchal authority has been rolled back some way. Working-class women have won more space and more resources. There is a cumulation, however modest each step in it has been.

Liberation Movements: Birth and Transformation

The articulation of interests in the women's liberation movement differs from the articulation in working-class feminism in a number of ways. Its main feature has been the construction of a collective project whose theme is the generalization of women's struggles across different settings, relationships and areas of life. It arose on a much narrower social base but achieved an intensity of commitment and degree of self-consciousness unparalleled in sexual politics.

Much has been made of the 'middle-class' character of this

movement, which orthodox marxists commonly lumped with liberalism as 'bourgeois feminism'. While there always have been working-class activists in women's liberation, its major social base is undeniable. Most of the early activists were white, tertiary-educated, belonged to a particular generation, lived in big cities and either came from well-off families or could expect to get well-paid jobs as teachers, journalists, welfare workers and the like. The movement has continued to recruit more from students in higher education than from elsewhere, though there is now a second generation of activists. Broadly it is a movement of the intelligentsia, if that is taken to include professions and semi-professions.

To recognize this base is not to discredit the movement, except on the crudest view of class interests. Rather it raises questions about the particular kind of articulation of women's interests accomplished here, and the particular circumstances that allowed such a project to emerge.

The first point is the more debated. The account of women's interests produced in women's liberation was for the most part based on categorical theory. As Hester Eisenstein argues, this easily led to a 'false universalism' that assimilated the situations of Third World, black and working-class women to the situation of affluent whites. This has changed, at least at the level of movement practice. There have been attempts to address the concerns of migrant and black women in the rich countries, and to take a less imperialist view of women's politics in the Third World. They remain an amendment rather than a reconstitution of the movement.

The impulse behind the earliest women's liberation groups was the contradiction between the radical democracy professed by the men of the 'New Left' and their actual exclusion and exploitation of women. Lynne Segal convincingly argues that 1960s radicalism was more than a target. Its critique of the family and its liberal attitudes to sex had helped emancipate younger women despite the alienated sexuality and frequent selfishness of radical men. The pursuit of personal freedom and attempts to build a 'radical self' highlighted questions of emotional relationships and personality, which were shortly to become central concerns of women's liberation consciousness-raising groups. The contrast between student activism and the workers in Cavendish's factory highlights the importance of free time and material resources in shifting the grounds of sexual politics. The movement has survived on a material base which working-class feminism does not have: the incomes of professional women (financing journals, films, conferences, women's houses etc.), access to the state for the funding of women's services, and the unpaid labour of women without young children.

The work of activists in the first half-dozen years created not only campaigns against injustices but also a political resource. The collective project was materialized, and to some extent institutionalized, in definite ways. First and most important was the allegiance of some thousands of women in each of the major cities of the rich capitalist countries. 'Allegiance' meant practices like CR groups, turning out for demonstrations, coming to meetings, reading and sometimes subscribing to feminist publications. It also meant a loyalty to the movement. Many participants came to define themselves politically as feminists before anything else, and to identify closely with the women who had been through the same campaigns and helped each other change their lives.

The second dimension of the resource was a network of institutions and enterprises based on feminist ideas or catering for a feminist clientele. The listings in the *New Woman's Survival Catalog* of 1973 are a measure of what had been established in the United States in a few years: feminist publishing houses, art galleries, rock bands, clinics, schools and courses, rape crisis centres, businesses, legal practices, women's centres, newsletters and magazines, theatre companies, and campaign groups of many kinds. Also growing by the mid-1970s was a feminist presence in the state, notably in the welfare bureaucracy and universities, and in political parties and unions.

Third, less tangible but also important, was the growing credibility of feminist ideas and of the movement as a representative of women's interests; credibility both among women outside the movement and among men. Ideas spread despite the lack of mass organization. Thus Elaine Markham stated a general principle of sex equality in language undoubtedly derived from feminism, and the workers in Ruth Cavendish's factory did much the same. We were surprised to hear, in schools like Elaine's, a considerable number of boys also endorsing the principle of equality. The funding of feminist refuges, with some difficulties but not intense resistance, illustrates the credibility acquired with men in the bureaucracy over an issue like domestic violence.

In a sense feminist theory predicted the creation of this resource: 'sisterhood is powerful', women together can make things happen. But categorical theory assumed it was a resource for women at large and had little to say about which particular women did or should direct it. In the mid-1970s several developments made this issue acute. The recession squeezed state expenditure on welfare and made it progressively harder to fund feminist welfare and education initiatives. It also led to mass unemployment among younger women and made it harder to open up new fields of employment. At the same time right-wing mobilizations developed against feminism on issues like abortion rights and the American ERA. Though there are no membership figures it seems likely that in the second half of the 1970s the women's liberation movement had either stopped growing, or at best was expanding much more slowly than the pace of the early 1970s.

In this context differences of opinion and strategy once easily accommodated were liable to harden into factional conflict. A struggle for hegemony developed within feminism whose stake was control of the political resource that the movement had created. None of the major tendencies proved strong enough to eliminate the others. In Britain for instance the result of a deepening series of conflicts, over issues of sexuality especially, was the shipwreck of the movement's national conferences, the last of which was held in 1978. In the first half of the 1980s the public face of women's liberation was increasingly presented by the 'woman-centred' ethos of cultural feminism, and by the political priorities of radical feminism (in the narrower sense) with a focus on 'male violence' as the means of oppression, men's hostility and power-seeking as the reason, and separatism as the strategic response. This strategy capitalized on resources generated within the movement and the possibility of turning it into a community, at the price of making the movement less accessible to those outside.

At one level this account reinforces a point already made, that there can be no single articulation of a structurally defined interest. The projects of socialist feminism, political lesbianism and so forth, have common ground but also cut across each other. At another level it shows the power of structural alignments once they are articulated at all. For the most remarkable feature of these events is the persistence of the movement despite sharp internal conflicts, changes of circumstance from boom to recession, changes of practice with the rise and decline of CR groups, and an increasingly hostile political environment.

In some ways the political history of gay liberation seems very like that of women's liberation. It emerged at much the same time and in the same metropolitan centres, used similar political tactics and rhetoric, grew rapidly in the same years, developed and factionalized in the 1970s. It too has been characterized by tension between a socialist wing and another more concerned to build a self-sustaining community and to develop gay culture. Like women's liberation it has had a highly ambivalent relationship with the state, often attacking it for anti-homosexual laws, police violence against gays and court discrimination against lesbian mothers, but also wanting to use it for antidiscrimination legislation and welfare provision.

In other ways the story is very different. Women's liberation developed out of a long history of women's mobilizations, and has operated as the radical end of a spectrum of women's organizations in parties, churches, charities and so on. While there is a history of homosexual rights groups going back to the turn of the century, among them Magnus Hirschfeld's 'Scientific Humanitarian Committee' in Germany, the Mattachine Society and Daughters of Bilitis in the United States, they had always been small. Modest successes in gaining toleration, for instance through the 1958 Wolfenden Report in Britain, were achieved by alliance with liberals in the establishment, not by mass mobilization of gays. It was assumed that was impossible because of legal repression and public hostility. The 'Stonewall riots' that launched gay liberation were sparked by a routine piece of policing by New York's Finest; only the response was not routine. Within a very short time the mobilization undoubtedly had brought into political campaigns more people than all previous homosexual organizations put together. Gay liberation stood alone to an extent women's liberation never did, and at least in its early days was the only significant articulation of the interest of gay people.

The second difference is that gay liberation, an articulation of interest based on the structure of cathexis, was built across the major divide in gender relations. So far as the interests of women and men diverge, the movement has an inbuilt tendency to divide. In law reform, for instance, lesbians are more affected by the operation of marital law, such as custody issues, and homosexual men more affected by the criminalization of sexual intercourse. What constitutes them as members of an oppressed group is in some ways different. There is much more violence against homosexual men than against lesbians, and male homosexuality has historically aroused more horror among straights. On their side lesbians suffer not only the stigmatization of homosexuality but also the social, psychological and economic penalties attached to being women. Politicized lesbians often have a stronger commitment to women's liberation as a movement than to gay liberation. For the most part 'gay politics' has been gay men's politics; the 1984 conference of the Campaign for Homosexual Equality (CHE) in Britain, to take one example, had five women and fifty men. It is understandable that the political relationship between lesbians and gay men has been complicated and often tense.

Third, the relationship between politics and community is different from that in women's liberation. To some extent a gay community existed before gay liberation, in clandestine networks and around beats and gay bars. The movement brought it into the open and gave it a massive stimulus. The growth of 'gay capitalism' since is familiar. There is some parallel in the growth of entrepreneurial feminism but the balance of forces is very different. By the late 1970s the proprietors of gay businesses had emerged in a number of cities as an alternative leadership. They articulated the interests of gay people in a very different way, having themselves a strong interest in the consolidation of gay identities and none at all in revolutionizing sexuality in the rest of society. The early gay liberation slogan that 'every straight man is a target for gay liberation' meant nothing in this context except an invitation to trouble. Dennis Altman points to the tendency to reconstitute gay politics as an interest group on the model of ethnic communities, seeking accommodations with the state and other interest groups.

As this tendency has gathered strength, the socially radical thrust of gay liberation easily becomes pitted *against* the trends that are giving social identity and personal self-confidence to homosexual people in their 'private' lives. Gay liberation increasingly was at risk of losing the base it had created. This strategic dilemma has not been easily resolved. The deconstructionist debate already discussed is one consequence. Another is a turn by political activists to electoral politics and the local state, with some success in San Francisco, Sydney and London. Thus gay politics have come by a different route from feminism to the problem of maintaining a radical presence inside the state.

Movements for a progressive sexual politics among heterosexual men have been on a very small scale by comparison. The 1970s talk about 'men's liberation' has already been mentioned. Most of it was based on a sex-role perspective on gender that ignored questions of power and exploitation. The group that holds predominant social power cannot be 'liberated'. The issues about the reconstruction of masculinity raised by this beginning were real enough and keep coming back, in feminist writing as well as men's. The difficulty of constructing a movement of men to dismantle hegemonic masculinity is that its logic is not the articulation of collective interest but the attempt to dismantle that interest. While there are good reasons to do this, some of which I listed in the Introduction, the chances of a widespread mobilization on this basis are slim.

The focus of counter-sexist politics among heterosexual men has therefore been domestic. I would guess that most energy has gone into the completely private renegotiation of relationships with feminist women in the context of individual sexual relationships and households. There has been little exchange of ideas or experience among the men involved. The exceptions to this are the 'men's groups', modelled on feminist CR groups, that still exist, and a degree of networking in the left-wing community politics discussed above.

NOTES

The Scope of Sexual Politics

(pp. 259–62). On conceptions of politics in the social sciences see Mackenzie (1967). There is no general survey of sexual politics in and around the state; for more specific references see chapter 6. For the sexual politics of labour markets and workplaces see O'Donnell (1984); Game and Pringle (1983); Eardley et al. (1980). The sexual politics of culture is formulated in many specific contexts, e.g., Easlea (1983). On the concept of the politics of the family see Morgan (1975). The politics of reproduction is explored in O'Brien (1981) and Sayers (1982); for erotica and the Sex Fairs see Lauret (1970). On the politics of movements see below.

Working-class Feminism

(pp. 265–71). Quotation from Davies (1978), (pp. 7–8); for the other British evidence see Reeves (1913) and Rice (1939). The Australian research discussed in the text should be compared with the American study by Lillian Rubin (1976); which in turn might be compared with the political mobilization of working-class women in earlier stages of American history, e.g., in Dancis (1976).

Liberation Movements

(pp. 270–77). 'Women's liberation' means the radical feminism that adopted this name at the end of the 1960s, partly to distinguish a revolutionary perspective from the gradualism and compromises of liberal feminism, partly to distinguish feminist priorities from those of the 'male Left'. It embraced tendencies later distinguished as socialist feminism, cultural feminism, eco-feminism. The term 'radical feminism' would be better, but during the 1970s was adopted by a specific tendency in women's liberation, particularly separatists, to distinguish their views from those of socialist feminists. Ellen Willis's argument that this narrower usage conceals a retreat from the radicalism of early women's liberation has force.

The best general account of a women's liberation movement I have seen is Coote and Campbell (1982); on the early stages in the United States see Willis (1984); on preconditions, Segal (1983). On the history of gay liberation see Gay Left Collective (1980) for Britain; D'Emilio (1983) for the United States; Thompson (1985) for Australia. Figures on the British CHE conference from Lumsden (1984). On the 'men's movement', Hanisch (1975) – *con.*; Bristol Anti-Sexist Men's Conference (1980) – *pro*; Lyttleton (1984) – thoughtfully mixed.

13

Present and Future

The Present Moment

Hegel invented, and Marx made popular, a way of schematizing history in which there is an origin, a dialectic of necessary stages and a culmination – the ethical state, the classless society. It is tempting to schematize the history of gender relations the same way. Thus the story of primitive matriarchy, disrupted by men who seized power and set up a patriarchal society, which has now matured a feminist revolution in its turn. Or the idea that the social subordination of women flowed from their place in biological reproduction, was therefore technically necessary while fertility was high, productivity low and life short, and is now able to be abolished because technological change has freed women from the need to spend their lives around babies.

In such thinking the present moment is one of culmination, or perhaps the dark just before the dawn, and previous history was a kind of preparation for the present. Interim oppressions and injustices may have been nasty but they were in some sense historically necessary; they allowed the maturing of the good society in the end. Indeed quite a lot of nastiness in the present may also be justified to allow the good society to emerge from the womb of history.

Hegelian thinking is seductive: it gives dignity to present oppressions, a sense of connectedness to the past and a vision of the future transfigured. But it is also slightly paranoid. The present we live in was no more a historically necessary development than any of our possible futures is. Human practice produced it, not the operation of a mechanism, whether cosmic, logical or biological. That means that patriarchy, sexism and sexual oppression have never been necessary. Every society has been able to abolish it, whatever the level of technological development; just as class inequality could be abolished at any stage of history. What is changed by the level of technology is not the possibility of altering gender relations but the consequences of doing so. For example sharing childcare between women and men in an agricultural society without scientific medicine means a different set of arrangements from shared childcare in modern low-fertility cities.

So we live in a world shaped by the collective failure of our forebears to abolish gender inequalities. The corollary is that our children may also live in such a world. An end of gender inequality is by no means inevitable now. This has been seen by some feminist critics of the idea of revolution by bottle-babies, the idea that technologizing reproduction will liberate women from the imperatives of the body and social subordination, or will end the oppression of homosexuals by abolishing distinctions of sex. There is no guarantee that the new technology of reproduction will be under women's control, or under any kind of democratic influence at all. Indeed there is reason to expect the opposite, given the current rapid development of genetic engineering by big business and the state, and techniques like *in vitro* fertilization by technocratic medical specialists. Our future could be one of rejuvenated high-technology patriarchy.

The present moment, then, is not a culmination but a point of choice. The purpose of analysis is to understand better the structure of the choice and the collective projects that are feasible responses to it.

The emergence of women's liberation and gay liberation reflect crisis tendencies of a general kind, and are historically novel in the depth of their critique of the gender order and the scope of the transformation they propose. This surge in the pace and depth of sexual politics and the power of theory opens the possibility of conscious social and personal transformation in a degree unthinkable before. Yet the liberation movements have nothing like the social power needed to push this transformation through, except in limited milieux. And in some respects their internal evolution has led them away from the project of general structural reform, to focus on problems of survival rather than on the fault-lines marking general crisis tendencies.

Other components of a larger transformative project, notably working-class feminism and counter-sexist politics among hetero-sexual men, exist in a dispersed state. The hegemony of an authoritative masculinity, guaranteed by science if not religion, has been disrupted. But the weakened integration of the gender order has led to a fragmentation of opposition as well. In the absence of a unifying practice this fragmentation could increase.

If some combination of social forces around a progressive programme were achieved, contemporary social and physical technologies would allow a collective choice of the following kind, at least in the richer capitalist and Soviet-bloc countries. Childbearing can be made a fairly short episode in any woman's life, and can be made socially equivalent to conception, pregnancy-support and infant care in men's lives. We have the knowledge and resources to share childcare and domestic work among adults to any extent desired in a balance between efficiency and privacy. Large numbers of men and women can choose to be childless without any danger of depopulation; a free choice of forms of cathexis becomes a general possibility. No average physical or psychological difference between the sexes has the slightest bearing on the efficiency of production in an age of numerically controlled machine tools, automatic data-processing and mechanized agriculture. Thus there is no economic sacrifice in a total abolition of the sexual division of labour. Hegemonic masculinity is no collective asset in a struggle for survival, in fact it is now a general menace. The social hierarchy of masculinities can be abandoned, and with it the definition of an emphasized femininity.

The situation in the rest of the world is different, and there is no reason to expect that Western patterns of gender relations must provide their model. I know so little about Third World situations that I hesitate to say anything about feasible futures. But one thing is clear, that the world has become an interconnected social order and this is true of the dynamic of gender as well as other structures. Global reconstructions of the sexual division of labour show this already. It is not impossible that low-technology methods of equalizing gender relations could emerge mainly from the poor countries. Such a development could be powerfully reinforced by a transfer of resources made possible by the pacification of gender relations in the rich countries.

Strategies

If this is a practicable world, what are practicable ways of getting there? The recent history of sexual politics offers two general strategies, which might be called intensive and extensive.

I have mentioned the attempts to construct, in the social networks involved in radical politics over the last two decades, households and sexual relationships based on thoroughgoing equality. This involves, first, finding ways of equalizing economic resources and decision-making power. This is often difficult in a mixed household given men's greater earning capacity in a gender-structured labour market. Sometimes the best that can be achieved is some guarantee of an economic 'floor' for women, for instance by having property in a wife's name rather than a husband's. Second, it involves the reorganization of relations between children and adults, in the teeth of a vast array of institutional and cultural arrangements that presuppose all early childcare is done by women. Third, it involves a reworking of sexual character and sexuality, on the run and often in the context of attachments to third parties and terrible doubts about loyalty and personal worth. The process sometimes feels like tearing out one's hair, clump by clump, with a badly adjusted mechanical harvester. It is no wonder that a good many people have abandoned the attempt and that those who stick with it can be reluctant to talk about it. It is perhaps important to make the experience more public and cumulative. It is also important to find ways of expressing its positive side: the generation of energy, the joys of being with children, the pleasures of love between equals.

The attempt to create 'liberated zones', as this kind of practice is sometimes called, may literally mean a physical space. A common demand of feminist groups in institutions has been a room for women. Refuges, rape crisis centres and women's centres have often operated on the principle of keeping all men out. More generally, however, a liberated zone is a social 'space', a particular institution or part of one, a network of relationships or simply a group of people, where a degree of sex equality has been achieved, heterosexism eliminated, or counter-sexist practice sustained.

The problems of sustaining such a 'zone' have something in common with the problems of other enclaves. They require a constant expenditure of energy to keep up. When it is a question of a radical departure from common social practice, as a serious effort at sex equality is, the energy level required is fairly high. People get tired of constant meetings, monitoring and mutual criticism. Egalitarian practices constantly confront hierarchical intrusions from outside the zone. An example is the radical health collective whose one qualified doctor is treated by the funding authorities, and many of the patients, as the head of a conventional medical practice. Such matters can be worked on, but at a further cost in energy, time and friction. Trade-offs have to be made, things let slide. One of the things most often let slide is the cleaning; liberated zones tend to be grubby.

Offsetting these costs are three kinds of gains. Bases are established for politics of wider scope. Marches and rallies, for instance, do not just happen; there have to be people who call them, people who get on the phone and spread the word, people who paint banners and provide places to store them. Next, liberated zones can generate energy by giving a taste of the social world to come, what Sheila Rowbotham called 'prefigurative' politics in *Beyond the Fragments*. The sisterhood of feminist activists, the solidarity generated in gay liberation campaigns, the sense of sharing in collective households, are real experiences and do matter in showing that the goals are practical ones.

Finally there is the personal dimension. Radical politics often presuppose superhuman energy and result in burnout, or presuppose superhuman virtue and result in disillusion. Critics of feminism rejoice in claiming that feminists with power behave as crassly as patriarchal men; and of course some do. Likewise some gay liberationists are self-interested or insensitive, and some anti-sexist heterosexual men fail dismally to love vegetables and babies. A relatively liberated zone provides some chance of working on these issues, taking up the politics of personality outlined in chapter 10. It may also provide an essential kind of support. The main resource of radical politics is its activists. Political practice can be personally demanding, wearing and damaging to a high degree. Daily confrontation with sexist business men or bureaucrats is no life for the thin-skinned. It matters to find ways of conserving the human resources and repairing damage.

This issue is common to all radicalism, but sexual politics has a unique personal dimension. Breaking down the gender system means, to some extent, tearing down what is most constitutive of one's own emotions, and occupying strange and ill-explained places in social space. The oldest jibe against feminists is that they are trying to turn women into men and men into women. In one sense this is right; reform of the division of labour must mean women doing things conventionally thought masculine. Yet 'role-reversal' of the kind often advocated in the early seventies has proved inadequate as a strategy. Feminism has attempted, not just for tactical reasons, to hold on to qualities and practices traditionally thought feminine too. Thus the movement has found itself weaving across the conventional gender boundaries of sexual character and the division of labour, and to the extent that bisexuality has commended itself as a sexual practice, across the boundaries of the structure of cathexis too.

To some theorists the occupation of what might be called 'border country' has seemed a basic strategy. Fernbach and Mieli both insist on the gender ambiguities of gayness. Chodorow and Dinnerstein derive psychoanalytic arguments for the importance of men taking an equal part in early childcare. The counter-sexist men's movement, at least its more radical wing, sought to purge masculinity of its connection with hierarchy and easily tipped towards 'effeminism', attaching a male tail-end to radical feminism.

'Border' like 'zone' is a spatial metaphor and perhaps too rigid for a dynamic process. The point may be better made by saying that practice on many questions of sexual politics requires living in and through contradictions about gender. Sometimes it is necessary to intensify the contradiction rather than try to resolve it. The problem with the 'androgyny' model discussed in chapter 8 is not with the idea that feminine and masculine qualities can be combined in the same person, a helpful if not wholly new insight. It is with the idea that combining them somehow resolves the tension between them. It may do just the reverse.

The domestic politics of the Left, the partly 'liberated zone' sketched above, has another strategic significance. The attempt to create egalitarian households and a non-sexist environment for children to grow up in is the only form of progressive sexual politics in which significant numbers of heterosexual men have become involved in a continuing and active way. It is therefore something of a laboratory for the possibility of alliance between groups normally divided by sexual politics.

Gay liberation is another. The tensions between women and men in homosexual politics mentioned in chapter 12 are real and continuing. Given these pressures the continued existence of the movement over fifteen years of fluctuating fortunes is a considerable achievement. Its experience of discussion and compromise, joint and parallel action and collective celebration is perhaps the most sophisticated practice of cooperation between women and men that has yet been developed in the radical reconstruction of gender relations.

These two cases raise the more general strategy of alliance, the 'extensive' side of sexual politics. Many, perhaps most, of the campaigns waged by feminists and gay activists have involved acting in alliance with people outside their ranks. Numbers, access, money or technical skills may be needed from outside. Movement rhetoric usually ignores this, stressing opposition from the rest of the world and attributing all gains to women's or gays' own determination and strength. The political reasons for talking this way are obvious enough; but the habit does make it difficult to discuss what is actually going on in sexual politics, and often creates an impression that alliance or support is not wanted.

Homosexual law reform, as one example, involves lobbying ministers and members of parliament, working on party platform committees, discussions with police, liaison with civil liberties groups, detail work with sympathetic lawyers, academics and journalists. Most of them are not gay or are not admitting it. As another example, setting up women's studies courses in universities involves working with curriculum committees, getting support from authorities who have money or staff to allocate, co-operation from other teaching staff in the reallocation of labour, organizing rooms, furniture, equipment, secretarial help, library facilities and so on. Most of this requires the co-operation and labour of people who are not feminists, a good many of them not even women.

These alliances are usually temporary affairs. The public side of sexual politics in the last two decades has mainly been a patchwork of campaigns. Local movements and alliances developed around particular issues: setting up a health centre here, demonstrating on Anzac Day there, organizing a lobbying day at Parliament House and so on. Each grouping was liable to disband as soon as some resolution of the particular matter was reached. There have been attempts to set up permanent formal organizations, the National Organisation of Women in the United States and the Campaign for Homosexual Equality in Britain among the most successful. Both of these have provided a framework for alliance in the context of pressure-group politics, for law reform and like purposes. Across the wider spectrum of sexual politics, however, permanent organization has been uncharacteristic. The continuity of women's liberation and gay liberation, considerable in both cases, is due to overlapping membership of many different campaigns and networks and to endless internal talk rather than to formal structures.

In the liberal capitalist countries this kind of politics could continue indefinitely. There is enough tolerance and enough intermittent support. It will sustain a feminist and gay political presence at the level of pressure-group politics. But to pursue the project of transforming the gender order something more formidable is required. This is a question of putting together radical majorities in sexual politics, and keeping them together for considerable periods of time.

This is an old aspiration, though it is one from which leading tendencies in both gay and feminist politics have now retreated. Majorities matter, if the process of social change is to come under conscious human control. On the argument of this book, structures cannot be levered into new shapes without mutations of grassroots practice. But majorities do not fall from heaven. They have to be constructed; and if they are to be constructed *against* the ruling powers, around a radical program of equality, then we need a clear understanding of the social dynamic that might make it possible.

The crisis tendencies discussed in chapter 7, which make radical majorities conceivable, also give some leverage on the main structural obstacle. The lion in the path is the calculus of interests. In a gender order where men are advantaged and women are disadvantaged, major structural reform is, on the face of it, against men's interests. Even subordinated masculinities share to some degree in this advantage – as Mike Broker puts it, 'I may be a queer, but at least I am a man'. With the considerable number of women who gain wealth, prestige or other advantage through their marriages or kin relationships, or through applying an emphasized femininity, there would seem to be a permanent majority for patriarchy.

For two reasons this calculation is not conclusive. First, 'interests' are relational as well as egocentric. A father, for instance, has an interest defined by the advantages of men, but also has an interest in the welfare of his children, and half of all children are girls. The practices that articulate interest may be organized around these relationships rather than around the gender category. The crisis of the sexual division of labour in childcare invites this. Second, even egocentric interests are liable to be ambiguous or divided. The 'men's movement' literature was wrong in thinking men had the same interest in liberation as women but was right in pointing to tensions, costs and unease with hegemonic masculinity as a fairly widespread experience. The crisis tendencies in structures of power and cathexis are likely to increase such internal divisions of interest.

Whether the gender order's tendencies towards crisis have gone far enough to provide a basis for majorities committed to major structural reform, is perhaps the key strategic question radical politics now faces. It involves, in some sense, a combination of intensive and extensive strategies; the former to define directions and feasibility, the latter to provide the muscle. That kind of combination has not so far been realized. Tendencies towards it seem stronger in relation to the sexual division of labour than elsewhere: one thinks of the breakdown of the 'family wage' concept, the crisis of childcare and changing views about fathering, the inability of the liberal politics of equal opportunity to deal with mass youth unemployment. Yet the main energies of movement radicalism are focused elsewhere. If radical majorities are to materialize it is not just a matter of the masses flocking to the banners already embroidered and raised. Some painful reorientations of present radicalism will also have to happen.

Concluding Notes on the World to which a Social Theory of Gender Might Lead

For the ultimate goal of the transformation of gender relations there are two logical candidates. One is the abolition of gender, the other its reconstitution on new bases.

Along the first track some bold spirits have proposed the abolition of sexual reproduction. David Fernbach, in a recent and sophisticated version of this argument, goes so far as to suggest that this transcendence of internal nature, modernizing our 'palaeolithic' system of reproduction, would be the equivalent of the human transcendence of external nature. Apart from the doubtful politics of reproductive technology already discussed, this vision is based – like the celebration of 'woman and nature' that is its mirror-opposite – on a misunderstanding of how the social world of gender is constructed. The gender order is not and never has been immanent in biology. Rather it represents a particular historical response to human reproductive biology. It is possible to make other collective responses. Attempting to abolish biological sex is certainly one among them. But this would not be a liberating transcendence of nature, because our existing gender order is not given in nature. It would be a collective mutilation, that would certainly reduce the diversity of human experience and very possibly reinforce existing structures of power.

If the abolition of gender is a worthwhile goal, then, it must be the abolition of gender as a social structure that is at issue. As defined in chapter 6 gender is ultimately the linking of fields of social practice to the reproductive division, the creation of a relevance. Its abolition would be, logically, a matter of disconnecting those fields. This implies no denigration or denial of biological difference; equally no celebration of it. Difference between sexes would be simply a complementarity of function in reproduction, not a cosmic division or a social fate. There would be no reason for this to structure emotional relationships, so the categories heterosexual and homosexual would become insignificant. There would be no reason for it to structure character, so femininity and masculinity would depart.

Such a future is implied in the deconstructionist wing of gay liberation theory, and as an ultimate goal is more convincing than as an immediate strategy. Its great virtue is that it eliminates the basis for gender inequalities. The way biological difference and similarity have got incorporated into structures of social inequality creates our dilemmas about 'nature', not nature itself. Inequality is the basis of the social constitution of interests, which generate the practices that institutionalize injustices, the politics that defend them, the ideologies that justify them. The concept of liberation is not about freedom, in the sense of lack of constraint on personal behaviour, so much as about equality.

That is easy to say, but as many details canvassed in this book show, more than a little difficult to achieve, even in narrow settings. Equality is an absolute concept. It allows of no qualifications however well intentioned. Equality would be wholly unrealistic as a criterion for practice if it required complete equality to be an immediately achievable state. The arguments on the stability of personality traversed in Part III are sufficient to demolish any idea of general deconstruction as an immediate option. A strong concept of equality can, however, be a practical criterion without being compromised, if it is taken as a *direction of movement* which is never given up. That is, the equality criterion of all practices is that they produce more equality than the conditions they started from, with no intention of stopping at the conditions produced. In that sense deconstructing gender is a feasible ethical programme. The criterion of political practice becomes the disconnection of some further area of social practice from the reproduction complex.

The standard argument against the abolition of gender, like the traditional argument against the abolition of class, is that it would result in sameness. Without sex difference we must have grey uniformity – we will all wear boiler suits and have hair just covering the ears. The claim is perhaps effective as rhetoric, but as analysis it is simply misconceived. The logical consequence of deconstruction is open-ended variety. Marcuse's discussion of 'polymorphous perversity' in *Eros and Civilization* is not a bad summary of this conception, though with rules dismantled nothing can be defined as normative and hence nothing as 'perverse'. Polymorphous eroticism, perhaps; and also polymorphous labour and polymorphous structures of decision-making.

The cost of the abolition of gender, then, is not sameness, but the loss of certain kinds of structure. A judgement of this conception of liberation turns on whether gender structures have any value. What would be our loss if they went down the gurgle-hole of history?

It has to be said that a great deal of our culture's energy and beauty, as well as its barbarism, has been created through and around gender relations. A gender-structured culture, and quite specifically sexist sensibilities, have given us *Othello*, the *Ring of the Nibelung* and Rubens portraits, to go no further. Much of the fine texture of everyday life, from the feel of our own bodies, through the lore of running a household, to popular songs and everyday humour, are predicated on gender. Our eroticism and our imagination seem to be both limited and fuelled by gender. To discard the whole pattern does seem to imply a way of life that would be seriously impoverished by comparison with the one we know. At best it would be so different from the world of our experience that we can hardly know whether it would be desirable or not.

Yet the constraints that produce this experience, this richness of culture, also produce the massive inequalities, bitter oppressions, violence and potential disaster that are the reasons for the critiques of gender discussed in this book. This raises the question whether the cultural energy can be disconnected from the structure of inequality, gender not abolished but reconstituted in unmurderous forms.

This implies restructuring rather than destructuring. It presupposes that the elements of gender orders can be reshuffled in some sense. The historical argument of Part II certainly supports this idea, though how far it can be pushed remains open. It implies a process at the collective level like what Piaget calls 'assimilation' in the psychology of intelligence, in which the existing materials of a sexist culture are taken up and made over to new purposes. A clear example on a small scale is the appropriation of punk styles by girls mentioned in chapter 6. Piaget defines play as almost pure assimilation, and it might be said that what is involved is a qualitative growth of our collective ability to play.

Playing with gender is not unknown at present. Elements of sexual character, gender practice or sexual ideology are often disconnected and recombined for enjoyment, erotic tension, subversion or convenience. Such games are most developed, perhaps, in sexual subcultures. Peter Ackroyd argues a historical connection between drag and the subversion of everyday custom in 'carnival'. Pat Califia describes how lesbian sado-masochism disconnects power from masculinity for erotic purposes. The erotica of fetishism – rubber, leather and others – systematically ring the changes on gender symbols and relationships. But the same kind of thing happens in less exotic contexts. Mass fashion began playing with gender recombination in the 1930s, and more vigorously in the 'unisex' styles of the 1960s. Gender ambiguity has been a theme of rock music presentation from David Bowie and the New York Dolls to Grace Jones and Boy George. In a different vein, the Soviets' creation of women cosmonauts as media figures is also a game with femininity/masculinity and the sexual division of labour, played for political effect.

However the implication of restructuring is more than the reshuffling of existing practices and symbols, more than the turning of a kaleidoscope; and the 'game' analogy only goes so far. When the relations between cultural elements change, new conditions for practice are created and new patterns of practice become possible. Deconstruction implies that the biology of sex would become a minimal presence in social life, a kind of sexual *cuisine minceur*. The restructuring conception would admit a cultural elaboration of difference and similarity in reproduction, though with the weight of power, divisions of labour and rules about cathexis lifted off it. The culture could attend to, and celebrate, the nuances and variations of conception, gestation, birth and suckling, growth and ageing.

More, it would be possible to explore and invent many different ways for people to become involved in the process. We have for the most part stuck at two sexes. But early gay theory conceived of a 'third sex', and Olaf Stapledon, in one of the first classics of science fiction, imagined human species in the far future with multiple sexes or sub-sexes. These were imagined as biological types; the real possibilities are social. While the 'third sex' concept is obsolete, it would be quite possible for gay women and men who do not have children of their own to be routinely involved in the raising of children. This would construct specific patterns of relationship between children and adults, able to complement and enrich the relationships constructed by heterosexual adults. Gary Dowsett points to historical examples of relationships between young children and adults who are not their parents, such as aunts and uncles in the nineteenth-century bourgeois family, as models that could be revived and given new meanings. The symbolic participation of men in birth through the 'couvade' is another historical experience that could be given a new meaning. If the inequalities of the sexual division of labour are to be dismantled, men must obviously take up much of the domestic work created by pregnancy, birth and early childcare. The somewhat fragile industrial concept of 'paternity leave' is a small beginning with a shift that needs to be given a much stronger social definition.

What would be lost in the restructuring conception of liberation is the necessary connection of the elements of gender relations to institutionalized inequality on one side and biological difference on the other. The depth of this change should not be underestimated. It would be a fundamental departure from a key condition of our present culture, which might be summarized as the sense that gender is fatality.

At present this sense runs through every area of gender practice, penetrating imagination and action alike. The naturalization of gender is the basic mechanism of sexual ideology. A leaden fatality invests the division of labour: 'woman's work', 'a man's responsibilities'. A sharper-edged fatality of cathexis is central to Western culture's treatment of the theme of love, from the *Medea* to *Casablanca*. A sense of the psychological fatality of gender is expressed in the doctrine of sexual character.

Given this, a society that eliminated sex inequality by the recomposition of gender must have a different structure of feeling. Much of the cultural inheritance will then only be recoverable as history, by a shift back into alien frames of thought. Not wholly alien, of course; there will still be love, hatred, jealousy and divided loyalties to keep life interesting. But they will be experienced as relationships between personal projects rather than as fatality. This may mean they have less cultural power. The sense of fatality is not a passive consciousness but a lever on experience and action, a generator (to change the metaphor) of tragedy and exhilaration. If it narrows the world it also makes parts of it more intense.

At that cost, a recomposed human society will gain a degree of practical equality never yet achieved, and an enormous enrichment of its cultural resources. This enrichment is worth spelling out. First there are more players in the game. The 'equal opportunity' argument that sex discrimination wastes human resources is, with all its limitations, correct – and can be extended far beyond the issue of employment. Second, the free reworking of gender relations which are at present strongly constrained, and psychological and cultural patterns at present strongly stylized, geometrically increases the possibilities of experience and invention. Hermaphroditism or androgyny is hardly even a beginning. Third, and perhaps most important, the emotional dimensions of life that are opened up for exploration in a sexually equal society are more complex than those of our own society because of the greater possibilities of creation and diversity. Love between equals is no less passionate than love under the star of gender inequality. It will be differently passionate as the business of protection and dependence is dispensed with. These themes in relationships will perhaps be replaced by the excitement of the unknown and unpredictable, and of constructing futures that are genuinely without preordained limits. Love will also have new difficulties, such as problems of constructing new forms of reciprocity and of balancing commitment with personal invention.

These possibilities, though argued here on the basis of change in the structure of gender relations, have other presuppositions. Notably they presuppose a move towards a society free of class and racial inequalities, and a world free of imperialism and the obscene inequalities of global living standards that we have today.

The analysis in this book rejects both the idea that gender is the basic oppression from which these others spring, so sexual politics must take priority, and the idea that gender inequalities are secondary, so sexual politics can be sidelined while the main event proceeds. The main event, the historic struggle for human equality which is now also a struggle for human survival, is a complex of these constituents. Global inequality is a composed structure in the sense of my argument about gender, on a larger scale again.

This implies that the constituents react on each other. It is therefore not possible to accept the arguments, which seem increasingly popular with radical intellectuals, that fragment radical politics into a plurality of struggles in different sites with no systematic connection to each other. These arguments reflect a well-justified discontent with attempts, for instance by orthodox Marxism, to hegemonize other groups, campaigns and social struggles. But they leave us with no way of making rational choices of strategy based on concepts like crisis tendencies. Movements for social change need strategies if their priorities are not to be set for them by the opposition.

It is possible to imagine a society with sex equality in which other kinds of inequality are far from dead. One thinks of the guardians in Plato's *Republic*, or the aristocracy and bureaucracy of Ursula LeGuin's *The Left Hand of Darkness*. Conversely there are socialist Utopias with a highly conventional idea of the naturalness of sexual character, like Edward Bellamy's *Looking Backward*. The connection between structures of inequality is not a logical connection: theorists who have assumed that have been seduced by another kind of Hegelianism. The connection is empirical and practical. As a matter of fact, the core institutions of the contemporary structure of gender power cannot be torn down without a class politics, because those institutions fuse gender and class domination. As a matter of practice, equality is difficult to contain; the origins of modern feminist radicalism in the New Left show that. The historic association between socialism and feminism, however tense and ragged it has been, expresses a basic truth about the global structure of inequality and what social forces might dismantle it. For all its resistances the British Trades Union Congress did march in support of women's abortion rights; the Confederation of British Industry did not.

There are other conceivable futures that are a great deal less attractive. Margaret Atwood's novel about a repressive future,

The Handmaid's Tale, is a satire but not wildly implausible. A recomposition of gender might well be undertaken as part of an authoritarian politics; the current development of birth technology points in that direction. A recomposition of gender that realizes the possibilities I have discussed, constructing an egalitarian form of life, is only a historical possibility and not a necessary future. If it is to happen then its practice, the projects in which we undertake recomposition, must be part of a politics that addresses oppression in all its forms, that sets no limit to the principle of human equality. In undertaking that we would be shifting the internal limits to our collective ability to shape a future that is physically and environmentally safe, rich in experience and historically open.

Bibliography

Abercrombie, N., Hill, S. and Turner, B. S. (1980) *The Dominant Ideology Thesis* (London: George Allen and Unwin).

Ackroyd, P. (1979) *Dressing Up: Transvestism and Drag* (London: Thames and Hudson).

Adler, A. (1956) *The Individual Psychology of Alfred Adler* (New York: Basic Books).

Adler, A. (1928) 'Psychologie der Macht', in F. Kobler, ed. *Gewalt und Gewaltlosigkeit* (Zurich: Rotapfelverlag), pp. 41–6.

Adorno, T. W., Frenkel-Brunswik, E., Levinson, D. J., and Sanford, R. N. (1950) *The Authoritarian Personality* (New York: Harper).

Alinsky, S. D. (1972) *Rules for Radicals* (New York: Vintage).

Allen, P. (1970) *Free Space: A Perspective on the Small Group in Women's Liberation* (United States: Times Change Press).

Altman, D. (1972) *Homosexual: Oppression and Liberation* (Sydney: Angus and Robertson).

Altman, D. (1979) *Coming Out in the Seventies* (Sydney: Wild and Woolley).

Altman, D. (1982) *The Homosexualization of America, the Americanization of the Homosexual* (New York: St Martin's Press).

Amato, P. R. (1980) 'Man in a Woman's World: The Hassles of a Male Homemaker', *Social Alternatives*, 1, 6/7, pp. 100–2.

American Psychological Association (1977) 'Guidelines for Nonsexist Language in APA Journals', *American Psychologist*, 32, 6, pp. 487–94.

Anti-Discrimination Board, NSW (1982) *Discrimination and Homosexuality* (Sydney: ADB).

Arendt, H. (1958) *The Origins of Totalitarianism* (New York: Meridan).

Aries, P. (1973) *Centuries of Childhood* (London: Jonathan Cape).

Atwood, M. (1986) *The Handmaid's Tale* (London: Jonathan Cape).

Bachofen, J. J. (1967) *Myth, Religion and Mother Right: Selected writings* (London: Routledge and Kegan Paul).

Baldock, C. V., and Cass, B., eds (1983) *Women, Social Welfare and the State* (Sydney: George Allen and Unwin).

Barbour, J. (1973) 'That Thing of Silk', *Refractory Girl*, 2 pp. 25–9.

Barnsley Women Against Pit Closures (1984) *Women Against Pit Closures* (Britain: WAPC).

Barrett, M. (1980) *Women's Oppression Today* (London: Verso).

Barry, K. (1979) *Female Sexual Slavery* (Englewood Cliffs, NJ: Prentice-Hall).

Bateson, G. (1973) *Steps to an Ecology of Mind* (St Albans: Paladin).

Beauvoir, S. de (1972 [1949]) *The Second Sex* (Harmondsworth: Penguin).

Bebel, F. A. (1904) *Women under Socialism* (New York: Labor News Company).

Bell, C. and Newby, H. (1976) 'Husbands and Wives: The Dynamics of the Deferential Dialectic' in S. Allen and D. Barker, eds *Dependence and Exploitation in Work and Marriage* (London: Longman).

Bellamy, E. (1888) *Looking Backward* (Boston: Ticknor and Co.).

Bem, S. L. (1974) 'The Measurement of Psychological Androgyny', *Journal Consult. Clin. Psychol.*, 42, 2, pp. 155–62.

Bertaux, D. (1981) *Biography and Society: The Life History Approach in the Social Sciences* Beverley Hills: Sage, Sage Studies in International Sociology, 23.

Biddle, B. J. (1979) *Role Theory* (New York: Academic Press).

Bland, L., Brunsdon, C., Hobson, D., and Winship, J. (1978) 'Women Inside and Outside' the Relations of Production', in Centre for Contemporary Cultural Studies, Women's Studies Group, *Women Take Issue: Aspects of Women's Subordination* (London: Hutchinson), pp. 35–78.

Bottomley, G. (1979) *After the Odyssey: A study of Greek Australians* (St Lucia: University of Queensland Press).

Bourdieu, P. (1977) *Outline of a Theory of Practice* (Cambridge: Cambridge University Press).

Bowlby, J. (1953) *Child Care and the Growth of Love* (Harmondsworth: Penguin).

Bowles, S. and Gintis, H. (1976) *Schooling in Capitalist America* (London: Routledge and Kegan Paul).

Branca, P. (1978) *Women in Europe since 1750* (London: Croom Helm).

Bray, A. (1982) *Homosexuality in Renaissance England* (London: Gay Men's Press).

Bristol Anti-Sexist Men's Conference (1980) 'A Minimum Self-Definition of the Anti-Sexist Men's Movement', *Achilles Heel*, 4, pp. 2–3.

Brohm, J-M. (1978) *Sport – A Prison of Measured Time* (London: Ink Links).

Broker, M. (1976) 'I May be a Queer, But at Least I am a Man: Male Hegemony and Ascribed versus Achieved Gender', in D. Leonard Barker and S. Allen, eds *Sexual Divisions and Society* (London: Tavistock), 174–98.

Brown, B. (1973) *Marx, Freud and the Critique of Everyday Life* (New York: Monthly Review Press).

296   *Bibliography*

Brown, N. O. (1959) *Life Against Death: The Psychoanalytical Meaning of History* (Middletown: Wesleyan University Press).

Brownmiller, S. (1975) *Against Our Will: Men, Women and Rape* (New York: Simon and Schuster).

Bryson, L. and Mowbray M. (1983) 'The Reality of Community Care', *Australian Society*, 2, 5, p. 13.

Bullock, A. (1962) *Hitler*, rev. edn (Harmondsworth: Penguin).

Bullough, V. L. (1979) *Homosexuality: a History* (New York: New American Library).

Bujra, J., et al. (1984) 'Challenging *The Feminist Challenge*: A Forum on Bouchier', *Network* (BSA Newsletter), 29, 6–7.

Bureau of Crime Statistics and Research, NSW (1978–9) *Homosexual Offences* (Sydney: BCSR), Research Report 3.

Burgmann, M. (1980) 'Revolution and Machismo', in E. Windschuttle, ed. *Women, Class and History* (Australia: Fontana).

Burnett, J., ed. (1982) *Destiny Obscure: Autobiographies of Childhood, Education and Family from the 1820s to the 1920s* (London: Allen Lane).

Burney, C. (1977) *From Village to Empire: An Introduction to Near Eastern Archaeology* (Oxford: Phaidon).

Burton, C. (1985) *Subordination: Feminism and Social Theory* (Sydney: George Allen and Unwin).

Cahill, S. E. (1983) 'Reexamining the Acquisition of Sex Roles: A Social Interactionist Approach', *Sex Roles*, 9, 1, pp. 1–15.

Caldwell, L. (1978) 'Church, State, and Family: The Women's Movement in Italy', in A. Kuhn and A-M. Wolpe, eds *Feminism and Materialism* (London: Routledge and Kegan Paul), pp. 68–95.

Califia, P. (1983) *Sapphistry: The Book of Lesbian Sexuality*, 2nd edn (United States: Naiad Press).

Campbell, B. (1984) *Wigan Pier Revisited: Poverty and Politics in the Eighties* (London: Virago).

Cancian, F. M. and Ross, B. L. (1981) 'Mass Media and the Women's Movement 1900–1977', *Journal of Applied Behavioral Sciences*, 17, 1, pp. 9–26.

Carey, G. and Lette, K. (1979) *Puberty Blues* (Melbourne: McPhee Gribble).

Carr, E. H. (1961) *What is History?* (London: Macmillan).

Carrigan, T. (1981) *The Theoretical Significance of the Arguments of the Gay Liberation Movement, 1969–1981*, Ph.D. thesis, Dept of Politics, University of Adelaide.

Carrigan, T., Connell, R. W., and Lee, J. (1985) 'Toward a New Sociology of Masculinity', *Theory and Society*, 14, 5, pp. 551–604.

Carroll, J. (1977) *Puritan, Paranoid, Remissive* (London: Routledge and Kegan Paul).

Carter, A. (1974) *Fireworks* (London: Quartet).

Carter, A. (1979) *The Sadeian Woman: An Exercise in Cultural History* (London: Virago).

Casner, M. B. and Gabriel, R. H. (1955) *The Story of American Democracy*, (New York: Harcourt, Brace, Jovanovich) 3rd edn.

Cavendish, R. (1982) *Women on the Line* (London: Routledge and Kegan Paul).

Central Office of Information, Great Britain (1984) *Women in Britain* (London: COI).

Centre for Contemporary Cultural Studies, Women's Studies Group (1978) *Women Take Issue* (London: Hutchinson).

Centre for Urban Research and Action (1976) *'But I Wouldn't Want my Wife to Work Here...' A Study of Migrant Women in Melbourne Industry* (Melbourne: CURA).

Chafetz, J. S. (1980) 'Toward a Macro-Level Theory of Sexual Stratification and Gender Differentiation', *Current Perspectives in Social Theory*, 1, pp. 103–25.

Chapkis, W. ed. (1981) *Loaded Questions: Women in the Military* (Amsterdam: Transnational Institute).

Chesler, P. (1978) *About Men* (London: Women's Press).

Childe, V. G. (1936) *Man Makes Himself* (London: Watts).

Childe, V. G. (1950[1925]) *The Dawn of European Civilization*, 5th edn (London: Routledge and Kegan Paul).

Childe, V. G. (1950) 'The Urban Revolution', *Town Planning Review*, 21, 1, pp. 3–17.

Chodorow, N. (1978) *The Reproduction of Mothering: Psychoanalysis and the Sociology of Gender* (Berkeley: University of California Press).

Chomsky, N. (1971) *Problems of Knowledge and Freedom* (New York: Vintage).

Cicourel, A. V. (1964) *Method and Measurement in Sociology* (New York: Free Press).

Clark G. and Piggott, S. (1965) *Prehistoric Societies* (London: Hutchinson).

Clark, W. (1983) 'Home Thoughts from Not so Far Away: A Personal Look at Family', in L. Segal, ed. *What is to be Done about the Family?* (London: Penguin), pp. 168–89.

Cliff, T. (1984) *Class Struggle and Women's Liberation* (London: Bookmarks).

Cockburn, C. (1983) *Brothers: Male Dominance and Technological Change* (London: Pluto Press).

Cockburn, C. (1986) *Machinery of Dominance* (London, Pluto Press).

Collingwood, R. G. (1946) *The Idea of History* (Oxford: Oxford University Press).

Collinson, D. and Knights, D. (1984) '"Men Only": Theories and Practices of Job Segregation' paper to Society for Study of Social Problems, San Antonio.

Comer, L. (1974) *Wedlocked Women* (Leeds: Feminist Books).

Connell, R. W. (1974) 'You Can't Tell Them Apart Nowadays, Can You?' *Search*, 5, 7, pp. 282–5.
Connell, R. W. (1983) *Which Way is Up?* (Sydney: George Allen and Unwin).
Connell, R. W. (1985a) 'Masculinity, Violence and War', in P. Patton and R. Poole, eds *War/Masculinity* (Sydney: Intervention), pp. 4–10.
Connell, R. W. (1985b) *Teachers' Work* (Sydney: George Allen and Unwin).
Connell, R. W., Ashenden, D. J., Kessler, S. & Dowsett, G. W. (1982) *Making the Difference: Schools, Families and Social Division* (Sydney: George Allen and Unwin).
Connell, R. W., Dowsett, G. W., Kessler, S., & Ashenden, D.J. (1981) 'Class and Gender Dynamics in a Ruling-Class School', *Interchange*, 12, 2–3, pp. 102–17.
Connell, W. F. (1980) *A History of Education in the Twentieth Century World* (Canberra: Curriculum Development Centre).
Connell, W. F., et al. (1975) *12 to 20* (Sydney: Hicks Smith).
Constantinople, A. (1973) 'Masculinity-Femininity: An Exception to a Famous Dictum?', *Psychological Bulletin*, 80, 5, 389-407.
Constantinople, A. (1979) 'Sex Role Acquisition: In Search of the Elephant', *Sex Roles*, 5, 2, pp. 121–33.
Cook, P., Davey, I. and Vick, M. (1979) 'Capitalism and Working Class Schooling in Late Nineteenth Century South Australia', *Australian and New Zealand History of Education Society Journal*, 8, 2, 36–48.
Cooper, D. (1968) *The Dialectics of Liberation* (Harmondsworth: Penguin).
Cooper, D. (1971) *The Death of the Family* (London: Allen Lane).
Coote, A. and Campbell, B. (1982) *Sweet Freedom: The Struggle for Women's Liberation* (London: Pan).
Corrigan, P. (1984) 'My Body, my "Self"? Trying to See my Masculine Eyes', *Resources for Feminist Research*, 12, 4, 29–32.
Costello, J. (1985) *The Pacific War* (London: Pan).
Court, D. (1986) *The State and Women's Liberation*, unpublished manuscript, Macquarie University.
Croll, E. J. (1983) *Chinese Women Since Mao* (London: Zed Press).
Cucchiari, S. (1981) 'The Gender Revolution and the Transition from Bisexual Horde to Patrilocal Band: The Origins of Gender Hierarchy', in S. B. Ortner and H. Whitehead, eds *Sexual Meanings: The Cultural Construction of Gender and Sexuality* (Cambridge, Cambridge University Press), pp. 31–79.
Curthoys, A. (1976) 'Men and Childcare in the Feminist Utopia', *Refractory Girl*, 1, pp. 3–5.
Dahrendorf, R. (1973) *Homo Sociologicus* (London: Routledge and Kegan Paul).
Dalla Costa, M. and James, S. (1975) *The Power of Women and the Subversion*

of the Community (Bristol: Falling Wall Press).

Daly, M. (1978) *Gyn/Ecology: The Metaethics of Radical Feminism* (Boston: Beacon Press).

Dancis, B. (1976) 'Socialism and Women in the United States, 1900–1917', *Socialist Revolution*, 6, 1, pp. 81–144.

Darwin, C. (1928[1859]) *Of the Origin of Species by means of Natural Selection* (London: Dent).

Darwin, C. (1890[1874]) *The Descent of Man, and Selection in Relation to Sex*, 2nd edn (London: John Murray).

Dasey, R. (1985) *Women Workers: Their Employment and Participation in the Labour Movement. Hamburg 1880–1914*. Ph.D. thesis, University of London.

David, D. S. and Brannon, R.(1976) *The Forty-Nine Percent Majority: The Male Sex Role* (Reading, MA: Addington-Wesley).

Davidson, B. (1974) *Africa in History: Themes and Outlines*, rev. edn (London, Macmillan).

Davies, M.L., ed. (1977[1931]) *Life As We Have Known It, By Cooperative Working Women* (London: Virago).

Davies, M. L. (1978[1915]) *Maternity: Letters from Working-Women* (London, Virago).

Dawkins, R. (1976) *The Selfish Gene* (Oxford University Press).

Delphy, C., (1977) *The Main Enemy: A Materialist Analysis of Women's Oppression* (London: Women's Research and Resources Centre).

D'Emilio, J. (1983) *Sexual Politics, Sexual Communities: The Making of a Homosexual Minority in the United States 1940–1970* (Chicago: University of Chicago Press).

Denno, D. (1982) 'Sex Differences in Cognition: A Review and Critique of the Longitudinal Evidence', *Adolescence*, 17, 68, pp. 779–88.

Department of Health, Australia (1984) *Alcohol in Australia: A Summary of Related Statistics* (Canberra: Australian Government Publishing Service).

Dinnerstein, D. (1976) *The Mermaid and the Minotaur* (New York: Harper and Row).

Dixon, B. (1977) *Catching them Young* (London: Pluto Press), Vol. 1: *Sex, Race and Class in Children's Fiction*.

Dobash, R. E. and Dobash, R. P. (1979) *Violence Against Wives: A Case Against the Patriarchy* (New York: Free Press).

Dollard, J. (1935) *Criteria for the Life History* (New Haven: Yale University Press).

Dollard, J. (1937) *Caste and Class in a Southern Town* (New Haven: Yale Univerity Press).

Dolto, F. (1974) *Dominique: Analysis of an Adolescent* (London: Souvenir Press).

Donzelot, J. (1979) *The Policing of Families* (New York: Pantheon).

Dowsett, G. (1982) 'Boiled Lollies and Bandaids: Gay Men and Kids', *Gay Information*, 11, pp. 34–8.

Du Bois, E., Buhle, M. J., Kaplan, T., Lerner, G., & Smith-Rosenberg, C. (1980) 'Politics and Culture in Women's History: A Symposium'. *Feminist Studies*, 6, 1, 26–64.

Duffy, M. (1972) *The Erotic World of Faery* (London: Hodder and Stoughton).

Dunbar, R. (1970) 'Female Liberation as the Basis for Social Revolution', in R. Morgan, ed. *Sisterhood is Powerful* (New York: Vintage), pp. 477–92.

Dworkin, A. (1981) *Pornography: Men Possessing Women* (London: Women's Press).

Dworkin, A. (1983) *Right-Wing Women* (London: Women's Press).

Eardley, T., Gould, S., Metcalfe, A. & Morrison, P. (1980) 'The Sexual Politics of Men's Work', *Achilles Heel*, 4, pp. 15–19.

Easlea, B. (1983) *Fathering the Unthinkable: Masculinity, Scientists and the Arms Race* (London: Pluto Press).

Edgar, D. and Ochiltree, G. (1982) 'Family Change and Early Childhood Development', *Institute of Family Studies Discussion Paper*, 6.

Edgar, P. and McPhee, H. (1974) *Media She* (Melbourne: Heinemann).

Edwards, A. R. (1983) 'Sex Roles: A Problem for Sociology and for Women', *Australian and New Zealand Journal of Sociology*, 19, 3, pp. 385–412.

Ehrenreich, B. (1977) 'Towards Socialist Feminism', *Heresies*, 1, pp. 4–7.

Ehrenreich, B. (1983) *The Hearts of Men* (London: Pluto Press).

Ehrenreich, B., and English, D. (1979) *For Her Own Good* (London: Pluto Press).

Ehrhardt, A. A. and Meyer-Bahlburg, H. F. L. (1981) 'Effects of Prenatal Sex Hormones on Gender-Related Behaviour', *Science*, 211, pp. 1312–18.

Eisenstein, H. (1984) *Contemporary Feminist Thought* (London: Unwin Paperbacks).

Eisenstein, H. (1985) 'The Gender of Bureaucracy: Reflections on Feminism and the State', in J. Goodnow and C. Pateman, eds *Women, Social Science and Public Policy* (Sydney: George Allen and Unwin), pp. 104–15.

Eisenstein, H. and Jardine, A., ed. (1980) *The Future of Difference* (Boston: Hall).

Eisenstein, Z. R. (1979) *Capitalist Patriarchy and the Case for Socialist Feminism* (New York: Monthly Review Press).

Ellis, A. (1976) *Sex and the Liberated Man* (Secaucus: Lyle Stuart).

Ellis, H. (1923[1897]) *Studies in the Psychology of Sex*, Vol. 2: *Sexual Inversion*. (Philadephia: Davis).

Engels, F. (1970[1884]) 'The Origin of the Family, Private Property and the State', in K. Marx and F. Engels *Selected Works* (Moscow: Progress Publishers), vol. 3.

Erikson, E. H. (1965) *Childhood and Society*, 2nd edn, (Harmondsworth: Penguin).

Esterson, A. (1970) *The Leaves of Spring: A Study in the Dialectics of Madness* (London: Tavistock).

Fairweather, H. (1976) 'Sex Differences in Cognition', *Cognition*, 4, 3, pp. 231–80.

Fanon, F. (1967) *Black Skin, White Masks* (New York: Grove Press).

Fanon, F. (1968) *The Wretched of the Earth* (New York: Grove Press).

Farrell, W. (1974) *The Liberated Man* (New York: Random House).

Fendrich-Salowey, G., Buchanan M. and Drew, C. (1982) 'Mathematics, Quantitative and Attitudinal Measures for Elementary School Boys and Girls', *Psychological Reports*, 51, 1, pp. 155–62.

Fernbach, D. (1981) *The Spiral Path* (London: Gay Men's Press).

Firestone, S. (1971) *The Dialectic of Sex* (London: Paladin).

Foucault, M. (1980) 'Introduction', in *Herculine Barbin* (Brighton: Harvester).

Foucault, M. (1980) *The History of Sexuality* (New York: Vintage), vol. 1: *Introduction*.

Franzway, S. and Lowe, J. (1978) 'Sex-Role Theory: Political Cul-de-sac?', *Refractory Girl*, 16, pp. 14–16.

Freud, S. (1905) 'Fragment of an Analysis of a Case of Hysteria', in his *Complete Psychological Works*, standard edn, (London: Hogarth, 1953), vol. 7, pp. 1–122.

Freud, S. 'Three Essays on the Theory of Sexuality', in his *Complete Psychological Works*, standard edn, (London: Hogarth, 1953), vol. 7, pp. 123–243.

Freud, S. (1908) '"Civilized" Sexual Morality and Modern Nervous Illness', in his *Complete Psychological Works*, standard edn, (London: Hogarth, 1959), vol. 9, pp. 177–204.

Freud, S. (1913) 'Totem and Taboo', in his *Complete Psychological Works*, standard edn (London: Hogarth, 1953), vol. 13, pp.1–161.

Freud, S. (1918) 'From the History of an Infantile Neurosis', in his *Complete Psychological Works*, standard edn, (London: Hogarth, 1955) vol. 17.

Freud, S. (1923) 'The Ego and the Id', in his *Complete Psychological Works*, standard edn (London: Hogarth, 1961) vol. 19.

Freud, S. (1930) 'Civilization and its Discontents', in his *Complete Psychological Works*, standard edn, (London: Hogarth, 1961), vol. 21.

Friedan, B. (1963) *The Feminine Mystique* (New York: Norton).

Friedan, B. (1982) *The Second Stage* (London: Michael Joseph).

Friday, N. (1979) *My Mother/My Self* (Glasgow: Fontana/Collins).

Fromm, E. (1942) *The Fear of Freedom* (London: Routledge and Kegan Paul).

Gagnon, J. H. and Simon, W. (1974) *Sexual Conduct: The Social Sources of Human Sexuality* (London: Hutchinson).

Gamarnikow, E. (1978) 'Sexual Division of Labour: The Case of Nursing', in A. Kuhn and A.-M. Wolpe, eds *Feminism and Materialism* (London: Routledge and Kegan Paul), pp. 96–123.

Game, A. and Pringle, R. (1979) 'Sexuality and the Suburban Dream', *Australian and New Zealand Journal of Sociology*, 15, 2, pp. 4–15.

Game, A., and Pringle, R. (1979) 'The Making of the Australian Family', *Intervention*, 12, pp. 63–83.

Game, A., and Pringle, R. (1983) *Gender at Work* (Sydney: George Allen and Unwin).

Garfinkel, H. (1967) 'Passing and the Managed Achievement of Sex Status in an Intersexed Person, Part 1', in his *Studies in Ethnomethodology* (Englewood Cliffs, NJ: Prentice-Hall), pp. 116–85.

Gay Left Collective, ed. (1980) *Homosexuality: Power and Politics* (London: Allison and Busby).

Genet, J. (1966) *Our Lady of the Flowers* (St Albans: Panther).

Giddens, A. (1979) *Central Problems in Social Theory* (London: Macmillan).

Giddens, A. (1984) *The Constitution of Society* (Cambridge: Polity Press).

Gilder, G. (1975) *Sexual Suicide* (New York: Bantam).

Gilding, M. (1984) *Theory and History of the Family. A Case Study: Sydney from the 1870s to the 1930s*, Ph.D. thesis, Sociology, Macquarie University.

Gilman, C. P. (1979[1915]) *Herland* (London: Women's Press).

Godelier, M. (1981) 'The Origins of Male Domination', *New Left Review*, 127, pp. 3–17.

Goffman, E. (1979) *Gender Advertisements*, (Cambridge, MA: Harvard University Press).

Goldberg, S. (1973) *The Inevitability of Patriarchy* (New York: William Morrow).

Goldberg, H. (1976) *The Hazards of Being Male* (New York: Nash).

Goldhamer, H. (1949) 'Public Opinion and Personality', *American Journal of Sociology*, 55, pp. 346–54.

Goldman, E. (1972a) 'The Traffic in Women', in her *Red Emma Speaks* (New York: Vintage), pp. 143–57.

Goldman, E. (1972b) 'Marriage and Love', in her *Red Emma Speaks* (New York: Vintage), pp. 158–67.

Goldmann, L. (1964) *The Hidden God* (London: Routledge and Kegan Paul).

Goldmann, L. (1977) *Cultural Creation in Modern Society* (Oxford: Basil Blackwell).

Goode, W. J. (1982) 'Why Men Resist', in B. Thorne and M. Yalom, eds *Rethinking the Family* (New York: Longman), pp. 131–50.

Goot, M. and Reid, E. (1975) *Women and Voting Studies* (London: Sage Publication), Sage Professional Papers in Contemporary Political Sociology vol. 1.

Gordimer, N. (1979) *Burger's Daughter* (Harmondsworth: Penguin).

Gough, K. (1971) 'The Origin of the Family', *Journal of Marriage and the Family*, 33, pp. 760–71.

Gouldner, A. W. (1979) *The Future of Intellectuals and the Rise of the New Class* (New York: Seabury Press).

Gramsci, A. (1971) *Selections from the Prison Notebooks* (London: Lawrence and Wishart).

Greene, G. and Greene, C. (1974) *S–M: The Last Taboo* (New York: Grove Press).

Greer, G. (1970) *The Female Eunuch* (London: McGibbon and Kee).

Griffin, C. (1985) *Typical Girls?* (London: Routledge and Kegan Paul).

Griffin, S. (1980) *Woman and Nature* (New York: Harper).

Griffin, S. (1981) *Pornography and Silence: Culture's revenge against nature* (London: Women's Press).

Habermas, J. (1976) *Legitimation Crisis* (London: Heinemann).

Habermas, J. (1979) *Communication and the Evolution of Society* (London, Heinemann).

Hacker, A. (1983) *US: A Statistical Portrait of the American People* (New York: Viking).

Hall, R. (1974[1928]) *The Well of Loneliness* (London: Corgi).

Hall, R. (1978) *Marie Stopes: A Biography* (London: Virago).

Hamilton, R. (1978) *The Liberation of Women* (London: George Allen and Unwin).

Hamilton, A. (1981) 'A Complex Strategical Situation: Gender and Power in Aboriginal Australia', in N. Grieve and P. Grimshaw, eds *Australian Women: Feminist Perspectives* (Melbourne; Oxford University Press) 69–85.

Hanisch, C. (1975) 'Men's Liberation', in *Feminist Revolution* (New York: Redstockings), pp. 60–4.

Hargreaves, D. H. (1967) *Social Relations in a Secondary School* (London: Routledge and Kegan Paul).

Harper, J. and Richards, L. (1979) *Mothers and Working Mothers* (Melbourne: Penguin).

Harré, R. (1979) *Social Being* (Oxford: Basil Blackwell).

Harré, R. (1983) *Personal Being* (Oxford: Basil Blackwell).

Harris, J. (1970) *The Bitter Fight* (St Lucia: University of Queensland Press).

Hartmann, H. I. (1979) 'The Unhappy Marriage of Marxism and Feminism: Towards a More Progressive Union', *Capital and Class*, 8, pp. 1–33.

Hartsock, N. (1979) 'Feminist Theory and the Development of Revolutionary Strategy', in Z. Eisenstein, ed. *Capitalist Patriarchy* (New York: Monthly Review Press), pp. 56–77.

Haug, F. (1987) *Sexualization of the Body* (London: Verso).

Henriques, J., Hollway, W., Urwin, C., Benn, C., and Walkerdine, V.

(1984) *Changing the Subject: Psychology, Social Regulation and Subjectivity* (London: Methuen).

Herdt, G. H. (1981) *Guardians of the Flutes: Images of Masculinity* (New York: McGraw Hill).

Heron House, ed. (1979) *The Book of Numbers* (London: Pelham Books).

Hicks, N. (1978) *This Sin and Scandal: Australia's Population Debate 1891–1911* (Canberra: Australian National University Press).

Hirschfeld, M. (1942) *Sexual Anomalies and Perversions* (London: Torch).

Hoch, P. (1979) *White Hero, Black Beast* (London: Pluto Press).

Hodson, P. (1984) *Men...An Investigation into the Emotional Male* (London: BBC Publications).

Hollway, W. (1984) 'Gender Difference and the Production of Subjectivity', in J. Henriques et al., *Changing the Subject* (London: Methuen), pp. 227–63.

Horkheimer, M., ed. (1936) *Studien über Autorität und Familie* (Paris: Alcan).

Horney, K. (1967) *Feminine Psychology* (London: Routledge and Kegan Paul).

House of Representatives, Australia, Standing Committee on Aboriginal Affairs (1979) *Aboriginal Health* (Canberra: AGPS).

Howe, L.K. (1977) *Pink Collar Workers: Inside the World of Women's Work* (New York: Avon).

Hunt, P. (1980) *Gender and Class Consciousness* (London: Macmillan).

Hyde, J. S. (1981) 'How Large are Cognitive Gender Differences?', *American Psychologist*, 36, 8, pp. 892–901.

Inglis, A. (1974) *'Not a White Woman Safe': Sexual Anxiety and Politics in Port Moresby, 1920–1934* (Canberra: ANU Press).

Irigaray, L. (1981) 'This Sex Which Is Not One', in E. Marks and I. de Courtivron, eds *New French Feminisms* (Brighton: Harvester), pp. 99–106.

Janeway, E. (1971) *Man's World, Woman's Place* (New York: Dell).

Johnson, O. and Harley, C. (1980) 'Handedness and Sex Differences in Cognitive Tests of Brain Laterality', *Cortex*, 16, 1, pp. 73–82.

Johnston, C. (1982) 'Foucault and Gay Lib', *Arena*, 61, pp. 62–70.

Johnston, J. (1973) *Lesbian Nation: The Feminist Solution* (New York: Simon and Schuster).

Jones, E., ed. (1924) *Social Aspects of Psycho-Analysis* (London: Williams and Norgate).

Joyce, J. (1960) *Portrait of the Artist as a Young Man* (Harmondsworth: Penguin and Jonathan Cape).

Jung, C. G. (1953[1928]) 'Anima and Animus', Part II, ch. ii of 'The Relations between the Ego and the Unconscious', in *Collected Works*, (London: Routledge and Kegan Paul), vol. 7, pp. 187–209.

Kelly, P. (1984) *Fighting for Hope* (London; Chatto and Windus).

Kenyon, K., et al. (1960-83) *Excavations at Jericho* (5 vols, London: British School of Archaeology in Jerusalem).

Kessler, S., Ashenden, D. J., Connell, R. W. & Dowsett, G. W. (1982) *Ockers and Disco-maniacs* (Sydney: Inner City Education Centre).

Kessler, S., Ashenden, D. J., Connell, R. W. & Dowsett, G. W. (1985) 'Gender Relations in Secondary Schooling', *Sociology of Education*, 58, 1, pp. 34–48.

Kessler, S. J. and McKenna, W. (1978) *Gender: An Ethnomethodological Approach* (New York: Wiley).

Kinsey, A. C., Pomeroy, W. B. and Martin, C. E. (1948) *Sexual Behavior in the Human Male* (Philadelphia: Saunders).

Kipling, R. (1908) *Just So Stories* (London: Macmillan).

Klein, V. (1946) *The Feminine Character* (London: Routledge and Kegan Paul).

Klima, B. (1962) 'The First Ground-Plan of an Upper Palaeolithic Loess Settlement in Middle Europe and its Meaning', in R. J. Braidwood and G. R. Willey, eds *Courses Toward Urban Life* (Edinburgh: Edinburgh University Press), pp. 193–210.

Kollontai, A. (1977) *Selected Writings* (London: Allison and Busby).

Komarovsky, M. (1946) 'Cultural Contradictions and Sex Roles', *American Journal of Sociology*, 52, pp. 184–9.

Komarovsky, M. (1950) 'Functional Analysis of Sex Roles', *American Sociological Review*, 15, pp. 508–16.

Komarovsky, M. (1964) *Blue-Collar Marriage* (New York: Vintage).

Konrad, G. and Szelenyi, I. (1979) *The Intellectuals on the Road to Class Power* (Brighton: Harvester).

Korda, M. (1973) *Male Chauvinism* (New York: Random House).

Kosík, K. (1976) *Dialectics of the Concrete* (Dordrecht: D. Reidel).

Kovel, J. (1981) *The Age of Desire: Reflections of a radical psychoanalyst* (New York: Pantheon).

Krafft-Ebing, R. von (1965 [1886]) *Psychopathia Sexualis*, 12th edn (New York: Paperback Library).

Kramer, S. N. (1963) *The Sumerians* (Chicago: University of Chicago Press).

Kristeva, J. (1981) 'Women's Time', *Signs* 7, 1, pp. 13–35.

Kuhn, A. and Wolpe, A-M. (1978) *Feminism and Materialism* (London: Routledge and Kegan Paul).

Lafitte, P. (1957) *The Person in Psychology* (London: Routledge and Kegan Paul).

Laing, R. D. (1960) *The Divided Self* (London, Tavistock).

Laing, R. D. (1968) *The Politics of Experience* (New York, Ballantine Books).

Laing, R. D. (1976) *The Politics of the Family* (Harmondsworth, Penguin).

Laing, R. D. and Cooper, D. G. (1964) *Reason and Violence* (London: Tavistock).

Laing, R. D. and Esterson, A. (1964) *Sanity, Madness and the Family* (London: Tavistock).

Lane, D. and O'Dell, F. (1978) *The Soviet Industrial Worker* (Oxford: Martin Robertson).

Lang, T. (1971) *The Difference Between a Man and a Woman* (New York: John Day).

Lasch, C. (1977) *Haven in a Heartless World: The Family Besieged* (New York: Basic Books).

Latin American and Caribbean Women's Collective (1980) *Slaves of Slaves* (London: Zed Press).

Lauret, J-C. (1970) *The Danish Sex Fairs* (London: Jasmine Press).

Lefebvre, H. (1976) *The Survival of Capitalism: Reproduction of the Relations of Production* (London: Allison and Busby).

LeGuin, U. (1973) *The Left Hand of Darkness*, (London: Panther).

Lepervanche, M. de (1984) 'The "Naturalness" of Inequality', in G. Bottomley and M. de Lepervanche, eds *Ethnicity, Class and Gender in Australia* (Sydney: George Allen and Unwin), pp. 49–71.

Lessing, D. (1962) *The Golden Notebook* (London: Michael Joseph).

Lewis, G. (1983) *Real Men Like Violence* (Sydney: Kangaroo Press).

Lévi-Strauss, C. (1969[1949]) *The Elementary Structures of Kinship*, rev. edn (Boston: Beacon Press).

Lewontin, R. C., Rose, S. and Kamin, L. J. (1984) *Not in Our Genes: Biology, Ideology and Human Nature* (New York: Pantheon).

Linstone, H. A., Lendaris, G. G., Rogers, S. D., Wakeland, W., and Williams, M. (1979) 'The Use of Structural Modeling for Technology Assessment', *Technological Forecasting and Social Change*, 14, 4, pp. 291–327.

Lipman-Blumen, J. and Tickamyer, A. R. (1975) 'Sex Roles in Transition: A Ten-Year Perspective', *Annual Review of Sociology*, 1, pp. 297–337.

Lippert, J. (1977) 'Sexuality as Consumption', in J. Snodgrass, ed. *For Men Against Sexism* (Albion, CA: Times Change Press), pp. 207–13.

Lloyd, S. (1955) *Foundations in the Dust: a Story of Mesopotamian Exploration* (Harmondsworth: Penguin).

Lukács, G. (1971) *History and Class Consciousness* (London: Merlin Press).

Lukes, S. (1974) *Power: A Radical View* (London: Macmillan).

Lumsden, A. (1984) 'Gayness is Good for You', *New Statesman*, (31 August), pp. 13–15.

Lyttleton, N. (1984) 'Men's Liberation, Men Against Sexism and Major Dividing Lines'. *Resources for Feminist Research*, 12, 4, pp. 33–4.

Maccoby, E. E. and Jacklin, C. N. (1975) *The Psychology of Sex Differences* (Stanford: Stanford University Press).

McIntosh, M. (1968) 'The Homosexual Role', *Social Problems*, 16, 2, pp. 182–92.

McIntosh, M. (1978) 'The State and the Oppression of Women', in A. Kuhn and A-M. Wolpe, eds *Feminism and Materialism* (London: Routledge and Kegan Paul), pp. 254–89.

MacKenzie, W. J. M. (1967) *Politics and Social Science* (Harmondsworth: Penguin).

MacKinnon, C. A. (1982) 'Feminism, Marxism, Method and the State: An Agenda for Theory', *Signs*, 7, 3, pp. 515–44.

McRobbie, A. (1978) *'Working class girls and the culture of femininity'*, in Centre for Contemporary Cultural Studies Women's Studies Group *Women Take Issue* (London: Hutchinson), pp. 96–108.

Magarey, S. (1985) 'Conditions for the Emergence of an Activist Feminism in Late Nineteenth Century Australia', paper to Sociological Association conference, Brisbane.

Mahler, V. (1981) 'Work, Consumption and Authority within the Household: A Moroccan Case', in K. Young, et al., eds *Of Marriage and the Market* (London: CSE Books), pp. 69–87.

Malinowski, B. (1955) *Sex and Repression in Savage Society* (New York: Meridian).

Mannheim, K. (1940) *Man and Society in an Age of Reconstruction* (London: Kegan Paul, Trench, Trubner).

Mannheim, K. (1954) *Ideology and Utopia* (London: Routledge and Kegan Paul).

Mannoni, O. (1964) *Prospero and Caliban: The Psychology of Colonization*, 2nd edn (New York: Praeger).

Marcuse, H. (1955) *Eros and Civilization* (Boston: Beacon Press).

Marcuse, H. (1964) *One Dimensional Man* (London: Routledge and Kegan Paul).

Marcuse, H. (1972) *An Essay on Liberation* (Harmondsworth: Penguin).

Marks, E. and de Courtivron, I. (1981) *New French Feminisms* (Brighton: Harvester).

Marshall, T. H. (1950) *Citizenship and Social Class* (Cambridge: Cambridge University Press).

Martin, W. (1972) *The American Sisterhood: Writings of the Feminist Movement from Colonial Times to the Present* (New York: Harper and Row).

Matthews, J. J. (1984) *Good and Mad Women: The Historical Construction of Femininity in Twentieth-Century Australia* (Sydney: George Allen and Unwin).

May, R. (1980) *Sex and Fantasy* (New York: Norton).

Mead, M. (1935) *Sex and Temperament in Three Primitive Societies* (New York: Morrow).

Mead, M. (1950) *Male and Female: A Study of the Sexes in a Changing World* (London: Gollancz).

Mellaart, J. (1967) *Çatal Hüyük: A Neolithic Town in Anatolia* (London: Thames and Hudson).

Men's Consciousness Raising Group (1971) *Unbecoming Men* (New York: Times Change Press).

Metcalfe, A. and Humphries, M., eds (1985) *The Sexuality of Men* (London: Pluto Press).

Meulenbelt, A. (1976) *Feminisme en Socialisme: Een Inleiding* (Amsterdam: Van Gennep).

Meulenbelt, A. (1980) *The Shame is Over* (London: Women's Press).

Mieli, M. (1980) *Homosexuality and Liberation* (London: Gay Men's Press).

Miles, K. (1974) *Women's Liberation, Class Struggle* (Sydney: Words for Women).

Mill, J. S. (1912[1869]) 'The Subjection of Women', in *Three Essays* (London: Oxford University Press) pp. 427–548.

Miller, C. and Swift, K. (1979) *Words and Women* (Harmondsworth: Penguin).

Miller, P. (1986) *Long Division: State Schooling in South Australian Society* (Adelaide: Wakefield Press).

Miller, S. M. (1971) 'The Making of a Confused, Middle-Aged Husband', *Social Policy*, 2, 2, pp. 33–9.

Millett, K. (1972) *Sexual Politics* (London: Abacus).

Mitchell, J. (1966) 'Women: The Longest Revolution', *New Left Review*, 40, pp. 11–37.

Mitchell, J. (1971) *Woman's Estate* (Harmondsworth: Penguin).

Mitchell, J. (1975) *Psychoanalysis and Feminism* (New York: Vintage Books).

Molyneux, M. (1979) 'Beyond the Domestic Labour Debate', *New Left Review*, 116, pp. 3–27.

Molyneux, M. (1981) 'Women in Socialist Societies: Problems of Theory and Practice', in K. Young, C. Wolkowitz and R. McCullagh, eds *Of Marriage and the Market* (London: CSE Books), pp. 167–202.

Money, J. (1970) 'Sexual Dimorphism and Homosexual Gender Identity', *Psychological Bulletin*, 74, 6, pp. 425–40.

Morgan, D. H. J. (1975) *Social Theory and the Family* (London: Routledge and Kegan Paul).

Morgan, L. H. (1963[1877]) *Ancient Society* (Cleveland World Publishing).

Morgan, M. (1975) *The Total Woman* (London: Hodder and Stoughton).

Morris, D. (1969) *The Naked Ape* (St Albans: Panther).

Morris, J. (1974) *Conundrum* (London: Faber and Faber).

Morrison, P., Holland, G. and Trott, T. (1979) '"Personally speaking …" 3 Men Share the Experience of their Men's Groups', *Achilles Heel*, 2, pp. 12–16.

Moses, J. C. (1978) 'Women in Political Roles', in D. Atkinson, A. Dallin and G. W. Lapidus, eds *Women in Russia* (Hassocks: Harvester).

Newland, K. (1975) *Women in Politics: A Global Review* (Washington, DC: Worldwatch Institute).

Newland, K. (1980) *Women, Men and the Division of Labor* (Washington, DC: Worldwatch Institute).

Nichols, J. (1975) *Men's Liberation* (New York: Penguin).

Niland, C. (1983) *Credit your Right*, speech to 'Money Matters' seminar, Woy Woy, 26 February.

Nye, F. I., et al. (1976) *Role Structure and Analysis of the Family* (Beverley Hills: Sage), Sage Library of Social Research, vol. 24.

O'Brien, M. (1981) *The Politics of Reproduction* (Boston: Routledge and Kegan Paul).

O'Donnell, C. (1984) *The Basis of the Bargain* (Sydney: George Allen and Unwin).

Offe, C. (1984) *Contradictions of the Welfare State* (London: Hutchinson).

Organisation for Economic Co-operation and Development (1980) *Women and Employment: Policies for Equal Opportunities* (Paris: OECD).

Orwell, G. (1962[1937]) *The Road to Wigan Pier* (Harmondsworth: Penguin).

Orwell, G. (1970[1941]) 'The Art of Donald McGill', in his *Collected Essays, Journalism and Letters* (Harmondsworth: Penguin), vol. 2.

Otto, R. (1982) *Occupational Stress Among Teachers in Post-Primary Education: A Study of Teachers in Technical Schools and Some Comparative Data on High School Teachers*, La Trobe University, Department of Sociology.

Owen, R. (1972[1813]) *A New View of Society, and Other Writings* (London: Dent).

Padgug, R. A. (1979) 'Sexual Matters: On Conceptualizing Sexuality in History', *Radical History Review*, (Spring/Summer), pp. 3–23.

Pahl, J. M. and Pahl, R. E. (1972) *Managers and their Wives* (Harmondsworth, Penguin).

Pahl, R. E. (1984) *Divisions of Labour* (Oxford: Basil Blackwell).

Parsons, A. (1964) 'Is the Oedipus Complex Universal? The Jones–Malinowski Debate Revisited and a South Italian "Nuclear Complex"', *The Psychoanalytic Study of Society*, 3, pp. 278–326.

Parsons, T. (1942) 'Age and Sex in the Social Structure of the United States', *American Sociological Review*, 7, pp. 604–16.

Parsons, T. and Bales, R. F. (1956) *Family Socialization and Interaction Process* (London: Routledge and Kegan Paul).

Pateman, C. (1983) 'The Fraternal Social Contract: some Observations on Patriarchal Civil Society', unpublished paper.

Perchenok, Y. (1985) *Women in the USSR: Facts and Figures* (Moscow: Novosti Press Agency Publishing House).

Pericot, L. (1962) 'The Social Life of Spanish Palaeolithic Hunters as Shown by Levantine Art', In S. L. Washburn, ed. *Social Life of Early Man* (London: Methuen), pp. 194–213.

Perkins, R. (1983) *The 'Drag Queen' Scene: Transsexuals in Kings Cross* (Sydney: George Allen and Unwin).

Piaget, J. (1962) *Play, Dreams and Imitation in Childhood* (New York: Norton).

Piaget, J. (1971) *Structuralism* (London: Routledge and Kegan Paul).

Pleck, E. H. and Pleck, J. H. (1980) *The American Man* (Englewood Cliffs, NJ: Prentice-Hall).

Pleck, J. H. (1976) 'The Male Sex Role: Definitions, Problems, and Sources of Change', *Journal of Social Issues*, 32, 3, pp. 155–64.

Pleck, J. H. (1981) *The Myth of Masculinity* (Cambridge, MA: MIT Press).

Plomin, R. and Foch, T. T. (1981) 'Sex Differences and Individual Differences', *Child Development*, 52, 1, pp. 383–5.

Plummer, K., ed. (1981) *The Making of the Modern Homosexual* (London, Hutchinson).

Plummer, K. (1983) *Documents of Life* (London: George Allen and Unwin).

Pogrebin, L. C. (1973) 'Rap Groups: The Feminist Connection', *Ms*, 1, 9, pp. 80–3, 98–104.

Polatnick, M. (1973–4) 'Why Men Don't Rear Children: A Power Analysis', *Berkeley Journal of Sociology*, 18, pp. 45–86.

Poole, R. (1982) 'Markets and Motherhood: The Advent of the New Right', *Intervention*, 16, pp. 37–52.

Power, M. (1975) 'The Making of a Woman's Occupation', *Hecate*, 1, 2, pp. 25–34.

Pringle, R. (1973) 'Octavius Beale and the Ideology of the Birth-Rate: the Royal Commissions of 1904 and 1905', *Refractory Girl*, 3, pp. 19–27.

Pringle, R. (1979) 'Feminists and Bureaucrats: The Last Four Years', *Refractory Girl*, 18/19, pp. 58–60.

Pritchard, J. B., ed. (1950) *Ancient Near Eastern Texts* (Princeton: Princeton University Press).

Ram, K. (1981) 'Sexual Violence in India', *Refractory Girl*, 22, pp. 2–8.

Raymond, J. G. (1979) *The Transsexual Empire* (Boston: Beacon Press).

Red Collective (1978) *The Politics of Sexuality in Capitalism* (London: Red Collective and Publications Distribution Cooperative).

Reeves, P. (1913) *Round About a Pound a Week* (London: G. Bell).

Reich, C. A. (1970) *The Greening of America* (New York: Random House).

Reich, W. (1970) *The Mass Psychology of Fascism* (New York: Farrar Strauss and Giroux).

Reiche, R. (1970) *Sexuality and Class Struggle* (London: New Left Books).

Reiger, K. M. (1985) *The Disenchantment of the Home: Modernizing the Australian family 1880–1940* (Melbourne: Oxford University Press).

Reik, T. (1967) *Of Love and Lust: On the Psychoanalysis of Romantic and Sexual Emotions* (New York: Bantam).

Reiter, R. R. (1977) 'The Search for Origins: Unravelling the Threads of Gender Hierarchy', *Critique of Anthropology*, 9/10, pp. 5–24.

Rice, M. S. (1981[1939]) *Working-Class Wives: Their Health and Conditions*, 2nd edn, (London: Virago).

Rich, A. (1980) 'Compulsory Heterosexuality and Lesbian Existence', *Signs*, 5, pp. 631–60.

Richards, L. (1985) 'A Man's Not a Neighbour? Gender and Local Relationships in a New Estate', paper presented to Sociological Association of Australia and New Zealand annual conference, Brisbane.

Riesman, D. (1950) *The Lonely Crowd* (New Haven, Yale University Press).

Robinson, P. A. (1972) *The Sexual Radicals* (London: Paladin).

Rosen, S. A. (1980–81) 'Police Harassment of Homosexual Women and Men in New York City', *Columbia Human Rights Law Review*, 12, pp. 159–90.

Rosenberg, R. (1982) *Beyond Separate Spheres: Intellectual Roots of Modern Feminism* (New Haven: Yale University Press).

Rosenthal, R. and Rubin, D. B., (1982) 'Further Meta-Analytic Procedures for Assessing Cognitive Gender Differences', *Journal of Educational Psychology*, 74, 5, pp. 708–12.

Rowbotham, S. (1973) *Woman's Consciousness, Man's World* (Harmondsworth: Penguin).

Rowbotham, S. (1974) *Women, Resistance and Revolution* (Harmondsworth: Penguin).

Rowbotham, S. (1974) *Hidden From History* 2nd edn (London: Pluto Press).

Rowbotham, S., Segal, L., and Wainwright, H. (1979) *Beyond the Fragments: Feminism and the Making of Socialism* (London: Islington Community Press).

Rubin, G. (1975) 'The Traffic in Women: Notes on the "Political Economy" of Sex', in R. R. Reiter, ed. *Toward an Anthropology of Women* (New York, Monthly Review Press), pp. 157–210.

Rubin, L. B. (1976) *Worlds of Pain: Life in the Working-Class Family* (New York: Basic Books).

Russell, G. (1983) *The Changing Role of Fathers?* (St Lucia: University of Queensland Press).

Ryan, E. and Conlon, A. (1978) *Gentle Invaders: Australian Women at Work 1788–1974* (Melbourne: Nelson).

Sade, M. de (1966[1791]) *Justine...and Other Writings* (New York: Grove Press).

Sade, M. de (1976[1797]) *Juliette* (New York: Grove Press).

Sahlins, M. (1977) *The Use and Abuse of Biology: An Anthropological Critique of Sociobiology* (London: Tavistock).

Sargent, D. (1983) 'Reformulating (Homo)Sexual Politics', in J. Allen and P. Patton, ed. *Beyond Marxism* (Sydney: Intervention), pp. 163–82.

Sartre, J-P. (1958) *Being and Nothingness* (London: Methuen).

Sartre, J-P. (1968) *Search for a Method* [The Question of Method] (New York: Vintage Books).

Sartre, J-P. (1976) *Critique of Dialectical Reason* (London: New Left Books).

Sartre, J-P. (1971–2) *L'Idiot de la famille* (Paris, Gallimard).

Sauer, C. (1962) 'Sedentary and Mobile Bents in Early Societies', in
    S.L. Washburn, ed. *Social Life of Early Man* (London: Methuen), pp.
    256–66.
Sawer, M. (1985) 'From Motherhood to Sisterhood: Attitudes of
    Australian Women MPs to their Roles', paper at Australasian Political
    Studies Association Annual Conference, Adelaide.
Sayers, J. (1982) *Biological Politics* (London: Tavistock).
Schlegel, A. (1977) *Sexual Stratification* (New York: Columbia University
    Press).
Schmidt, J. (1977) 'Praxis and Temporality: Karel Kosik's Political
    Theory', *Telos*, 33, pp. 71–84.
Schools Commission, Australia (1975) *Girls, School and Society* (Canberra:
    Schools Commission).
Scott, J. W. and Tilly, L. A. (1975) 'Women's Work and the Family in
    Nineteenth-Century Europe', *Comparative Studies in Society and History*
    17, 1, pp. 36–64.
Scutt, J. A. (1983) *Even in the Best of Homes: Violence in the Family*
    (Melbourne: Penguin).
Scutt, J. (1985) 'In Pursuit of Equality: Women and Legal Thought
    1788–1984' in J. Goodnow and C. Pateman, ed. *Women, Social Science
    and Public Policy* (Sydney: George Allen and Unwin), pp. 116–139.
Seale, P. and McConville, M. (1978) *Philby*, rev. edn (Harmondsworth:
    Penguin).
Secord, P. F., ed. (1982) *Explaining Human Behavior* (Beverley Hills: Sage).
Segal, L., et al. (1979–80) 'Family Life: Communal Living and Childcare.
    Living Your Politics: A Discussion of Communal Living Ten Years
    On', *Revolutionary Socialism: Big Flame Magazine*, 4, pp. 4–8.
Segal, L. ed (1983) *What is to be Done About the Family?* (Harmondsworth:
    Penguin).
Segal, L. (1987) *Is the Future Female?* (London: Virago).
Seidler, V. (1979) 'Men and Feminism', *Achilles Heel*, 2, pp. 32–6.
Sennett, R. (1970) *Families Against the City* (Cambridge MA: Harvard
    University Press).
Shaver, S. (1983) 'Sex and Money in the Welfare State', in C. Baldock
    and B. Cass, eds *Women, Social Welfare and the State in Australia* (Sydney:
    George Allen and Unwin), pp. 146–63.
Sichtermann, B. (1986) *Femininity* (Cambridge: Polity Press).
Silverstein, C. (1982) *Man to Man: Gay Couples in America* (New York:
    Quill).
Silverstein, M. (1977) 'The History of a Short, Unsuccessful Academic
    Career', in J. Snodgrass, ed., *For Men Against Sexism* (Albion, CA:
    Times Change Press), pp. 177–97.
Smith, C. (1959) *The Speaking Eye* (Harmondsworth: Penguin).
Smith, R. and Knight, J. (1981) 'Political Censorship in the Teaching

of Social Sciences', *Australian Journal of Education*, 25, pp. 3–19.
Smith-Rosenberg, C. (1975) 'The Female World of Love and Ritual: Relations Between Women in Nineteenth-Century America', *Signs*, 1, 1; reprinted in E. Abel and E. K. Abel, *The Signs Reader* (Chicago: University of Chicago Press, 1983), pp. 27–55.
Smout, T. C. (1969) *A History of the Scottish People 1560–1830* (Britain: Collins).
Snodgrass, J., ed. (1977) *For Men Against Sexism* (Albion, CA: Times Change Press).
Spence, J. (1978/9) 'What do People Do all Day? Class and Gender in Images of Women', *Screen Education*, 29, pp. 29–45.
Spence, J. T. and Helmreich, R. L. (1978) *Masculinity and Femininity* (Austin: University of Texas Press).
Spender, D. (1982) *Women of Ideas and What Men have Done to Them* (London: Routledge and Kegan Paul).
Stacey, J. (1979) 'When Patriarchy Kowtows: The Significance of the Chinese Family Revolution for Feminist Theory', in Z. R. Eisenstein, ed. *Capitalist Patriarchy and the Case for Socialist Feminism* (New York: Monthly Review Press), pp. 299–348.
Stapledon, O. (1937) *Last and First Men* (London: Penguin).
Stearns, P. N. (1979) *Be a Man! Males in Modern Society* (New York: Holmes and Meier).
Steinmann, A. and Fox, D. J. (1974) *The Male Dilemma* (New York: Aronson).
Stevens, G. L. (1984) 'The Flowering of Sex', *The Sciences*, 24, 3, pp. 28–35.
Stevens, J. *The First Ten Years* (forthcoming).
Stille, A. (1985–6) 'Election v. Appointment: Who Wins?', *National Law Journal* (US), (30 Dec. 1985–6 Jan. 1986), pp. 1–9.
Stolcke, V. (1981) 'Women's Labours: The Naturalisation of Social Inequality and Women's Subordination', In K. Young et al., eds *Of Marriage and the Market* (London: CSE Books), pp. 30–48.
Stoller, R. J. (1968,1976) *Sex and Gender*, (London: Hogarth Press and Institute of Psychoanalysis), vol. 1: *On the Development of Masculinity and Femininity*; vol. 2: *'The Transsexual Experiment'* (New York: Aronson).
Straus, M. A. (1978) 'Wife Beating: How Common and Why?', *Victimology*, 2, 3–4, pp. 443–58.
Strober, M. H. (1976) 'Toward Dimorphics: A Summary Statement to the Conference on Occupational Segregation', *Signs*, 1, 3, part 2, pp. 293–302.
Strouse, J. (1975) *Women and Analysis* (New York: Laurel).
Sullivan, E. V. (1984) *A Critical Psychology* (New York: Plenum).
Szasz, T. S. (1978) *The Myth of Mental Illness* rev. edn, (New York: Harper and Row).

Task Force on Domestic Violence, New South Wales (1981) *Report* (Sydney: Government Printer).

Taylor, B. (1983) *Eve and the New Jerusalem: Socialism and Feminism in the Nineteenth Century* (London: Virago).

Taylor, G. R. (1959) *Sex in History*, 2nd edn (London: Thames and Hudson).

Tension, E. (1978) *You Don't Need a Degree to Read the Writing on the Wall* (London: No Press).

Thomas, D. (1976) *The Marquis de Sade* (London: Weidenfeld and Nicolson).

Thomas, W. I. (1907) *Sex and Society* (Chicago: University of Chicago Press).

Thompson, D. (1985) *Flaws in the Social Fabric: Homosexuals and Society in Sydney* (Sydney: George Allen and Unwin).

Thompson, E. P. (1968) *The Making of the English Working Class*, 2nd edn (Harmondsworth: Penguin).

Thompson, E. P. (1978) *The Poverty of Theory* (London: Merlin Press).

Tieger, T. (1980) 'On the Biological Basis of Sex Differences in Aggression', *Child Development*, 51, 4, pp. 943–63.

Tiger, L. (1969) *Men in Groups* (London: Nelson).

Tiger, L. and Fox, R. (1971) *The Imperial Animal* (New York: Holt, Rinehart and Winston).

Tolson, A. (1977) *The Limits of Masculinity* (London: Tavistock).

Tomasetti, G. (1976) *Thoroughly Decent People* (Melbourne, McPhee Gribble).

Touraine, A. (1981) *The Voice and the Eye: An Analysis of Social Movements* (Cambridge: Cambridge University Press).

Trigger, B. G., Kemp, B. J., O'Connor, D., and Lloyd, A. B. (1983) *Ancient Egypt: A Social History*, (Cambridge University Press).

United Nations–Asian and Pacific Centre for Women and Development (1979) *Draft Report of International Workshop on Feminist Ideology and Structures in the First Half of the Decade for Women, 24–30 June 1979* (Bangkok: United Nations).

Vatsyayana (1963) *Kama Sutra* (London: Panther).

Wajcman, J. (1983) *Women in Control: Dilemmas of a Workers' Cooperative* (Milton Keynes: Open University Press).

Wallace, A. (1986) *Homicide: The Social Reality* (Sydney: NSW Bureau of Crime Statistics and Research).

Walter, A., ed. (1980) *Come Together: The Years of Gay Liberation 1970–1973* (London: Gay Men's Press).

Ware, H. (1981) *Women, Demography and Development* (Canberra: ANU Development Studies Centre).

Weeks, J. (1977) *Coming Out: Homosexual Politics in Britain, from the Nineteenth Century to the Present* (London: Quartet).

Weeks, J. (1985) *Sexuality and its Discontents* (London: Routledge and Kegan Paul).

Wesley, F. and Wesley, C. (1977) *Sex-Role Psychology* (New York: Human Sciences Press).

Wesson, G., (1975) *Brian's Wife, Jenny's Mum* (Melbourne: Dove).

West, J. (1978) 'Women, Sex and Class', in A. Kuhn and A. Wolpe, eds *Feminism and Materialism* (London: Routledge and Kegan Paul), pp. 220–53.

White, A. (1939) *Frost in May* (Harmondsworth: Penguin).

White, P. (1979) *The Twyborn Affair* (London: Jonathan Cape).

White, R. W. (1975) *Lives in Progress: A Study of the Natural Growth of Personality*, 3rd edn, (New York: Holt, Rinehart and Winston).

Whyte, W. F. (1955) *Street Corner Society*, enlarged edn, (Chicago: University of Chicago Press).

Williams, C. (1981) *Open Cut* (Sydney: George Allen and Unwin).

Williams, G. (1960) 'Gramsci's Concept of Egemonia', *Journal of the History of Ideas*, 21, 4, pp. 586–99.

Williams, T. R. (1959) 'A Critique of Some Assumptions of Social Survey Research', *Public Opinion Quarterly*, 23, pp. 55–62.

Willis, E. (1984) 'Radical Feminism and Feminist Radicalism', in S. Sayres, et al., eds *The 60s Without Apology* (Minneapolis: University of Minnesota Press/Social Text), pp. 91–118.

Willis, P. (1977) *Learning to Labour: How Working Class Kids get Working Class Jobs* (Farnborough, Saxon House).

Willis, P. (1979) 'Shop Floor Culture, Masculinity and the Wage Form', in J. Clarke, C. Critcher and R. Johnson, eds *Working Class Culture* (London: Hutchinson), pp. 185–98.

Wilson, E. O. (1978) *On Human Nature* (Cambridge MA/London: Tavistock).

Wilson, E. (1977) *Women and the Welfare State* (London, Tavistock).

Wilson, E. (1982) 'Women, the "Community" and the Family', in A. Walker, ed. *Community Care: The Family, the State and Social Policy* (Oxford: Basil Blackwell and Martin Robertson).

Wilson, J. A. (1951) *The Culture of Ancient Egypt* (Chicago: University of Chicago Press).

Wolfe, S. J., and Stanley, J. P. (1980) *The Coming Out Stories* (Watertown MA: Persephone Press).

Wollstonecraft, M. (1975[1792]) *Vindication of the Rights of Woman* (Harmondsworth: Penguin).

Women's Bureau, Department of Employment and Youth Affairs, Australia (1981) *The Role of Women in the Economy*, Position paper for OECD High Level Conference on the Employment of Women 1980 (Canberra: AGPS).

Wylie, P. (1974[1951]) *The Disappearance* (St Albans: Panther).

Yates, L. (1983) 'The Theory and Practice of Counter-Sexist Education in Schools', *Discourse*, 3, 2, pp. 33–44.

Young, I. (1981) 'Beyond the Unhappy Marriage: A Critique of the Dual Systems Theory', in L. Sargent, ed. *Women and Revolution* (Boston: South End Press), pp. 43–69.

Young, K. (1978) 'Modes of Appropriation and the Sexual Division of Labour: A Case Study from Oaxaca, Mexico', in A. Kuhn and A-M. Wolpe, eds *Feminism and Materialism* (London: Routledge and Kegan Paul), pp. 124–54.

Young, K., Wolkowitz, C. and McCullagh, R., eds (1981) *Of Marriage and the Market: Women's Subordination in International Perspective* (London: CSE Books).

Young, M. and Willmott, P. (1962) *Family and Kinship in East London* (Harmondsworth: Penguin).

Zaretsky, E. (1976) *Capitalism, the Family and Personal Life* (London: Pluto Press).

Ziller, A. (1980) *Affirmative Action Handbook* (Sydney: Review of NSW Government Administration).

Zmroczek, C. (1984) 'Women's Work: Laundry and Technical Change in the Last 50 Years', paper at British Sociological Association conference, Bradford.

Index

abolition of gender, 286–8, 289
abortion, 37, 261, 292
accumulation, gendered logic of, 105–6
Ackroyd, P., 289
actor and script in role theory, 47
additive concept of society and nature, 73–5
adjustment, gender, 33
Adler, A., 82, 199, 206–7, 211
adolescents, 80, 195
  and housework, 122
  and sex, 115
  see also children; education; family
adornment see clothing
Adorno, T.W., 200, 201
advertisements, 102, 115, 133, 246–7; see also media
affirmative action, 49
Africa, 58, 125, 138, 154; see also Egypt
agencies of socialization, 49; see also institutions
aggression
  and genetics, 69
  and hormones, 38, 70
  physical see violence
Agnes' (case study), 76
agricultural civilizations, 154
AIDS, 37, 186, 233
alcoholism, 86
Algeria, Kabyle society in, 138
Alinsky, S. D., 65
allegiance, 272; see also alliance
Allen, P., 237
alliance, strategy of, 284; see also liberation; mobilization; solidarity

Althusser, L., 44, 62, 92, 96, 202, 221
Altman, D., 36, 37, 208
Amato, P. R., 100
ambiguity, gender, 289
Anatolia, 151
ancient civilizations, 144–6, 150–5
Andrews, B., 176, 177, 224–5
androgyny, 33, 47, 171, 291
Anglo-Saxons, 155
antagonisms, gender, 97, 114
Anthony, S. B., 131
anthropology/ethnomethodology, 26, 27, 30–1, 62, 194
  and archaeology, 146
  culture-and-personality school, 194
  and natural difference theory, 75
  structural, 45
anxiety, 82
appearance, see clothing
appropriate technology, 102
archaeology, see prehistoric
Arendt, H., 228
Aries, P., 155, 206
armies see military
articulation of interests, 262–5
ascendancy see hegemonic
Ashenden, D. J., xiv, xvii, 18
Asia, 8, 9, 72, 126, 128, 136, 158, 176, 260; see also China; India; Japan
assertiveness training, 37
Assyrians, 144
attribution, gender, 75–6, 78–81

Atwood, M., 292
Australia
    Aborigines, 125
    ancient, 154
    capitalism, 44
    case study *see* Prince
    education, 34, 120, 177–9, 192,
        225–6, 244, 261
    equal opportunities, 49
    family, 100, 120, 122–5, 135,
        195, 225–6
    health care, 250
    homosexuality, 36, 232, 260
    psychiatric incarceration, 177–8
    state, 126, 129
    street life, 133, 134, 135
    taxation, 260
    transsexuals, 76
    violence, 11–14
    women: movement, 44, 45, 230,
        262, 270, 284; in power, 15;
        working, 10, 103, 162, 260,
        268
authority, 109, 224
    see also power

Bachofen, J. J., 26
bad faith, 213
Baldock, C. V., 65
Bali, 136
Bangladesh, 128
Barassi, R., 185
'Barbin, H.' (case study), 76, 148
Barbour, J., 83
'Barr, Angus' (case study), 177, 178,
    189
Barrett, M., 95
Barry, K., 58
Bateson, G., 123
Beale, D., 86
Beauvoir, S. de, 31–2, 175, 211,
    213, 214, 217
Bebel, F. A., 26, 44
Bell, C., 110, 122
Bellamy, E., 292
Bem, S. L., 33, 47, 64, 171, 174
    Sex Role Inventory, 47
Bertaux, D., 236
Biddle, B. J., 48, 52
biology/biological
    dichotomy/reductionism *see* natural
    evolutionary, 26–7

pseudo *see* sociobiology
birth, 290
    control *see* contraception
bisexuality, 27, 28
Bland, L., 65
block differences, 168–70
body
    history of, 83, 86–7
    see also natural
Bogart, H., 184–5
Bottomley, G., 123
boundary exchange, capitalism and
    patriarchy as, 46
Bourdieu, P., 44, 62, 65, 94–5, 117,
    138
Bowlby, J., 200
Bowles, S., 237
Branca, P., 65, 147
Brannon, R., 65
Bray, A., 148
Brazil, 8, 9
Britain
    abortion, 260, 292
    contraception, 86
    co-operatives, 266, 270
    education, 193
    family, 121, 122, 270; housework,
        100
    feminism *see* women *below*
    homosexuals, 36, 126, 137, 147–8,
        284
    industry, 243
    men's groups, 235
    military, 14
    miners' strike, 143, 270
    personality, 176, 225
    sex roles, 32, 175, 180–1
    sexual ideology, 243, 247, 255
    state, 126, 131
    street life, 133
    violence, 11
    women: movement, 45, 230,
        266–8, 270; in power, 15
Brohm, J.-M., 88
Broker, M., 285
Broughton, F., 181, 189
Brown, N. O., 207
Brownmiller, S., 35, 55, 56
Bryson, I., 230
Bujra, J., xvii
Bullock, A., 142
Bullough, V. L., 147, 163

Burgess, G., 185, 190
Burgmann, M., 180
Burnett, J., 142, 189
Burney, C., 164
Burton, C., xv, 35, 40, 64, 146

Cahill, S. E., 218
Califia, P., 84, 88, 182, 289
Campaign for Homosexual Equality
    (Britain), 284
Campbell, B., 64, 65, 106
Canada, 13, 14, 129, 139, 223, 230
Cancian, F. M., 258
capitalism
    and crisis, 159–63
    and family, 125
    mode of production, 103
    reproduction of, 35–6
    and socialization, 42, 43, 45–6
    and women's subordination, 41–7
Carey, G., 115, 228
Carr, E. H., 163
Carrigan, T., xv, 39, 40, 64, 65, 163
Carroll, J., 224
Carter, A., 39, 88
Carter, J., 126, 128
case studies, 76, 148, 200; *see also*
    'Barr'; 'David'; 'Markham';
    'Prince'; 'Wolf Man'
Casner, M. B., 237
Cass, B., 65
castration anxiety, 82, 205
Çatal Hüyük, 151
categorical gender theory, 54–61, 65,
    135–9, 271
cathexis
    defined and described, 98, 111–16,
        118
    and domestic power, 124
    and feminism, 269
    in future, 280, 290
    and psychoanalysis, 212: displaced,
        201–2; *see also* Oedipus
    reciprocity of, 161
    and street, 134
    and structures, 181–2, 245
    see also love; sexuality
Catholicism, 108, 160, 161, 255, 261
Cavendish, R., 45, 99, 101, 102,
    162, 268, 269, 271
Central America *see* Latin and
    Central

Chafetz, J. S., 55
Chapkis, W., 20
Chesler, P., 124
Childe, V. G., 77, 144, 152
children *see* adolescents;
    psychoanalysis; socialization;
    sexual reproduction *and under*
    family
Chile, 7
China
    ancient, 152, 154
    contraception, 126
    extrinsic theories, 42
    patriarchal atrocities, 58
    secular morality, 23
    women, 8, 9
Chodorow, N., 56, 167, 201–5, 283
choice of gender, 75–6; *see also*
    transsexualism; transvestism
Chomsky, N., 83, 98
chromosome testing, 75; *see also*
    genetics
Cicourel, A. V., 189
civilization *see* ancient; social
Clark, G., 163
Clark, W., 136, 237
class
    and categorical theory, 59
    and disease and malnutrition, 86
    produced by state, 127–8
    relations/struggle, 42–3, 46, 221
    see also middle class; working class
Cliff, T., 42
clothing and adornment
    emphasizing differences, 73,
        79–80, 81, 151, 178, 181–2
    history of, 151
    and liberated femininity, 179
    playing with, 289
    and sexuality, 113, 289: in street,
        133; symbolic purpose, 115;
        transvestism, 75–6
    and textile industry, 102, 103
Cockburn, C., 36, 105, 186, 216,
    243–5
collective practices, 222; *see also*
    projects
Collingwood, R. G., 163, 164
Collinson, D., 101, 243
Colombia, 9, 15
colonialism *see* imperialism
Comer, L., 36

competition
　with men, 226, 228
　in sport, 75, 85
compliance, 187
　praxis of, 123
computer industry, 99, 100, 104
Confucianism, 154
Conlon, A., 164
Connell, R. W., xiv, xvii, 18, 39,
　64–5, 88, 117, 142, 189
Connell, W. F., 122, 218
consciousness-raising, 230–2, 235
Constantinople, A., 172, 174, 218
constitution of interests, 263, 285
consumption, gender structure of,
　103–4
contestation, 251
contraception, 86, 160, 261; *see also*
　abortion
control *see* power
Cooper, D., 36, 258
co-operative movement, 255, 266
Coote, A., 64
core
　figure, mother as, 93, 124
　in power structure of gender, 109
Corrigan, P., 88
cosmetics *see* clothing and adornment
Costello, J., 164
counter-position in role theory, 47
Court, D., xv, 64
CR (consciousness-raising), 230–2, 235
credit, 10–11
crime, 13–14, 128–9; *see also* police
criminalization of homosexuality, 28
crisis tendencies, 158–63, 164, 264,
　285–6
Croll, E. J., 64
Cucchiari, S., 164
cultures/cultural
　dynamics and sexual ideology,
　　250–3, 258
　enrichment, 291
　marginalization of women, 30
　other *see* anthropology; ethnicity
　and personality, 31
current frameworks of gender theory,
　41–65
　categorical theory, 54–61, 65
　extrinsic theories, 41–7, 64
　practice-based theory, towards,
　　61–4, 65

sex role theory, 47–54, 64–5
Curthoys, A., 106
cyclical practice, 141
Czechoslovakia, 7, 151

Dahrendorf, R., 48, 221
Dalla Costa, M., 46
Daly, M., 34, 55, 58
Dancis, B., 39
Dante, 24
Darwin, C., 26, 27, 29, 37
Dasey, R., 39
'David' (case study), 214, 233
David, D. S., 65
Davidson, B., 154
Davies, M. L., 43, 142, 258, 266
deconstruction of gender, 286–8, 289
Delphy, C., 34, 42, 56, 64, 105,
　122, 138, 145, 163
Denmark, 261
Denno, D., 189
depression, 82
desemanticization, 173
design of work, 101–2
desire/desirability, 97, 112–13
determinism, 50, 67; *see also* natural
deviation
　biological bases for, 57
　of family, 51
　from sex role, 30, 49, 50, 52
　sexual, 27: *see also* bisexuality;
　　homosexuality; transsexualism;
　　transvestism
　and socialization, 194–5
dichotomy
　biological *see* natural
　public/private 248; *see also* family;
　　workplace
dictionaries, 242
diet, poor, 86, 108
dimorphism, 16, 55
Dinnerstein, D., xi, 65, 218
　on childcare, 35, 202–3, 205, 227,
　　278
　on emotional interactions, 202–3,
　　204, 209, 216–17
　on masculinity and femininity,
　　205–6
　on women's liberation, 207–8
disarmament, 262
discourse and practice and sexual
　ideology, 241–5, 258

disease, 37, 86, 186, 233
division of labour
    sexual, 29, 268–9, 285: and
        categorical theory, 56; in
        family, 121–3, 125; *see also*
        family, childcare *and*
        housework; history of 150,
        157–58; reform, 277–8
    and sexual ideology, 243–4, 245
    and structuralism, 91, 96, 98–100,
        116
    see also sex roles *and under* industry
        social 103, 105
divorce, 108, 160, 261
Dixon, B., 246
Dobash, R. E., and R. P., 19
Dollard, J., 220
Dolto, F., 193
domestic *see* family
Donzelot, J., 108, 127, 148, 228
Dowsett, G. W., xiv, xvii, 18, 290
drama *see* media
Du Bois, E., 118
dual systems theory, 46, 128
duality of structure, 94–5
Duffy, M., 84
Dunbar, R., 54–5
Duncan, G., 12
Dworkin, A., 35, 55, 56, 255, 257
dynamic
    in history, 224–8, 237
    unconscious, 196–211, 218
    and cultural and sexual ideology,
        250–3, 258

Easlea, B., 57
ecology, 262
Edgar, D., 164
Edgar, P., 246
education, 1, 8–9, 19, 99, 192,
        195–6
    differential training, 100
    and gender regime, 120
    gender formation in, 195–6
    physical, 87
    reform, 25–6: counter-sexist, 49;
        and new feminism, 260–1
    and sexual character, 177–9, 225
    and sexual ideology, 244, 252
    of women, 109, 160
Edwards, A. R., 51, 54, 65
ego, 208

egocentric interests, 285
Egypt, 7, 9
    ancient, 144, 151–3
Ehrenreich, B., 46, 138, 161, 185,
        250, 254
Eisenstein, H., 40, 58, 65, 67, 142,
        271
Eisenstein, Z. R., 46, 128
El Salvador, 7
Ellis, A., 235
Ellis, H., 27
embedding, theory of, 201–4
empires *see* imperialism
empirical psychoanalysis, 211
employment *see* labour
Engels, F., 26, 44, 144, 145, 163
English, D., 250, 254
Enlightenment, 24–5
environment
    damaged, 57–8
    and sexual character, 175–7; *see
        also* social; structures
equal rights, movements for and
        against, 37, 49, 126, 136,
        259–60
equality and reconstitution of gender,
        286–91
Erhardt, A., 71
Erikson, E. H., 194, 200, 206
eroticism, 113
    symbolic, 83–4
    see also libido; pornography; sexual
Esterson, A., 121, 193, 212, 214, 216
ethnicity, 59, 71
ethnomethodology *see* anthropology
Etruscans, 144
Europe
    ancient, 144, 150, 154
    Eastern, 7, 8, 9, 151
    Western, 7, 8, 9, 25, 87, 261: *see
        also* Britain; France; Germany;
        Italy
evolutionary biology, 26–7
    pseudo *see* sociobiology
exchange system, 92–3
exclusion of women *see* invisibility
existential
    phenomenology, 31; *see also* Sartre
    psychoanalysis, 210, 211–17, 218
expectations, role, 47
expressive
    sex roles, 32

traits, 167
extensive strategies, 284–6
extrinsic gender theory, 41–7, 64

Fairweather, H., 189
family
  and categorical theory, 56
  childcare and rearing: birth, 290;
      bonding, 38; and emotional
      relationships, 93, 97, 114,
      187; liberal parenting, 227;
      men and, 100, 106, 275, 283,
      290; and socialization, 71; as
      structural basis of feminism,
      106; as women's role, 35, 42,
      45, 56, 96, 106, 122; and
      working women, 80, 134–5;
      see also mothers; Oedipus
  crisis of, 158–60, 161–2, 205
  division of labour in, 121–2; 125,
      134–5; see also childcare above;
      housework below
  housework, 45, 86, 96, 100,
      225–6: new attitudes to, 280;
      technology of, 102; wages for,
      35; and working women,
      134–5
  as institution, 121–5, 142, 192
  nuclear: Chinese attempt to create,
      42; as norm, 36, 38, 51–2,
      57, 226; as restraint on
      inequality, 105; and
      sociobiology, 72; unwanted,
      94
  power in, 36, 97, 110–11, 123–4,
      276
  prehistoric, 144–6, 150–1, 152
  sex role, 32, 34, 51–2
  violence in, 11, 13, 51, 58, 123
  violence produced by, 123, 124–5
  working class 93–4, 111, 121–2,
      265–8
  see also adolescents; children;
      divorce; kinship; marriage;
      mothers
Fanon, F., 158, 223
fantasy, 168, 185, 248, 256
Farrell, W., 65, 185, 234, 235
fascism, 131, 200, 224
fashion see clothing and adornment
fatality, 290–91
fatigue of political practice, 282

femininity
  and cathexis, 112–13
  constructed, 80
  emphasized, 183, 186–8, 190, 255
  and masculinity see personality;
      psychoanalysis and gender
      formation; sexual character and
      under masculinity
  structured in work, 103
  see also gender; women
feminism, 162–3, 234
  and capitalism, 42–3
  and categorical theory, 54–5, 60,
      62
  and gay liberation, 32–7, 39
  liberal, 33–4, 73–4, 193, 127,
      227–8
  and Marxism, 35, 40, 42, 45, 54,
      56, 64, 127, 140
  middle class, 269–72
  and natural difference theories,
      73–4
  new, 260–1
  radical, 34–5
  and social production, 67
  socialist, 29, 35, 287
  working class, 265–70, 274
Fendrich-Salowey, G., 189
Fernbach, D., 37, 63, 115, 128, 152,
      233, 278, 281
fertility and state, 130
fetishism, 84, 115, 289
fiction see media
films see media
Firestone, S., xii, 34, 54–5, 204,
      217, 223
Foch, T. T., 169
foot-binding, 58
Foucault, M., 37, 76, 111, 127, 148,
      221, 228, 250, 254
Fox, D. J., 64
Fox, R., 67, 87
France
  class struggle, 42
  health care, 250
  marriage, 105
  military, 14, 126
  revolution, 24
  semiotics, 241
  sex roles, 34, 175
Franzway, S., 50, 65
Freud, S./Freudian, x, xii, 49, 82

on ambivalence, 203
biological determinism of, 67
on bisexuality and homosexuality,
27, 28
and cathexis, 112
on emotional conflict, 27
on femininity and masculinity,
168, 173, 200, 202–6, 209
Left, 36, 127
on primary process, 194
on psychic and social, 197–9,
210–11
on repression, 207–8
on self-knowledge, 212
on symptomatic acts, 219
on 'Wolf Man', 204, 209, 221
see also Oedipus; psychoanalysis
Friday, N., 114, 115
Friedan, B., 33, 37, 48, 74, 142,
193
friendship, 85, 109; *see also* solidarity
Fromm, E., 200, 201, 224
functionalism, 62
future of social theory of gender,
281–8
and present, 273–5

Gable, C., 256
Gabriel, R. H., 237
Gagnon, J. H., 111
Gamarnikow, E., 101
Game, A., xv, 36, 99, 104, 225, 226
Gandhi, I., 159
gangs, 133
Gardiner, N., 202
Garfinkel, H., 76
gay people *see* homosexuality
gender
abolition and reconstruction,
286–93
adjustment, 33
ambiguity, 289
attribution, 75–6, 78–81
defined and institutionalized,
139–41
dynamic *see* history
formation *see* psychoanalysis
identity, 194
order, 91, 98–9, 134–9, 142
patterns, 31–2
regimes and institutions, 99, 120,
119–42, 255; definition and

institutionalization of gender,
139–41; gender order, 134–9,
142; street, 132–4, 142; *see
also* family; state
relations, structure of, 16–17, 79:
see also gender regimes;
history; structures
scaling *see* tests
theory *see* current frameworks;
history, roots; natural
Genet, J., 84, 214
genetics, 98
explanation for differences, 69–71,
75
genital
mutilation, 58
primacy in sexuality, 161–2
valorization, 213
George, J., 260
Germany
Frankfurt School, 200, 207, 224
personality, 176
prison and military, 14
women in, 7, 9; movement, 29, 270
Giddens, A., 62, 94–5, 117, 140–1
Gilder, G., 38, 68
Gilding, M., 96, 122, 225
Gilgamesh, Epic of, 153
Gilman, C. P., 252
Gintis, H., 237
Godelier, M., 146
Goffman, E., 79
Goldberg, H., 33, 235
Goldberg, S., 38, 69–70, 74
Goldhamer, H., 189
Goldman, E., 112, 113, 123, 134,
241
Goldmann, L., 98, 245
Goode, W. J., 223
Groot, M., 119, 141
Gordimer, N., 61, 256
Gough, K., 146
Gouldner, A. W., 254
Gramsci, A., 184, 254, 255, 263
Grant, C., 182
Greece, ancient, 144, 154
Greek families in Australia, 123–4
Greene, G. and C., 88
Greer, G., 243
Griffin, C., 18, 180
Griffin, S., 55
guilt, 235

Habermas, J., 77, 136, 158, 203
Hacker, A., 20
Hall, R., 86
Hamilton, A., 125
Hamilton, R., 241
Hargreaves, D. H., 178
Harley, C., 169
Harper, J., 110
Harré, R., 219, 220
Hartmann, H. I., 40, 46
Hartsock, N., 46
hatred and love, 114–15
    see also Oedipus
Haug, F., 223
health care, 45, 108
    collective, 281–92
    see also medicalization
Hegel, G. W. F., 273, 292
hegemonic masculinity, 183–6, 190,
    199, 206, 215
Helmreich, R. L., 171, 172, 174
Henriques, J., 220
Herdt, G. H., 72
hermaphroditism, 291
Herrick, R., 83
heterosexuality
    as category, 137, 159, 161
    dismantling, 161–2
    as front, 233
    presumed, 36
    see also sexual
Hicks, N., 88
hidden nature of women's experience,
    188, 247
Hirschfield, M., 28
history, 143–64, 273–4
    course of, 150–8, 164
    crisis tendencies, 158–63, 164
    dynamic in, 224–8, 237
    historicity, 63–4: and origins, 26,
        143–50, 163–4
    process concept, 198
    roots of contemporary gender
        theory, 23–40: feminism and
        gay liberation, 32–7, 39;
        reaction and paradox, 37–8;
        science and radicalism, 26–9;
        secular morality, 23–6; sex
        roles and syntheses, 29–32
    textbook, biased, 229
    women invisible in, 188, 247
Hitler, A., 131, 142

Hittites, 144
Hoch, P., 224
Hollway, W., 241
home *see* family
homosexuality/lesbianism
    and categorical theory, 62–3, 137
    egalitarian, 116
    and feminism, 32–7, 39
    frequency of, 51
    history of, 147–9
    homophobia, 12–13, 19, 60:
        sanctions, 28, 72
    and jobs, 103
    liberation and 'coming out', 32–7,
        39, 62, 110, 148, 162–3,
        231–4, 248, 260, 262, 283–4
    as mental illness, 250–1
    as natural, 200, 246: genetic
        explanation, 69
    production of, 97
    and psychoanalysis, 28
    social definition, 80–1
    solidarity, 182: *see also* liberation
        above
    and state, 28, 126, 129, 130, 131,
        136, 159
    and subordination, 186
    as symbol of disorder, 248
Horkheimer, M., 200
hormones and aggression, 38, 70
Horney, K., xv, 200
hostility *see* antagonism
house-husbands, 100: *see* also family,
    housework
housewife as construction, 226
Howe, L. K., 36
Humphries, M., 252
Hungary, 7
Hunt, P., 110, 121, 243
Hyde, J. S., 189
hysteria, 82

id, 208
ideology, sexual *see under* sexual
illiteracy, 8
images *see under* media
imperialism 86–7, 157–58
income/wages *see under* working
    women
India
    ancient, 152
    contraception, 126

education, 8, 9
  illiteracy, 8
  patriarchal atrocities, 58
  secular morality, 23
  women in power, 15
individual *see* personality
Indonesia, 8
industry
  power in, 109
  and sexual character, 180–1
  sexual division of labour in,
    99–106, 243, 260, 269
inequality *see* power
Inglis, A., 158
institutions
  crisis of, 159–60
  and personality, 222
  and psychoanalysis, 192–3
  violent *see* military; police; prison
  see also gender regimes
instrumental sex roles, 32
instrumental traits, 167
intellectuals and gender order,
    254–7, 263–4
intelligence, 71, 98
intensive strategies, 281–4
interactionism, symbolic, 62
interests
  articulation of, 262–5
  constitution of, 263, 285
  formation of, 102–3
  and ideologists, 253–8
  social, 137–8
invention/inventiveness, 94, 95
inventories, structural, 91: *see also*
    gender order
invisibility of women, 188, 247
Iran, 126, 260
Ireland, 136, 195–6
Irigaray, L., 183, 202

Jacklin, C. N., 33, 66, 73–4, 87, 88,
    169, 170, 189
James, S., 46
Japan
  education, 8, 9
  personality, 176
  prison, 14
  women in power, 15
  women's wages, 7
Jardine, A., 67
Johnson, O., 169

Johnston, C., 163
Johnston, J., 54, 65, 162
Jones, E., 223
Joyce, J., 195–6
Jung, C. G., 114, 175, 206–7, 209

Kabyle society in Algeria, 138
Kamin, L. J., 88
Kelly, P., 65
Kenyon, K., 164
Kessler, S., xiv, xvii, 18, 75–6, 78,
    141
Key, E., 195, 218
Kidd, H., 255, 256, 258
Kinsey, A. C., 51
kinship, 26
  and sex roles, 31
  structural view of, 92, 98
  as system of categories, 79
  see also family
Kippax, S., xv, 117
Klein, V., 39, 168, 183, 245, 253,
    254, 258
Klima, B., 164
Knights, D., 101, 243
knowledge, sociology of, 245, 253
Kollontai, A., 29, 39, 136
Komarovsky, M., 30, 32, 39, 48, 52,
    110, 111, 122, 193
Konrad, G., 254
Korda, M., 101, 243
Kosik, K., 62, 79, 88, 211
Kovel, J., 88, 218
Krafft-Ebing, R. von, 27
Kramer, S. N., 164
Kristeva, J., 241
Kuhn, A., 64

labelling, 52
labour
  market/jobs, 6–7, 9–10, 19
  and structure, 99–106, 118
  see also division of labour; equal
    opportunities; industry;
    working
Lafitte, P., 173, 189
Laing, R. D., 121, 123, 173, 193,
    195, 212, 214, 222, 233, 259
Lane, D., 138
language
  sexist, 242, 247
  structure of, 94

'Larry' (case study), 200
Lasch, C., 254
Latin and Central America, 7, 8, 9, 75, 25, 152, 154
laundries, communal, 102
layering, 209
Lee, J., xv, 39, 64, 65
Lefebvre, H., 65, 116
legislation: equal opportunities and rights, 37, 49, 259–60
LeGuin, U., 287
Lepervanche, M. de, 68, 246
lesbians *see* homosexuality
Lessing, D., 61
Lette, K., 115, 228
Lévi-Strauss, C., 45, 62, 92–3, 98, 202
Lewis, G., 182
Lewontin, R. C., 88
liberal feminism, 33–4, 73–4, 127, 193, 227–8
liberated zones, 281–2
liberation, 270–2, 284: *see also* feminism; mobilization *and under* homosexuality
libido, 207–9, 212–13: *see also* sexual
life history analysis, 27–8, 219–23, 236–7
linking concept, gender as, 140
Lipman-Blumen, J., 65
Lippert, J., 180
literature *see* media
Lloyd, S., 163
Locke, J., 131
love, 185–6
    and hate, 114–15: *see also* Oedipus project of, 216–17
Lowe, J., 50, 65
Lukács, G., 245
Lukes, S., 118

Maccoby, E. E., 33, 66, 73–4, 87, 88, 169, 170, 189
McConville, M., 190
McGill, D., 65
machinery, 109–10
McIntosh, M., 128, 163
'Mack' (case study), 200
McKenna, W., 75–6, 78
MacKinnon, C. A., 128
McRobbie, A., 243
Magarey, S., 226

magazines *see* media
Mahler, V., 125
majorities, construction of, 285
Malinowski, B., 30
malnutrition, 86, 108
Mannheim, K., 200, 251–4
Mannoni, O., 158, 223
Marcuse, H., 63, 83, 115, 127, 161, 198, 200–1, 207, 228, 288
'Markhams' (case study), 266–7, 268
marriage, 223
    divorce, 108, 160, 261
    gender structure of, 105
    and psychoanalysis 197
    and role theory, 48
    and state, 130
    see also family
Marshall, T. H., 160
Martin, W., 39
Marx, K./Marxism, ix, xii, 17, 96, 145, 262, 272, 292
    on class relations and modes of production, 45, 103
    and feminism, 35, 40, 42, 45, 54, 56, 64, 127, 140
    and psychoanalysis, 200
masculinity
    and cathexis, 112–13
    constructed, 81, 83–6
    and femininity *see* personality; psychoanalysis and gender formation; sexual; tests
    hegemonic, 183–6, 190, 199, 206, 215
    and power, 107–9
    protest, 199, 207
    and state, 126, 128, 130, 155–7
    see also gender; hegemonic; men; patriarchy; violence
mass media *see* media
matriarchy, primitive, 145
Matthews, J. J., 63, 98–9, 225
May, R., 67, 168
Mead, M., 30–2, 33, 72, 119, 176
media (literature and mass)
    and capitalism, 45
    fantasy and science fiction, 256, 292–3
    and gender relations, 61
    images: of feminism, 45, 267; of masculinity, 184–5, 236; of women, 48, 102, 113, 179,

188, 226, 246–8, 289; *see also* advertisements
sexist and homophobic, 108, 229 *see also* images *above*
and sexuality: cathexis, 115–16; character, 182; ideology, 246–9, 252; love, 217, 248; morality, 24; symbolic eroticism, 83–4; *see also* images *above*
medicalization of sexual ideology, 250–1, 254, 279; *see also* health care
Mellaart, J., 151
men
  as category, 137–8
  movement, xi, 34, 234–6, 252, 264, 285–6
  see also gender; masculinity; sexual
menstruation, 82
mental illness, 197, 213, 250–1
Mesopotamia, 151
Metcalfe, A., 252
Meulenbelt, A., 46, 61, 115, 256
Mexico, 75, 125
Meyer-Bahlburg, H., 71
middle class
  and categorical theory, 59
  feminism, 269–72
Middle East, 7, 9, 126, 151, 260
Mieli, M., 36, 162, 208, 233, 283
migration and decline of patriarchy, 123–4
Miles, K., 42–3
military, 14, 20, 107, 109, 126, 129, 135–6, 152–3
Mill, J.S., 25, 131
Miller, C., 242
Miller, P., 192
Miller, S. M., 195
Millett, K., 259
miners' wives, 143, 270
Minnesota Multiphasic Personality Inventory 171
Minoans, 144
Mitchell, J.
  on kinship, 92–3
  on patriarchy, 43, 241
  on psychoanalysis, 202, 203, 207
  on social reproduction, 35, 64
  structuralist model, 56, 62, 96, 149

MMPI *see* Minnesota Multiphasic etc.
mobilization 284; *see also* feminism; liberation; men, movement
modelling, structural, 91, 98: *see also* sex roles; socialization *and under* sexual character
modes of production, 103
Mohammed Ali, 185
Molyneux, M., 19, 40
Money, J., 51, 65
Monroe, M., 188
morality
  crisis of, 160–1
  panic about AIDS, 37
  secular, 23–6
Morgan, L. H., 26
Morgan, M., 123–5, 188, 255–7, 261
Morocco, 125
Morris, D., 68, 87
Morris, J., 134
Morrison, P., 234
mortality rates, 108
Moses, J. C., 109
mothers, 202, 204
  as core figures, 93, 124
  relationships with, 38, 93, 114, 187
  see also family, childcare, Oedipus; women
Mowbray, M., 230
multiple models of sexual character, 175–9, 189
Mycenaeans, 144
myths, 98
  love, 217
  mental illness, 213
  of Origin, 26, 143–50, 163–4

narcissism, 115
National Organization of Women (USA), 284
natural/nature
  deviance as, 28, 57, 200
  difference theories, 17, 26, 64, 66–88, 137, 245–6, 253, 280, 290: additive, 73–5; objections to, 74–7; practical transformation of, 83–7, 88; sociobiology, 66, 68–73; transcendence and negation, 78–82, 88;

homosexuality as, 200
and science, additive concept of,
   73–5
sex roles as, 50–1, 53
and social, conflict between, 197–8
negation of body and transcendence,
   78–82, 88
neurosis, 197
neutral arbiter, state seen as, 127
New Caledonia, 126
new feminism, 260–1
New Guinea (Papua), 72, 158
New Left, 100, 160, 203, 217, 227,
   271
New Right, 38, 126, 136, 229–30,
   236
New Zealand, 25, 126
Newby, H., 110, 122
Newland, K., 16, 19, 20
newspapers *see* media
Nichols, J., 34, 235
Nightingale, F., 101
Niland, C., 19
norm/normative: not standard, 51–4:
   see also family, nuclear;
   heterosexuality
North America, 28, 75, 154; *see also*
   Canada; United States
novels *see* media
nuclear complexes, 206
nursing, 101, 181
Nye, F. I., 65

object, woman as, 92–3, 108, 113
Ochiltree, G., 164
O'Dell, F., 138
O'Donnell, C., xv, 36, 100
Oedipus complex, 27, 112, 124
   and castration fear, 213
   and cathexis, 205
   and embedding theories, 204
   and guilt, 198
   non-Oedipal nuclear complex, 141
   twofold nature of, 114
   universality assumed, 30, 206, 218
   see also Freud; psychoanalysis
office, work in, 101, 225, 243
Olympics, 75, 85
oppression, collective project of,
   215–16
order, gender, 91, 98–9, 134–9, 142
organic intellectual, 263

Organization for Economic Co-
   operation and Development, 10,
   34
Origin myths, 26, 143–50, 163–4
Orwell, G., 29, 39, 65
Otto, R., 236
Owen, R., 25

Padgug, R. A., 147
Pahl, J. M., 223
Pahl, R. E., 100, 122, 135, 223
Pakistan, 128, 151, 260
Palestine, 151
Panama, 7
Papua *see* New Guinea
paradox and reaction, 37–8
parenting *see* family, childcare;
   mothers
parliaments
   women in, 15–16
   see also power; state
Parsons, A., 124, 141, 206, 218
Parsons, T., 30–3, 38–9, 46, 49, 53,
   62, 72, 119, 161, 167–8
Pateman, C., 128, 130
paternity leave, 290; *see also* men
patriarchy, 34–5, 264, 285
   and capitalism, 43–6
   and categorical theory, 55, 56
   Chinese attempts to change, 42
   and exchange system, 93
   in family, 123–4
   and state, 128–30
   see also masculinity; power
patriotism, 86–7; *see also* imperialism
patterns, gender, 31–2
Paul, St, 222, 236
penis, valorization of, 213
Perchenok, Y., 20
Pericot, L., 164
Perkins, R., 76
personality, 30–1, 287
   as practice, 219–37: historical
      dynamic in, 224–8, 237;
      politics of, 228–36, 237;
      society and life history,
      219–23, 236–7;
   and sex roles, 48–9
   see also sexual character; tests
phenomenology, existential, 31; *see*
   also Sartre

physical
  body *see* natural
  sense of masculinity, 83–6
Piaget, J., 92, 98, 117, 289
Piggott, S., 163
Plato, 292
playing with gender, 289
Pleck, E. H., 147
Pleck, J. H., 33, 65, 147
Plomin, R., 169
Plummer, K., 236
poetry *see* media
Pogrebin, L. C., 237
Poland, 7, 8, 9
Polatnick, M., 106
police, 11–14, 20, 109, 129, 133, 136
politics/political
  and body, history of, 83, 86–7
  and categorical theory, 60
  economy of masculinity, 106
  of personality as practice, 228–36,
    237
  practice, 259–72: articulation of
    interests, 262–5; liberation
    movements, 270–2; scope of
    sexual politics, 259–62;
    working-class feminism,
    265–70
  of reform and sex role theory, 49
  sexual *see* gender
  women in, 15–16, 20
  see also state
polymorphous gender, 288
Poole, R., 164
pornography, 261–2
  campaigns against, 167
  and categorical theory, 55, 58
  fetish, 84
poverty, feminization of, 136
Power, M., 56, 101
power
  absent in role theory, 52
  of adults, 195, 199
  and analysis of gender, 34–5
  conflicts of interest, 54–61
  and masculinity, 107–9
  physical, 85
  and sex roles, 32
  and structure, 107–11, 118, 269
  top jobs, 10, 15–16, 20, 107, 126
  see also patriarchy; state; violence;
    and under family

practical transformation of body,
    83–7, 88
practice
  -based gender theory, towards,
    61–4, 65
  and discourse and sexual ideology,
    241–5, 258
  and institutions, 140–1
  natural, 78–82
  routine, 203
  social *see* natural
  and structure, 62
  structure of power as, 107–8; *see
    also* personality as practice
practico-inert practices, 81
prefigurative politics, 277
prehistoric family, 144–6, 150–1,
    152
present and future, 278–93
primitive societies *see* ancient
'Prince, Delia' (case study), 1–6, 17,
    18, 111, 120, 121, 193, 223,
    266
Pringle, R., xv, 36, 88, 99, 104, 142,
    225, 226
prisons, 14, 20, 109
Pritchard, J. B., 164
private *see* public/private
process, gender as, 140
processes, ideological, 245–9, 258
production
  modes of, 103
  relation of, 43–6, 56
projects, collective 263, 264, 270–2
  of oppression, 215–16
  see also existential psychoanalysis;
    liberation; mobilization;
    solidarity
property *see* object
prostitution, 103, 134
protest, masculine, 199, 207
pseudo-biology/pseudo-evolutionism
    see sociobiology
psychoanalysis
  and ambivalence, 114
  and family, 124
  and gender formation, 191–218;
    classical, 196–211, 218;
    existential, 211–17, 218; *see
    also* socialization
  life history analysis, 27–8
  and personality, 31

and sex roles, 30
and social reproduction, 45
see also Freud
psychology, 30
public/private dichotomy, 248; *see also* family; workplace

race *see* ethnicity
radical/radicalism, 271
  feminism, 34–5
  politics, 230, 282
  and science, 26–9
Ram, K., 58
rape, 11, 55, 56, 107, 128
Raymond, J. G., 65
reaction and paradox, 37–8
Reagan, R., 136, 236, 262
reciprocity, 113
reconstruction
  of gender, 286, 289–93
  of personality, 230–4
Red Collective, 111, 114–15, 210–11, 218
reductionism, biological *see* natural; sociobiology
regimes *see under* gender
regulation and soft domination by state, 127; *see also* legislation
Reich, C. A., 224
Reich, W., 127, 199, 200
Reiche, R., 207
Reid, E., 119, 141
reification, 245: of gender scaling, 174–5
Reiger, K. M., 96, 132, 225, 250, 254
Reik, T., 67, 168, 200
Reiter, R. R., 146
relational interests, 285
relations
  of production, 43–6, 56; *see also under* gender
  and morality, 23–4, 25
  and sexual ideology, 250, 251, 255–6
  and women, 108; *see also* Catholicism
religion, 25
repression, 31, 114, 197–208
reproduction
  of capitalism, 35–6
  social, 35–6, 43–6

as structure, 96
  see also under sexual
resistance, 52–3
Rice, M. S., 86
Rich, A., 62, 141, 161
Richards, L., 106, 110
Riesman, D., 167, 224
ritual and sexuality, 84
Robinson, P. A., 39, 254
rock music, 284; *see also* media
Roheim, G., 30
role theory, 47–8, 50, 170; *see also* sex roles
role-reversal, 277–8
Roman Empire, 144, 154
romanticism, 248; *see also* love
Rose, S., 88
Rosen, S. A., 19
Rosenberg, R., 39, 168, 258
Rosenthal, R., 189
Ross, B. L., 258
Rousseau, J.-J., 197
Rowbotham, S., 39, 149, 188, 216, 247, 282
Rubin, D. B., 189
Rubin, G., 16, 56, 62, 79–80, 88, 92–3, 140
Rubin, L. B., 110, 121, 123, 193
Russell, G., 100
Russia, 221; *see also* Soviet Union
Ryan, E., 164

Sade, M. de, 24, 39
Sahlins, M., 68–9
Samoa, 176
sanctions in role theory, 47, 50
Sargent, D., 163
Sartre, J.-P., xv, 62, 65, 88, 195
  on consciousness and motivation, 210
  on existential psychoanalysis, 211, 212–15, 218; bad faith, 213; class dynamics, 215
  on practico-inert and seriality, 80–1, 137, 256–7
  on unification, 221, 222
Sawer, M., 20
Sayers, J., 69
scaling, gender *see* tests
schizophrenia, 121
Schlegel, A., 55

Schmidt, J., 88
schools *see* education
science/technology
  appropriate, 102
  and masculinity, 58, 279
  nature and, additive concept of,
    73–5
  and power, 109–10
  pseudo-, *see* sociobiology
  and radicalism, 26–9
  see also medicalization
Scientific Humanitarian Committee,
  28
Scotland, 11, 247
Scutt, J. A., 19, 260
Seale, P., 190
Secord, P. F., 220
secular morality, 23–6
Segal, L., 100, 118, 242, 271
Seidler, V., 234
self *see* personality
self-knowledge, difficulty of, 212
semiotics, 45, 241
Sennett, R., 192
seriality, 81
sex roles, 33–4
  deviation from, 30, 49, 50, 52
  history of, 146–7
  and psychoanalysis, 192
  socialization and, 33, 34, 49, 73
  syntheses, 29–32
  theory, 47–54, 64–5, 73
  see also division of labour; sexual
sexism *see* sexual ideology
sexual/sexuality
  bisexuality, 27, 28
  character, 167–90, 224–5, 286;
    multiple models, 175–9, 189;
    reworking, 281; unitary
    models and sex difference
    research, 167–71, 189; *see also*
    hegemonic; femininity,
    emphasized
  crisis of, 160–2
  differences in work *see* division of
    labour
  fetishism, 84, 115, 284
  harassment, 12, 260, 269
  history of, 147
  ideology, 241–58: cultural
    dynamics, 250–3, 258;
    discourse and practice, 241–5,

258; ideologists and interests,
    253–8; processes, 245–9, 258
  intercourse, 51, 82
  marketing of, 103, 104; *see also*
    advertisements
  morality, 23–6, 37, 160–1
  non-heterosexual *see* deviation;
    homosexuality
  pornography, 55, 58, 84, 167,
    261–2
  and psychoanalysis, 197, 200,
    204–5, 207–10; *see also*
    Oedipus
  rape, 11, 55, 56, 107, 128
  reproduction, 34, 72, 81, 286
  sexology, 27
  socially constructed *see* cathexis
  and state, 126
  stratification, 55
  as structure, 96
  taboos, 112, 161
  see also cathexis; gender; politics,
    practice; present and future;
    sex roles; *and under* media
Shakespeare, W., 24
Shaver, S., xv, 108, 132
Sichtermann, B., 216
significance testing, 168–9
Silverstein, C., 237
Silverstein, M., 195
Simon, W., 111
Smith, C., 249
Smith, K., 242
Smith-Rosenberg, C., 109
Smout, T. C., 102, 258
Snodgrass, J., 235, 252
social/society
  bases of sexual politics *see* gender
  determinism, 50
  division of labour, 103, 105
  interest, 137–8
  and life history, 219–23, 236–7
  and nature, conflict between,
    197–8
  practice *see* natural
  production of sexual differences, 67
  reproduction, 35–6, 43–6
  space, 276
  structure, gender as *see* gender
    relations
  as unnatural, 78
socialism, 29, 35, 104, 292

socialization
  and capitalism, 42, 43, 45–6
  and psychoanalysis, 191–6, 218
  and sex roles, 33, 34, 49, 73
  as structure, 96
sociobiology, 38, 66, 68–73
sociology, 30, 31, 62
  of knowledge of, 245, 253
soft domination by state, 127
South America *see* Latin and Central America
South Korea, 9
Soviet Union, 289
  extrinsic theories, 42
  family, 136
  militarism, 109
  women, 15, 29; workers, 8, 9, 126, 138
  see also Russia
space, 281–3
Spain, 150
Spence, J., 171, 172, 174, 241, 247
Spender, D., 65
Spenser, E., 84
sport, 75, 85
Stacey, J., 64
Stalin, 29, 217
Stanley, J. P., 237
Stapledon, O., 290
state, 11–18, 19, 45, 259
  control, 96, 109; *see also* legislation; military; police; prisons
  crisis of, 160
  history of, 152–3
  as institution, 125–32, 135–6, 142
  reconstruction of, 155–7
  welfare, 127, 129, 131–3; cuts, 135–6, 230, 260
  see also politics; power
Stearns, P. N., 38, 147
Steinmann, A., 64
stereotypes, 33–4, 73; *see also* sex roles
Stevens, G. L., 87
Stevens, J., 64
Stille, A., 20
Stolcke, V., 246
Stoller, R. J., 194
Stopes, M., 86
strategy, present and future, 280–86
Straus, M. A., 19, 51

street as institution, 132–4, 142
Strober, M. H., 55
structures/structuralism
  and anthropology, 45
  and cathexis, 111–16, 118
  and labour, 99–106, 118
  loss with abolition of gender, 288–9
  and power, 107–11, 118
  and practice, 62
  and sexual character, 180–3, 189
  social gender as *see* gender relations
  structural analysis, 92–9, 117–18
  system and composition, 116–17
subordination
  of men, 186
  of women, 41–7, 73, 92–3, 96, 183
  see also sex roles
suffrage *see* voting
Sullivan, E. V., 220, 223
Sumer, 144, 151, 152–3
super-ego, 197, 208
Sweden, 87
symbolic
  eroticism, 83–4
  interactionism, 62
  purposes of sex, 115
symbolization, 241–2, 248
system idea of, 46
systems theory, 62
Szasz, T. S., 213
Szelenyi, I., 254

taboos, sexual, 112, 161
Taft, J., 30
taxation, 230, 260
Taylor, B., 39
Taylor, F., 227, 228, 237
Taylor, G. R., 146
technology *see* science
television *see* media
testosterone, 70; *see also* hormones
tests of sexual character and personality, 30, 47, 168, 169, 171–5, 189, 221
textiles *see* clothing
Thatcher, M., 159
theatre
  homosexuals in, 103
  street as, 133
  see also media

theory *see* gender theory
therapy for men, 235–6, 264
third sex, 285
Third World, 271, 280
  aid to, 18
  industry, 158
  radical movements, 104
  industry, 158
Thomas, D., 39
Thomism, 17
Thompson, D., 65
Thompson,. E. P., 65
Tickamyer, A. R., 65
Tieger, T., 87
Tiger, L., 68, 87, 145
Tolkein, J. R. R., 248
Tolson, A., 43, 59, 175, 235
Tomasetti, G., 266
top jobs *see* power
Touraine, A., 126, 163
tradesmen, 181
training *see* education
transcendence and negation of body,
  78–82, 88
transformation of body, practical,
  83–7, 88
transsexualism, 57, 76, 81, 148
transvestism, 75–6
Trigger, B. G., 164
Tristan and Isolde, 24, 217
Trotskyites, 42

Ulrichs, K., 28
unconscious, dynamic, 196–211, 218
unification, 222
unions, 29, 45, 214, 260, 292
unitary models of sexual character,
  167–71, 189, 206
United Nations
  Asian and Pacific Centre for
    Women and Development, 59
  International Decade for Women,
    260
United States, 16
  anthropology, 31
  black people, 160
  capitalism, 44
  education, 8, 9, 228–9
  equality *see* equal rights
  extrinsic theories, 42
  family, 48, 121, 122, 123, 139,
    193

health care, 250
homosexuality, 36, 37, 51, 162,
  232; 260
illiteracy, 8
industry/workplace, 101, 109
intrinsic theories, 62
marriage, 111
men: flight from commitment, 161;
  movement, xi, 34, 235; role
  models, 185
military, 14, 109, 126
New Left, 160, 203, 227
New Right, 126, 136, 229–30,
  236
personality, 221, 227, 228
pornography, 58, 262
religion, 262
sex roles, 30, 33, 34, 38, 53, 180
  tests, 169, 171
sexual ideology, 243, 247, 255
state, 126, 128, 131, 136; welfare
  cuts, 37
street life, 133
violence, 11, 12, 13–14
women: movement, 24–5, 29–30,
  44, 203, 230, 234, 284; in
  power, 15; working, 9, 10
universalism, false, 58, 271
urban civilizations, history of, 154,
  155
Utopianism, 26, 29, 251–2, 264,
  292

Vatsyayana, 115
Vikings, 155
violence, 11 14, 19, 37, 85, 96, 128,
  249, 260
  domestic *see under* family
  and masculinity, 57–8, 85–6;
    hegemonic, 184, 185
  organized *see* military; police;
    prisons
  and power, 107
voluntarism, 62
voting rights for women, 24–5, 131

wages *see under* working women
Wajcman, J., 268
Wallace, A., 19
Walter, A., 40
war
  and conscription, 135

genetic explanation of, 69
Ware, H., 107
Wayne, J., 185
wealth, 6–7, 18–19
    accumulation of, 105–6
weapons, 107; *see also* military
Weeks, J., 39, 111, 127, 147, 250
Welch, R., 256
welfare, state, 127, 129, 131–3
    cuts, 135–6, 230, 260
Wesley, F. and C., 64
Wesson, G., 43
West, J., 141
White, P., 61, 202–3, 256
White, R. W., 122, 221
wife-burning, 58
Wilde, O., 28
Williams, C., 45, 110
Williams, T. R., 189
Willis, E., 40, 65
Willis, P., 88, 178, 180
Willmott, P., 32, 93
Wilson, E., 141, 230
Wilson, E. O., 69–70, 73–4, 87
Wilson, J. A., 164
'Wolf Man', 204, 209, 221
Wolfe, S. J., 237
Wollstonecraft, M., 24, 25, 131, 241
Wolpe, A.-M., 64
women
    as category, 137–8
    invisible, 188, 247
    voting rights for, 24–5, 131
    see also education; femininity;
        feminism; gender; mothers;
        sexual; working women
Women Against Pit Closures, 143,
    270

Women Who Want to be Women,
    262
Women's Christian Temperance
    Union, 25
Women's Co-operative Guild, 255
work *see* labour
Working class
    and capitalism, 42
    and categorical theory, 59
        education, 1, 193
    family, 93–4, 111, 121–2, 265–8
    feminism, 265–70, 279
    movements, 29
    and physical aggression and
        toughness, 85, 109
    women, 35
working women, 35–6, 45, 162, 260
    numbers of, 9, 52
    part-time, 134–5
    wages, 6–7, 8–10, 18–19, 42, 45,
        96, 103, 162, 267
    see also division of labour
workplace, 243–4; *see also* industry;
    labour; office; working women
World Bank, 8–9
writing, 151–2
Wylie, P., 248

Yates, L., 252
Young, I., 64
Young, K., 16, 125
Young, M., 32, 93

Zaretsky, E., 104
Zetkin, C., 29
Ziller, A., 49
zones, liberated, 281–2

Index by Ann Hall